The Reciprocity of Perceiver and Environment

RESOURCES FOR ECOLOGICAL PSYCHOLOGY

A series of volumes edited by:
Robert E. Shaw, William M. Mace, and Michael T. Turvey

The Reciprocity of Perceiver and Environment

The Evolution of James J. Gibson's Ecological Psychology

Thomas J. Lombardo, Ph.D.

Illinois Department of Mental Health and Developmental Disabilities

College of DuPage

Loyola University

LEA LAWRENCE ERLBAUM ASSOCIATES, PUBLISHERS
1987   Hillsdale, New Jersey   London

Lawrence Erlbaum Associates, Inc., Publishers
365 Broadway
Hillsdale, New Jersey 07642

Library of Congress Cataloging in Publication Data

Lombardo, Thomas J.
  The reciprocity of perceiver and environment.

  Bibliography: p.
  Includes index.
  1. Environmental psychology.   2. Perception—Philosophy.
3. Gibson, James Jerome, 1904–   . I. Title.
BF353.L55   1987   155.9   86-24011
ISBN 0-89859-885-0
ISBN 0-8058-0049-2 (pbk)

Printed in the United States of America
10 9 8 7 6 5 4 3 2 1

TO MY PARENTS
RICHARD AND ANGELA LOMBARDO

RESOURCES
for ECOLOGICAL PSYCHOLOGY

Edited by
Robert E. Shaw, William M. Mace, and Michael Turvey

This series of volumes is dedicated to furthering the development of psychology as a branch of ecological science. In its broadest sense, ecology is a multidisciplinary approach to the study of living systems, their environments, and the reciprocity that has evolved between the two. Traditionally, ecological science emphasizes the study of the biological bases of *energy* transactions between animals and their physical environments across cellular, organismic, and population scales. Ecological psychology complements this traditional focus by emphasizing the study of *information* transactions between living systems and their environments, especially as they pertain to perceiving situations of significance to planning and execution of purposes activated in an environment.

The late James J. Gibson used the term *ecological psychology* to emphasize this animal-environment mutuality for the study of problems of perception. He believed that analyzing the environment to be perceived was just as much a part of the psychologist's task as analyzing animals themselves, and hence that the "physical" concepts applied to the environment and the "biological" and "psychological" concepts applied to organisms would have to be tailored to one another in a larger system of mutual constraint. His early interest in the applied problems of landing airplanes and driving automobiles led him to pioneer the study of the perceptual guidance of action.

The work of Nicolai Bernstein in biomechanics and physiology presents a complementary approach to problems of the coordination and control of movement. His work suggests that action, too, cannot be studied without reference to the environment, and that physical and biological concepts must be developed together. The coupling of Gibson's ideas with those of Bernstein forms a natural basis for looking at the traditional psychological topics of perceiving, acting, and knowing as activities of ecosystems rather than isolated animals.

The purpose of this series is to form a useful collection, a resource, for people who wish to learn about ecological psychology and for those who wish to contribute to its development. The series will include original research, collected papers, reports of conferences and symposia, theoretical monographs, technical handbooks, and works from the many disciplines relevant to ecological psychology.

Series Dedication

To James J. Gibson, whose pioneering work in ecological
psychology has opened new vistas in psychology and
related sciences, we respectfully dedicate this series.

CONTENTS

INTRODUCTION: GIBSON and the HISTORY OF SCIENCE

The most incomprehensible thing about the universe is that it is comprehensible.

—Albert Einstein

I first met J. J. Gibson in 1971 at the University of Minnesota in Minneapolis. I was a second-year psychology graduate student when Gibson stopped over for a few days to visit some friends on his way back to Cornell University. As an undergraduate at the University of Connecticut, I had read Gibson's *Senses Considered as Perceptual Systems* (1966a), and his ideas had slowly but steadily and quite significantly impressed me. Gibson's ideas are deceptively simple, the mark of a good writer and an insightful thinker, and as a graduate student I found myself drawn to his writings. My main interests in graduate school were perception, the history of psychology, and the philosophy of science. From an historical perspective it seemed to me that Gibson was the most original theoretician in the world in the psychology of perception. Further, from a philosophical perspective Gibson appeared to be moving toward a reconceptualization of the nature of knowledge that ran counter to most of modern western thought. One of my teachers at Minnesota, Dr. Herb Pick, had worked with Gibson at Cornell, and while I was sitting in my office, Dr. Pick walked in with Gibson and introduced me to him. I distinctly remember butterflies materializing in my stomach as my Adam's apple surged up in my throat. Gibson, though, was so unpretentious and engaging that I quickly found myself at ease, drawn into a conversation with an extremely fascinating personality and mind. That morning a friendship and professional association began that would last almost 10 years until Gibson passed away in 1980. That first meeting also laid the seeds of a project that, with detours, outbursts, and periods of hibernation, grew into this book.

My graduate advisor at Minnesota, Dr. Robert Shaw, had studied with Gibson a couple of years earlier at Cornell. Bob has a very eclectic background, and is a person of prodigious philosophical imagination. When I became his advisee in 1970 he allowed me considerable intellectual freedom as I moved from a strict experimental focus into the philosophy and history of psychology. The sharp academic distinction between philosophy and science, so prevalent in the 1940s and 1950s, was losing its hold, and Minnesota was one of the places to be for someone who wished to bridge the gap between science and philosophy. What attracted Bob (and later me) to Gibson was the philosophical intent and ramifications of his thinking. Having more than the usual philosophical background for a psychologist (a bachelor's degree in philosophy from Princeton), Gibson was familiar with philosophical theory and was not hesitant to grapple with fundamental issues regarding reality and the nature of knowledge. Bob allowed me to pursue in my studies the historical and philosophical aspects of Gibson's ideas.

Through history, an overview and integration can be achieved of the philosophical and scientific worlds. Viewed from the vantage point of history, the interconnections between scientific and philosophical thought become apparent; the histories of philosophy and science overlap, cross-fertilizing each other. Often what begins as a philosophical doctrine over time becomes a basic assumption or conceptual scheme in a scientific theory. The variety of modern scientific disciplines, such as biology, physics, or psychology, presuppose in language, practice, and beliefs numerous ideas first found in the history of philosophy. Novel scientific theories are original to the degree to which they challenge the philosophical underpinnings of accepted theories. The theoretical scientist will engage in "philosophical" thinking along the path to a new theory or concept of nature. Novel scientific theory causes one to think differently, to reject old questions and to ask new ones. The psychology and biology of perception, as traditionally understood, rests upon a philosophy of science expounded in the writings of Descartes, Berkeley, and Newton among others. Descartes' philosophy is the modern starting point of *mind-body (matter) dualism*, whereas Berkeley and Newton significantly contributed to the *elementaristic* philosophy of nature. Gibson was clearly intent on challenging this philosophical foundation underlying contemporary perceptual psychology. Conversely, new science impacts upon philosophical thinking. Prime examples of scientific theories that have significantly influenced philosophy include Copernicus' heliocentric astronomy, Galileo's mechanistic physics, Darwin's evolutionary biology, and more recently, relativity and quantum mechanics. In many ways, Gibson's ecological psychology addresses modern philosophical thinking. During the 20th-century, a variety of distinctions have been drawn between philosophy and science (Carmap, 1936; Hamlyn, 1961, 1977; Popper, 1959, 1963; Reichenbach, 1938). Aside from the fact that such distinctions keep shifting and are open to a variety of criticisms, the historical fact is that science and modern philosophy have not developed in isolation of one another (Agassi, 1964; Wartofsky, 1976). The history of Gibson's development seemed a prime example of how philosophy influenced science and vice versa.

For me, one fascinating philosophical feature to Gibson's thought concerned its implications on issues within theories of scientific knowledge. For most scientists, perception (or observation) is the expressed starting point and foundation of all scientific knowledge, yet philosophical theories of scientific knowledge assumed ideas that Gibson, as a psychologist of perception, questioned. Contemporary philosophy of science was in a period of flux, controversy, and revision (Agassi, 1963, 1966, 1975; Bartley, 1964; Feyerabend, 1962, 1964, 1965, 1970a, 1970b, 1970c, 1976; Kuhn, 1962, 1970a, 1970b; Lakatos, 1968, 1970, 1971; Maxwell, 1962; Sellars, 1965b; Suppe, 1977). In particular, the apparent objectivity of science had come under attack. Aside from critiques centering on the logical justification of scientific theory, observation—the empirical "bedrock" of theory—was seen to possess an intractable subjective contamination. My judgment was that traditional theories of perception had generated the problem of subjectivity in observation. I believed Gibson's ecological direct realism provided a basis for understanding the objectivity inherent in observation. Gibson was offering a new approach to knowledge about the world.

After meeting with Gibson, I suggested to Bob the idea of writing my dissertation on Gibson, an historical thesis, examining in detail both relevant history and Gibson's own historical development. My motivation was twofold: to historically reveal, through tracing Gibson's development, the substance of his views and how they bore upon general philosophical issues in theories of knowledge, and to investigate in detail the historical context of Gibson's theoretical position within psychology. I believed that the substance or meaning of an idea could only be understood by examining its development and historical-theoretical significance. Ideas are historically dynamic and interactive.

Bob suggested I go to Cornell to study with Gibson while I wrote my thesis. He also suggested that the Center for Research in Human Learning, then under the directorship of James Jenkins, might fund the project with a fellowship. Bob wrote Gibson who approved the idea. The Center, with Jim and Bob's support, granted me a one-year fellowship. In the summer of 1972, I left Minneapolis and headed for Ithaca, New York.

James Jerome Gibson was born January 27, 1904 in McConnelsville, Ohio. He attended Northwestern and Princeton Universities, graduating from the latter with a major in philosophy. He stayed on at Princeton as a graduate student in psychology, received his Ph.D., and accepted a position at Smith College. He taught at Smith until joining the Air Force as a research psychologist during World War II. At the end of the war, he left the armed services, and he and his wife Eleanor came to Cornell University in Ithaca. Gibson published his first book, *The Perception of the Visual World* (1950a) soon after coming to Cornell, and when I arrived in 1972 he was working on his grand synthesis, *The Ecological Approach to Visual Perception* (1979a).

The terrain around Ithaca is cut through with ravines, gorges, and cliffs, and covered with forest and foliage. There is little if any flat open terrain—most of the space is filled and carved into variegated structures. Vistas open up in the most surprising places and the dense foilage noticeably disentangles and separates in depth. One can see Gibson's theory of "space" perception embedded in the surroundings. Of course, one has to move about and explore to fully experience the terrain. Getting to know Gibson was a similar experience. One had to engage, to participate, to educate one's attention, and the "terrain" was full of surprises.

Gibson and I talked. At first, more accurately, we argued. He was extremely meticulous with terminology and meaning and would question almost everything I'd say. He read all my papers on perception and filled the pages with comments. He invited me to his home, and both he and his wife, Eleanor, were very hospitable and personable. Both of them loved to talk and socialize. Gibson and I were night owls and at least once a week we'd sit up until 2 in the morning discussing the history of science, epistemology, ecological optics, plus a never ending variety of other topics. During this time I met Rik Warren, a graduate student in psychology, and Rik, Gibson, and I formed a discussion group on the philosophy of perception. Gibson was always willing to discuss his ideas or listen to mine. He was a fascinating, animated, and lovable man and was tremendously supportive.

By the summer of 1973 I had completed my history of Gibson. My historical treatment of pre-Gibsonian thinking emphasized *empiricist* psychology and philosophy, which was the intellectual establishment in the late 19th and early 20th centuries. It was here that I initially found the strongest contrasts with Gibson's views. American psychology has been most strongly influenced by the British empiricism of Locke, Berkeley, Hume and Mill. My own education in the history of psychology emphasized empiricist thought. Gibson's education as a graduate student had emphasized traditional empiricist thought, and though Gibson's mature thought is adamantly empiricist (viz., knowledge can be achieved through the senses), Gibson, in challenge to his education, developed a different *theory* of empiricism, in particular, a *wholistic* as opposed to an *elementaristic* empiricism.

Gibson, in 1973, was working on his final book, *The Ecological Approach to Visual Perception,* but it was still quite a few years from completion. There were rough drafts on some of the earlier chapters plus typed seminar notes from the period (1965–1973), but the ecological approach was still forming. My history of Gibson, though titled "J. J. Gibson's Ecological Approach to Visual Perception: Its Historical Context and Development" (Lombardo, 1973) emphasized the period 1930–1966, and did not fully develop Gibson's ecological themes. Gibson's development can be divided into two periods: His *psychophysical* theory (1930–1960) and his *ecological* theory (1960–1980). Gibson's psychophysics was a stepping stone to his ecological approach. My thesis, in actuality, focused on the psychophysical approach and the historical background relevant to it. Through the publication of the *Senses* (1966a), Gibson's psychological theory was engaged in a challenge with traditional elemental empiricism. The basic contrasts I developed at this time were Gibson's wholistic treatments of physiology, stimulation, and the environment versus the elementaristic theories of Descartes, Berkeley, Müller, Helmholtz, and Mill. The challenge of Gibson's ecological psychology goes beyond the wholism-elementarism issue. In the 1940s and 1950s Gibson, in his psychophysics, was reconceptualizing space—it is only with a similar reconceptualization of time and the dynamic features of perception that Gibson's ecological approach fully emerged. This rethinking was still in process in the 1970s. Gibson's ecological psychology would challenge more than elementaristic empiricism. It would challenge dualism.

During the next 3 years Gibson and I kept in close touch. I was an assistant professor in psychology at Indiana University Northwest, teaching history of psychology and perception, while I worked on filling in certain weak spots in my thesis. In particular, I discovered the relevancy of Greek philosophy, especially Plato and Aristotle. The historical issues became deeper, going beyond visual perception to include all of psychology. Aristotle's functional psychology now seemed the pivotal historical antecedent of those intellectual trends that positively influenced Gibson. Toward the end of this period, it appeared to me that Berkeley's empiricist psychology was the basic historical contrast for Gibson's psychophysical approach, but in the broader context of Gibson's ecological approach, it was Plato's dualism that epitomized the most fundamental contrast. Gibsonian history, especially the most recent period, became clearer by looking further into the past. Bob Shaw had left Minnesota and come to the University of Connecticut beginning a series of collaborative studies in ecological psychology with Dr. Michael Turvey. Turvey had been my undergraduate advisor and in the winter of 1975–76, Mike invited me to Connecticut to speak on Gibson (Lombardo, 1975). I was very pleased to learn that he had read my thesis and he was very supportive of me in completing the historical study.

In the fall of 1979, I returned to the University of Connecticut as a postdoctoral fellow. What followed was an extremely stimulating year. There were numerous discussions with an old friend from graduate school, Bill Hazelett, on the comparative philosophies of Plato and Aristotle and the continental philosophers Leibnitz and Spinoza. Bob Shaw for years had been talking about the relevance of Leibnitz's concept of *harmony* to Gibson's ecological psychology. Leibnitz in many respects, stands in the Aristotelian tradition, and along with other continental thinkers, provides connecting links between Aristotle and Gibson. In my thesis I had not given wholistic continental philosophy sufficient attention, but this historical one-sidedness toward the British empiricists simply reflected the one-sidedness embodied in traditional treatments of the history of psychology (Boring, 1950). That fall I became interested in J. T. Fraser's philosophy of time after attending a lecture by him in which he attacked Plato's dualistic philosophy. It seemed to me that Plato was the source of the dualism that, through various modifications and embellishments, was carried over into British empiricism and Newtonian science. Aristotle had rejected Plato's dualism and Gibson, in his ecological approach, was attaking the physics of Newton, as well as British empiricism. I attended Shaw and Turvey's seminars listening to how Gibson had inspired their own work in ecological psychology. Turvey and Shaw also provided invaluable interpretative studies of Gibson's theory (Shaw & Bransford, 1977; Shaw & Pittenger, 1978; Shaw & Turvey, 1981; Shaw, Turvey, & Mace, 1981; Turvey & Shaw, 1979).

In the winter of 1980 Gibson passed away. I had been in correspondence with him since the fall, but I had not made the trip to Cornell. I regretted missing this final opportunity to see him. Throughout the spring I tried my hand at updating my thesis and I met with Lawrence Erlbaum for the first time to discuss its publication. By the summer I realized that much of the manuscript needed to be reorganized or rewritten. In 1972–73, my thesis was to demonstrate how Gibson's psychology of perception went beyond empiricist philosophy and psychology. By 1980, the focus, encapsulating the earlier one, was Gibson's ecological psychology and how it differed from a philosophical-scientific tradition best epitomized by the dualism of Plato, Descartes, and Newton, among others. The intellectual antecedents of Gibson had become clear, with Aristotle standing out, followed by "process" and "wholistic" philosophy. Aristotle saw nature as dynamic and integrated, as did Gibson, where Plato had bifurcated nature, placing order above and separate from the flux of time. These conclusions went far beyond my ideas of 1972–73. In the summer of 1980 I left Connecticut and headed west, beginning a process of thinking through the ideas of the previous year.

History and historiography (the study of history) are complex and intertwining. Gibson read my 1973 thesis and acknowledged its influence on his thinking (1979a, p. xiv). In some manner or form, my ongoing historical interest in Gibson influenced the history I studied. Equally true, it was the students of Gibson, including myself and Bob Shaw, who because we found his ideas so theoretically fascinating, thought it worthwhile to promote Gibsonian history. The positivist-empiricist ideal of a dispassionate empty recorder of facts is a theoretical fiction of dualistic philosophy. The mind does not stand apart from the world it studies. History is blind without theory and vapid without conviction.

The events and ideas of a period in time guide the eyes of an historian. The 1970s saw the rise of ecological biology, renewed interest in evolution, plus an incredible amount of study and discussion in the philosophy and science of time (Fraser, 1978, 1982; Prigogine, 1976, 1980, 1984). Through my eyes, Gibson and much of this newer thinking, especially as it pertained to ecology and life, complimented and reinforced each other (Jantsch & Waddington, 1976). When, in 1982, I returned to the University of Connecticut, it was Peter Kugler who helped me to further see the modern scope of the issues being addressed in Gibson's ecological psychology. Peter, a graduate student under Bob and Michael, was temporarily back in Connecticut completing his thesis. Peter has a broad range of interests, but in particular was fascinated with the development and organization of natural systems. More than anyone else, Peter gave me the necessary final impetus to complete this book.

Gibson was a psychologist whose main interest was perception, in particular vision. But throughout his life his theoretical motivation became increasingly more generalized in scope. In effect, he outlined a new concept of psychology, and a new empiricist epistemology, as well as developing a general critique of many basic features of the life sciences. Perception, which at the "naive" level seems the most innocuous of topics, has been a pivotal concern in the development of many philosophies and basic sciences. A significant shift in our attitude toward perception would require a corresponding shift in our attitude toward ourselves and the world around us. Though the following history emphasizes the psychology of perception, its ground work is laid in basic intellectual traditions, notably of Plato, Aristotle, Descartes, Newton, and Darwin. Gibson saw himself as a theoretical scientist and a naturalistic philosopher and his ideas on perception led him to reconsider many basic concepts about nature, e.g., space, time, life, the brain, and the mind.

There are numerous reviews and studies of Gibson which either focus on his experimental research or selected aspects of his theory. Turvey, Shaw, and Ed Reed have looked at a main theoretical issues in the context of recent history. Though I have included a history of Gibson's perceptual research and experimentation, my focus is to explicate the "dynamic abstract form" of Gibson's ecological approach. My emphasis is philosophical and theoretical, attempting to bring out the direction Gibson was moving in and how such changes could restructure the theoretical fabric of psychology. I devote considerable attention to the Greeks, Medievalists, and the founders of the Scientific Revolution. I do this because Gibson's theoretical challenge runs deep into the structure of western thought. My central goal is to set Gibson's ecological theory within the historical context of fundamental philosophical-scientific issues.

In the final analysis, what I present as a history of Gibson and significant antecedents is founded upon my interpretation of Gibson and intellectual history. Though I have been influenced and educated in numerous ways by Shaw, Turvey, Kugler, and others, the basic themes of this study ultimately depend on my individual historical theoretical perspective. There are other approaches to interpreting Gibson or the history of perceptual history; my intent is not necessarily to compete with them for there can be multiple yet equally valid interpretations of the same ideas. Yet I do believe in the ideals of truth and understanding and have striven to work toward these objectives in my study.

One final note of acknowledgment and appreciation is extended to Lois Baker and Kathy Holmes, who typed earlier drafts of this book, and Donna Skala, who while working a full-time job, typed the final draft in less than one month.

Part I

THE PHILOSOPHY
of KNOWLEDGE
and the SCIENCE
of PERCEPTION

Chapter 1_____

ECOLOGICAL PSYCHOLOGY
and MIND-MATTER DUALISM

GIBSON'S THEORY OF PERCEIVER-ENVIRONMENT
RECIPROCITY

The central insight within J. J. Gibson's ecological psychology is the principle of reciprocity. Reciprocity means distinguishable yet mutually supportive realities. Animate life forms and their environment taken together comprise a reciprocally integrated ecosystem; life functions such as perception and behavior, necessarily involve an environment, and, complimentarily, environmental properties necessarily involve animate life forms. Gibson's main interest throughout his life was visual perception and it was as it pertained to the perceiver and its environment that Gibson initially applied the principle of reciprocity; Gibson's ecological approach to visual perception involved describing vision as a fact of an ecosystem, rather than just a fact of physiology or the mind. The term *ecological* signifies animal-environment reciprocity. Later in his career Gibson extended the principle of ecological reciprocity to cover all of psychology. Further, in his developing understanding of an ecosystem, Gibson reconceptualized such fundamental ideas as permanence and change, whole and parts, knower and known, and even space and time as reciprocal pairs. In his mature ecological theory, his direct realist epistemology, as well as other central substantive and methodological principles, follow from the idea of reciprocity.

Owing its genesis to Plato, the predominant philosophy in western

3

civilization of "what exists" (ontology) has been mind-matter dualism: Mind and matter are independent, absolute, and distinct. Mind and matter may "somehow" affect or parallel each other, but existentially and qualitatively each is a world unto itself. The epistemology (theory of knowledge) of indirect perception historically follows from Plato's dualistic ontology. Mind can only be acquainted with itself—the material world is known indirectly through representation, inference, or effect. Plato's dualism extended to separating permanence (eternity) and change (time) and universals (order) and particulars (individuals). Aristotle, Plato's most illustrious student, would challenge this dualism of thought, and in accepting the absolute incommensurability of mind and matter, many others would try to eliminate one half or both halves of Plato's dualism. With all the twists and turns of history, none of these solutions or alternatives have succeeded and Plato's dualism has remained the predominant mode of thought in western science and philosophy.

Initially, Gibson was strongly influenced by traditional theories in perception and psychology, but over a 50-year period he came to challenge both mind-matter dualism in his ecological theory and the epistemology of indirect perception in his direct realist philosophy of perception. Gibson's theory of ecological reciprocity avoids both the absolute philosophical dichotomies inherent in Platonic thinking, and the one-sided treatments of reality in monistic philosophies. Though Gibson's thorough and uncompromising development of ecological reciprocity is theoretically unique, there exists an historical-intellectual lineage for his views. History exhibits both continuous and discontinuous elements, and both constancy and novelty. In examining the growth of Gibson's ecological psychology, one can find numerous roots. Aristotle, as a single theorist, probably anticipates Gibson more than any one, and in modern times, functional psychology, process ontology, Gestalt wholism, and the evolutionary-ecological view of nature have all influenced Gibson's thinking. Not surprisingly, many of these later developments can be traced back to Aristotle. History is intertwining—a bramble bush rather than a simple hierarchical tree—and it would be inaccurate, in fact an example of historical dualism, to divide history into two absolute, opposed lines of development. Yet within the confines of this study of Gibson an historical distinction will be made between the Aristotelian and Platonic lines of thought. Later scientific and philosophical developments usually represent in lineage some mixture of selected aspects of each line but a basic historical contrast can be delineated between the predominant heritage of absolute dualism, reactionary monisms, and related doctrines, and the Aristotelian "ecological" heritage. Within this historical theoretical framework Gibson's own development chronicles a movement away from dualistic and monistic influences toward the Aristotelian lineage and the concept of ecological reciprocity.

Plato separated the knowing mind with its capacity to apprehend eternal and universal truths from the fluctuating, individualized world of matter. Within the Scientific Revolution (1550–1750), matter and energy (especially light) were progressively reduced (or analyzed) into an impoverished structure of localized particles and lines. Mind was elevated to a detached and ethereal creator and manipulator of abstractions, generalities, and ideas. With the rise of reductionistic biology (1650–1850), neural and sensory physiology was analyzed into independent, simple elements. Monistic trends inspired by the success of physicalism and elementism in science attempted to reduce and/or eliminate the mind. Instead of becoming more intelligible, perceptual experience, as well as other psychological phenomena became increasingly unintelligible and divorced from the supposed real (elementaristic) world of physics, chemistry, and biology. Reflecting these earlier intellectual trends, the standard modern explanation of perception ran as follows: Beginning from an order-imposed world of localized elements in an instantaneous present, lines of energy are transmitted through space to a physical mosaic of sensory receptors. In turn lines of energy are transmitted along neurons to a brain where organizational processes transform this "blooming, buzzing, confusion" into a spatial-temporally ordered experience. The resultant experience is qualitatively and ontologically distinct from the world at the beginning of this chain of events.

Aristotle logically distinguished the knowing mind (or "subject") from the known "object," but stated that in reality the two were inseparable. Aristotle saw knower and known united in a functional interdependency. Although the dualistic picture of reality reigned supreme throughout the Middle Ages and into the Scientific Revolution, a variety of philosophical and scientific movements challenging the dualistic world view had gained a considerable following by the end of the 19th century. Reflecting an Aristotelian heritage, the "dynamic wholism" of process ontology, functionalism, evolutionism, and related theoretical perspectives attacked the analytic, static, and segmented science and philosophy of previous centuries. Drawing upon these newer ideas, Gibson put spatial and temporal order back into the environment of matter and energy. The structures and capacities of animals were described relative to their ways of life within an environment; in turn, the environment was described relative to the ways of life of animals. An explanation of perception involved a dynamic interdependency of animal and environment. Gibson's epistemology is direct realism, as was Aristotle's—the "object" of perception is the real world, viz., the environment. Perhaps the most difficult and unique point to grasp is treating perception as an ecological phenomenon rather than a mental or physiological event, yet Gibson's direct realism only follows if perception is defined ecologically. Perception does not reside in the brain or the mind any more than life resides in cells or in some inexplicable living spirit. Neither mentalism nor physicalism is correct. Perception, as well as life, is ecological; perception exists at the reciprocal interface of animal and environment within an ecosystem.

The ensuing history follows a chronological order beginning with the ancient Greeks, tracing the development of the basic theoretical issues Gibson addresses. The development of Gibson's ideas is divided into two major periods: his psychophysical approach (1930–1960) that breaks with many traditional ideas in the history of perception and his increasingly novel ecological approach (1960–1980) covered in the last chapters of this history. The remainder of this chapter provides a more detailed road map of the historical-conceptual connections between Gibson and relevant intellectual tradition.

THE SCIENTIFIC REVOLUTION
AND MIND-MATTER DUALISM

Much of what Gibson explicitly critiqued as he was developing his views on perception and psychology can be found in the scientific-philosophical tradition articulated during the Scientific Revolution and the rise of modern philosophy (circa 1550–1750). The modern distinction of the mental and the physical as ontologically different realms can be found in seminal scientific treatments of perception and related psychological topics. At the beginning of the 17th century, Johannes Kepler, using principles of physical optics and geometry, was able to scientifically explain how a focused image of light was produced on the retina of the eye. At the time, this explanation was considered one of the significant achievements of early modern science and presumably clarified the physical component of visual perception. His explanation was intentionally formulated in abstract physical concepts utilizing a mathematical methodology—it was mechanistic, analytic, and geometric. Elements of light and matter causally interacted to produce a geometrical relationship between external physical objects and the retinal image. When it came to explaining how these physical facts were related to the mental side of visual perception, viz., the conscious experience of colors and visual space, Kepler acknowledged it as a legitimate problem, but was hesitant in applying the concepts and methods of the burgeoning physical sciences to the "spirit" or "mind." Kepler did tread upon the spiritual-mental waters with certain geometrical notions, but basically he avoided such issues, for the incorporeal soul was initially considered off limits to scientific investigation—a methodological and political policy fostered by the Medieval theological separation of "spirit" and "physical matter." Both mind and spirit possessed attributes that could not be incorporated into the analytical and mechanical picture of early physical science.

Psychological "explanations" early in the Scientific Revolution elevated mind above matter, making it either mysterious or literally opposite to matter. The transformation from the world of matter to the world of mind, as in perception, was nothing short of miraculous. Kepler geometrically analyzed matter and energy into individualized points and lines, and the mind, like a geometer, presumably calculated the distances of objects. Elements of matter and energy obeyed geometrical and optical laws, whereas the mind used abstract knowledge of such laws to calculate physical relationships.

Kepler's contemporary, the philosopher-scientist Rene Descartes, popularized and carried further this split of reality. According to Descartes, one set of principles and concepts applies to physical objects, viz., they are divisible into aggregates of measurable units and they are related to each other in absolute causal determinism. Conversely, the mind is unified, possessing free will, and does not have any spatial attributes. The conscious qualities of perception, such as color and sweetness, are distinguishable from the actual properties of matter. Perception is an experience that is somehow "connected" with physical brain states, but it is nevertheless a separate mental reality. Because Descartes placed the perceiver's body in the deterministic physical world (thus setting the stage for the rise of scientific biology), Descartes advocated a dualism of mind (perceptions, ideas, emotions) and the body-brain, but his mind-body dualism was a consequence of his mind-matter dualism.

Descartes' dualism led him into various puzzles and perplexities: How could matter (brain states) effect mind in producing perception? In reverse, how could mind effect matter, as in intentions of will, producing physical behavior? And if perception is a state of mind distinct from the physical world, how can there be any real knowledge of the physical world? A significant logical implication of mind-matter dualism is the theory of indirect perception. The epistemological counterpart to Gibson's ecological reciprocity is his theory of direct perception where perception is not seen as a mental state isolated from the physical world. Perception is *of* the environment, because the perceiver is within the environment. Ascribing perception to an isolated mind leads to the idea of a "homunculus" (a little man or observer in the mind) who looks at the mental pictures and draws inferences about what they represent in the physical world.

Descartes believed in causal interaction between mind and brain, thus he took at least one concept from the physical sciences and applied it to the mind. Yet he never overcame his belief in their ultimate separability. Later philosophers and scientists, in various ways, applied physicalistic concepts to the mind, such as quantification and analysis as well as causality. Mind became methodologically homogenized to matter. The materialistic principles applied to the mind were elementaristic and analytic, mirroring the dualistic philosophy of physical nature developing in science. Descartes believed in limited spheres, that precise psychophysical laws of brain and mind could be discovered, but he nevertheless preserved areas of the mind beyond scientific investigation, viz., free will and the unified ego. Even if monistic trends in philosophy and science intermittently attempted reductions of mind to physical principles, treatments of matter as such remained elementaristic throughout the 17th and 18th centuries. Order, both spatially and temporally, was divorced from the constituents of matter and energy. In spite of such monistic trends in psychology and philosophy, dualism, in one form or another, has remained to the present the more popular view where matter is analyzed into ultimate units and mind (or psychological processes) is imbued with abstract, constructive forms of order.

The medieval separation of spirit and matter set up an important condition for the Scientific Revolution. It was considered justifiable to develop atheological and areligious principles for understanding the physical world as long as they were considered irrelevant and non-threatening to spiritual matters. Recall that Galileo found himself in hot water for defending Copernicus' heliocentric theory because it seemed to conflict with Biblical-Christian cosmology. The Scientific Revolution saw the beginnings of modern mechanics, astronomy, geology, optics, chemistry, electricity, and magnetism, all sciences of matter. This universe of matter, mathematics, and scientific law in following centuries would begin to encroach upon the mental realm. Initially, though, the universe of the Scientific Revolution was an absolute dualism, substantively and methodologically, and this view set the stage for later philosophies and scientific theories. Monism can be seen as a way to avoid Platonic-Cartesian dualism. Both Aristotle's and Gibson's attempts to develop an alternative picture of nature, must be seen relative to this historical contrast.

NEWTONIAN SUBSTANCE ONTOLOGY

Considerably reinforced by Isaac Newton's theoretical advances in physics and optics, mind-matter dualism enters the Age of Enlightenment (1700–1800) in the philosophy of John Locke. Consciousness contains ideas, feelings, and sensations, whereas Newton's physical world, inferred through scientific experimentation and mathematical hypotheses, presumably consisted of colorless, odorless atomistic particles in absolute empty space. According to Locke there were some "resemblances" between perception and the physical world, such as extension, shape, and spatial location, but the worlds were clearly different. Though Locke did believe that though a distant realm, perceptual experience could be similar to features of the physical world and thus represent it, his idea of similarity is difficult to understand, given his ontological dualism. Later philosophers, notably Bishop Berkeley, would attack Locke's concept of mind-matter similarity and his representative (indirect) theory of perception. For Locke and Descartes, perception is indirect because there is no direct aquaintance of mind with matter. In order to avoid this absolute dualism, Berkeley had to resort to an idealistic philosophy, which denied the separate world of matter.

Monistic trends can be seen in both Locke and Berkeley. Locke adopts the elementaristic picture of physical nature found in Kepler and further developed in Newton and applies it to the mind. Berkeley goes further, not only applying the elementaristic picture to the mind, but also trying to reduce everything to mind. Berkeley's monism (idealistic and elementaristic) is therefore more thorough than Locke's (empiricists after Berkeley would continue this trend), yet Berkeley still retains an indirect theory of perception for there are still elements of dualism in his thought.

A core assumption of the eighteenth century was the almost universal acceptance of the ontological primacy of substance. Newton's world consisted of material substances (particles of matter) contained within empty space; analogously, Locke's world of consciousness was an empty mind containing mental elements. The eighteenth century universe consisted of entities, composed of substances, intrinsic, independent, and self-contained. Substance had an absolute existence—its nature remained unchanged regardless of whatever relationships it might have to other substances. Secondly, all complex forms of substances were merely concatenations of elements—these elements preserve their inner nature however combined or related they are to other elements.

Though Locke ontologically separates mind from matter as two distinct substances, he initiated the monistic trend of describing the composition of the mind in terms of the elementaristic principles popularized in physical science. This elementaristic orientation prevailed in 18th and 19th century empiricist philosophy and psychology, turning the mind into a concatenation of units (elements) of mental substance.

If we recall that, initially, the Scientific Revolution separated the study of matter from the study of mind by describing the world of matter independent of mind, then the role of a substance ontology makes sense. Substances are conceived of as distinct and by describing mind and matter as substances, as Descartes and Locke did, the ontological split is made absolute. Yet, the Newtonian ontology of units of substance fosters a more general problem of understanding any type of relationship between absolutely distinct entities. Physical laws were seen as imposed upon matter and following the later critique by the Scottish philosopher David Hume, causal "connection" within this model was shown to reduce to nothing more than a regular sequence (assuming a universe of distinct entities). Generally, the elementaristic philosophy of distinct units of substance, whether it was applied to matter or mind, had difficulty with the concepts of order and relationship. In effect, if fostered a dualism of elements (particulars) and order.

To a measure, the idea of a psychophysical causal connection addresses the problem of relatedness but makes perception representative and causally indirect. Gibson's efforts to establish a psychophysics of perception in some ways draws from this dualistic theory of perception. Though mind and brain are ontologically distinct, they are causally and lawfully connected. How this happens is a mystery of nature and its eternal, imposed laws, but psychophysical correspondence as understood in Descartes and Locke's psychology comes down into Fechner's 19th century psychophysics of sensations and is taken up in spirit by Gibson in his psychophysics of perception (1930–1960). Gibson, though, would eventually abandon his psychophysical approach in favor of an ecological theory that dropped mind-matter dualism and the causal theory of perception. A psychophysics of perception still implied an indirect theory of perception and by the 1960s, Gibson was moving toward a direct perceptual epistemology. Gibson's psychophysics did move away from an elementaristic treatment of matter and energy and this was a significant step away from mind-matter dualism. Gibson, significantly influenced by Gestalt psychology's emphasis on organization, looked for order, not only in perceptual experience, but also in stimulation and the environment.

Commensurate with Newton's substance ontology, 18th century science contains a very limited conceptualization of change. A substance is intrinsically inert. Particles are moved about by physical forces; ideas and perceptions consist of elements connected together through mental laws. The Newtonian cosmos was divided into absolute elements, unrelated to each other and intrinsically incorrigible, created instantaneously, and kept in motion by the unchanging laws of nature. Change is not intrinsic to substance, it is merely the rearrangement of substances. The importance of the concepts of change and relationship do not emerge until the 19th century with Hegelian philosophy and Darwinian science. These intellectual turns eventually spelled the end of the Newtonian world view. The modern heritage of Gibson's ecological psychology lies in the newer ideas that dethroned Newton. If Gibson's psychophysics can be captured in the ideas of order and relationship carried consistently through in his treatment of perception, stimulation, and the environment, then Gibson's ecological approach can be captured in the ideas of change and order in change, for Gibson's concept of reciprocity is bound together with an intrinsically dynamic picture of nature.

Preceding the intellectual changes of the 19th century, there were diverse reactions to mind-matter dualism that attempted to solve the problem while still retaining the idea of independent static substances. The most popular were idealism, materialism, and neutral monism. Idealism, advocated by Bishop George Berkeley, assimilates matter to mind— everything is mental and there is no independent physical world. Conversely, scientific materialism, inspired by the success of Newton's physics, assimilates everything to matter—there is no mind. In the monistic philosophy of Spinoza, mind and matter are treated as different aspects of a unitary underlying substance. Phenomenalism, a popular 19th century version of neutral monism, dropped the idea of substance, but retained the idea of elements and proposed that the worlds of mind and matter were two alternate ways of descriptively organizing the same entities. In effect, both mind and matter were thrown out. Phenomenalism finds its philosophical origins in David Hume, John Stuart Mill, and Ernest Mach, but it would become the accepted scientific ontology in Wundt and Titchener's structuralist psychology, the first form of scientifically acceptable psychology late in the 19th century.

EVOLUTION, PROCESS ONTOLOGY, AND ECOLOGICAL PSYCHOLOGY

During the 18th and 19th centuries a set of ideas alternative to Newton's developed that Gibson would later draw upon in his own theoretical growth. The German philosophers Leibnitz, Kant, and Hegel would all argue that mind was an activity rather than a thing; all three, in different ways, would emphasize the importance of relationships and attack the idea of absolute elements and substances. Leibnitz saw space and time as relational, contrary to Newton's absolute space and time, and the constituents of the universe as intrinsically transforming processes as contrary to Newton's inert substances. Leibnitz saw spatial and temporal order as intrinsic to the constituents of nature. Further, Leibnitz rejected the causal chain model, replacing it with the connected ideas of intrinsic dynamism and harmony of events. Kant described the mind as an organization of capacities wherein individual experiences are meaningful only in the context of the whole mental network—there are no absolute mental elements—the whole is not a concatenation of parts. Hegel attempted to turn all natural and human history into interdependent processes where nothing stood as static and intrinsic in nature. Hegel, continuing a tradition begun with Leibnitz and Spinoza, believed that any entity in nature derived its nature from its relationships with the whole of nature.

Darwin would challenge the absolute separation of mind and matter in his evolutionary view of life. Mind evolved as an adaptive function geared to the material environment. It was not placed "within" the body from some independent spiritual realm. Darwin's emphasis on change in biological forms came to challenge, more than any other single idea, the static Newtonian universe. Within the 19th century, geology, archaeology, paleontology, and astronomy were all coming to a similar conclusion that natural forms changed rather than remaining static. The Darwinian Revolution intoduced the idea that the mind was a developing capacity intrinsic to nature and not a fixed form extrinsic to nature.

Toward the end of the 19th century, three forms of psychology would emerge that ran counter to the traditional structuralist-psychophysical views spawned from Descartes, Locke, and Hume. Act psychology, drawing from Leibnitz and Kant, provided the first real alternative to Wundt's psychology of mental elements. Basic to act psychology was the concept of intentionality—the intrinsic relatedness of mind to its object of knowledge or affect. This view of mind historically derives from Aristotle's psychology. Drawing upon Darwin's idea of adaptation, functional psychology developed a similar theory of mind in which psychology studies "functions": Activities adapted to the world for the purpose of maintaining the life of the organism. The mind was active and inextricably connected to its objects of knowledge. For functionalism, the object of knowledge was nature—in essence a modern restatement of another aspect of Aristotle's psychology. Gestalt psychology would be very critical of structuralism's emphasis on absolute mental elements and mental concatenation. A German movement drawing upon the heritage of German philosophy, Gestalt psychology proposed that organized forms were not reducible to their parts. The importance of relationships, as in a melody or a visual form, took precedence over analyzing the world into atomistic elements.

Gibson was philosophically and scientifically educated in the mainstream traditions of structuralism and empiricism but was also exposed to functional and Gestalt psychology and evolutionary biology. In his ecological psychology, his two basic concepts are the animal and the environment, and all of his more modern views play into his understanding of these reciprocal concepts. An animal is a being-in-a-world and the environment is the world-of-animals. Each is functionally and structurally tied to the other. The animal and the environment are both organized wholes, and each is characterized by numerous types of change or processes. Due to evolutionary adaptation, the structures and capacities of an animal "fit" or "harmonize" with the make-up of the environment. Surrounding and containing animals is an environment of objects, surfaces, and a medium; and the animal moves across and over surfaces through a medium, using objects to perpetuate its existence. The environment is used to accomplish the animal's ends or goals providing "affordances" for the animal's ways of life. Animal and environment form a functional whole, an ecosystem. This position is neither materialistic nor idealistic for neither matter nor mind is an absolute in Gibson's ecological psychology.

Gibson's direct realism is theoretically united with his ecological psychology and challenges most modern scientifically based epistemologies of perception. Absolute dualism clearly implied indirect perception—perception is both representative and causally separated from the external physical world. Furthermore, because idealism, materialism, and neutral monism involve the theoretical construction of one ontological realm out of the other, perception (experience, consciousness) and the world are separated by inferential derivation. Gibson's ecological ontology of animal and environment treats perception as an ongoing ecological event because it is not localized, hence isolated, within the mind or brain. The animal and environment are united in perception. In order to better understand this epistemological unity, Gibson's ideas can be compared with the two fountainheads of Western thought, Plato and Aristotle.

PLATONIC DUALISM
AND PARMENIDIAN RATIONALISM

Plato's theory of knowledge is intimately related to his theory of being. He divides the cosmos into abstract eternal forms (or eternal ideas) and transitory particulars; the latter is a world of appearances, whereas the former is a world of truth and ultimate reality. Genuine knowledge is abstract and eternal and reached through reason or the rational soul; the perceived world of particular physical objects is illusory and subjective. The senses of the body presumably reveal a flux without inherent order. The rational soul, because it is eternal and distinct from the mortal physical body, can reach abstract eternal knowledge or universal truths. Hence Plato adopted both an ontological dualism of mind (eternal) and matter (transitory) and an epistemological dualism of universals (real) and particulars (appearance). What is real is eternal and what is transitory is mere appearance.

The relationship between Plato and the Scientific Revolution is significant. Plato's dualism of mind and matter was retained. Whereas Plato had accorded physical objects an illusory status (thus he often is referred to as an idealist), modern science treats matter as an ontological reality. Both dualisms, though, end up treating the world of perception as only appearance. For Plato, the world of abstract ideas is real and for dualist scientists it is the theoretically inferred world of matter beyond perception that is real. In both cases order and ultimate reality lie beyond sensory perception; in both cases order and reality are found through reason. There is an empirical element in science, for scientists supposedly start from observation or perception. But true knowledge in Newton's physics pertains to abstract laws that are eternal and changeless within the physical universe. These laws describe the regularities of change. The particulars observed through perception are unique and no two events are ever exactly alike. Newtonian science was Platonic in placing true knowledge beyond transitory, unique perceptions in an eternal realm. Epistemologically and psychologically, sensory and rational consciousness are sharply distinguished.

Plato's hierarchical ontology and epistemology derive from his intellectual predecessors, Pythagoras and Parmenides. Ancient Greece had its own metaphysical controversy over the ultimate foundation to the universe, with materialists, such as Thales, Empedocles, and Democritus, and idealists, such as Pythagoras and Parmenides. Parmenides, in his *Way of Truth,* argued that the transitory world of particulars can be only appearances—what is real must be eternal and unified. Conversely, Democritus reduced everything to physical "atoms," arguing that perceived changes in the world were due to rearrangements of intrinsically inert atoms.

Democritus accepted the reality of motion whereas Parmenides did not, and the former developed a theory of the physical world very similar to Newton's. Yet underneath these disagreements was a common separation of the real world from the world of appearance plus an attempt to reduce everything to one ontological substrate, either mind or matter. In fact, it is with the Greeks that the theory of a primary single principle or substance initially comes on the philosophical scene, but because this universal element was thought to be timeless, it had to exist behind the scene of fluctuating perceptions.

Parmenides rejected the reality of time (change) because it apparently contradicted the Law of Identity. Change involves becoming and passing away; what is not becomes what is, and what is passes away into what is not. The Law of Identity states that a thing either is or it is not: It cannot be both. Thus for Parmenides and his follower Plato, the world-as-it-appears-to-be is unreal and illusory. What is true must be eternal without change. The idea that the universe consists of an absolute substance (or substances) is a reification of this rationalistic principle, and though both Plato and his descendents in the Newtonian age wanted to unite reality under the umbrella of an eternal substrate, the world became dualistic because they distinguished and separated the diversified flux of perception from an eternal and unified substrate known through reason. The ontological and epistemological dualisms of the Scientific Revolution can therefore be traced back to the Parmenidian-Platonic elevation of the eternal one over the temporal many.

At this point several fundamental themes in Gibson's ecological psychology can be introduced and contrasted with Plato. For Gibson, invariance and change are reciprocal and relative. Second, Gibson contends that there is considerable order, both spatially and temporally, within perception per se, because there is a corresponding order within stimulation and environment. Reason is not privy to order. The sharp distinction between the objective and subjective is also questioned; again they are relative and reciprocal. Finally, the whole (unity) and the parts (diversity) are also relative.

Plato's philosophical dualism rests upon a reified logical distinction between identity (order, constancy, homogeneity) and diversity (flux, variation, heterogeneity). Though an eternal unity gives the cosmos coherence, it is ontologically separated from the observed temporal diversity of the everyday world. Aristotle clearly wished to avoid this dualistic picture, and though in some respects he retained Platonic ideas, he moved in the direction of integrating Plato's dualistic philosophy. At a logical level, Gibson's use of the concept of reciprocity addresses the same issue, viz., is nature unified or divided? In essence, Gibson's answer is that the question is wrong. Unity and diversity, and permanence and change are reciprocals. At least at the ecological level, nature is necessarily both unified and diversified, persistent and transforming.

ARISTOTELIAN FUNCTIONALISM
AND GIBSON'S ECOLOGICAL REALISM

Aristotle began his philosophical career as a Platonist and retained some of his teacher's ideas in his mature system of thought, but Aristotle's functional approach to the science of life, as well as his philosophy of science are significantly different from Plato's views. The contrast pivots on a shift of emphasis, for Plato attempted to unite Parmenides with Heraclitus, Parmenides' philosophical adversary, putting Parmenides' ideas above the latter's philosopy. Heraclitus is noted for his pronouncement that "the only thing that stays the same is that nothing stays the same." Change is fundamental. Aristotle attempted a theoretical synthesis as well, but began with Heraclitus as his starting point in attempt to find order within change rather than separate from it.

Following Plato, Aristotle saw the world of observation as fundamentally a world of change but he believed true knowledge could be gained about this perceivable world. In this respect Aristotle is closer to the empiricist spirit of the Scientific Revolution than Plato. Aristotle's main goal as a scientist and philosopher was to understand, rather than reject, change. Thus where Plato's ultimate reality was static and timeless, Aristotle's world was dynamic or temporal. Certain exceptions aside (the Platonic residue in his thinking), everything is in a state of becoming and passing away. Becoming involves "movement" toward some end, and the nature (form) of a thing is defined in terms of the power to reach its actualization or ends. "Psyche" is the "form" of life or the power to achieve its ends, hence life is what life does. This is Aristotle's functionalism. Functioning means the process of achieving ends. Everything in nature moves toward achieving ends, and a thing's form or identity is its powers to achieve ends, hence identity is understood as the potential for action.

Aristotle avoids Plato's mind-body dualism, for mind is "psyche" or the "form" of the body and not a second substance. In general, mind-matter dualism is rejected by Aristotle, for mind is to matter as function is to substance; mind is the power of a living substance. This position is neither materialistic nor idealistic—function and substance stand related but distinct. The substance of a thing is its parts, hence the "psyche" is the integration of the body. Secondly, the form of a thing turns out to be its functioning powers—the "psyche" is a functional integrity. Third, each part has a form, hence substance keeps decomposing into integrated functions. Whole and parts, and substance and function are relative concepts. In neither case do these distinctions reify into absolute and independent ontological realms.

For Aristotle, every function of the "psyche" has a "correlative object." This "object" is what is used in carrying out the function. All functions are understood relative to their correlative objects, for example, to nourish (eat and digest) is understood relative to food and its procurement. Perceiving is defined relative to what is perceived. In fact for all the psychological functions, the correlative object is the world or the environment. This general formula even includes reason, for abstract knowledge is *about* the perceived world and not some separate ethereal realm. Universals (or forms) are revealed through particulars; order is revealed through the flux. Though Aristotle did not use the expression, the meaning is clear: Mind has an ecological reality grounded in the body but actualized in the world. Aristotle, in concordance with this theory of mind and ontology, was an epistemological realist. Whether we are simply opening our eyes to the morning sun or scientifically studying the world with all our rational faculties, our knowledge is direct and the world reveals its true nature as opposed to simply giving a veil of appearances. The "psyche" possesses the power to know; the correlative object, the power to be known. The form or identity of an object is not something hidden away beyond its dynamic actualizations.

Functionalism, act psychology, Gestalt psychology, and process ontology all owe a great deal to the heritage of Aristotle's philosophy, and historically as well as conceptually tie Gibson to Aristotle. There are a great number of limited parallels between Gibson and earlier theorists, but the strongest, most essential theoretical connection is to Aristotle's functionalism. The connecting themes are the reality of change and the emphasis on natural organization, and the resultant ecological psychologies and direct realist epistemologies. During his psychophysical period, Gibson attempted to demonstrate that considerable spatial order and structure existed within the physical world, where others before him had analyzed (e.g., Kepler) matter and energy into elementary simple units. Beginning in his psychophysical period, and becoming increasingly more important in his ecological period, Gibson investigated temporal order within stimulation and the environment. Further, Gibson became increasingly critical of the idea that there was a single, ultimate level to reality, whether it be mental or physical; instead reality reveals a "nesting" of units within units (to be compared with Aristotle's idea of multiple equally real levels of reality).

Early in his education, Gibson was introduced to both Gestalt psychology and functionalism and they are both essential ingredients in his early work, but he progressively begins to tie them together throughout the 1950s and 1960s. In particular both perception and the environment become much more dynamic concepts with his introduction of the ideas of "perceptual systems" and "environmental events." Each end of the polarity, though given a Gestalt interpretation in his psychophysical program, remained relatively inert "spatial" configurations. The duality was, so to speak, energized into an ontological and epistemological merging with Gibson's increasing emphasis on change. In the late 1950s and early 1960s Gibson pays increasing attention to evolution and the dynamic nature of animals and adaptation. In this respect, he goes beyond Aristotle's understanding of change. From 1960 onward, perception was defined as an activity, an integrated set of functions tied to organized perceptual systems. The knowing mind was no longer "localized" in some specific part of the nervous system. In turn, the environment was described as possessing "affordances" that are defined relative to the ways of animate life—analogous to Aristotle's "correlative objects." In turning in this direction, the barrier between mind and matter comes down and Gibson becomes increasingly Aristotelian in his ecological psychology. Animal and environment are a reciprocity, but they are reciprocal because they are dynamic in form. Perceiving is an ecological event that does not take place within the animal—it is an ecological process involving both perceiver and environment.

If Plato split the world with his subjugation of time to eternal absolutes, Aristotle and Gibson, much later, attempted to reunite the world through time. For Gibson the animal and environment are a dynamic ecosystem; in a sense a functional Gestalt. It is a truism to say Gibson was into "space," but he once said to me that the real puzzle was time and that's where he headed.

Chapter 2 _____

PRE-SOCRATIC PHILOSOPHY
and SCIENCE

HERACLITIAN AND PARMENIDIAN PHILOSOPHY

Western philosophy begins in the intellectual conflict between Heraclitus (540–480 B.C.) and Parmenides (515–445 B.C.). This conflict revolved around the relative importance of time in formulating a metaphysics of ultimate reality and an epistemology of knowledge. The beginnings of the philosophical controversies between dualism and monism and rationalism and empiricism are to be found in the writings of these two seminal thinkers and their followers and commentators. This period, preceding the time of Aristotle and Plato, also saw the beginnings of Greek science. Early Greek science combined elements of mathematics, descriptive analysis of nature, and speculative explanatory schemes. Many significant themes that would later influence the philosophy and science of perception have their written origins during this period. Correspondingly, many of the classically intractable problems and puzzles in understanding perception emerge from this intellectual context. The indirect theory of perception, the dualism of thought and perception, and the theory of inner observation all derive from Pre-Socratic thought. Such ideas were developed to solve a set of problems, but they also created problems. Many of these resultant problems would become the grist for the mill of Gibson's criticisms of traditional approaches to perception, optics, and epistemology.

Parmenides argued that true knowledge pertained to an eternal realm of changeless and unified being achieved through reason, whereas Heraclitus believed knowledge was about the rhythm ("Logos") of temporal flux. Parmenides is viewed as a rationalist; Heraclitus more an empiricist. Basically, rationalism is the epistemological position that reason yields knowledge; empiricism, the position that observation yields knowledge. Traditionally, reason is the domain of order, and rationalism is the attempt to derive diversity from order. Perception is the domain of diversity, and empiricism is the attempt to derive order from diversity. Parmenides saw universality and reality beyond perception, whereas Heraclitus saw perception as the "door" into knowledge. Perception reveals diversity and flux and thus, according to Parmenides does not possess order. Oppositely, for Heraclitus, the "Logos" is embodied within the world of perception, thus empiricism is the path to knowledge.

Taking the observed flux of perception as his starting point, Heraclitus described the natural ebb and flow of time as a conflict of opposites. The "Logos" is the form or rhythm of temporal oscillations. (For further duscussion see Kirk and Raven, 1966, pp. 187–196; Sherover, 1975, pp. 11–13.) Aristotle and, much later, modern science, would extend this idea that a law of nature was a constancy in the form of natural change. Everything may change, but everything may change in a repeatable constant way. The significant point in Heraclitus' philosophy is to treat order and constancy as a dynamic principle, rather than as something standing above the flux of perception and time. Further, though this insight became increasingly lost in later empiricist philosophy, order is seen as embodied within the flux of perception, rather than in addition to it.

Parmenides' philosophy, on the other hand, initiates the tradition of rejecting perception as a source of knowledge about objective reality—perception is subjective. Perception reveals a flux of particulars. It is thought which yields unity, organization, and stability (Kirk & Raven, 1966; Sherover, 1975, pp. 265–278). Beginning with the Law of Identity, Parmenides arrives at the conclusion that what is true and real must be both timeless and homogeneous, i.e., reason leads to the idea of an "eternal one" existing beyond perception. The term *diversity* can designate either temporal diversity, i.e., change; spatial diversity, i.e., variations of material distribution; or substantial diversity, i.e., variations in substances. All three types of diversity are associated with the world of perception, and Parmenides' "eternal one" is diametrically the opposite. Being—the eternal one—is omnipresent and ever present, continuous and without variation. It is a reality known only through reason. The objects of perception and reason are ontologically and epistemologically distinguished; perception yields a diversity of what seems to be, and reason yields unity and truth. Parmenides' rationalistic philosophy epitomizes a dual-world view, one in which order and unity are contrasted with diversity and change, thought contrasted with perception, and reality contrasted with appearance.

Plato is the intellectual descendent of Parmenides, attempting through reason and dialectical narrative, to explain the world of perception in terms of a transcendent eternal one. Aristotle is the intellectual descendant of Heraclitus, emphasizing the importance of observation, and believing order could be embodied in change and diversity. Parmenides and Heraclitus represent general philosophical positions not specifically directed toward vision or perception, although they do establish certain general themes that will deeply influence-perceptual theory. We can see an anti-dualistic element to Heraclitus' empiricism, and a decided dualistic ontology and rationalist epistemology in Parmenides. Also time is more fundamental in Heraclitus' basic concept of order ("Logos"). Within Parmenides, time is the anathema of order. Contemporary with these general philosophies of reality and knowledge, specific explanations of perception, in particular vision, were being developed in ancient Greece.

THE PHYSICS AND OPTICS OF VISION

From a scientific or naturalist point of view, one basic requirement the earliest Greek theories of perception addressed was how perceiver and world made "contact" with each other. The philosophical consensus was that there could not be "action-at-a-distance." Causal explanations fell into three main groups: Something ("rays") go out of the eyes and contact the world; something (eidola) comes from the world and contacts the sense organs; or sense organs and world are united through a medium. Corresponding to these causal explanations, there existed various ontological theories of perception. Perception was described exclusively in physical terms (materialism); perception was described as a product and reality of the mind (idealism or mentalism); or perception was described as a combined product of mind and matter (dualism). Various scientific-philosophical theories embodied different aspects of these basic perspectives.

The beginnings of the concept of emanation have been traced back to Pythagoras (ca. 580–530 B.C.) (Polyak, 1957; Ronchi, 1957, 1967). According to proponents of the emanation hypothesis, the eye emitted rays that traveled through space and came in physical contact with objects. Vision occurred when these "visual rays" took on the shape of the contacted object and returned with these forms to the eyes. According to the emanation hypothesis, the world does not send forms to be received by the eyes, rather the eyes send out "carriers" to bring back the forms of the world. The visual rays producing perception are contingent upon the outgoing process of emanation from the perceiver.

Euclid (ca. 330–260 B.C.), a supporter of the emanation hypothesis, further articulated the position in his studies of optics and perspective. For Euclid, visual rays were thought to be rays of light propagated rectilinearly from the eyes. Euclid, though, did not exclusively identify light with visual rays, since he also thought the sun emitted light. Early optics, in fact, identified two types of light: The "outer light" having its source in the physical world and the "inner light" emanated by the perceiver. Euclid was primarily interested in developing a geometry of visual perspective rather than a physical optics of vision, and he described perspective in terms of rays going from eye to object.

In investigating the geometry of the eye-object relation, Euclid developed the idea of the visual cone. "The figure enclosed by the visual rays is a cone which has its apex at the eye and its base at the edge of the object looked at" (Euclid, *Optica,* Postulate 2). The visual cone provided Euclid with a geometrical model for describing the direction of motion of visual rays and the relationship between the eyes and viewed objects. In initiating the geometrical approach to perspective, Euclid was providing a key mathematical conceptualization for later optical theories of perspective, for example, Kepler's optics. Geometrical perspective or projection is a way of understanding the relationship between the world and perception. Perception of the world is founded upon geometrical projections of the world. Within such a model, perception is exclusively based on a spatial representation. There is no temporal dimension.

Euclid's concept of the visual cone is secondary to his concept of rays. Euclid's perspective geometry is logically constructed out of points and lines. Besides initiating the spatial-geometrical perspective approach to optics, Euclid also lays the seeds of the elementaristic approach in visual optics. Light is primarily a punctate phemonemon. The cone is built up from rays. Treating light as a collection of points or lines has a long-standing tradition in optics. Elementaristic optics "creates" the perceptual problem of how the units of light are coalesced together into continuous and organized visual impressions. (Perceptual awareness does not seem to be a mosaic or a collection of pointillistic impressions—it appears to be organized.) Because Euclid's primary concern in his *Optics* was a geometrical rather than physical understanding of light, the concept of rays and cones can be seen as logical artifacts of his treatment, rather than representing real things. Regardless, the use of such geometrical constructions biases "physical" theories of light. Kepler employed a geometry of points and lines in describing light. What begins as a methodological convenience may later be seen as an ontological reality.

Light energy was analyzed into elemental units, and the classic tradition of physical optics thereafter assumed light possessed such a limited structural complexity. Gibson would be critical of traditional optics, in particular "pointillism," because it impoverished optical stimulation, and a second major approach, the pictorial model, because it misconstrued the nature of optical stimulation, as well as impoverishing it.

Euclid's *Optica* constitutes the beginning of the study of perspective. It should be noted that Euclid's "natural" perspective is not identical with "pictorial perspective." In natural perspective the form of an object adopted by visual rays is projected to a point (the apex of the visual cone). Pictorial perspective is the geometrical projection of forms to a plane which intersects the visual cone; this second approach was developed much later by the artists of the Renaissance. (See Diagrams 1 and 2).

Visual perception can be compared to viewing pictures projected into the eye. The optics of vision becomes a study in how pictorial representations of reality get projected to the perceiver. The popular analogies of the eye being like a camera and the retinal image being like a picture are associated with this tradition. Natural perspective does not represent projected light as if it were something that could be seen because all forms are projected to a point. For the picture model, perception will be indirect. What the perceiver actually sees are "flat" pictures of the world, rather than the world. Alternatively, Gibson, (1961a) in denying any functional similarity between visual optics and pictorial representations, dropped the pictorial perspective approach to optics in favor of natural perspective. Even natural perspective has its inherant limitations. As Gibson would note, it disregards time.

Another historically interesting aspect of Euclid's *Optica* (Postulate 23) is his explanation of seen distance. Depth or distance is not something embodied in either points or pictures. A long standing problem in the history of vision is explaining how distance is visually perceived. According to Euclid, the visually perceived distance of an object is a function of the length of the "visual rays." This hypothesis could be interpreted, states Ronchi (1957), to imply that the eye somehow measures the length of the rays it emits. This hypothesis also characterizes seen distance as the line-length of empty-space between objects and the eye. In developing

DIAGRAM I

NATURAL PERSPECTIVE

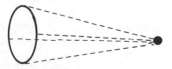

DIAGRAM 2

PICTORIAL PERSPECTIVE

his theory of depth perception, Bishop Berkeley (1709) adopted this concept of distance, and his views would dominate visual psychology for the next 250 years. Though he was Berkeley's archenemy, Newton's concept of empty space is historically related to this description of distance. Generally, in 18th and 19th century science, the physical spatial world consisted of "objects" (static, self-contained things) possessing size, shape and location within space (a void). Explaining perception meant explaining how this kind of spatial world could be perceived. Distance was the length of empty space between objects. Central to Gibson's reconceptualization of ecological space was his ground theory developed in his *Perception of the Visual World* (1950a). Space was no longer described as a void containing detached objects, but rather as intersecting surfaces; space was structurally more complex and differently organized.

The main alternative to the emanation hypothesis was provided by the Greek atomists Democritus and Leucippus (ca. 450 B.C.) in their *eidola* hypothesis. Physical objects, according to the atomists, continuously give off "hollow and thin frames" *(eidolae)* that strike the eyes of perceivers. These *eidolae,* which were thought to be material complexes of atoms, would transfer their shapes to the "soul atoms" and produce awareness of these forms. The main difference between the eidola and emanation hypotheses lies in whether perception is seen as instigated in the perceiver or the world.

The *eidola* hypothesis contained the idea that the observer sees objects because replicas of the objects reach the eye. Objects are represented to the observer by means of simulation. Hereafter, in accordance with Boring (1950, p. 672), this belief is referred to as the simulative assumption. Both the *eidola* and emanation views supposed the function of "light" (whatever its origin) was to provide a representation by means of which the world is perceived. Perceiver and world were connected, though in effect, separated by means of a representation. Simulation is one possible form of representation, where the representation replicates the actual form (shape) of the perceived object. However construed, the idea of representation places an intermediary between the perceiver and the world. Treating light as an intermediary simulation makes vision indirect. Simulation, I believe, is connected with mind-matter dualism. Light as a copy of the world serves as an intermediary between the mind and the world. As I will explain momentarily, it is connected with the idea that perception involves an "inner observation" of forms within the mind.

Epicurus (342–270 B.C.), another advocate of the *eidola* hypothesis, was fairly explicit in his belief in simulation. "There are images like in shape to the solid bodies . . . these models similar in colour and shape, leave objects and enter . . . into our sight and mind" (Epicurus, ca. 300 B.C., Oates, pp. 5–6). The *eidolae* produce *phantasiae* through impressions upon the soul, which in turn are replicas of the object's form. The soul (mind) perceives the world because it contains replicas within itself of the world.

The simulative assumption has been extremely influential within the history of perceptual theory. Ultimately, it is connected with mind-matter dualism though it was accepted by numerous thinkers in later centuries who were not ontological dualists, notably Berkeley. Conceptually it is tied to the picture theory of perception, as well as the homunculus hypothesis (the theory of inner observation is discussed in the next section). Additionally, it is one of the pillars of indirect realism, and significantly directed thinking and investigation regarding perceptual stimulation. Also, Gibson's attack on the simulative assumption, beginning very early in his career, led to many of his novel ideas about perception. It is definitely the crux of his disagreement with Berkeleian theories in his *Perception of the Visual World*. "Perception is by means of replication." It is a simple idea, yet perhaps because of its simplicity it has often been taken for granted. More generally, where light or any other type of stimulation is viewed as a connecting or interposed link between mind (perceiver) and matter (world), the perceiver and the world are separated.

Democritus, though a materialist, attempted to combine the emanation and *eidola* hypotheses. He argued that emanations from the eye must meet the incoming *eidolae* and form in the air, an impression of the forms of the *eidolae*. He pictured this physical interaction as comparable to a seal impressing its form on wax. The forms were only then transmitted to the eye affecting the "soul atoms" (Stratton, 1917). This explanation parallels the "inner light" and "outer light" view found in Plato and other Greek thinkers making perception a dual product of perceiver and the world.

Later philosophers and psychologists invariably thought the role of the perceiver as contributory or constructive, as adding something to the component offered from the world. Epicurus, for example, believed the images of *phantasiae* were fitted to concepts that had been built up through experience. Seeing was described as a judging of incoming phantasiae in accordance with learned concepts. The physics and optics of perception are seen as providing the raw material upon which perceptual experiences are built. This view fits into the Platonic dualistic scheme, where the senses yield particulars and the mind brings them together through thought. Physical atomism, which breaks the world down into physical particulars, robs the world of order. The analytic approach in physics, initiated with Democritus, would eventually become the dominant view in modern physical science. Mind adds order to matter. The general, extremely pervasive view that the mind contributes order to perception is a direct implication of mind-matter dualism.

According to the atomists, such as Democritus, individual atoms do not have color. They only have size, shape, position, and spatial order. Democritus believed that color was a property only of interacting atoms. Color is seen (not heard or smelled) because only the visual sense is constructed to receive this property of *eidolae*. Later scientists, such as Galen, would provide an alternative explanation placing color exclusively within the perceiver. This became the more popular explanation, later developing into Johannes Müller's (1843, 1848) "specific energies of nerves" hypothesis. Either view, though, turns actual reality into something different in quality from perceptual experience. "Color," in this case, is not intrinsic to the world. Democritus' atomism was a philosophical attempt to reduce the common sense world to a more fundamental level that eliminated the apparent Heraclitian flux of "becoming" and "passing away," making atoms indestructible and unchangeable (like little models of Parmenides' eternal one). Change is reduced to rearrangement at the fundamental level of physical reality. Perception takes on a false quality in this sense, making actual reality not only ontologically distinct but qualitatively different.

THE PSYCHOPHYSIOLOGY OF VISION

Both the eidola and emanation hypotheses assume something is sent through space in vision. An alternative view, to be more fully explained in discussing Aristotle, is the medium hypothesis. For example, Chrysippus, (280–212 B.C.), a leading Stoic thinker on vision, opposed the *eidola* hypothesis and the simulative assumption associated with it. For Chrysippus, there was no image or copy of an object transmitted to the eyes. Instead, vision was described as a "modification" of the "soul" that occurred when "visual *pneuma*" was sent from the brain to the eyes and "stressed" the air between the visual organ and the seen object. Chrysippus utilized Euclid's visual cone in describing the form of the stressed air between objects and the eyes. This cone of stressed air formed with its base at the object and apex at the pupil (Sambursky, 1959).

Galen (131–201 A.D.), following the Stoic theory of vision, supposed that a modification (stressing) of the medium of air transpired only in the presence of light. Like the Stoics, Galen used Euclid's visual cone to describe perspective or "what will be seen." Though it may be obvious that "external" light is necessary for sight, what light is and how it is involved in vision have been ongoing issues in the history of thought. The medium of air, actualized in the presence of light, becomes "endowed with sensory power" (Lindberg, 1976) by means of which objects are seen. Strictly speaking, *no thing* is transmitted. Is light a medium or a thing? The answer one chooses for this physical question will in turn affect the approach one takes to the physiology and psychology of vision. Does vision require mediating copies either inside or outside the perceiver? Is perception the result (or end point) of a transmission?

The physiology of perception contained in Galen's works (Galen, ca. 200), was the authoritative physiology through the Middle Ages. It began to lose its prominence in the 16th century with the advent of Vesalius' studies (1543). In particular, later thinkers inherited through Galen's writings two hypotheses that proved extremely influential. The lens, first described by Rufus (ca. 100 A.D.) (Singer, 1959), was hypothesized by Galen to be the sensitive portion of the eye. Galen, following Erasistratus (fl. 300–260 B.C.) (Mason, 1962; Singer, 1959), assumed the eyes contained a "visual *pneuma*"—a type of "animal spirit"—that reacted to the forms enclosed in the visual cone. (The terms *pneuma* and *spirit* indicate a medium rather than a thing.) Not until Kepler's time (1611) was it accepted that the retina was the sensitive anatomical structure of the eye.

A second hypothesis found in Galen's writings has proved to be of greater and more lasting significance. He contended that there was a specific pneuma for every different type of sense organ, each of which responded differently to physical effects upon it. Galen's hypothesis was an alternative to the atomist's explanation of special sensory qualities for different senses. For Galen, the sensory differences are inner-determined. The idea that sensory impressions are specific to the affected sense organ or pneuma evolved into Müller's "specific energies of nerves hypothesis." It came to signify to thinkers, notably Müller and his illustrious student, Hermann von Helmholtz (1866), that sensory awareness was of the specific nerves being stimulated. Perception involoves an "inner" awareness of physiological states. This hypothesis of "inner awareness," along with the representative theory of stimulation, historically provided two basic starting points for indirect theories of perception.

In modern times indirect realism (Hirst, 1965; Mandelbaum, 1964), or as it has been alternatively called "the representative theory of perception" (Armstrong, 1961; Hamlyn, 1961; Hirst, 1959; Smythies, 1965), has become the accepted epistemology in scientific theories of perception. Another one of its theoretical seeds, the homunculus hypothesis, combines elements of both the "inner awareness" and "representation" hypotheses. Images (in some form) are transmitted to the brain where the soul observes them.

The homunculus hypothesis implied a particular functional conception of the visual image. It is something that is "internally" observed. Within the 17th century, the idea of internal observation was influential in describing the retinal image; the retinal image was compared to an internal picture. In the 18th century it became unpopular to say the mind (or brain) actually observed incoming images, yet visual experience was still described as if it were a literal observation of the retinal image. The homunculus hypothesis separates perceptual experience from the physical world. The perceiver experiences some state or thing within the body or mind; consequently knowledge of the outside world is epistemologically indirect.

Two basic stages can be noted in the transmission depicted in Diagram 3. First, an image is transmitted from the object to the sense organ. Second, an image, e.g., by means of "animal spirits," is transmitted from the sense organ to the mind. With the rise of modern biology, nerve impulses would take the place of animal spirits as conductors, but the general psychophysiological model proposed by the ancient Greeks (hereafter referred to as the causal theory of perception) has remained popular in modern times. Both light and neural impulses are propagated, carrying a representation of the world to the mind. Light and neural impulses are mediators in a casual chain. A mediator may causally (or spatially) connect two distinct things (mind and world), yet in effect it separates through interpolation. Both the representational and causal theories lead to indirect realism for in both cases something is placed between the mind and the world.

If visual awareness is of anatomically internal images, a property of the physical world must be simulated in the image for there to be awareness of that property. If the image is what is seen, anything not in the image is not seen. Although the simulative assumption presupposes the homunculus hypothesis, it remained influential long after explicit defense of the homunculus disappeared. Berkeley (1709) seems to have believed in simulation, yet not in homunculus. Why must a literal copy of X transmit-

DIAGRAM 3

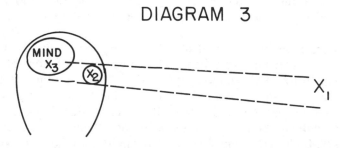

X_1 is a physical object. X_2 is the corresponding image (e.g., *eidola*) in the eye. X_3 is the transmitted image located in the area of the brain where the mind is located.

ted to the perceiver be a necessary condition for the perception of X? To repeat, simulation is only one form of representation, but if perception involves something functionally analogous to inner observation of inner representations (a functional homunculus), then whatever is sensed (rather than inferred or derived) must be simulated in these inner representations.

At this point, it is possible to summarize those ideas or hypotheses so far discussed that formed the historical starting points for theories that perception is ontologically and epistemologically indirect. They include:

1. Pictorial perspective and the representative theory of simulation.
2. Inner awareness of physiological or neural states.
3. The homunculus hypothesis of inner observation.
4. The causal theory of perception.
5. Appearance versus scientific reality.
6. Mind-matter dualism, in particular the separation of order and diversity.

The last idea, though grounded intellectually in Parmenides, is a basic and extremely influential theme in Plato. More is said on this idea in the next chapter. The separation of order and diversity is one facet of mind-matter dualism. It is notable that other ideas just listed (e.g., item 3) also follow from mind-matter dualism.

In the foregoing discussion, several basic themes in the history of perceptual theory have been uncovered in ancient Greek thought; simulation, the homunculus, the causal theory, indirect realism and the separation of mental unity and physical diversity all originate during this period. Gibson, at different points in his career, would challenge all of these ideas, not insofar as critiquing the ancient Greeks themselves, but in attacking the modern renditions and elaborations on these ideas. The remaining portion of Greek philosophy and science, in effect its intellectual culmination, can be found in the works of Plato and Aristotle. Both were familiar with many of the ideas discussed above, but in breadth and depth of treatment each in his distinctive way went far beyond their predecessors or contemporaries and left a more lasting impression on the history of thought and perceptual theory.

Chapter 3 _____

PLATONIC
and ARISTOTELIAN PHILOSOPHY

PLATO'S THEORY OF REALITY AND KNOWLEDGE

> *we must make a distinction and ask, what is that which always is and has no becoming; and what is that which is always becoming and never is? That which is apprehended by intelligence and reason is always in the same state; but that which is conceived by opinion with the help of sensation and without reason, is always in a process of becoming and perishing and never really is.*
>
> —Plato, *Timaeus*

Plato is generally regarded as the most influential writer and thinker in western intellectual history. During his time (427–347 B.C.), Greek civilization was entering a period of flux and instability, and differing philosophies proliferated. Plato's quest for stability and certainty in philosophical knowledge was motivated in part by his disillusionment with the seemingly disordered world around him. His philosophical dualism, reflecting the mytho-religious dualism Greek culture inherited from ancient Egypt, psychologically provided an escape from the world of change, ontologically provided an explanation of time, and philosophically provided for subsequent intellectual history an abstract scheme of thought that would be incorporated and developed in western philosophy, science, and religion.

Following the intellectual tradition epitomized in Parmenides, Plato divides existence into a unified eternal realm of abstract forms and a diversified temporal flux of particulars. Plato's epistemological goal is certainty, which according to him can be reached through reason: Reason deals with logic and abstractions that are eternal truths. Also following Parmenides, Plato believed that certain knowledge could not be obtained through perception because perception reveals flux, ambiguity, and a vast array of unique particulars and differences. Medieval Europe would theologically follow Plato for it fitted well with the religious dualism of the Judeo-Christian tradition. Plato's rationalist epistemology would be incorporated into modern science: What is abstract and eternal explains the observed flux. Initially, the scientific endeavor was viewed as a quest for certain knowledge in the form of universal laws and principles from which the observable universe could be deduced. (Deduction is to derive particulars from abstractions.) Though eternal abstractions give the total cosmos order, these "forms" are distinguished from what they are intended to explain, viz., in the Scientific Revolution laws were viewed as imposed upon matter. The origin of these laws was the divine mind of God.

Plato's theory of man mirrors his general cosmological theory and sets the stage for modern mind-body dualism. The rational mind is eternal whereas the physical body is mortal and perishing. Only through something eternal can eternal truths be known. Through the physical senses, the body is the source of "opinions" about the fluctuating world, but the senses are open to ambiguity, uncertainty, and relativity of perspective. Ontologically, Plato divides reason and bodily perception because reason deals with abstractions while perception deals with particulars. Given this dualistic position, Plato offers a two-fold explanation of the relation of the knower and the physical world. His explanation combines a physical-sensory dimension (temporal world) and a mental-conceptual dimension (eternal forms).

According to the emanation hypothesis, perception was instigated by the transmission of an "inner light" outward towards the physical world. The thesis that there is an inner fire (light) residing in the eyes originated with Parmenides (Kirk & Raven, 1966) and was popularized and elaborated by the physician-philosopher Alcmaeon. The *synaugy* hypothesis advocated by Empedocles (500–430 B.C.) incorporated the idea of an "inner light." Empedocles argued that "external elementary fire" in the form of *aporroiai* was given off by objects and met with an inner fire coming from the eyes (Beare, 1906; Lindberg, 1976). Substituting atoms for light, Democritus would later provide a similar explanation of vision involving a synergy of inner and outer factors.

Plato's physical explanation of vision involved a dual concept of an inner and outer light. The inner light traveled from the brain to the eyes where it was impressed with the forms of the outer light. (In Democritus, physical entities carry the forms; in Empedocles and Plato, forms are carried by light.) Plato emphasized the importance of light as a medium through which objects were sensed. Inner and outer light coalesced "like to like" to form the medium of light in which impressions of objects were formed. Strictly speaking, the instrument of sight was not the eye but the synergized body of light from the eye to the object. The Stoic explanation of vision discussed in the previous chapter adopted a similar conception of light as a synergistic medium (Lindberg, 1976). Knower and known in perception form a "merging" through the medium of light. It is historically noteworthy that the concept of an "inner light or fire" would be transformed in later centuries into "animal spirits" and finally "neural impulses." "Animal spirits" would be distinguished ("like to like") according to the different objects of sense (Galen's specific *pneuma*). Emanation, "inner light," "animal spirits," and "specific energies" all belong to a similar, connected heritage of thinking. The general problem addressed in the synergistic explanation is how the knower and known made "contact": The answer is through a medium (of light) that allows for a merging.

Though Plato's synergistic explanation of perception appears to bridge the gap between the perceiver and the world, it only allows for a physical contact between the world and the perceiver's body. As we have seen, both the emanation and *eidola* hypotheses attempted to explain "physical contact" between the perceiver and the world. Forms may be transmitted across a physical connection, but a problem arises regarding how these forms are made known to the mind. How is the ontological gulf bridged? For Democritus there was no problem, for, being a materialist, the "mind" was nothing more than atomic complexes. For Plato there was a real problem for the mind knows of abstraction; it is the body that senses particulars.

Through abstraction, man does make judgments about the world of perception but these judgments can be no more than approximations. The particulars of time do approximate ideal forms, but there cannot be any real embodiment of eternal forms in temporal particulars. A drawn or painted square may approximate an ideal square (the abstraction) but no more. Abstractions for Plato are ideals, and abstractions cannot contain any specific features. The "perfect square" cannot possess any specific size, though all particular squares have a determinate size. According to Plato, to perceive a square means to sense a particular form and judge it to be an approximation to the ideal square, an idea of the rational mind. Note that in perception, the senses deliver particulars and the mind adds abstractions, which could never be derived simply from the senses.

It can be argued that Plato's dualistic treatment of perception is the progenitor of all subsequent enrichment theories of perception. The theory under consideration is that the mind adds order to the effects of the physical senses. Plato's mind-matter dualism placing order exclusively in the mind, necessitates that in perception, the mind must contribute the apparent degree of order in perceptual awareness or consciousness. Later enrichment theories roughly divide into two groups: the empiricist school where mental order depended on memory generalizations of sense impressions and the nativist school, of which Plato is the first outstanding member, arguing that mental order is inherent to the mind itself. Mental order for empiricists was learned, whereas for nativists mental order is innate (Hochberg, 1962).

Historically, Plato's mind-matter dualism had a similar and mutually reinforcing effect upon both the theory of science and theories of perception. Order resides in an eternal realm; reason can know this order and "explain" the flux, but the temporal world of matter neither reveals nor embodies this order. In science, abstractions of the mind refer to laws of nature. In perception, abstractions of the mind are used to judge sense-impressions and give them some semblance of order. Ontologically, unity is seen as residing at some deep, ultimate level beyond observation. Epistemologically, this unity cannot be known through perception but only through the separate faculty of reason. Scientific explanations of perception in later centuries accepted the diversified flux of matter, energy, and the senses and then tried to give it order through some set of mental principles.

ARISTOTLE'S PHILOSOPHY OF SCIENCE

J. H. Randall, in his book *Aristotle* (1960), has strongly and convincingly argued that as a student of nature, Aristotle (e.g., in his *Physics*) was first and foremost a functional-teleologist. During the Sciencific Revolution it was Aristotle's teleological concept of final causes that came under attack by Galileo, yet according to Randall, Aristotle's teleology needs to be understood in the context of his functionalism. Aristotle's philosophy is naturalistic rather than supernaturalistic, and his doctrine of final causes refers to observable processes within nature. Final causes are the outcomes of natural functions, and provide a conceptual tool for describing and categorizing natural activities. Aristotle's functionalism provided an alternative to Plato's dualism and "other-worldly" or supernatural theories. What is especially relevant is how central the functional theme is in Aristotle's biological-psychological works (*De Anima, De Partibus Ani-*

malium, De Generatione Animalium). If one looks at his biology and psychology from this functional perspective, it seems to anticipate Gibson's ecological approach in many important ways.

It should be noted that historical and philosophical interpretations of Aristotle are diverse and numerous. One significant complication is the strong possibility that Aristotle considerably modified his views between his earlier period when he studied with Plato and his mature period when his views turned both more anti-Platonic and biological-functional in emphasis. Randall emphasizes Aristotle's mature views, to the degree that they can be reasonably extracted from the total corpus of his surviving works. My remarks on Aristotle and comparisons between Aristotle and Gibson take Aristotle's more mature views as their basis. Interestingly, it is Gibson's most mature views (1966–1980) that bear the strongest resemblance to Aristotle.

Aristotle's functional-teleological framework is apparent in his general philosophy of nature (ontology) and theory of scientific knowledge (epistemology). Nature involves *telos* (purpose), and a scientific explanation involves understanding this telos. Aristotle is a realist in his philosophy of science contra Plato, for *telos* is revealed within the observable world of particulars—it is not supernatural or transcendent of the observable world. Knowledge is empirical for it derives from what is sensed or perceived. *Telos* means goal, purpose, or end. A natural process is directed toward an end, but this direction comes from within the natural world, and not from beyond it, as in Plato. Randall has arugued that Aristotle based his philosophy of nature on a biological model. Life shows purpose through various functionings or activities that achieve ends; living forms go through developmental processes that lead to maturation, reproduction, and eventual death. Natural biological processes are goal-directed. This is Aristotle's basic model for all nature.

Heraclitus' emphasis on the primacy of change is Aristotle's philosophical starting point. Aristotle's goal is to explain or understand change, rather than to develop a philosophical system that relegates change to an illusory or secondary status. For "things undergoing change" four questions require answers that explain a change. What is it that is changing? (Formal cause) Out of what is it made? (Material cause) By what agent is the change instigated? (Efficient cause) For what end? (Final cause) If any of these four questions is left unanswered the change is not sufficiently understood. Second, all four causes are to be found within nature. ·

In his atomistic philosophy, Democritus proposed that change occurs due to atoms moving each other about by impacting upon each other. There is no "action at a distance" (thus his eidola theory), and change is instigated from past to present. The future does not affect the present.

This corresponds to the mechanistic view of causality developed during the Scientific Revolution. Aristotle, aware of this type of causality, referred to it as "efficient causality," yet felt it was only part of a complete understanding of change. The efficient cause is that event (to kick the ball) that sets the change going (the ball moving). It was the mechanistic view of causality that Galileo developed in opposition to Aristotle's teleologism, arguing that it was sufficient for understanding natural processes. The model for mechanistic causality was also applied to perception within the Scientific Revolution. Perception was treated as a consequence of a successive series of events initiated in the physical world and terminating in the brain and/or mind.

The material cause in Aristotle corresponds to Democritus' elementaristic view of physical nature. Within elementarism, everything in nature consists of parts, and each entity's identity is reducible to its parts. Along with the mechanistic view of causality, Newtonian science adopted an atomistic view of matter. This reductionist (analytic) theory of nature would influence scientific treatments of light and neurophysiology. The elementaristic treatment of physical nature and Plato's theory of the temporal world reinforce each other, for in both cases the world of matter and time is robbed of order. Aristotle, though, goes on to include two other "causes" that set him apart from the Democritus-Newtonian tradition. In this regard he anticipates the Gestalt-Gibsonian rejection of the atomistic view of nature.

Aristotle does not identify the "what is it?" of a natural entity with its parts. The whole is not reducible to its parts. He notes that processes have consequences. These consequences can be purposes, as in human action, but also they may be simply the natural result of growth and development in all living things. (Acorns grow into oak trees.) The natural end of any process is the "final cause," and the power within a thing to reach its final cause is its "formal cause." Aristotle identifies the "what is it?" of a thing with its formal cause, i.e., its power (potentiality) to achieve its natural ends. The final cause realized is the "actuality" of the process. The former cause designates the powers that the parts possess in unison—in fact, the former cause (the whole) is the order (or organization) of the parts (material cause). The parts are necessary, but they are not identified with the power or identity of a thing.

Aristotle's teleologism is not supernatural or Platonic. Processes move toward natural ends—a child grows into an adult. This actualization of what is potential involves accomplishments, thus the end (final cause) of a process is a natural, observable event. It is an intrinsic and essential feature of the nature of the change. The final cause is the determinate actualization of the formal cause of the change. Natural change is described as general powers actualized as determinate and regularly repeating ends. Aristotle sees nature as would a developmentalist. He avoids the extremes of Democritus' atomism, which eliminates order and *telos* from the physical world, and Plato who places order and *telos* in a second realm beyond the observable world. What Aristotle does believe, quite significantly, is that order and change are tied together: The processes (or powers) of a thing reveal order for such processes achieve determinate yet general ends.

This anti-dualistic ontology is reflected in Aristotle's epistemology. Knowledge of all four causes is to be found within the temporal world. Aristotle rejects Plato's eternal realm of ideal forms. Order, direction, and universality can be found within the flux of particulars. Plato sees knowledge as transcendental to observables; Aristotle is an arch-empiricist. Knowledge is about observables. Consequently, he is an epistemological realist. The powers (formal cause) of a thing can be known without recourse to a world beyond perception. Where Plato separated particulars and universals ontologically and epistemologically, Aristotle wishes to unite them. Universals, in fact, are embodied within their actualizations. Universals are powers (potentialities) revealed through activity. The power or potential (e.g., the ability to move) is the universal and the actualization (e.g., a specific movement) is the particular.

ARISTOTLE'S BIOLOGY AND PSYCHOLOGY

Aristotle's books that are most exclusively concerned with biology and psychology include *de Anima, de Generatione Animalium,* and *de Partibus Animalum.* According to Aristotle, the *arche* (form) of *zoa* (living things) is *psyche. Psyche* is the general principle of life. It is first the "power of living" (the power to live) and secondly the actual process (operation) of living. For any living thing there is first its specific material composition (material cause), and second is its form (formal cause). The form of the body is the *psyche,* i.e., what identifies it as a living thing; the matter of a body is its parts. Aristotle does not identify the principle of life with material composition—he does not reduce a living form to its parts. The principle of organization within the parts of the body is cooperation of action (or process), hence the power of life refers to the functional organization of the body's parts working together. Further, in his hierarchical view of life, Aristotle avoids the idea of ultimate parts or an ultimate substance. Any part of the body itself is intrinsically complex and possesses some activity peculiar to it. Any part itself has parts. There is no formless matter, no simple elements. If Aristotle wished to avoid the dualism of Plato, equally so he wished to avoid the reductionism of the Greek atomists.

For each operation of the body (seeing, eating, movement), there is an accomplishment. Eating accomplishes nourishment—perceiving produces knowledge. A body (material cause), instigated by some efficient cause, acts (formal cause) yielding an end (final cause). The *psyche* is an integrated set of functions; it is the powers (potentialities) and functions (actualities) of the physical body. Power and functioning are dynamic principles, but they are manifested only within matter—there is no matterless form. Aristotle, therefore, rejects the ontological dualism in Plato's theory of man. Thinking and perceiving are capacities of a physical thing (the body) rather than a second thing.

Aristotle would say a power is understood in terms of its actualizations, and the actualizations (the activity-functions) are understood in terms of its correlative object. What is the power to write? The potential for actual writing. And what is writing? An activity that produces written words. Functions are not simply muscular movements, for something is achieved and these achievements involve the use of something beyond the living form. Aristotle ties the *psyche* to the natural world. There is no separate realm of forms or ideas, as in Plato, that are known through the mind. For Plato, the mind was separate from the body and its "objects" were separate from the material world. For Aristotle, the mind is not separate from the body and its "correlative objects" are not distinct from the material world. Aristotelian biology and psychology has an ecological dimension for functions are tied to correlative objects in the world.

Several important parallels exist between Aristotelian and Gibsonian psychology. For Aristotle, mind is an activity or functioning rather than a separate thing from the body. Beginning in the early 1960s, Gibson used functional-dynamic concepts to define perception and in a variety of ways attacked "mentalistic" theories of perception. Psychological processes are ecological, tied to the environment through their distinctive functions. Gibson, in fact, avoided the term "mind" because of its common dualistic interpretation and meaning. Because both Aristotle and later Gibson define perception functionally and do not invoke a "separate reality" beyond the physical environment, perception is tied to the observable world. For both Aristotle and Gibson, psychological processes are integrated—the body is organized in terms of "co-operative" interdependent activities. Both Aristotle and later Gibson treat a life form as a functional whole, where organization involves cooperation of activities toward common ends. Reduction of reality to atomistic elements is rejected, yet equally so is a supra-natural metaphysics that ties the universe together from "above and beyond." Neither Gibson nor Aristotle was a materialist or reductionist because complexity and integrated activities exist at all "levels" within the natural world. There are no simple, segregated elements (atoms) of nature. Order is embodied throughout the physical world. Finally, both Aristotle and Gibson saw reality as fundamentally dynamic. Both the living form and its world are conceptualized in terms of processes. It should be noted though that in some respects Gibson's view of nature is even more dynamic than Aristotle's. Gibson saw nature through 20th century evolutionary eyes. These are ontological similarities between Aristotle and Gibson. I interpret the Aristotelian-Gibsonian view of nature and mind as theoretically distinct from both Platonic dualism and materialistic reductionism. Epistemologically, there are also parallels that can be highlighted through examining Aristotle's views on perception.

ARISTOTLE'S THEORY OF PERCEPTION

For Aristotle, sense-perception involves a sense-organ, a medium through which the sense-organ is acted upon, and a sensed-object. Looking at sense-perception from this perspective, Aristotle could distinguish five senses each with a separate sense organ. For each sense (seeing, hearing, smelling, tasting, touching), there is also a specific object of sense, e.g., color for vision, sound for hearing. For each sense, the sense organ is the material cause, the power and activity of sensing is the formal cause, and the specific object sensed, the correlative object. The medium is the efficient cause. Aristotle's idea of "special sensibles" ultimately was connected with the "specific energies of nerves" hypothesis, though Aristotle did not believe that the peculiarity of a special sensible resided in the body. He did believe that each sense had a distinctive organ that was receptive to a different sensory quality of an external object.

Aristotle also believed that the specific senses were functionally united through a "common sense" for there are sensibles not peculiar to just one sense, e.g., shape, duration, size, and movement. The unity of the senses is functional for there is no special sense organ for the common sense, but only a commonality and cooperation of function across the senses. The five senses are functionally integrated. The specific energies of nerves hypothesis is frequently connected with the heterogeneity of senses hypothesis (Berkeley): Each sense is distinct and separate in function and qualitative experience. One important parallel between Aristotle and Gibson is the concept of the functional unity of the senses. Gibson rejected both the specific energies of nerves hypothesis, with its subjective implications for perception, and the heterogeneity of senses hypothesis. Though Aristotle emphasized analysis in his scientific discussions, he believed in the reality of organization in nature. The *psyche* and the body can be analyzed into parts but there exists a functional unity of the parts, including the senses. This wholistic orientation is also very pronounced in Gibson's "system" approach to the senses.

Aristotle views a sense as a power (a capability) to sense some property of the physical world. The power becomes actualized in the process of sensing. Prior to the actual sensing of X, X as a sensible property is defined as a power to be sensed as "X." For example, "blue" exists potentially in the object as "to be seen as blue," and "seeing blue" (the sensing activity) exists potentially in the perceiver. In "seeing blue" both powers are actualized as "the seeing of blue." Aristotle views sensing as a unitary process involving the perceiver and the world. Although there are two separate powers (to sense X and to be sensed X), in their actualization there is a unitary event. The actualization of the sensible depends upon both the perceiver and the world. The sensing power and potential sensible are each defined relative to each other, giving them ecological realities. "Ecological" in this context means that an interdependency exists between the perceiver and the natural world.

What is sensed is a "form" of the sensed object. The sense-organ becomes like this form; it receives its formal nature (formal cause) without actually receiving the object (matter) itself. Aristotle sees the medium as revealing forms rather than transmitting something material (*eidola*). The medium is a field actualized through light. It is not a void or an empty space—it possesses the power of "transparency". The perceiver sees forms through the medium; the perceiver does not see the medium. Aristotle rejects modeling all the senses on touch. Instead there is always a medium, and the perceiver need not be in physical contact (touch) with something to sense it. The perceiver senses a form through a medium. What is sensed is not matter as such but the form of material things.

Given Aristotle's ecological concept of perception and his treatment of the medium, he anticipates Gibson's direct realist theory. Perception is an ecological event, rather than a state of an isolated *psyche*. Second, Aristotle does not hypothesize an intermediary between perceiving and the environment. Light is the actualization of transparency. As Gibson would say, the perceiver does not see "light"—the perceiver sees by means of light. For Aristotle, the medium unites the sensing and sensed powers—it does not separate them. Form is revealed through the medium. Aristotle's perceptual realism also comes through in his concept of "sensibles." Perceived properties of objects exist within those objects as powers; they are not simply states of the nerves of the perceiver. Perception is veridical rather than a false veil. Both Aristotle and Gibson are realists, believing perception yields knowledge about an objective reality.

Whereas Plato was a rationalist in his epistemology, Aristotle was an empiricist. Plato saw universals as lying beyond perception (sensing);

Aristotle believed universals were known through perception. For Plato, order could only be known through reason for order pertained to the realm of ideas, and not the world of senses. As a scientist and a theorist of perception, Aristotle believed order could be known through observation. The world of the senses, though spatially and temporally diversified, possessed form. *The psyche* is a *tabula rasa* (blank tablet) with the potential to become any *archai* (general form) of nature. In perception, the *psyche* does not add mental elements to what is sensed. It does not need to for there is order within what is sensed. *Nous* (the power to know) is pure potentiality having no actual determinant structure that would distort what is known. Further, no sharp dividing line exists between sensing and higher mental powers ("the intellect"). When a universal is thought of, *phantasia* (images) from sense perception are always involved. Aristotle's empiricism was realistically motivated—the world could be known. The world, in point of fact, possessed the power to be known. Theories of perception that postulate a mental contribution imposed upon what comes through the senses separate perception from the physical world. One basic function of a perceptual intermediary is to represent the world in an intelligible or meaningful form. Aristotle, as a realist, found this type of theory of perception objectionable: the physical world is knowable as it is without embellishment or transformation.

Aristotle's realistic epistemology rests on an extreme empiricism, where the mind does not add anything to sensory experiences nor does the mind go beyond perception to gain universal knowledge. Gibson's view that perception can be of ordered properties of the environment without mental contributions places him also in the extreme empiricist perspective. Both Gibson, in his ecological theory, and Aristotle were direct realists in their epistemologies of perception. First, for both Gibson and Aristotle the world possessed the necessary order to be known contra Plato and materialistic elementarism. (To demonstrate and describe this order would be one of Gibson's main goals.) Second, the power of a sense is to know this natural order rather than to construct or receive an intermediary or representation. Using an Aristotelian metaphor, the senses are "transparent" to the world. In contrast, later empiricist theories of perception lost their realist emphasis and substituted a combination of Platonic dualism and materialistic elementarism, the two philosophical extremes Aristotle had tried to avoid. Later empiricists took the stance that only particulars could be revealed through the senses. This idea corresponds with Plato's theory of the material-temporal world. Taking such a stance, Berkeley, Hume, and Helmholtz attempted to derive order from generalizations of particulars. The mind, as a storehouse of memories, gives perception order.

Chapter 4 _____

MEDIEVAL PSYCHOLOGY, OPTICS, and PHILOSOPHY

ALHAZEN AND THE SCIENCE OF VISION

According to Polyak (1957), Ronchi (1957, 1961, 1967) and Lindberg (1970, 1976), the emanation hypothesis emerged as the most widely accepted explanation of vision during the first millennium. Into this intellectual atmosphere stepped Islam's greatest student of vision and optics, Alhazen (965–1038), attempting to prove experimentally the falsity of the emanation hypothesis. Avicenna (980–1037), an Aristotelian contemporary of Alhazen, also set out at this time to disprove the emanation hypothesis, but Alhazen was the scientist and provided, where Avicenna did not, a well developed alternative experimental optics of vision (Avicenna, 1952). Alhazen's theory of optics and vision sets the stage for Kepler's elementaristic optics and Berkeley's empiricist theory of perception. In terms of both influence and anticipation of modern (1600–1900) trends in perceptual theory, Alhazen is the most important person of the Medieval period. He is one of the progenitors of the elementaristic empiricism that supplanted Aristotle's wholistic empiricism. For Alhazen, physical nature is experienced in an elemental form requiring mental organization.

Before turning to Alhazen, another Arab scientist and philosopher Alkindi (813–880) should be mentioned for Alkindi would provide Alhazen with a key optical concept in the latter's new theory of vision. Euclid had geometrically treated visual rays analytically, reducing the visual cone to a set of distinct and discrete lines. Alkindi, in his *De Aspectibus* (ca. 850 A.D.), extended the geometrical analysis to the actual physics of light by developing a pointillistic theory of emanation. This elementaristic treatment of visual rays entailed that vision was built up out of "elements" in the same fashion that physical objects were built up out of atoms (Democritus). Alhazen seems to have been the first theorist to apply the pointillistic treatment to an intromission (e.g., *eidola*) theory of vision and light.

Though historically its birth is officially reserved until the sixteenth and seventeenth centuries, the scientific tradition has many threads running back to the times of the ancient Greeks and Egyptians. In the Middle Ages the traditions of mathematics, naturalistic analysis, and experimental observation and demonstration are well developed in Islamic culture. Alhazen antedates Kepler and other theorists in later centuries because Alhazen shares many basic epistemological beliefs and methodological principles with the modern scientific tradition. His geometrical treatment of analytic elements of light stands within the tradition of Kepler, Descartes, and Newton. Familiar with Greek science and philosophy, Alhazen's optics reflects the geometric treatment of perspective in Euclid and the atomistic reductionism of nature in Democritus.

Alhazen *(Opticae Thesauras,* ca. 1000) approached the study of vision through his investigations into physical optics. By means of optical principles as he understood them, Alhazen resolved two related and extremely perplexing problems for intromission theories of vision. If vision is dependent upon something coming from physical objects to the eye and not vice versa, how is the spatial order in the physical world preserved in the transmission? And how does the image or form of a physically large object get into a physically smaller eye? Alhazen's solution is based upon treating the eye as an optical instrument that forms an image. In accordance with his laws of refraction, an eye should form an image *(eidola, forma,* or *species)* due to its inherant optical (physical) properties. Alhazen's explanation turned out to be faulty in detail, but in general conception it anticipates Kepler's accepted solution to the formation of the retinal image. More generally, Alhazen's optics of vision placed the support of physical science clearly behind the intromission model, and in the following centuries the intromission model eventually won the day in scientific theories of perception. Perception involves something physical being propagated or transmitted from the world to the perceiver. This idea became one key component in Descartes' causal theory of perception.

According to Alhazen, when light is emitted from a luminous source, it travels outward in all directions in rectilinear paths. An opaque physical object, upon illumination, reflects light back in all directions from any point illuminated on its surface. Hence the *diaphonous* medium will be filled with light reflected from illuminated opaque bodies (see Diagram 4). *Diaphonous* is from the Greek "to shine through" or be "transparent." Light, a punctate physical reality, is what is transmitted through the transparent medium. It is a physical and elemental intermediary transmitted (reflected and propagated) from the physical world to a physical sense organ in the perceiver.

Alhazen assumed that in refraction through a transparent surface (the eye), only the perpendicular rays to the anterior surface pass through without a significant reduction in intensity. These perpendicular rays strike the lens, (considered by Alhazen to be the sensitive portion of the eye) forming an optical projection of the viewed physical world (see Diagram 5).

What is significant in this optics of vision is that the eye forms an image on the lens in accordance with its refractive properties. It does not receive a ready-formed or unitary image. The *eidola* theory described images as sent ready-made from object to eye. *Eidola* had form and integrity. The eye, for Alhazen, receives a set of distinct points of light. Correspondingly, for Alhazen, the lens is a set of sensitive points, each of which reacts specifically to the discrete visual ray striking it. By the nineteenth century, this pointillistic view of stimulation and reception had become very influential and well developed, e.g., through Helmholtz and his followers. Helmholtz's theory was that each receptor cell in the eye reacts to the quantitative variations of intensity and wavelength inherent in individual points of light discretely striking it. Consequently, visual experience is of elemental sensations of brightness and color and nothing more complex.

From the Parmenidian split of reality and Plato's solid reinforcement of it, the physical-temporal world is treated as an unorganized diversity that

DIAGRAM 4

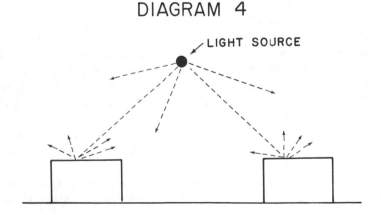

LIGHT SOURCE

DIAGRAM 5

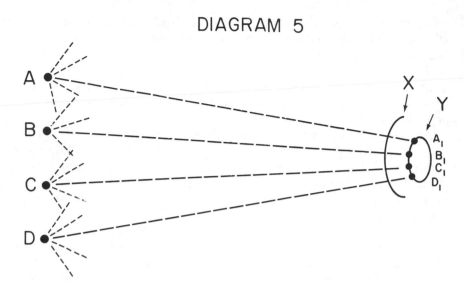

Points A, B, C, . . . send light in all directions, but only those rays perpendicular to the anterior surface (X) pass through with full intensity forming an image A, B, C, D, . . . which is a geometrical projection of physical points $A_1 B_1 C_1 D_1$ . . .

the perceiver must order. Alhazen's optics is a scientific elaboration on this ontological theme. Gibson objected to this impoverished view of the physical world and optical stimulation and the implication that the perceiver must contribute mental principles of order to complete the perception. For one thing, from early on in his career (circa 1945–1950), Gibson would deny that sensory anatomy was sensitive to just points of stimulation. Just as importantly, Gibson would propose (circa 1960) and develop an alternative optics ("ecological optics") that described light differently, emphasizing optical structure above the level of points and rays. For both stimulation and sensory mechanisms there is order or organization above light rays and individual receptor cells.

As can be ascertained from Diagram 5, if the paths of perpendicular rays were allowed to continue in the same direction past the lens, they would converge and then diverge forming an inverted image on the back of the eye. Insofar as Alhazen believed the image was conveyed through the optic nerve to the brain, he thought that if an inverted image was transmitted to the brain, the effect would be an inverted mental representation of the world. In order to avoid this result he supposed the lens, through refraction, modified the paths of the rays preserving the upright orientation of the image (see Diagram 6).

The often discussed problem of the inverted image is historically noteworthy because it presupposes that the perceiver is aware of the

DIAGRAM 6

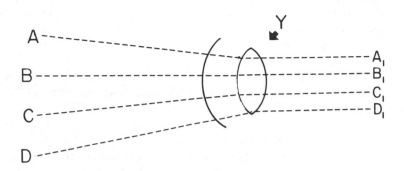

Y is the lens. An alteration of the direction of rays ABCD preserves an upright representation of $A_1B_1C_1D_1$ going into the optic nerve.

anatomical (retinal) image. Relative to retinal anatomy the image can be either erect or inverted. If it is concluded that the perceived world will be inverted, given an inverted image, then the simulative assumption is being presupposed. Why else should the world look upside given an inverted image? According to the simulative assumption, what the perceiver is aware of should be equivalent to viewing the image itself. Later optical theorists (e.g., da Vinci) continued to believe that an inverted image would produce an inverted perception. Until Kepler, the truth that the image is physically inverted was not accepted.

Alhazen's concern over inversion would seem to indicate that he thought of visual stimulation as more than a set of points because inversion is a spatial relationship. If the eye was sensitive only to variations of independent points of light, the corresponding impressions would have no spatial arrangement. Alhazen, though, was concerned over the spatial arrangement of light points on the eye—in fact, this was a central issue: How is the spatial arrangement of the external world preserved in the eye? Alhazen's optics therefore contains both an analysis of light into discrete elements and a geometrical representation of perspective and optical images.

Alhazen believed that the optical image is transmitted to the brain where the "ultimate sentient" is located. The pure sensory impressions which result are only of light (brightness) and color. Visual impressions also have spatial extent, but it is primitive, without form or order. Via additional psychological and muscular processes, Alhazen completed his explanation of visual perception. Because the set of points constituting the image geometrically preserves the world's spatial arrangement, the image can be "looked over" and judged. Memory is included in this explanation. The process of psychologically putting together the image heppens automatically and habitually. Alhazen has been seen as the Medieval Helmholtz (Brett, 1962). Helmholtz believed that unconscious inferences were involved in constructing perceptions out of elemental sensations. For Alhazen, the perception of location, size, and object shape involves a mental process being added to the purely optical-sensory effects. What the "inner perceiver" gets is a mosaic, and it is left to mental processes to form a spatial integration and understanding of this mosaic of points. Consequently, perception is epistemologically indirect. Alhazen gets the image into the eye, but he must break it apart to accomplish this feat, and then he needs something mental to put it together. Kepler's accepted explanation of the formation of the image essentially produced the same result, viz., a set of points that needed to be put together.

Alhazen forms a significant link between a variety of Greek ideas regarding perception and more modern viewpoints. His elementaristic treatment of light continues the atomistic and analytic traditions begun with Euclid and Democritus. His theory of mental contributions in perception follows from Platonic dualism, but for Alhazen the contributions of the mind derived from previous experiences (memory). Alhazen antedates the whole empiricist school (Berkeley, Helmholtz, and their followers) where mental contributions were believed "learned" rather than derived from reason or inherited abilities. He combines in his optics both the pointillistic and pictorial views of light, the two most popular models of the retinal image after Kepler.

MEDIEVAL PSYCHOLOGY AND PHILOSOPHY OF PERCEPTION

Alhazen's optical theory of vision exerted a tremendous influence upon European science and philosophy. Through his ideas and their dissemination in the thirteenth and fourteenth centuries, the stage was set for the great theoretical synthesis of Johannes Kepler, thus ushering in the "modern" period of optical and perceptual science. According to Lindberg (1976), prior to the translation of Alhazen from Arabic into Latin, European thinking consisted mainly of a conglomeration of Platonic and Aristotelian philosophical traditions, Galenist anatomy, Euclidean perspective, versions of intromission and extromission theories and scholastic-theological writings. It should be added though that many of the thematic elements of modern science existed prior to the late Middle Ages. Both Alhazen and Kepler, though theoretically creative, were equally synthesizers of ideas with a long, if not ancient tradition.

Turning to some selected European thinkers and Medieval themes significant within the history of perception, Plotinus (204–270 A.D.), a spiritual philosopher influenced by Plato, had several historically interesting ideas concerning vision. In his *Enneads* Plotinus argued that perception occurs when the soul matches present impressions to existing memory images. Concerning the role of memory images in perception, of particular significance was his hypothesis that the standard adopted for the size of an object is supplied not through vision but touch. In visually recognizing an object, the soul remembers its "touched-size" and judges its size according to this standard. This is a clear anticipation of Berkeley's theory of visual perception. Plotinus, again anticipating Berkeley, argued that visual perception of distance is dependent upon the faintness and distinctness of seen colors. The soul "reads" this degree of faintness as a sign of the distance of the seen object.

Plotinus, in the above hypotheses, was providing specific examples of how the soul is actively involved in vision. From Plato he took the idea that the soul's mental activities are necessarily involved in visual perception. Both Plato and Plotinus conceived of this process as contributory. Plato had given the physical world an impoverished existence that required mental supplementation; later, as evident in Alhazen's optics, physical stimulation to the eye was found lacking. By the time of Berkeley, one main reason for postulating some sort of contributory mental activity was the belief that optical stimulation provided an inadequate basis for perceiving spatial dimensions and relationships. Gibson's objection to contributory processes in perception stemmed from his conviction that the optical basis for visual perception was adequate. The kernel of the problem though, and this could account for the popularity of the emanation hypothesis in Medieval Europe from St. Augustine (354–430) to Roger Bacon (1215–1292), was the Platonic belief that the mind (or soul) was necessary to give perception intelligible form and organization.

The most influential philosopher between the times of Aristotle and Descartes was St. Thomas Aquinas (1225–1274). Though a follower philosophically more of Aristotle than Plato, Aquinas also involves mental processes in perception, and interestingly falls within the Alhazen-Helmholtz line of thought in making such processes "unconscious." According to Aquinas (*Summa Theologica*, Book I, Questions 75–87, ca. 1270), images entering the eyes produce *phantasmata* in the mind. In addition, he postulated an "active reason" that abstracts from the *phantasmata* their general forms. Aquinas contends that normally there is no awareness of these *phantasmata*. The idea of an unconscious element in perception seems theoretically motivated by the conviction that the mind "receives" morsels and must be doing something to build them into a full course meal. Because the perceiver does not seem to be conscious of such mental activities, these processes must be unconscious. Taking Plotinus and Aquinas as two significant and representative philosophers not usually associated with the scientific tradition of the Medieval period, it is clear that the contributory theory of perception rests upon more than just optical considerations. Further, it should be noted that *phantasmata* function as an intermediary between perception and the world. Consequently, perception is indirect.

One Medieval thinker who seems to have broken out of traditional modes of thought concerning perception was the arch-realist and empiricist William of Ockham ("Ockham's Razor") (1280–1349). In his *Sententiarium* (1495) Ockham attacked Plato's eternal forms, arguing that only individuals (or particulars) have real existence. In this respect, his philosophy is sympathetic more with Aristotle, and anticipates the analytic empiricist philosophy of Berkeley, Hume and Mill. Modern empiricism would attack the reality of the abstract, assuming that the ground of all reality and knowledge was particulars, as revealed through observations. The empiricist or observational tradition becomes analytical in modern times, assuming, in agreement with Platonic dualism, that observation only yields a diversity of particulars. Plato argued that abstractions are limited to the intellect and reason. Modern analytic empiricism attempted to chop off the top half of Plato's dualism, but assumed still Plato's theory of sensory observation. Ockham's empiricist philosophy is the intellectual counterpart of the analytic-empiricist methodological philosophy developed in Medieval optics. Secondly, Ockham rejected the idea of any type of mediator in perception. Perception is *of* particulars in the physical world without the necessity of mediating contact through either "visual rays" or *eidola*. Perception involves instanteous "action-at-a-distance" (i.e., Ockham rejected the causal theory of perception). Ockham seems to have been one of the main Aristotelian threads running through the Middle Ages, but the most influential theories of perception derived more from Plato's epistemology and later, Alhazen's optics.

Robert Grosseteste (1168–1253) is to be remembered for his *species* hypothesis that would work its way into later optical theories, especially Roger Bacon's and derivative views (Lindberg, 1976; Reisch, 1486). A species is distinguishable from an *eidola,* in that the latter was thought of as a physical entity, whereas the former, for Grosseteste, was the form of an object transferred through the physical medium. Objects propagate their "power" in all directions. This projected power is the *species* and is not restricted to just optics and light. It is a general property of effluence that all natural forms possess. Regarding optics, *species* are propagated by means of *lumen* (light), and visual perception occurs through the reception of *species* (*De Iride,* ca. 1230). Grosseteste's species hypothesis closely resembles ideas found in da Vinci's physics and Leibnitz's philosophy and can be related to certain aspects of Gibson's ecological optics. Theoretically, light is treated as a medium rather than a transmitted entity, and "forms," following Aristotle, are not material complexes, as in Democritus' *eidola,* but powers embodied within things.

MEDIEVAL EUROPEAN OPTICS

The most widely used textbook on optics during the Middle Ages was John Pecham's (1230–1292) *Perspectiva Communis* (ca. 1275). Alhazen's impact on European thought was substantially mediated through Pecham's book. According to Lindberg (1970) (see also Crombie, 1968; Polyak, 1957; Ronchi, 1967), the *Perspectiva* basically was a condensed and simplified version of the recently accessible *Opticae* by Alhazen, the latter work having been translated from Arabic into Latin during the twelfth century (Singer, 1959).

Pecham attempted to combine Grosseteste's *species* hypothesis with Alhazen's visual rays by defining a ray as the *species* of an object "fashioned into a straight line". Pecham adopted the perpendicular ray hypothesis of Alhazen as an explanation of how the optical image is formed. Where he differed from Alhazen was in supposing the eye contains a "natural light" *(lumen oculi naturale)* that must be emitted before the optically formed image affects the mind. Influenced by Platonic and emanation theories, Pecham backslides on Alhazen's purely intromission theory.

Pecham's discussions of distance, size and shape perception are extremely noteworthy. Through specific issues they elucidate the respective roles of psychological factors and sensory impressions in vision. Following Alhazen, Pecham viewed the "proper objects" of the "naked" sense of vision as only light and color. All other "visible intentions" require acquired knowledge, reasoning, and other psychological activities.

The projected sizes and shapes in the optical image are "certified" through eye movements in that the movements of the eye must trace the optical forms. Only after this process is there awareness of these forms and their visual angles. This explanation, similar to Alhazen's, anticipates Helmholtz's local sign hypothesis and presupposes an elementaristic view of sensory impressions.

The observer perceives the real size of an object through a knowledge of its distance and its visual angle. The projected angle (perspective size) of an object will vary as a function of its distance, so the distance must be known in order to know the actual size of the object. Basically this is the same explanation of size perception offered by Berkeley and his followers. The shape of an object is perceived through knowledge of the distance of its parts because otherwise objects would appear "flat." The presupposition of this argument is the simulative assumption, i.e., that objects should appear "flat" since the optical image is bi-dimensional and not tri-dimensional. In general, distance must be inferred rather than seen because the optical image is "flat." This also was Berkeley's belief. For example, Pecham argued that through apprehension of the number of intervening objects, the distance of an object can be known.

Between their optics and psychology of perception, Alhazen, and derivatively Pecham antedate many of the important elements found in Berkeley's theory of perception and its psycho-physiological development in Helmholtz a century later. The visual image is treated as flat or as a mosaic of points and all other spatial attributes of perception are added through inference or some other higher mental process.

Aside from a few divergencies, the treatment of optics and vision by Roger Bacon (1215–1292) in his *Opus Majus* was based primarily on Alhazen's *Opticae*. As Pecham before him, Bacon also attempted to synthesize disparate views, combining together Alhazen's theory with *species,* visual rays, and the medium concept. Europeans prior to Kepler seemed generally unwilling to completely give up the emanation (or extromission) view of vision. One noteworthy exception was Witelo's (ca. 1275) *Opticae,* another widely read medieval text that followed Alhazen's optics more closely and attacked the idea of emanation.

DA VINCI'S THEORY OF VISION

Through Filippo Brunelleschi (1377–1446), Leon Battista Alberti (1404–1472) and other Renaissance artists, the principles of pictorial perspective were developed (Alberti, 1435). Renaissance artistic views reinforced the "picture analogy" in theories of vision. Aside from this artistic influence, another concept that fostered the pictorial model was the *camera obscura,* a device first noted by Alhazen, but only theoretically developed much later by Leonardo da Vinci (1452–1519) (Lindberg, 1976; Singer, 1959).

The *camera obscura,* or pinhole camera, consists of an enclosed chamber (e.g., a box) with only a small aperture through which light can enter the chamber. An inverted image of the source of the light that passes through the aperture will be formed on the back interior of the chamber (see Diagram 7).

Da Vinci made several noteworthy advances in using the *camera obscura* as a model of the eye though it did, as mentioned earlier, tend to reinforce the pictorial view of the visual image. For one thing, da Vinci correctly believed that the image was formed on the retina (back of the

DIAGRAM 7

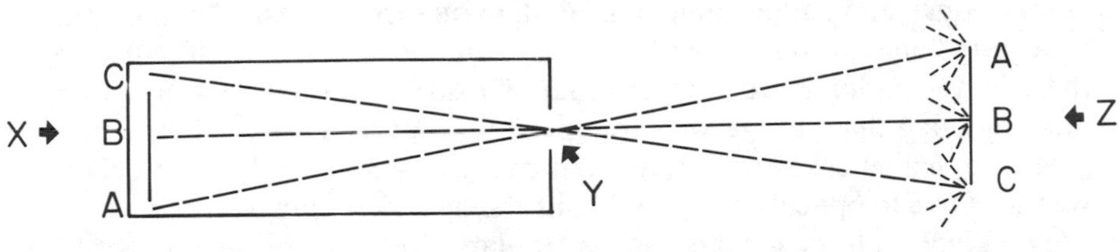

Light from points A, B, C, . . . passing through the aperture marked Y produces an inverted image of the figure Z upon the back surface of the *camera obscura* marked X.

eye) and that the retina, rather than the lens, was the sensitive portion of the eye (Ferrero, 1952). The optic nerve with its termination in the retina was the source of the "visual power," and the lens, as da Vinci correctly noted, possessed only a refractive power. Another 100 years would pass before the hypothesis of the retinal image was corroborated by Kepler and Scheiner. Da Vinci, however, seems to be the first theorist to have clearly supported and understood the idea of the retinal image.

If the eye is analogous to the *camera obscura,* would it not also form an inverted image? Because Leonardo, for reasons comparable to those of Alhazen, could not accept an inverted image (the world would look upside down), he postulated a double inversion in the eye. Da Vinci apparently had a variety of schemes for producing this double inversion, yet he had indeed hit upon the correct solution: the retinal image is inverted. But he couldn't accept it.

Though Lindberg (1976) has argued that da Vinci did not compare the retinal image to a picture, why else would inversion be a problem? The same question was raised regarding Alhazen's problem with inversion. If the image is not seen (inner observation), then it is irrelevant whether it is erect or inverted as long as the internal spatial arrangements are preserved. Kepler and Berkeley both realized this fact. It seems that da Vinci was caught in the picture analogy of the image implicitly, even if he explicitly rejected it. Though Kepler and Berkeley recognized how the pictorial model created the problem of inversion, in other respects they both assumed the image was like a picture.

One noteworthy and natural result of the retinal image-picture analogy has been to view optical stimulation as having values or properties of momentarily fixed conditions, viz., as a series of separate static pictures. The corresponding visual impressions would also be a succession of mental pictures. More generally, what emerges from the Middle Ages and gets passed on to modern thinking is a static view of visual optics. Change is not a property of optical forms (*eidolae, species,* images), and correspondingly visual impressions are static. The popular view of perception of motion was that it was based upon mental comparisons across sequences of static, but different, visual impressions. The picture model gives optical stimulation some spatial structure (more than treating light as a set of points), but because change is not a property of stimulation there is no temporal structure or order. Gibson would take the opposite view, arguing that change was an inherent property of optical structure given a dynamic environment, and a moving observer, and the perceiver was sensitive to optical changes without the need of mental computations.

Da Vinci's physical optics is particularly noteworthy and sophisticated, anticipating both Leibnitz and Gibson. Da Vinci explains his concept of radiant pyramids as follows:

> Necessity causes that nature ordains or has ordained that in all points of the air all the images of the things opposite to them converge, by the pyramidal concourse of the rays that have emanated from these things; and if it were not so the eye would not discern in every point of the air that is between it and the thing seen, the shape and quality of the thing facing it. (da Vinci, 1910, p. 965)

The medium is filled with observation points of converging *species*. Except for the terminology, this is very similar to Gibson's ecological concept of the ambient optic array. Reflected light diverges outward into the medium, but at any given point in the medium, light is converging from surrounding (ambient) objects. What da Vinci proposed is the concept of ambient optical structure. This represents a shift from describing a "cone" of light connecting an eye and a single object. Light is conceptualized as surrounding an observer. Such convergent patterns of light are complex and ambient or omnidirectional. When light is described as points or lines of radiation it is elemental and simple. We can see a significant shift in emphasis from Alhazen to da Vinci, but Alhazen's optics was more compatible with Newtonian science and the dualistic predilection to rob the physical world of order.

In adopting Grosseteste's notion of *species* as the power of an object propagated radiantly, da Vinci also anticipates Leibnitz's concept of monads and the relational view of nature. Da Vinci states that *species* are "all throughout the whole and all in each smallest part; each in all and all in the part" (da Vinci, 1939, Vol. I., p. 138). Leibnitz's "monad" was described as the embodiment of the surrounding whole within the part, an entity "mirrors" its relationships to all surrounding entities. The monad provided an alternative building block to Newton's atom, offering a relational view of reality. Instead of intrinsically independent atoms (elements), each of which is internally simple, the relational view rejects the idea of absolute parts independent of the whole. Further, within a relational view of nature, parts are not described as simple but rather as complex.

Connecting together certain basic themes found in the Medieval period, a tradition of analysis and empiricism emerges in Islamic science, and scholastic philosophy (Alhazen, Ockham, and Pecham). This concern for naturalistic detail and observation also comes through with the Renaissance painters—witness da Vinci's numerous and exacting anatomical drawings. Nature should be observed and analyzed in detail. Alhazen breaks down light into simple elements. This general epistemology and theory of physical nature coupled with the mathematical tradition, develops into modern science, as well as anticipating British empiricist philosophy. One basic theoretical point mentioned regarding Gibson's ideas is his rejection of the elementaristic treatment of physical nature (including light). Gibson, following certain relational and wholistic concepts would attempt to describe both the environment and light in terms of higher order relationships.

The wholistic tradition in modern thought is spawned from Platonic rationalism. Plato saw order as revealed through reason, and those philosophers in later centuries who emphasized order and abstraction above analysis and particulars, were historically identified as rationalists. Implicit in rationalism is the Platonic thesis that order is revealed through reason. The Medieval period includes some individuals such as Grosseteste and da Vinci who advocated relational views of nature in contrast to elemental views. Gibson rejects Platonic dualism finding something faulty in both analytic-empiricist and wholistic-rationalist philosophies. For Gibson, order exists in the environment, and this order is perceived rather than rationally constructed. Gibson, along with Aristotle, could be described as a wholistic empiricist, in contrast to an analytic empiricist, such as Berkeley and Alhazen.

The casual and indirect theories of perception also find further support and development in the Medieval treatment of perception, particularly through the influence of Alhazen's intromission theory and European optics. Perception is treated as the "inner" effect of external optical causes. This approach is taken up by Kepler and Descartes in the seventeenth century. The theories of "inner observation" and "external" causation become two basic points of criticism in Gibson's ecological approach. It has already been mentioned that Gibson objected to the "inner awareness," pictorial representation, and homunculus ideas. His views on such issues were fairly well developed by the 1950s. In the 1960s and 1970s he developed a variety of criticisms regarding causal models of perception.

Although the Aristotelian tradition of final causes worked its way into physics, astronomy, and scholastic theology in the Middle Ages, Aristotle's wholism, biological functionalism, and epistemological realism did not exert as strong an influence on theories of mind and knowledge as did Plato's dualism. The scientific tradition cultivated in Islam and passed on to Europe in the 13th and 14th centuries emerged in Kepler, Galileo and Newton with an analytic, mathematical emphasis that reinforced elementarism and dualism. The wholistic and dynamic views of nature would be taken up by continental rationalist philosophers, such as Leibnitz, Spinoza, and Kant. Wholism and dynamism would not work their way into the "official" scientific mainstream until the 19th century. The theorists and theories discussed in the next few chapters (5–7), represent the modern (1600–1900) orthodox approach to perception that Gibson would criticize. In heritage, it continues and further develops Platonic dualism, physical elementarism, Alhazen's optics and theory of vision, and both the simulative assumption and homunculus hypothesis. The major figures of this intertwining scientific-philosophical network include Kepler, Descartes, Newton, Berkeley, Müller, and Helmholtz. All these individuals, though diverse in their ideas and practices, accepted concepts with a history running back through the Middle Ages to the time of the Ancient Greeks. Together they are the major architects of the standard modern treatment of perception.

Part II

THE PSYCHOLOGY
and BIOLOGY
of KNOWLEDGE

Chapter 5 _____

THE SCIENTIFIC REVOLUTION

KEPLER'S OPTICS AND THE SCIENCE OF VISION

Leonardo da Vinci's particular references to the *camera obscura* as a model of the eye were not publicly accessible until after Kepler. It was Giambattista della Porta (1536–1615) in his *Magia Naturalis* (1589) who convinced Kepler of the appropriateness of the *camera obscura*-eye analogy. Della Porta still thought that the image was located on the lens and not on the retina (della Porta, 1593), and with this hypothesis Kepler disagreed.

A few years earlier Felix Platter (1536–1614) in his *De Corporis* (1583) had suggested that the image was actually formed on the retina by the lens.

> the crystalline humour . . . collects the images *(species)* or rays flowing into the eye and, spreading them over the area of the whole retiform nerve, it presents *(repraesentent)* these magnified, acting like an internal eyeglass, so that the nerve can take possession of them more easily. (1583, p. 187)

It appears that Kepler's source for the idea of a retinal image was this work of Platter. Though da Vinci also anticipated this idea, his writings on vision were not read within the mainstream of scientific research.

Although della Porta provided the *camera obscura* model, and Platter the hypothesis of an image on the retina, it took the genius of Johannes Kepler (1571–1630) to discover the correct optical analysis of the eye that connected these two ideas. Kepler, along with Galileo, Descartes, and Newton, was one of the premier minds of the Scientific Revolution. Though most often associated with his three laws of planetary motion, Kepler was as influential in optics as in astronomy. His predilection for detailed analysis and description, as well as his mathematical and historical sophistication, accounts for his broad and varied achievements. To vision and optics he brought a strengthened emphasis on empirical analysis and mathematical-geometrical formulation.

Kepler defined a ray as the direction of motion of light, as did Alhazen. Still following Alhazen, Kepler argued that, when illuminated, opaque objects reflect light in all directions from every point on their illuminated surfaces. Where Kepler differed from Alhazen was in his solution of how light rays are collected by the eye to form a distinct image of the illuminated object. Diagram 8 is a simplified version of Kepler's model found in his *Dioptrics* (1611). Kepler's conception of this optical process was pointillistic. In Kepler's (1604, 1611) works on vision, the illuminated object was represented as a set of points, and the retina was stimulated by a set of points of light, hence the idea of a retinal mosaic. To quote Kepler (1604), "The retina is illuminated distinctly point by point from individual points of objects" (p. 158) (see Diagram 8).

Kepler's retinal optics became the accepted treatment of light in later centuries and was incorporated into Berkeley's psychology of vision. For Berkeleians, such as Helmholtz, visual sensations are correlative to the points of retinal stimulation in having hue and brightness without any

DIAGRAM 8

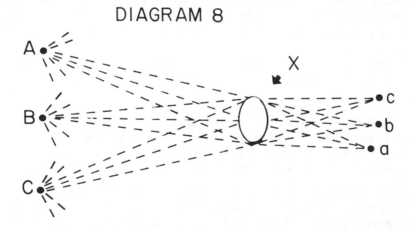

A, B, C are three illuminated points on an object which reflect light rectilinearly in all directions. The lens (X) refracts these rays, forming an inverted group of points behind it (on the retina). Although the diagram does not actually depict it, the reversal is both vertical (up-down) and horizontal (right-left).

extent, pattern, or spatial relationship with one another. Insofar as visual perception is evidently of more than just extensionless sensations, Berkeley and his followers were led to postulate supplementary perceptual activities that added to the strictly visual effect of points of light. Pointillism implied optical inadequacy in vision and indirect visual awareness of the spatiality of the physical world. Visual space perception was epistemically indirect because a mental step was required to go from visual sensations to an awareness of spatiality. In effect, the optical principle of the retinal mosaic was taken to imply that the physiological starting point of vision possessed no intrinsic spatial structure, let alone any temporal structure. Because perception possesses order, the brain and/or the mind must be contributing the integrating order.

Kepler also characterized the retinal image in a different way than as points of light. According to him, the retina is "affected" *(impressio)* by a picture or representation *(pictura seu illustratio)*. This image *(species)* passes to the brain as an immaterial image *(species immateriata)* where it is impressed on the *sensus communis* (Crombie, 1968, p. 66). Here Kepler spoke as if the *sensorium* were aware of not just a set of points, but of an image. An image is an integrated and ordered two dimensional form. Further, Kepler functionally describes the image as if it were a picture and, correlatively, as if the *sensus communis* were a homunculus.

> Vision is the sense of the stimulated retina . . . To see is to be aware of the extent that the retina is stimulated. The retina is painted with colored rays of visible things. This picture or representation . . . does not complete the act of vision until the image so received by the retina passes . . . to the brain. . . . Inside within the brain is something called the *sensus communis,* on which is impressed the image. . . . (1611, prop. 61)

The same dual meaning of the optical image is found in Alhazen. Should we think of the optical basis of vision as just a set of points producing impressions without any extent or order? Or should we think of it as an image—a *pictura*—giving the mind a corresponding picture?

Either way, Kepler noted the lack of three dimensions in the retinal image. The image described by Kepler is only two dimensional, whereas the physical world has three spatial dimensions. The image was physically flat, the world was not. Kepler concluded distance could not be seen. Why? Kepler, in this respect, appears to have accepted the Greeks' belief that physical simulation was the basis of what could be seen, and if there wasn't simulation of the third dimension, it must follow that it was not seen. Recall that the function of *eidola* or images was to replicate the world. Outer vision could then be explained by an inner vision (the homunculus).

At this point we can comment upon Kepler's approach to the problem of the inverted image. As was mentioned earlier, both Alhazen and da Vinci rejected the idea of an inverted image. Kepler did not believe that an inverted image would produce a visual inversion. In this respect Kepler did not treat the image as something observed. Yet we see that in other respects he did speak as if the image were observed. If we also bear in mind Kepler's dual treatment of the image as either a picture or a set of points, there appear to be multiple perspectives Kepler adopted in his understanding and description of the retinal image. If the image could not furnish an optical basis for seeing the solid shapes and distances of objects, Kepler was obliged to postulate some other means to explain our awareness of these aspects of the physical world. The two hypotheses Kepler proposed were the "Telemetric Triangle Hypothesis" (see Diagram 9) and the "Angle of Convergence Hypothesis" (see Diagram 10).

Kepler, within these hypotheses, was proposing specific types of inferences involved in the perception of distance. Note they are types of mathematical (geometrical) deduction involving a particular concept of physical distance. Distance (the third dimension) is the length of empty space from the eye to the object, and distance is computed in a rationalistic manner. Kepler appears to have extrapolated one aspect of the

DIAGRAM 9

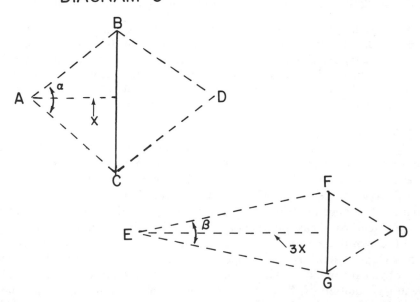

A and E are two points in the physical world at distances X and 3X from the eye. Both produce the same point D on the retina. The rays to the pupil (BC) show greater divergence than (FG) i.e., a > b. The eye could register the base angles of ABC and EFG. Given this, the mind could deduce X and 3X, respectively, from the angles.

scientific method (mathematical reasoning) to the study of perception and to have given space a meaning he took from astronomy.

DIAGRAM 10

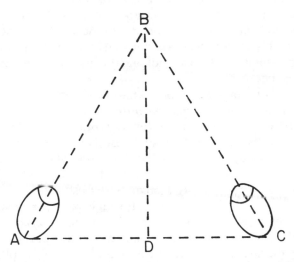

The angles BAC and BCA will vary as a function of the distance of B from D. The smaller the angles BAC and BCA, the closer will be B. If the distance of the base AC of the triangle ABC is known (the distance between the two eyes), then the distance BD can be computed from AC and the angles BAC and BCA.

The question may arise as to whether Kepler actually presumed that there were literal geometrical computations going on in the observer's mind. Both Kepler and Descartes (the latter having adopted Kepler's "Angle of Convergence" hypothesis), wrote as if there were such capabilities in the perceiver. They gave perception a Platonic flavor, separating the particularized flux of material processes from the ordered and logical processes of the abstracting mind. This dichotomy mirrors the Platonic dualism found in early science. Second, it draws upon astronomy, a science known to both of them, to depict space and how it is apprehended. Perceived distance is apprehended the way an astronomer calculates the distances of planets. It is a space of distinct objects suspended in a void. The astronomical concept of space continues and reinforces the theory of space developed in perspective optics. Space is empty and distance is linear extent through space from object to eye. Though critical of Kepler in other respects, Berkeley accepted Kepler's concept of distance as did many others who followed Berkeley. The proposal, developed in early Gibson, for a more ecologically representative conception of distance defined relative to the ground constituted one of the first significant departures of Gibson from traditional views.

These hypotheses of Kepler are also relevant because of the reaction they instigated in Berkeley. Berkeley's theoretical starting point was an attack on Kepler and Descartes. Instead of invoking mathematical abstractions that could not be derived from the experienced flux of particulars, Berkeley proposed that experience teaches the perceiver how to correctly apprehend distance. This theoretical disagreement is an instance of the historically well known nativism-empiricism controversy. Empiricism assumes that a psychological capability is learned; nativism assumes it is inherited.

In explanations of perception, what is significant in the nativism-empiricism issue is *the assumption both sides shared in common*. This presupposition is that the mind (or the brain) contributes to visual perception. For the empiricists, such as Berkeley, what was added to the psychological (or physiological) result of the retinal image was a correlate or consequence of past experience stored in the mind or brain. Conversely, for nativists, such as Kepler and Descartes, the contributory factor was not derived or obtained through past experience, but was either psychologically or physiologically innate. (Berkeley considered Kepler and Descartes to be nativists, since the geometrical abilities assumed by the later two theorists could not be learned. Following Plato, many philosophers and scientists of the Scientific Revolution believed mathematical reasoning could not be derived from sensory experience.) Either way, the presupposition of contributory factors was grounded in the conviction that the optical basis for vision was deficient. But as we are beginning to see, this assumption is based upon a particular way of describing light and the physical world. Secondly, the implication followed for either empiricist or nativist approaches that visual perception was epistemologically indirect in that it was mediated by organizing operations upon the incoming input. In this historical sense of nativism and empiricism, Gibson's direct realist approach is antagonistic to both views. For Gibson, the perceiver, however construed, does not contribute to optics either correlates of past experience or innate organizational or supplementary operations. Ecological optics developed to demonstrate that visual stimulation, if described differently, was not impoverished in structure.

DESCARTES' PHILOSOPHY AND PSYCHOPHYSIOLOGY

Though an important figure in the history of science, Descartes (1596–1650) is also thought of as the father of modern philosophy. His mind-body dualism set the stage for numerous philosophical debates and conflicts in forthcoming centuries, and his quest to find a sound philosophical method (harkening back to Plato) provided both inspiration for positivists and grist for the mill for philosophical skeptics. His famous pronouncement, "I think, therefore I am," is one of the few lines of mainstream academic philosophy to work its way into popular usage. His more general philosophical positions, such as his dualism and treatment of the "ego" or *cogito,* influenced his more specific ideas on perception. What Descartes provided for the history of perception was a dualistic psychophysiology consistent with Kepler's optics.

After Kepler, the eye was generally considered a picture (image) forming device analogous to a *camera obscura* with a refractive lens (e.g., Huygens, 1667–1691; Kohlhans, 1663; Scheiner, 1619). Secondly, the retinal image was thereafter considered the optical basis for vision. Rene Descartes' *Dioptric* (1638a) incorporated these developments as well as containing several other theoretical contributions of comparable significance. Descartes' ideas on vision are scattered throughout many of his works (1628, 1637, 1638a, 1638b, 1641, 1644, 1649). Within these books are found the reflex-arc and physiological projection hypotheses, his body-machine analogy, a theory of psychophysical correspondence, explanations of distance and size perception, and a discussion of the simulative assumption and the homunculus hypothesis.

The simulative assumption has been historically connected with the homunculus hypothesis, i.e., the idea of an internal observer. If vision occurs by means of internal observation, the rationale for the simulative assumption is evident, but if the relation of the transmitted image to the brain and the *sensorium* is not observation, then the necessity of simulation vanishes. In principle, though not always in practice, Descartes abandoned the homunculus hypothesis and with it belief in the necessity of simulation. Other individuals, such as Kepler and Berkeley, also only partially relinguished the simulative assumption. At best, the history of perception has shown only a gradual bit-by-bit abandonment of this idea, though both the simulative assumption and the homunculus hypothesis have frequently been criticized. One noteworthy feature of Gibson's approach is how thoroughly he has rejected both ideas, both in general theory and in specific cases.

Descartes argued against the necessity of resemblance between the retinal image and sensations. He stated:

> Now, while this picture, in thus passing into our head, always retains some degree of resemblance to the objects from which it proceeds, we yet need not hold . . . that it is by means of this resemblance that it enables us to perceive them, as if there were again in our brain yet other eyes with which we are able to apprehend it. . . . (1638a, p. 151)

Within this excerpt, Descartes' realization of the relationship between the simulative assumption and the homunculus hypothesis is apparent.

The basis of Descartes' rejection of the necessity of simulative representation was his mind-body dualism. The mind, although intimately related
to its seat in the brain, viz., the pineal gland, is ontologically distinct from
it. Activity in the brain causes sensations in the mind, but the two are
separate events. Therefore, qualities of sensation such as color may have
specific causes in the brain without resembling these causes. A sensation
is not what is observed by the mind in the brain (homunculus view) but is
a correlated effect of movements in the brain (1638a, 1638b, 1641, 1649).
Or as he said,

> rather that it is movements that go to compose the picture, which acting
> immediately on our mind, in as much as it is united to our body, are so
> instituted by nature as to make it to have such and such sensations. . . . Yet
> in all this there need be no resemblance between the ideas apprehended and
> the movements which cause these ideas. . . . (1638a, p. 151–152)

Descartes' mind-body dualism followed from his mind-matter dualism,
and so while he rejected the homunculus hypothesis, he still accepted an
absolute separation of perceiver (mind) and world (matter). In coming to
the assertion "I think, therefore I am", Descartes found himself certain
of the existence of his own mind (a thinking thing) but also trapped within
it. How could anything beyond one's own mind and experiences be
known? (In essence this is Berkeley's argument for idealism.) Descartes
introduced the concept of psychophysical causality to save himself from
being stuck in such a solopsistic conclusion. He argued that every event
must have a cause (a basic premise of early science), therefore sensory
experiences must be caused by something outside the mind. This something was the physical world, distinct both qualitatively and ontologically,
yet producing mental effects. Though a representation is not presented to
the mind, a physical effect must be transmitted to the brain to produce a
mental effect.

It could be argued that the homunculus hypothesis is a consequence of
mind-matter dualism, at least in so far as mind is identified with the
perceiver and matter with the external world. In this sense, mind cannot
observe the world but can only "observe" something "within" it, or in
"contact" with it (All these quoted words have perhaps only a metaphori-
cal or analogical meaning.) It is interesting then that Descartes rejected
the homunculus hypothesis because of his mind-body dualism. On the
other hand, to treat mind as a substance or thing, as Descartes and others
did, turns perception into something intrinsic to a self-contained entity (a
substance). In this sense perception is "contained within" the mind, i.e.,
it is an inner experience. At best, following Descartes, perception can be
a consequence or effect of the external world.

Connected with Descartes' dualism was his hypothesis that sensory qualities (color, sound, oder, etc.) are specific to the nerves stimulated in the brain. Each quality has some unique, though non-simulative, correlate in the brain. Although not in all respects identical with Johannes Müller's "specific energies of nerves" hypothesis, Descartes' conception of sensory quality-neurological correlation stands with Müller in contrast to Gibson's contention that visual perception is specific to optical information and the physical environment. To correlate sensory experience with the brain and nerves separates perception from the physical world; though experience is not *of* the brain (homunculus), it is specific to the brain rather than the world, making perception inherently subjective and ontologically distinct from the world.

Descartes' dualism of mind and matter, coupled with his view of their causal connectivity, lead him to anticipate the concept of psychophysics as developed by Fechner, Troland, and early Gibson. Though mind and matter are distinct, they are causally connected, and "lawful" relationships should exist between physical and mental events. Fechner would apply this idea to sensations (simple sensory experiences), and later Troland and Gibson would apply it to perceptions (more complex experiences). Psychophysics though, as traditionally conceived, tends to be both dualistic and mechanistic. Experiences are conceptualized as distinct events caused by physical stimulation (e.g., light). Psychophysics is mechanistic because experience is seen as unidirectionally dependent upon physical stimulation.

Descartes' opposition to a necessary resemblance between sensations and the retinal image was most pronounced in his discussion of the qualitative dimensions of consciousness, such as color, sound, etc. This rejection of the simulative assumption was not consistently carried over in his explanations of shape, size, and distance perception. He described the observer as being aware of the size, figure and movement of forms in the retinal image. The visual impressions of a perceiver would supposedly replicate these aspects of the retinal image (1638b; 1644, Bk. II, IV). Since there is this correspondence (simulative), one consequence noted by Descartes is that the visual impression of an object's size is not a reliable indicator of its magnitude (a specific example of the belief in optical inadequacy). The optically projected size on the retina of a physical object varies with respect to its distance as well as its size. Therefore, Descartes argued that mediation is required for cognizance of the actual physical sizes of objects. It is "estimated" by comparing the seen sizes with perceived distance (1638b, p. 156–157). This is essentially Alhazen's view, some sophisticated version of which most psychologists still hold.

Descartes' implicit distinction between the qualitative and quantitative attributes of visual experiences corresponds to John Locke's distinction between primary and secondary qualities. For Locke, primary qualities, such as size, shape, and location, are actual properties of physical objects, whereas secondary qualities are only qualities of experience and do not bear any resemblance to properties within the physical world. In effect, Descartes's position on visual experiences is very similar: For those qualities Locke called "secondary," there is no resemblance between experience and the world, and for those properties Locke called primary, there is for Descartes a resemblance between experience and the physical world.

Descartes' physiological hypothesis of retinal projection to the brain is another indication of his belief that sensations simulate the geometry of forms in the retinal image. His hypothesis (1637) was that the arrangement of points on the retina is projected to the brain. Further, each point on the retina is connected to the brain by a neural pathway whose own activity is unaffected by activity in neighboring pathways. Hence, the activity for a neural pathway is specific to the excitation of the retinal unit with which it is connected. Resultantly, the spatial pattern of excitation on the retina is replicated in the brain. The mind, being "connected" most intimately with the brain, is thus causally connected with the retina.

Within the context of this discussion of Descartes, the concept of simulation can be further clarified. It was within the earlier discussion of the *eidola* theory that the simulative assumption was introduced: *eidola* simulate or copy the physical world. With the development of optics and the theory of the retinal image (Alhazen through Kepler) the retinal image took the place of *eidola*. The issue now became to what degree the retinal image simulated the physical world. A second, though related question, was to what degree visual awareness resembled this image. Perhaps awareness does not copy the retinal image. Perhaps, at least in some respects, it only corresponds or correlates with properties in the image. The relationship between stimulation and experience has traditionally been called the psychophysical relationship. Descartes believed in psychophysical correspondences, though for him these correspondences, e.g., regarding color, may involve only lawful correlations rather than actual resemblances of properties. Qualities such as color do not resemble anything in the retinal image or in the physical world, whereas quantitative (e.g., visual size) or spatial (e.g., visual shape) properties of experience do resemble and are proportional to properties in the retinal image. Interestingly, given our historical starting point in the *eidola* theory, a central conclusion of the seventeenth through nineteenth centuries was how poorly the retinal image did copy or simulate the physical world. This conclusion, however, depended upon modes of description for visual stimulation and the physical world that Gibson would strongly criticize. One could argue that the reason why visual perception seems so different from visual stimulation (e.g., we perceive distance despite the image having no depth) is because our descriptions of stimulation and the physical world are inadequate.

The projection hypothesis in later centuries came to serve as the physiological underpinning for the psycho-physical hypothesis that visual sensations simulate the retinal image. The projection hypothesis forms part of a more encompassing proposal of Descartes, viz., his reflex-arc hypothesis (1628, 1637). What is significant in this influential doctrine is the entailed unidirectional nature of causation in visual perception. Each stage in the chain of causation from the retinal image to the brain is contingent upon the preceding more peripheral event, but never contingent upon any succeeding more central event (see Diagram 11).

Diagram 11   Unidirectional Causal Chain

A through E are events proceeding from most peripheral to most anatomically central in location. (These stages suggested are, of course, not necessary. Other segmentations of this causal chain are possible.) A is the light entering the eye; B is the retinal image; C is activity in the optic nerve; D is activity in the brain; and E is a sensation. Each succeeding stage is anatomically more central and temporarily subsequent to the preceding stage. The arrows (———➤) depict the direction of causal dependency between events. Causal dependency does not occur in the opposite direction anywhere in the chain. Muscular reactions (R) are indirectly contingent upon A. Hence, in modern terminology A is an independent variable with respect to E or R which are dependent variables.

The concept of causality fostered by Galileo in his attack upon Aristotle's teleologism was mechanistic and the mechanistic view became part of the accepted ontology in physical science. Each succeeding event is determined by some previous event(s)—causality runs from past to present. Further, all events in the physical universe are strictly determined, where if present conditions are completely known, consequent future conditions can be infallibly predicted. Events are analyzed into distinct units, yet connected causally through strict determinism.

Descartes applied this mechanistic view to the human body arguing that it was essentially a machine whereby each and every physiological process followed by absolute necessity from immediately prior processes. The "causal chain" is simply a laying out of the anatomical flow of sequential bodily processes which start outside the body, pass through the nerves, and terminate in the brain. The body reacts like a billiard ball being struck by another billiard ball. Something impacts upon it from the external world, and it causally reacts (is affected) by moving itself. Experience caused by incoming effects is produced at the middle point of the chain in the brain. Though a mental vent, perception is a causal consequence of a unidirectional series of physical events. Simple projection or transmission of retinal excitation is unidirectional but a unidirectional series of causal relations in visual perception does not entail projection. For example, a more central state in a causal chain may be a function of the sum or relationship of several events at the next more peripheral stage. Hence, the idea of unidirectionality in visual perception is greater in scope or generality than anatomical projection. The reflex-arc hypothesis can be seen as the physio-anatomical extension of the mechanistic concept of causality and physical transmission begun with Democritus' atomic physics and reinforced in Galileo's scientific treatment of physical causality. Further, it became the general neurological framework for sensory and perceptual psychophysics.

The use of the term *mechanistic,* though popularly contrasted with *teleologism,* is also used in this description of Descartes' views to underscore his idea that perception is a *reactive sequential* process. Light is a consequence of the world, sense organs are effected by light, nerve impulses, in turn, are determined by the sense organs, etc. There is no reference to interdependency or circular processes—two of Gibson's main themes. Further perception turns into a passive process, where even if mental or rational activities intervene between sensory input and motor output, such mental activities do not have any control or effect on input. They simply react to it within their modes of operations. Gibson's ecological approach, based on the ideas of reciprocal interdependency, circular activities, and active perceptual systems attacked the above mechanistic theory of perception.

It should be remarked that Descartes adopted Kepler's "Angle of Convergence" hypothesis. Descartes appeared to have thought of the relation between convergence and visual perception of distance as quasi-mathematical. In his criticism of the deductive or "necessary connection" account of convergence, Berkeley (1733) believed that Descartes did think a mathematical type of reasoning was involved in the perception of distance by means of convergence. The idea of signs or depth cues was proposed by Berkeley in opposition to this Keplerian-Cartesian hypothesis. Two translations of Descartes' description of this process are included, and it does appear that Berkeley was correct in his interpretation of Descartes.

And this action of thought which, quite simple though it may be as an imagination, none the less in itself covers a reasoning quite similar to that which surveyors make. . . . (1638a, p. 155)

This will be accomplished by an operation of the mind which although it is only a simple set of imagination involves a calculation very similar to that made by surveyors. . . . (1638c, p. 30)

Nativism and rationalism, though historically connected, are logically distinct ideas. Plato believed that rationality could not be acquired through perceptual experiences, i.e., it could not be learned, hence he supposed reason to be "innate"—in the soul at birth. Modern philosophy has tended to follow Plato's distinction between reason (logic) and sensory experinece for how can abstractive necessary relations (such as in mathematics) be derived from segregated particulars? Rationalism is the view that knowledge comes through reason; nativism is the view that knowledge is inherited rather than learned. Rationalists (like Descartes) tend to be nativists, for they cannot see how abstract reason could be learned. (But they beg the question, in describing sensory experience as unrelated particulars.) Empiricism, as advocated by Berkeley, objected to both rationalism and nativism. Knowledge is not inherited; it is learned, and the road to knowledge is not through reason but through observation. In his psychology and his general epistemology, Berkeley saw knowledge developing from an empirical base. It was his empiricist psychology that became the prevalent theory of perception, at least in the English speaking world. Rationalists, on the other hand (such as Descartes and Kepler), believed that the mind (or perceiver) used logical-abstractive activities in perception, and though not as influential as empiricists, they still had some influence in the 18th and 19th centuries.

THE NEWTONIAN WORLD VIEW AND THE PHILOSOPHY OF SCIENCE

The Scientific Revolution was an intellectual and social change in the sixteenth and seventeenth centuries. Its major figures, Galileo, Descartes, Kepler, Francis Bacon, and Newton, saw themselves breaking with past beliefs and practices. In essence, science is a particular method or approach for gaining knowledge but aside from its methodology and epistemology, it also embodies a general ontology. Though to a degree its spokesmen (Bacon and Descartes) and practitioners were right in believing they were emancipators from the past, they carried with them various ideas whose sources lie in the Middle Ages and Ancient Greece. There was, though, a general orientation to knowledge and nature that emerged between the time of Copernicus (1473–1543) and Newton (1642–1727) that differed considerably from the world view of the Middle Ages and would eventually affect all areas of human thought.

Theories of perception in the seventeenth century reflected both the epistemology and ontology of early science. Both Kepler and Descartes adopted a metaphysical dualism, one aspect of early science derivative from the past. They also brought to perception mathematical and geometrical analysis, physical analysis and elementarism, and the principle of mechanistic causation. Each of these concepts or principles has historical roots extending backward prior to the Scientific Revolution, but by the 17th century these numerous ideas had coalesced into an integrated outlook. Not only is the ontology of 17th century science dualistic, but the epistemology also reinforced the dualistic approach to perception found in Kepler and Descartes. Beginning with Francis Bacon and culminating in Newton's physics, it is important to look more closely at the philosophy or theory of science as formulated and practiced. Expanding on an earlier thesis, Gibson's ecological approach clashes with both the ontology and epistemology that developed during the time of Kepler, Descartes and Newton. This clash is not limited to the study of perception but extends to ideas regarding the ontology and epistemology of science. This deeper theoretical clash makes sense for classic theories of perception reflected ideas or themes embodied in this traditional philosophy of science.

Francis Bacon (1561–1626), one of the earliest spokesmen of the Scientific Revolution, characterized much of "pre-scientific" thinking as based on tradition, prejudice, faith, and empty speculation. In contradiction to these unempirical practices of religion, philosophy, and mythology, secure knowledge about nature can only be obtained through observing nature and drawing generalizations well-supported by repeated observations of facts. Scientific knowledge consists of empirical generalizations "induced" from observations of particulars. Though Bacon advocates an empiricist epistemology, he distinguishes (following Plato's dualistic epistemology) observations of particulars and abstraction or generalization. The method of induction is proposed to bridge the gap between particulars and universals. For Bacon, science involved a turning away from "hearsay." Nature should be studied without theoretical presuppositions. But Bacon, by arguing that observations of particulars should not involve abstractive presuppositions, assumed that "pure" observation involved only particulars—abstraction, generalities, universals, and order were relegated to the realm of thought. Where Bacon differed from Plato's dualism, and this would become a basic assumption of modern science, was in assuming an epistemic certainty and clarity could be obtained through observation or perception, and abstractions could be inductively derived from repeated observations of particulars.

Prior to the Scientific Revolution there were numerous philosophies and belief systems (mythologies, cultures, religions) that contained theories, however well explicated, of the world (and often beyond). These ontologies, in some manner or form, were justified or supported, even if the justification was no more rational than authority or materialistic-political power. Implicit within any ontology is a theory of knowledge— its source(s), its nature, and its form. *What* is known is related to *how* it is known and supported by a particular epistemology. Historically, the Scientific Revolution can be seen as an epistemological revolution in which a new method and theory of knowledge developed. Only those ontological claims supported by the new epistemology and consequent methodology would be accepted as valid. For Bacon, the scientific method involved unbiased repeated observations and cautious generalizations. Yet, in general form, this epistemology delineated a domain of scientific knowledge. This domain with its causal relations, general laws, quantitative properties, and elementaristic composition constituted the ontology of science. Bacon accepted aspects of Plato's dualistic ontology—the predominant ontology of the Middle Ages—and though Bacon's contemporary, Descartes, also attempted to start afresh, his epistemology also presupposed an ontology derivative from the Middle Ages.

Descartes proposed that all ideas or beliefs not self-evident should be doubted. Only from indubitable axioms could conclusions about the world be deduced. Descartes, as a rationalist, emphasized the logical demands of the quest for knowledge, whereas Bacon, as an empiricist, had emphasized the observational demands. As part of the logical demands of science, Descartes also emphasized the role of mathematics and quanitative relationships, where scientific ideas, e.g., the axioms within deductions, required mathematical formulation whenever possible. With his concern for careful, detailed observation, Bacon also brought to science an emphasis on physical analysis. Descartes' proposed methodology proceeds in the opposite direction from Bacon's, but assumes the same basic distinction of observational particulars and intellectural abstractions. Descartes' indubitable starting point is abstraction or thought (making his epistemology more Platonic than Bacon's); logical reasoning goes from abstractions to particulars. Descartes' rationalism emphasizes the role of mathematical formulation in abstractions;. Bacon and other subsequent empiricists emphasized the role of detailed analysis in observation.

Logic, observation, analysis, and mathematics are all methodological principles advocated and practiced by individuals prior to the seventeenth century. Within the Scientific Revolution these principles were socially and intellectually united under the general principles of experimentation and hypothesis testing. Hypothesis testing, as practiced by Galileo, Kepler, and Newton represents an intellectual reconciliation of empiricist and rationalist epistemologies and provided a social forum for ideas to be compared and evaluated. In essence, abstractions are tested through experimentation. An abstract hypothesis should have testable observational implications and the truth or falsity of an abstraction can therefore be checked against observations. The arbiter of truth is observation, but the hypothesis itself may not refer to anything observable. Some of its deductive implications, though, must be empirical. Ideally, the implications of a hypothesis should also be formulated in terms of mathematical or quantitative relationships. Science then introduces a concern for the measurement, as well as the analysis, of observables.

Though the increasing use of hypothesis testing through experimentation may be the most distinctive feature of science, the epistemological structure presupposed in its methodology reflects elements found in Platonic rationalism and Aristotelian empiricism. Further, this new theory of scientific knowledge, while more empirically oriented than the speculative philosophies of the Middle Ages still retained a fundamentally dualistic epistemology to complement and reinforce its dualistic ontology. Recall from previous discussions that Kepler and Descartes assumed mind-matter ontological dualisms, in part due to the rationalistic (Plantonic) belief that mind, in its capacity for abstractive thought, transcended the nature of matter. Despite science using observations of nature "ideally" as the arbiter of the truth or falsity of abstractions, the persumed reference of abstract scientific knowledge is clearly distinguished from the objects of perception. Perception supplies particular examples, illustrations, or manifestations of general laws and primordial matter. Thought is the creator and storehouse of abstraction and fundamental truths; perception supplies particulars. Such abstractions, as we will see, go beyond the world of perception.

Finding its antecedents in Greek and Medieval physical thought, the causal theory of perception reinforced the epistemological dualism of science. It also provided an almost universally accepted general framework for scientific explanations of perception. In 17th century physics, the body is treated a complex physical object, localized in space, composed of matter, and effected through transmission and contact of matter and/or energy with the body. Sense-organ and nervous system activity (as in Descartes' machine model) is caused by externally originating physical forces; in turn, these physical imprints upon the body have a casual line running back to the world. Perception is seen as ultimately based (as in Descartes' psycho-physical causality) on a linear series of cause-effect relations originating "outside" or "beyond" the mind. The world that causes or triggers perception is separated from it. Consequently, abstractive thought, in scientific physical theories, not only comprehends universal laws or truths, but deals with a distinguishable realm from what is revealed through the senses.

The relationship between unobservable matter and the laws of nature seems to have been originally based on the idea of control, where the motions and states of matter "conform to" or "obey" general laws. The abstractions of theories describe these natural laws. A scientific explanation provides deductions from these abstract formulations, e.g., $F = ma$

designates a universal relationship, so for any particular situation, what is observed and measured must confrom to this quantitative proportion. Since the actual occurrence lies beyond sensory consciousness, what observation provides need not be qualitatively identical; for instance, color is a quality of visual experience but not a quality of matter. Scientific laws designate universal relationships within a world of matter only indirectly accessible through perception.

In summary, sensory experience consists of particulars possessing some qualities identical with matter but others, such as color, not actually being qualities of matter. Matter exists separate from mind (i.e., the object or content of sensory experience is not matter). Finally, there are natural laws that determine or control the processes of matter, e.g., the revolutions of planets or the falling of objects to the earth. These laws are known through rationality or thought, though they are tested or substantiated through observation. Much of this epistemology and supporting ontology is developed during Galileo and Descartes' time (early 17th century).

Along with the general causal model of physical interaction there eventually developed a specific quantified theoretical explanation that subsumed a substantial portion of all such interactions. Newton's (1687) laws of mechanics brought together under a small set of abstractive relationships both Galileo's terrestrial physics of motion and Kepler's laws of astronomical physics. Incorporated into Newton's laws was an ontological description of the physical world. Using a small set of basic concepts (e.g., mass, gravity, velocity, and distance), Newton's physics offered a general description of the behavior of nature. In a variety of ways, the Newtonian world view would influence scientific and philosophical treatments of perception. Isaac Newton is generally considered the greatest scientist of the Scientific Revolution and for 200 years his ideas were the dominant authority in physical science. Newton's theory was so successful it fostered a subsequent rise in materialism where all of nature was hypothesized as reducible to the laws and substrate of matter. Newtonian science, strictly speaking, involved both an ontological and epistemological dualism, but the effect of his success within physics gave rise to a movement toward a universal monistic materialism. Berkeley's whole philosophical development was motivated toward undercutting this materialsim by disproving the existence of matter.

Like Bacon, Galileo, and Kepler before him, Newton wished to emphasize the central importance and epistemic reliance of his physics upon observation. Though he wished to contrast his methods with Medievalists, Newton's description of the world was theoretically biased because it contained concepts that did not designate anything observable; e.g., gravity is not perceived but rather known only through the presumed observable effects of it. As mentioned earlier, space was conceived as an absolute void *in which* units (elements) of matter existed and moved around. Both motion and location were fixed relative to the coordinates of absolute space. Absolute space existed independent of matter and motion. Such a theory of space implies that the location and movement of any object is not fixed relative to the disposition of other objects, hence the ideas of absolute rest, absolute location, and absolute movement. Space, thus conceived, gives rest, location, and movement objective values, but this absolute void, modeled on an astronomical view of nature, does not designate anything observable.

Newton also conceived time as an absolute. Time has a uniform and universal flow throughout the entire universe, occurring regardless of what, if anything, is actually happening within the universe. If everything were still and without change, time would still march on. In effect, space and time are absolutes existing independently of matter and material processes. Further, space and time are considered independent of each other. Each is an absolute, universal "containment" co-existing with the other, but without any ontological connection. In principle, space could exist without time, and time without space.

Matter and motion are placed within space and time. Matter is a substance possessing intrinsic mass as a measure of its quantity. Matter is analytically and existentially broken down into elements (mass points or localized particles). Anything complex is built up out of these ultimate units. Motion is an absolute displacement of material elements through space requiring some duration fixed relative to absolute time. The concept of a physical object designates a localized aggregate of elements within space. An object is effected by the transmission of force or energy across the intervening space between objects as is the case with gravity or through material contact as is the case with mechanical impact. The laws of physics designate the universal regularities of motion and material interaction, e.g., for every action there is an equal and opposite reaction.

It is interesting to note, within the context of our history of perceptual theory, how light as a physical phenomena was treated during Newton's time. Light is a form of energy, but a point of debate in modern times has been whether to describe it as waves or localized particles. If light consists of waves, what are these waves transmitted through? The void? The Greeks had proposed the concept of a medium through which forms make contact with the perceiver, but for the Greeks light was the medium. Within the history of visual optics and geometrical perspective, light is treated as localized, though the notion of "scattering" implies a wave. Kepler's optics of the lens though provided an explanation of how such scattering or spreading could be refocused to localized points. In essence, the pattern of light effecting the eye was a set of points.

Associated with Newtonian science is the general tendency to analyze the complex into the simple, supposing the simple, more punctate was also more fundamental. Locke, Berkeley and later empiricist psychologists and philosophers would generally adopt this building block theory of reality, applying it to the mind and sensory-perceptual experience. Because space and time are made independent absolutes, spatial and temporal relationships are not intrinsic to matter but are fixed relative to dimensions existing independent of matter. For the particulars of the physical universe (elements of matter), there are intrinsic properties (e.g., mass) and there is a dimensional order that is imposed upon the units. The building block model of the universe, though historically traceable to Democritus' atomism, rests ultimately upon Plato's dualism where particulars are separated from order. Though empiricists rejected the nativist-rationalist hypothesis that order in the mind derived from a source other than sensory particulars, empiricists assumed that sensory elements did not possess any order—order derived from accumulated and generalized memories (or habits).

To review, 17th century science, as developed by Galileo, Kepler, Descartes, Newton, and others accepted the mind-matter dualism of the Middle Ages. The physical world consisted of objects in space that conformed in behavior to universal laws. Physical change followed cause-effect chains through space. The body, as a physical object, was causally effected by distant objects through the transmission of forces. Mind added order and truth to sensory-bodily effects. Perceptual awareness was of such "internal" representations. The elements of matter and the hypothesized laws of nature are known through abstraction and inference, though such knowledge is tested or evaluated through observational particulars.

The subject matter of perception can be divided into considerations about: (a) the physical world and stimulation (e.g., light, sound, etc.); (b) anatomical-physiological features of the body, sense-organs, and nervous system; (c) psychological processes of the mind; and (d) epistemological issues regarding the nature and scope of human knowledge. Physical science and philosophical epistemology in the 17th century, incorporating a variety of ideas going back to the Middle Ages and Ancient Greeks, addressed itself to each of these main topics relevant to understanding perception. Equally, the stage was set for the psychological theories of perception developed in the 18th and 19th centuries. In terms of modern intellectual heritage, Gibson's two main sources of conflict derive from the scientific-philosophical outlook of the 17th century and the psychological-philosophical views developed in the 18th and 19th centuries. Gibson's ecological optics and ecological theory of the environment clashed with the Newtonian picture of physical nature. Second, Gibson's functional concept of perceptual systems clashed with the physiology of Descartes, as well as 19th century physiology. Finally, Gibson's direct realist theory clashed with the psychology-epistemology beginning with 17th century philosophy and extending into later psychological theories of perceptual knowledge, e.g., Berkeleian views.

Various themes have been introduced in these early chapters: the objects-in-space substance ontology of Newton can be contrasted with Gibson's wholistic and dynamic theory of the environment. For Gibson, features of the environment are spatially related to the ground. Further, Gibson rejects a reductionistic analysis of the physical world and stimulation into ultimate elements. There are levels of analysis or description pertaining to the physical world and there exists an intrinsic order, both spatially and temporally, to the environment. Basically, Gibson begins an ecological description with differences, relationships, and structure rather than ultimate elements (or particulars). For Gibson, there is no dichotomy, as in Platonic-Newtonian thought between order and particulars. Gibson describes light the same way, contra Alhazen and Kepler; light possesses order.

On the physiological side, Gibson eventually rejected the unidirectional causal chain model and the projection-representation model of the brain. Gibson proposed instead the idea of perceptual systems. The camera analogy of the eye is also dropped, as well as the simulative assumption, which in modern times is supported by the camera model of the eye. Because stimulation is not seen as impoverished, the function of perceptual systems is not to enrich (or organize) input. Thought is not absolutely distinguished from perception as the sole source of order and generality. How the "enrichment" or constructive theory of perception developed through the writings of Locke, Berkeley, and Helmholtz, among others, is the next topic discussed. To recall, though empiricist theories of perception were the more popular explanations of enrichment, nativist and rationalist explanations (e.g., Kepler and Descartes) also offered enrichment theories, and Gibson, in both his physiology and psychology of perception, rejected any kind of enrichment theory.

Chapter 6 _____

BERKELEY
and EMPIRICIST PSYCHOLOGY

LOCKEAN EMPIRICISM

There is the normative or prescriptive epistemological position that all knowledge should be gathered through observation, e.g., Bacon's inductivism. (A more modern, slightly watered down view of epistemological empiricism is that all knowledge should be evaluated through observation.) This view is conceptually distinguishable from the idea that all knowledge by *natural necessity* comes through observation. Both views are labeled *empiricism,* and historically, individuals who subscribe to one idea subscribe to the other. Epistemological empiricism is usually contrasted with rationalism; naturalistic (or psychological) empiricism is contrasted with nativism. The two main psychological theories of perception in modern times (1650 to the present) have been empiricism and nativism, where the main theoretical disagreement has been how much of perception is a product of learning (empiricism) and how much is a product of inherited abilities (nativism). While he was a student, Gibson's education in theories of perception consisted of empiricist and nativist approaches and the particular controversies between these views. The empiricist view dominated early 20th century American psychology; consequently, Gibson's own position (circa 1930) was basically empiricist as it was historically and theoretically developed from the time of Locke and Berkeley through Helmhlotz and Titchener.

Although the hypothesis that all knowledge (by natural necessity) comes through the senses dates back to Aristotle and St. Thomas Aquinas, it is the English philosopher Thomas Hobbes (1588–1679) who is the modern starting point of this consequential position. He wrote in his *Leviathan* (1651), "There is no conception in a man's mind which hath not at first, totally or by parts been begotten upon the organs of sense" (p. 159).

Empiricism puts increasing importance on perception. How is it that all knowledge derives from perception? What, in fact, is involved in the process of perception, and how does perception relate to "higher" cognitive abilities such as thought, imagination, and memory? Given the general empiricist thesis, a specific formulation of how knowledge is acquired through perceptual experience developed soon thereafter that was extremely influential in the scientific investigation of perception. This particular hypothesis was associationism, and it provided the *modus operandi* of knowledge acquisition (learning) through the senses. Locke hinted at its utility but it was only adequately developed by Berkeley and Hume.

The theory of associationism was developed not only within a psychological context but also within a anatomical-physiological context. (Later it also would be applied to behavior.) The physiological counterpart of Berkeley and Hume's associationism was supplied by David Hartley (1705–1757), but Hobbes anticipated an important ingredient of Hartley's physiology. Hobbes (1651, Chapter 1) argued that after the brain has been stimulated in sensory experience, *phantasms* remain in the brain forming the physiological basis of memory. For Hobbes, perception involved a memory component, and this was contingent upon the rearousal of the *phantasms*. The memory component supplements the sensory component. It is "associated" with the sensory component, so it is rearoused when the sensory component is present. Subsequently, a similar physiological hypothesis was presented by Hartley that eventually became part of the associative explanation of visual perception.

Locke's epistemological starting point is Aristotle's concept of the *tabula rasa* or "blank tablet." For Locke, the mind is empty or blank at birth and all its content is provided through the senses. Locke's adversary is Descartes and his theory of innate ideas. Nativism, originating with Plato, placed "ideas" or knowledge in the mind prior to any experiental learning. Locke argued against this view (though his motivation was partially political), contending that the mind is a pure receptacle that does not contain any innate ideas.

Knowledge, according to Locke, consists of ideas which are either simple or compounds of simple ideas (complex ideas). Consequently, the mind could be described in terms of compounds and elements. This view evolved into the general hypothesis that perceptual experience consisted of concatenations of mental elements. These elements were sensations and ideas, the latter being copies (memories) of the former. Locke's building block theory was probably inspired by Newton's elemental view of physical nature, Locke assuming that the mind could be built up in a similar manner to that of the physical world.

Locke's simple "ideas of sensations" were especially significant. Afterwards traditionally termed "sensations," they were thought to correspond to the effects of elements of sensory stimulation. "Ideas of sensations" were not that simple for Locke, but later individuals took the notion of a simple constituent to the analytic extreme. The general assumption that sensations were elements and that perceptions were compounds found its inspiration in Locke and supplied an appropriate psychological counterpart for optical elementarism. The next step in the development of this psychological theory was Berkeley's *minima sensibilia*.

Another idea that influenced thinking regarding the nature of sensations was the primary-secondary quality distinction. Granting that the distinction between secondary and primary qualities is usually credited to Locke and that its influence upon later thought derives from him, it did not originate with him. The idea in explicit form can be found in Galileo's (1564–1642) *Il Saggiatore* (1624) (Singer, 1959, p. 246) and Robert Boyle's (1627–1691) *Origins of Forms and Qualities* (1666, p. 214–215). The primary-secondary quality distinction actually bears a close resemblance to Aristotle's distinction between common and special sensibles, though there are certain important differences.

For Locke, secondary qualities, such as colors, tastes, smells and sounds, were not qualities of physical objects, but only effects of the primary qualities of objects upon the perceiver. Primary qualities, such as spatial location, movement and size and shape, actually exist in the external physical world. Locke again seems to have followed Newton, for Locke's primary qualities consisted of those physical attributes Newton included in the physical world within his physics. Later, Locke's secondary qualities were thought of as the qualities of sensations that corresponded with points of stimulation. Pointillism in the 19th century entailed that the perceiver was presented with sensations whose qualities did not have any counterpart in the physical world. Visual cognizance of any property of the physical world would have to be inferential and indirect. Both the elementarism of early science and the distinction between sensory experience and the actual physical world are carried over and reinforced in Locke's philosophy.

The simulative assumption is presupposed in Locke's discussion of visual perception. He depicted the retinal image as a "picture" and the corresponding "ideas of sensation" as "only a plane variously colored".

"When we set before our eyes a round globe of any uniform color . . ., it is certain that the idea thereby imprinted in our mind is of a flat circle." (Locke, 1690, p. 91). This same assumption is also discoverable in the following statement:

> The idea we have of them and their grandeur being proportioned to the bigness of the area, on the bottom of our eyes, that is affected by the rays which paint the image there, and we may be said to see the picture in the retina, as, when it is pricked, we are truly said to feel the pain in our finger. (Locke, 1706, section 11–12)

We can compare these statements with the previously quoted statement by Kepler regarding visual experience and the retinal image. In the next section dealing with Berkeley's theory of visual perception, we find similar comments that further reinforce this simulative approach to the retinal image.

The concept of association owes its origins to Aristotle, but it was the empiricists Berkeley and Hume who took this simple idea and extended its applicability, making it the universal explanatory principle of empiricist psychology. Although the phrase "association of ideas" first occurred in Locke's *Essay* (1690) (Warren, 1921), he did not explicitly utilize it in his general treatment of visual perception. It is, as least, implicit in his explanation of the visual perception of the solidity of objects. Locke characterized the ability to know the solid dimensions of an object through vision as a judgment based upon "habitual custom." The eye, according to Locke (1690), provides the mind only with "flat" figures, whereas through touch, the "idea of solidity" is obtained (p. 73). Because of the "habitual custom" the visual ideas are judged in terms of these ideas of touch (1690, p. 91). (Recall a similar explanation from as far back as Plotinus.) What we do see in Locke is the hypothesis that the mind, specifically through memories, adds (contributes) to the visual sensations in the perception of solidity. Locke did not explain why visual ideas are judged in accordance with touch ideas in any clear or detailed fashion. Neither was this explanation extended systematically to all cases of visual space perception. It was Berkeley in his *New Theory* (1709) who went much further in both these directions and synthesized many of Locke's ideas into a coherent theory of perception.

BERKELEY'S PSYCHOLOGY, EPISTEMOLOGY, AND IDEALISTIC ONTOLOGY

In several respects, Bishop George Berkeley (1685–1753), is an astonishing figure. *An Essay Toward a New Theory of Vision* (1709) is the most influential single work in the history of the psychology of visual perception, whereas his *Principles of Human Knowledge* (1710) has instigated more controversy and commentary in the philosophy of perception than any other work in the history of philosophy. Amazingly, both books were completed by the time he was 25 years of age. Empiricist psychology of perception in the next 2 centuries owes more to Berkeley than to anyone else. It is several of Berkeley's key theoretical assumptions that Gibson explicitly attacks in his *Perception of the Visual World*. In point of fact, though Gibson was educated as an empiricist psychologist, it is Berkeley, more than anyone else, who is the focus of criticism in the *Perception of the Visual World*.

As the notoriety and influence of Berkeley's visual theory grew throughout the 18th and 19th centuries, critiques, defenses, and counter-rebuttals proliferated (Abbott, 1864, 1879; Bailey, 1842, 1843; Fraser, 1864, 1871; J. S. Mill, 1842, 1843, 1871). His theory found a place in theoretical reviews of visual psychology, and became one of the mainstays of 19th century psychology. Even if it is granted that the theory no longer commands the influence it once did, (and this is debatable) the large number of contemporary studies devoted to it offering philosophical, psychological and historical interpretations indicates that scholarly interest has not waned (Armstrong, 1956, 1960; Hicks, 1932; Luce, 1944, 1946, 1967; Pastore, 1965, 1971; Ritchie, 1967; Turbayne, 1956a, 1956b, 1961, 1962, 1963, 1966). Though the specifics of his psychological theory of perception have been altered and replaced in 20th century empiricist psychology, his general orientation to perception can still be found beneath the modern jargon of 20th century theory.

Berkeley's primary intellectual motivation behind all his works was a refutation of Newtonian materialism. Berkeley was a strategist who introduced his ideas in a step-by-step fashion beginning with a study of vision and the psychology of perception. His main philosophical goal was metaphysical: He wished to construct an idealistic and theistic picture of the universe. Along the way he developed a theory of perception that became the psychological cornerstone of empiricist and associative accounts of vision. In developing his theory of vision and his metaphysics of reality, he made many important theoretical contributions relevant to the history of perception.

Berkeley's logical starting point in his *Essay* is a denial that distance can be seen. Instead, he proposes that distance is suggested through signs that acquire meaning through association with tactual-muscular experiences. He attacks nativist and rationalist explanations of perception and provides the first detailed application of associationism and the building block theory (elementism) to the mind. Phenomenologically, he introduces the *minima sensibilia* hypothesis, later to be theoretically connected with neurological units of sensation, and the *heterogeneity of the senses* hypothesis, which is connected with Müller's specific energies of nerves hypothesis. He carries empiricist epistemology to an extreme, way beyond Locke, and arrives at an empiricist metaphysics of idealism as his grand philosophical conclusion, thus refuting materialism.

Berkeley's argument in the *Essay* begins with the often cited statement of the invisibility of distance. "It is, I think, agreed by all, that distance of itself, and immediately, cannot be seen. For distance being a line directed end-wise to the eye, it projects only one point in the fund of the eye. Which point remains invariably the same, whether the distance be longer or shorter" (1709, sec. 2). In the *Alciphron* (1732, sec. 8) Berkeley is somewhat more explicit, "Therefore the appearance of a long and short distance is the same magnitude, or rather no magnitude at all, being in all cases one single point." This argument deserves close attention. First, it is a modification of a similar argument presented in Molyneux's (1656–1698) *Dioptrika Nova* (1692) with which Berkeley was familiar. "For distance of itself, is not to be perceived; for 'tis a line (or a length) presented to our eye with its end toward us, which must therefore be only a point, and that is invisible" (Molyneux, 1692, proposition 31).

Berkeley's claim that distance is invisible is not original with him, but it was his "sign" theory that became the popular explanation of how distance is *indirectly* apprehended through vision. It was Berkeley's denial of visual depth that served as the actual starting point for most later students of vision. Most noteworthy among those that followed Berkeley were Hartley, Hume, Condillac, Reid, James and J. S. Mill, Müller, Helmholtz, Wundt, Titchener, and Brunswik. There have been some psychologists who have objected to Berkeley's theory, but it has stood the test of time, and when Gibson in 1950 reexamined the problem of distance perception, it was Berkeley's theory that Gibson attacked in formulating his views.

Though Berkeley refers to the invisibility of distance, he must have taken the above argument as demonstrating the invisibility of the distance of objects. His concern in the *New Theory* was with explaining how we know the distance of objects. Unless this statement constitutes proof of the invisibility of the distance of objects for Berkeley, he could not conclude, as he did, that distance of objects is only suggested through sight. Later in *Essay* he states."I say, neither distance nor things placed at a distance are themselves or their ideas, truly perceived by sight" (1709, section 45).

The line argument from Berkeley's *New Theory* appears to imply that distance is not seen because nothing on the retina varies with change in the distance. (If, of course, distance is depicted as the length of a line.) The quote would then be misleading because Berkeley later described several retinal correlates of the distance of objects. Also the *Alciphron* quote reveals that it was a lack of the dimension of length ("no magnitude") on the retina rather than a lack of correlation that is significant.

Berkeley defined ideas as the "immediate objects of the understanding" (1713, 3rd dialogue). This general definition of ideas should be kept in mind, because what later came to be referred to as "visual sensations" were "visible ideas" for Berkeley. For each sense there are certain "sensible objects" "properly perceived" by a sense that are the immediate ideas of a sense. The question is, how did Berkeley decide what are the immediate objects of vision? For some reason he concluded that the distance of objects was not an immediate object ("idea") of vision.

Tangible objects project tangible images, or "figures" on the retina. Corresponding to this retinal image, Berkeley hypothesized a "visible picture." The "visible picture" rather than the retinal image is the immediate object of vision. The figures in the visible picture will be "proportional" to the magnitude and situation of parts in the tangible retinal image (1709, section 50-56). Berkeley summarized in the following this relation between the "visible picture" and the tangible retinal image. "There is, at this day, no one ignorant that the picture of external objects are painted on the retina or the fund of the eye; that we can see nothing which is not so painted" (1709, section 88).

In Berkeley's *Visual Language* (1733) the following reasoning is expressed,

> these inverted images on the retina . . . although they are in kind altogether different from the . . . pictures (experiences), they may nevertheless be proportional to them . . . the diameters of the image, to which, images the pictures are proportional. . . . There are pictures relative to . . . (the) . . . images; and those pictures have an order among themselves, answering to the situation of the images. . . . Therefore, what hath been said of the images must in strictness be understood of the corresponding pictures, whose faintness, situation, and magnitude, being immediately perceived by sight. (sec. 53, 57)

Berkeley's belief in the invisibility of the distance of objects was based upon the aforementioned reasoning. It was the simulative assumption and its implied restrictions upon what can be seen that constituted Berkeley's starting point. There will only be visible ideas that are proportional (not just correlative) with what the tangible image replicates of the physical world. (One qualification for Berkeley was color; it is a "visible idea" although it is not a property of the "tangible" retinal image or the "tangible" physical world.)

Some who are familiar with Berkeley's metaphysics (1710, 1713) may wish to argue that for Berkeley, the retinal image does not copy anything in the physical world, because Berkeley's physical world did not exist independently of minds. On the contrary, there is a physical world that the retinal image copies. It consists of the "tangible ideas" of objects that exist, at the very least, in God's mind. (Berkeley replaced Newton's world of matter with the mind of God that "housed" all that exists.) The retinal image, also a "tangible idea," replicates these "tangible ideas" to a limited extent. Of historical interest is the fact that Berkeley accepted the restrictions of the simulative assumption without adopting the homunculus hypothesis. The simulative assumption exists in Berkeley's writings totally devoid of any vindication or explanation.

Because distance is not seen, Berkeley concluded that knowledge of distance through vision must be indirect, i.e., not immediate. Berkeley approached the problem of ascertaining the general nature of this mediational process. It is here that he mentioned the "writers of optics" (e.g., Kepler, Descartes, and Molyneux) who argued that judgment of distance, in certain cases, is a type of natural geometry. Berkeley characterized this view as follows:

> There appears a necessary connection between an obtuse angle (angle of convergence) and near distance, and an acute angle and farther distance. It does not in the least depend upon experience, but may be evidently known by any one before he had experienced it, that the nearer the concurrence of the optic axes, the greater the angle, and the remoter their concurrence is, the lesser will be the angle comprehended by them (Berkeley, 1709, section 5). . . . they imagine men judge of distance, as they do of a conclusion in mathematics: betwixt which and the premises, it is indeed absolutely requisite there be an apparent, necessary connexion. (Berkeley, 1709, section 24)

The arguments Berkeley presented against this "necessary connexion" hypothesis need not concern us. What matters is that his explanation of how distance is "suggested" is the antithesis of the nativist view (although, of course, both Berkeley and Kepler assumed psychological mediation). For example, according to Berkeley convergence of the eyes produces an "idea" of muscular strain that will increase in intensity as the degree of convergence increases. The distance of a seen figure is "suggested" because the idea of strain occurs together, in experience, with the idea of distance. The idea of distance is a "tangible idea" that is received through touching and moving towards objects. There is no "necessary connexion" between the idea of muscular strain of the eyes and the idea of distance. The former "suggests" the latter *only* because they are experienced together in time; hence, it is nothing but an arbitrary *sign*. He said,

> Ideas which are observed to be connected with other ideas come to be considered as signs, by means where of things not actually perceived by sense are signified or suggested to the imagination . . . where there is no

such relation of similtude or causality nor any necessary connexion whatso-
ever, two things by their mere coexistence, or two ideas by being perceived
together, may suggest or signify one the other—their connexion being all
the while arbitrary. (1733, section 39)

Throughout his *New Theory,* Berkeley listed various possible signs of
distance for vision, e.g., faintness, interposition, accomodation, etc.
These signifiers must be experienced together with tangible ideas to
"suggest" distance. The sign does not "resemble" what it signifies and
would therefore not "suggest" distance if it was never experienced
together with tangible ideas. Visual ideas do not resemble tangible ideas
because they involve different senses and for Berkeley, each sense is
qualitatively distinct (the heterogeneity of the senses). It should be
stressed that this is the reason a sign only "suggests" distance. It is not
because signs are thought only to be probabilistically correlated with
tangible ideas of distance. This did not enter into Berkeley's reasoning
precisely because he thought signs were reliable correlates of distance.
For example, regarding convergence, he remarked "which never fail to
accompany (changes in distance) . . . varies with different degrees of
distance" (1709, Section 18).

Whether Berkeley is correct concerning the reliability of signs is beside
the point. What is important is that he thought there were reliable
correlates of distance and, hence, this was not his reason for believing
distance was only suggested and not seen. The retinal image doesn't
simulate distance, and therefore visible ideas, although correlated in
variation with the distance of an object, cannot be of the distance of an
object.

In the subsequent discussion of Helmholtz, Brunswik, and Gibson,
several important conceptual ties and divergencies between these individuals and Berkeley's views of signs will be demonstrated. For example,
Berkeley's "signs" differ from Helmholtz's and Brunswik's "cues" in
that, for the latter, the psychological process from cue to visual perception was quasi-rational whereas it was quite automatic for Berkeley. On
the other hand, the role of association, however interpreted, is essential
to Helmholtz and Brunswik, as well as Berkeley. Secondly, it is shown
that one significant difference between Gibson's and Berkeley's starting
points is that Gibson rejected the old notion of simulation that Berkeley
accepted.

The psychological elementarism inspired by Locke emerged clearly in
Berkeley's treatment of the visual perception of the distance of objects.
For Berkeley, the experience of an object at a specific distance consisted
of a visible idea and a suggested tangible idea. These tangible ideas, in
being connected with visible ideas, do not alter the visible ideas; hence,

their occurrence together in the mind is simply a concatenation of elements. For Berkeley, perceptual learning consisted of the adding of psychological elements of memory ("tangible ideas") to "visible ideas" (visual sensations).

Berkeley's empiricist theory of distance perception was actually only one component, albeit a central one, of a more encompassing explanation of visual perception. Visual experiences serve as "signs" of various spatial properties of objects experienced through touch and movement. These properties would include, besides distance, the size, shape, and location of objects. Such properties are suggested through signs; a perceiver learns the meanings of the signs by experiencing them in conjunction with tactual-muscular experiences of an object's size, shape, and location. This general theory is similar in concept to Alhazen's view.

In considering why Berkeley's view became so popular, one should compare it with its major alternative, viz., nativism. For the last 200 years the simple fact has been that to have rejected Berkeley's empiricist theory would have been tantamount to accepting nativism. One primary factor that worked against a nativist theory of visual perception was the almost universal acceptance of an empiricist-associative theory of general mental development. A nativist theory of perception would have been inconsistent with the general empiricist theory of how knowledge develops. Another factor that helped Berkeley's view was its relative explicitness compared to the vague character of nativist theories. Associationism's ubiquitous hold on 18th and 19th century psychology derived from its analytic and elementaristic nature. Analyzing the mind into elements connected by associations gave associative empiricism a "scientific" character and detail that nativist theories lacked.

When Berkeley first published his theory in 1709, it was not a set of inductive generalizations based upon experiments; rather, his conclusions were arrived at through speculation and reason. One implication of the theory was that a man born blind and later made to see, when first presented with a cube and sphere, could not identify them correctly. Cheselden, an English physician, soon thereafter removed cataracts from a blind person and tested this implication. The patient, after being resighted, appeared unable to recognize which was the cube and which was the sphere until he touched them. Berkeley (1733) and others took this as support for his theory, but this operation plus other ones seemed to constitute the only type of early experimental support for his theory.

During the 19th century, other possible observational tests of Berkeley's theory were suggested by his critics (Bailey), and Berkeley's theory appeared to be refuted. Apparent falsifications, however, were argued away, for example, by J. S. Mill; Berkeley's theory had become the accepted view, and it was not easily dethroned. Only toward the end of the 19th century did a well developed alternative theory really unsettle Berkeley's hold. This new view was Gestalt psychology which reflected the new ("field theory") approach in physical science. Still, Gestalt psychology was essentially a nativistic approach, explaining perception by means of innate principles of organization. The real alternative to both nativism and empiricism as traditionally conceived comes with Gibson's theory of perception. As an important point to be reemphasized, Gibson's theory of perception is opposed to both traditional empiricist and nativist therories of perception, because both views assumed that perception involved an enrichment process.

Before leaving Berkeley's discussion of distance perception, note should be made of his formulation of the problem. Berkeley attempted to explain the perception of the distance of objects where distance was defined as the length between an object and the eye. Berkeley's framing of the problem followed the traditional way of describing the problem. Distance was understood as something between surfaces (e.g., the eye and objects), and was always described with respect to individual objects. This model of distance is the astronomical conception of detached objects in a void (space). In 1947, Gibson reformulated the problem quite differently. For him, distance is a dimension, not between surfaces, but across surfaces. Secondly, for Gibson, the distance of objects was considered with respect to the physical surface they rested upon and not as lying at the end of an imaginary line through a void.

Berkeley's solution to the problem of the inverted image, on the contrary, contained a positive anticipation of Gibson's 1950 treatment of the visual stimulus. If the retinal image is described with respect to the anatomy of the observer, it is inverted. The observer's legs, for example, are represented in the upper portion of the image, whereas the observer's nose is in a lower portion. This is an anatomical depiction of the retinal image. In order for the perceiver to be aware of such an inversion, he would have to be sensitive to more than just the image, but also its relation to his anatomy. Berkeley contrarily argued. "For, if you take the little images of the pictures in B (an eye) and consider them by themselves, and with respect only to one another, they are all erect and in their natural posture" (1709, section 116).

Thereafter, Berkeley's solution to the inverted image became popularly accepted. The solution simply was to consider the retinal image independently of its spatial relations to the anatomy of the perceiver. Gibson argued precisely this in 1950, but he applied the idea to all his characterizations of the image. This is what thinkers after Berkeley did not do. Except for the fact of inversion, most 19th century psychologists still assumed the perceiver to be sensitive to the anatomical location of the retinal image. The "local sign theories" of Lötze, Helmholtz, Hering, and Wundt, among others, implied the perceiver was sensitive to the anatomical location of points in the optical retinal mosaic. Hereafter this view of the retinal image will be referred to as the *anatomical retinal image*. Note that the anatomical retinal image involves an "inner sensitivity" of the image as if there was a homunculus.

Although the local sign explanation of visual perception of location and form is connected with the anatomical retinal image, Berkeley did present a hypothesis in his *New Theory* (1709) that is similar in many respects to the "local sign theory" of Lötze. Berkeley argued that the proper objects of vision are totally dissimilar to the proper objects of touch, i.e., there are no common sensibles. Hence, even if there is a "visible extent" proportional to the extent of the retinal image, these visible extents need to be associated with "tangible ideas" of direction supplied through eye movements to have a tangible spatial meaning. The theory of eye movement sensations being conjoined with visual sensations had been first expressed by Alhazen, and after Berkeley the local sign theory emerged as quite an important element in empiricist explanations of perception.

Two significant ideas emerge in this explanation associating visual sensations with muscular sensations. Berkeley's elementism led him to conclude that there were irreducible units of sensory experience; these units were *minima sensibilia*. For vision there existed a smallest discernible extent of color, a *minima visibilia*. Visual extent was built up out of color-atoms. Second, Berkeley rejects the notion of similarity between visual extent and tangible (muscular-tactual) extent because he believes that each sense has qualities peculiar to it. Berkeley rejects Aristotle's common sensibles and Locke's primary qualities. There are distinct groups of qualitatively different sensibles, and they need to be associated together if one is to signify the other. The units of visual extent need to be associated with tangible extent. If a blind man who knew the shape of a square through touch were resighted, he would not be able to visually identify a square.

One of the key terms in 19th century psychology was *sensation;* the word referred to the conscious effect or concomitant of sensory excitation. In 19th century neuro-physiology we find that the brain and the sensory nerves were thought to consist of functionally and anatomically distinct units labeled *neurons*. Also, areas of the brain and of the sensory nerves were segregated in an analytic fashion. Upon excitation of a sensory nerve and connected areas of the brain, sensations supposedly result. Any sensory experience consists of a large number of individual sensations; each sensation was believed to be the effect (or concomitant) of excitation in one neuron. Berkeley's *minima sensibilia* was conceptually connected and reinforced by the neuron theory of sensations and his heterogeneity of sensory qualities was likewise connected with the segregated view of distinct areas of the brain and distinct sensory nerves.

Berkeley's context theory of meaning was one of his most lasting and important contributions to psychology. Not only did Berkeley apply this theory to his treatment of perception, but he explained the meanings of words and any other type of signs in terms of associative context. Later associative psychologists generally supported the context theory of meaning. In the 19th century Helmholtz and especially Titchener argued that the meaning of perceptual experiences was the associated context (memories) of present sensations. Titchener, indeed, is remembered for explicitly contending that all meaning is context.

Berkeley's empiricism provided the basis for both his phenomenalist epistemology and his idealistic ontology. The empiricist theory of knowledge entails that all ideas must derive from sensory observation; therefore Berkeley concludes that inferences to "entities" beyond observation are unjustified and meaningless. Matter, as an inference, is thrown out and the world is reduced to what is actually experienced. Berkeley, in accepting a clear cut distinction between observation ("immediate ideas") and inference ("mediate ideas"), comes to an empiricist idealism based on the premise that only what is "perceived" ("immediate ideas") actually exists. If a mediate idea is a memory of an immediate idea, it has a real reference though not momentarily present. Matter as an inference has no real referent for it is never experienced directly—what is experienced are "sensibilia" or sensory qualities. Fundamentally, what Berkeley asks is how anything can be known beyond what is experienced? And as an empiricist, Berkeley answers that there is no meaningful basis for believing anything exists beyond experience. Berkeley argues that where there are ideas, there must be a mind; hence, what exists are ideas and minds. Note this argument is similar to Descartes' "I think, therefore I am." Phenomenalism, as an epistemology, entails that only observables can be known. Berkeley's inclusion of the "mind" oversteps this restriction, for the mind is not a sensory quality. Including the mind makes Berkeley an idealist. Berkeley wished to rid the world of the threat of Newtonian materialism, but his idealism was equally susceptible to the same empiricist restrictions. Hume would carry empiricist epistemology further, ending with a more through phenomenalism. Through his extreme empiricism Hume would rid the "world" of both matter and mind, and end up with just qualities, rather than substances or entities.

It has been supposed that Berkeley's rejection of the visibility of distance was basic to his defense of idealism. The reverse view has also been held that Berkeley used his idealism to refute the visibility of distance (Armstrong, 1956, 1961; Luce, 1934, 1946; Turbayne, 1963;

Watson, 1968). The correct conclusion seems to be that although Berkeley entertained the idea that there was a connection between his perceptual psychology and idealism (1707–1708, 1710 sec. 43), in his mature thinking he did not see the two ideas as logically connected (1713, pp. 201–202). On the other hand, the idea that the mind is "thing-like," somehow localized in the perceiver with an inside and outside, does suggest, if one holds an empiricist epistemology like Berkeley, that anything "external" to the mind (e.g., objects in space) cannot be known. Such reasoning assumes the mind is localized in physical space and for the mind to experience something it must "contain" it. For Berkeley, beyond the mind could not possibly mean at a distance in physical space for there is nothing "beyond" minds and there is no physical space. Berkeley's idealism follows from his empiricism and theism; his rejection of visual distance follows from the simulative assumption. His mature theoretical position involves an idealistic monism and, though empiricist in conception, an indirect (mediate) theory of perception.

The thrust of Gibson's attack on Berkeley initially was the indirect, sensation-based psychology of perception and the building block view of consciousness. This attack focused on Berkeley's theory of distance (depth) perception and branched out into other aspects of spatial vision. Later Gibson would also develop countertheories to Berkeley's context theory of meaning and his heterogeneity of the senses hypothesis. Berkeley's idealism, though both controversial and influential, was not popular in twentieth century psychology, yet Gibson's theory of ecological reciprocity dealt with the problem of mind and matter as had Berkeley's metaphysics. Gibson's conclusion is much different, opposing any type of reductionistic monism yet equally opposing an absolute dualism such as in Descartes or Plato.

EMPIRICIST PHENOMENALISM AND ASSOCIATIONISM

I open my eyes, and I see at first only an obscure haze. I touch, I move forward, I touch again: a chaos gradually unravels itself in my gaze. Touch in some way decomposes the light; it separates colors, distributes them on objects, separates a luminous space, and in this space of sizes and shapes, leads my eyes up to a certain distance, uncloses to them the road through which they must fly far and wide over the earth, and ascend up to the heavens; before them, in a word, it unfurls the universe. (Condillac, 1754, Ch. 8, sec. 8)

The French philosopher Etienne Bonnet de Condillac (1715–1780) in his *Essai* (1746) was decidedly critical of Berkeley, but Condillac underwent a change of opinion in his *Traite des Sensations* (1754). Condillac, adopting Berkeley's conception of signs, endeavored to describe how visual awareness of all geometrical porperties could develop through associations with tangible ideas. For Condillac, the retinal image yielded nothing but extensionless visual sensations that only after associations with tangible ideas came to signify spatial ideas. In the 19th century this corresponded to treating the optical basis for vision as just a set of independent points having no spatial structure. Condillac's theory typlified popular empiricist thought during the next 150 years.

David Hume (1711–1776) in his Treatise (1739) accepted the Berkeleian hypothesis of signs of distance. He also argued similarly that, "bodies . . . appear . . . to the eye . . . as if painted on a plain surface?" (Hume, 1739, Bk. I, ii5).

His explicit and systematic formulation of the principles of association, in particular association by contiguity, clarified for later Berkeleians the *modus operandi* of distance signs or depth cues and subsumed them under a general psychological principle (law). Association, for Hume, serves the general function of uniting together the flux of particulars produced through sensory awareness. Association is a principle used to explain memory, thus it is memory for the associative empiricist that relates the unordered particulars of sensory awareness.

Hume, with his phenomenal distinction between impressions and ideas, clarified Berkeley's and Locke's dual meaning of their term *idea*. Hume's "impressions" came to be referred to as "sensations" in the next century. Hume decomposes consciousness into two basic elements and eliminates any vestiges of non-elemental aspects of the mind still contained in Berkeley and Locke. Taking a strict empiricist stance, Hume believed "ideas" were nothing but memories of "impressions."

Berkeley introduced the hypothesis of *minimum visibilia* in his *New Theory* (section 80) where he argued that visible extent is not infinitely divisible; hence, there must be non-divisible extents. Hume, who also supposed that visible extent is composed of these *minimum visibilia*, contributed to this idea the hypothesis that these *minimum visibilia* have no extent since they cannot be divided (*Treatise*, Bk. I, iv, 5, 1739). Locke's simple ideas of sensation, Hume's minimum visibilia, and optical pointillism merged to form the psychological theory of unextended elemental visual sensations.

Hume, in his extreme associative empirisism, achieves a very economic philosophical system. He reduces consciousness to a world of particulars and eliminates any wholistic or relational characteristics to the mind. In fact, Hume rejects both mind and matter as empirically unjustified inferences and arrives at a phenomenalist ontology that became the basis of structuralist psychology.

In the previous section, the rationale behind Berkeley's denial of the visibility of distance was examined in considerable detail. In understanding Locke, Berkeley, Hume and their followers, a general and quite significant point to be raised is upon what criteria did such early empiricists decide what was directly experienced through sensory observation. It may seem a simple matter for an empiricist to describe what is sensed, distinguishing such immediate experiences from inferences and speculations. (Recall Bacon's conviction that the facts of observation can be distinguished from speculation.) Yet empiricists such as Berkeley and Hume make a variety of assumptions (e.g., particulars and intrinsic qualities are immediately sensed rather than universals and relationships) and invoke a variety of arguments (e.g., simulation, optical pointillism, the primacy of analytic elements) in their descriptions of what is sensed. Historically, the distinction between direct acquaintance and inference is controversial, rather than intuitively obvious. Analogously, in science, the distinction between fact and theory has been disputed, and there have often been significant transformations of the facts of science. A fact of science is not necessarily a fact of sensory experience but scientists and philosophers who advocate an empiricist epistemology historically have used theory and argumentation in their descriptions of experience and fact. Berkeley's simulative assumption derives from Kepler's optics and Greek theory, and Hume's phenomenal reductionism derives from the analytic tradition of early science. Simply, there is no purely empricial way (through observation) to decide or discover what is empirical (observational). Gibson would question traditional empiricist descriptions of sensory experience, invoking alternative theoretical notions anathema to optical and experiential elementism, arriving at a quite different description of what is perceived.

David Hartley's (1705–1757) *Observations on Man* (1749) includes several further developments on Berkeley's theory. Although soon outmoded, his physiological conception of association initiated a new direction of inquiry for later thinkers. Hartley, in conjunction with his psychological associationism, proposed a physiological distinction between ideas and sensations. For Hartley, sensations are contingent upon peripheral neurological excitation. Cerebral excitation ("vibration") caused by sensory peripheral activity is the physiological concomitant of sensations. Cerebral "vibrations" that occur together often enough cause the activated nerves to become anatomically connected. Later, when one nerve of a connected pair is excited, it will cause vibrations in the other nerve. Ideas correspond to the temporally latter physiological event, whereas sensations are the temporally prior occurrence. This provided an explanation of how visual sensations come to suggest tangible ideas.

Tangible ideas for Berkeley resulted from bodily movement and touching. Hartley suggested a demarcation between tactual sensations that were caused by bodily contact with an object and motor sensations that resulted from movement. The latter eventually carried for many (Bain, Helmholtz, etc.) the full burden of furnishing the ideas of distance in visual perception. This occurred first in Thomas Brown.

In his *Lectures* (1820), Brown (1778–1820) provided the Berkeleian approach with several significant ideas. First, unlike Berkeley, he distinguished between muscular and cutaneous (skin) sensations and attempted to explain visual perception of distance completely in terms of the former. Muscular sensations of resistance in combination with an innate idea of causality supply the ideas of distance, solid shape, and object size in visual perception. Visual sensations serve as signs of the ideas of distance in the same sense as in Berkeley, viz., they "suggest" these spatial ideas only after experienced in temporal contiguity with ideas of distance.

Brown's treatment of visual perception is also of historical consequence because of his introduction of the concept of mental chemistry. This idea was to occupy an important role for some later thinkers, notably John Stuart Mill and Wilhelm Wundt. In the following passage is an explication of this hypothesis by Brown.

> In this spontaneous chemistry of mind, the compound sentiment that results from the association of former feelings has in many cases, on first consideration so little resemblance to these constituents of it, as formerly (existed) in their elementary state. (1820, p. 156)

If visual sensations have either only two-dimensional extent or no extent at all, mental chemistry would explain why they are not noticed as such. In combination with ideas of distance derived from touch and/or muscular effort, they may no longer appear to the mind (perceiver) as in this primitive or original state. Consequently, the phenomenal elementarism prevalent in associative empiricism was of two distinct forms. Either elements merely combine in the mind to yield perceptions or they somehow "fuse" or "blend" together in visual perception. Either type of phenomenal elementarism is clearly distinguishable from Gibson's theory of perception. Gibson rejected the building block theory in either form. Yet note that mental chemistry is a theoretical or hypothetical process. The whole thrust of empiricism had been to restrict description to what was experienced, yet because of a variety of assumptions about what shoud be immediately experienced, empiricist theories of perception began to introduce a variety of mental entities and processes that were inferential and not directly experienced.

Thirdly, Brown supplied empiricism with an explicit formulation of the secondary laws of association. Of particular interest are Brown's third and fifth laws (1820, p. 44–45). The third law is that of "relative frequency"; for example, "the parts of any train are more readily suggested in proportion as they have been more frequently renewed," whereas the fifth law is that of "fewer alternative associates," e.g., "the song which we have never heard but from one person can scarcely be heard again by us without recalling that person to our memory." Together these laws were utilized by Egon Brunswik in his description of the probabilistic nature and "weights" of depth cues for visual perception.

The following excerpt is taken from James Mill's (1773–1836) *Analysis of the Phenomena of the Human Mind*, (1829):

> Yet, philosophy has ascertained that we derive nothing from the eye whatever, but sensations of colour; that the idea of extension, in which size, and form, and distances are included, is derived from sensations, not in the eye, but in the muscular part of our frame. (p. 95)

Recall that the simulative assumption implied visual sensations would have two-dimensional extent and form, whereas optical pointillism entailed that visual sensations would have neither extent nor form of any kind. Although Mill did not rely upon optical considerations, he reached a decision concerning visual sensations that is commensurate with optical pointiliism. Mill's mental elementism, in this respect, stands more with Hume's philosophical elementism than with physical or scientific elementism. The philosophical assumption is that the particulars of analysis are the ultimate constituents of reality. In his hypothesis of *minimum visibilia*, Mill identified visual sensations with these unextended visual impressions. Later, many empiricists followed Hume and Mill in viewing visual sensations as nothing but signs for all spatial ideas; hence, visual perception of the physical worlds was, in its entirety, epistemologically indirect.

Paralleling Brown, Mill relied strictly upon muscular sensations to explain the origin of spatial ideas in visual perception. One difference between them was that Brown included in visual perception an innate idea of causality. For Mill, it was solely an association of visual sensations with muscular sensations that yielded visual perception of form, size, distance, etc.

James Mill's characterization of visual perception represents the paradigm historical case of the elementaristic conception of sensations. Visual perceptions consist of mere combinations of sensations and ideas. Following Mill, Bain and Helmholtz further developed this form of phenomenal elementarism. Again in the spirit of Hume's empiricism, Mill attempted to eliminate any vestige of nativist or rationalist features in his theory of perception.

John Stuart Mill (1806–1873), in his *System of Logic* (1874, Bk. III, Chapter VI), distinguished between two forms of natural laws, which he designated respectively as mechanical and chemical laws. In opposition to his father, he proposed that perceptions are not merely concatenations of sensations and ideas but "blendings," i.e., cases of mental chemistry. Space, according to John Stuart Mill, is originally an idea of succession derived from bodily movement. It fuses with visual sensations to form the idea of space in visual perception, altogether different in quality from the muscular idea from which it was "generated."

Because of his belief that spatiality was not supplied through vision, Mill envisioned his position as an extension of Berkeley's views (Mill, 1865–1868a, 1865–1868b, 1871). What the Berkeleian approach especially owed to Mill was his hypothesis that the perceived meaning (including spatial) of objects is analyzable into the expected permanent possibilities of sensation. This hypothesis is contained in Berkeley's writings, (e.g., 1710, p. 252), but Mill systematized it.

Through associations, any small set of visual sensations can serve as signs for whole groups of visual and non-visual ideas. The mind "expects," says Mill certain sensations to follow other particular sensations (the signs). These expected sensations can be visual ideas which correspond to various "perspectives" of an object, tactual ideas corresponding to feeling an object, and muscular ideas of resistance corresponding to pressing against an object. Any object will have an ordered and constant series of sensations specific to it that are obtained again and again by the perceiver. All the concomitant ideas will be associated together, and thereafter any subset of the total group of sensations produces an expectation of the remaining sensations of the set, viz., the remaining associated ideas. Of particular interest is that in visual perception, a set of visual sensations produces associated ideas (visual, tactual and muscular) that are the permanent possibilities of sensations for an object and the perceptual meaning of the object (J. S. Mill, 1865, Chapter 11). A major implication of this view of visual perception is that visual sensations are supplied with meaning. Meaning is not obtained through vision, but supplied by the mind in the form of concurrent ideas. This general theory of perceptual meaning was accepted by Helmholtz and Titchener.

Mill's theory of perceptual meaning, which essentially is an extension of Berkeley's theory of signs, falls within the general Platonic perspective on meaning. The mind supplies meaning and in the case of Berkeley and Mill, meaning is associated ideas or memory. The mind also gives order and coherence to the fleeting and sketchy world of sensations by "filling in" the missing parts of an object or total situation. Gibson would address the general problem of coherence throughout his career and would offer a decidedly anti-Platonic solution, where the coherence of perception was explained through stimulus invariants within the total ecological context. For Gibson, perceiving the continuity of the surrounding scene, for instance, where things are relative to each other and how they fit together into a meaningful whole, does not involve a "filling in" or a "connecting together" by the mind. Stimulus invariants specify continuity and coherence within the environment. Eighteenth and nineteenth century British empiricism, with its analytical bias, breaking the world into elemental independent pieces, was faced with the "Humpty Dumpty" problem of trying to put the pieces together again using the glue of associative memory.

The empiricist philosophical tradition, initiated by Locke and Berkeley and developed by Hume, J. S. Mill and others would provide the basic conceptual framework for much of neural and sensory physiology in the 19th century. In fact, the work of Müller, Helmholtz, Wundt, and other experimentally oriented students of perception can be viewed as a merging of the empiricist philosophical tradition and the scientific tradition of Kepler, Descartes, and Newton. Basically it was this late 19th century scientific empiricism that constituted the intellectual establishment in perceptual theory when Gibson was a student at Princeton. It would be the modern source for Gibson's major critical objections to theories of perception. All Gibson's major works are directed against some fundamental idea embodied in this tradition.

Chapter 7

NINETEENTH CENTURY STRUCTURAL PSYCHOLOGY

MÜLLER, LÖTZE, AND EMPIRICIST PSYCHOPHYSIOLOGY

Each of Gibson's three books had one predominant historical figure that was the focus of theoretical criticism. Berkeley was the central adversary in the *Visual World*, as was Newton in Gibson's *Ecological Approach*. Johannes Müller, the great 19th century physiologist and teacher of Helmholtz, was the focus of attack in Gibson's *Senses*. Gibson attacked Berkeley's psychological theory of space perception in the *Visual World*. In his *Ecological Approach*, Gibson attacked Newton's theory of nature, and in the *Senses*, it was Müller's explanation of sensory physiology, the "specific energies of nerves hypothesis", that Gibson would criticize and reject.

Müller's doctrine of the "specific energies of nerves" is said to have been anticipated by such individuals as Charles Bonnet, Thomas Young, and Charles Bell (Boring, 1950). We have seen that its beginnings can be glimmered as far back as in Galen's specific *pneuma* hypothesis. It was Müller though who crystallized the concept. Descartes' mind-body dualism led him to deny that simulation was a necessary condition for a corresponding visual sensation. Johannes Müller's (1801–1859) "specific energies of nerves" hypothesis (1843, 1848) was basically in accordance with the simulative assumption. Neither Descartes nor Müller believed color was a property of the physical world, but Müller did believe, because of his "specific energies of nerves" hypothesis, that simulation was required for the spatial properties of sensation. For example, Müller asserted that, "The immediate objects of the perception of our senses are merely particular states induced in the nerves and felt as sensations" (1843, p. 707).

The "specific energies" hypothesis entails an ontological identity between sensory consciousness and neurological states. Inasmuch as for Müller, sensations are the states of nerves experienced, he concluded that the spatial pattern of nervous excitation is sensed and that any pattern of visual sensations is nothing but the spatial pattern of the nerves excited. A square pattern is experienced if there is a corresponding square pattern of excitation because the latter is *identical* with the former and not just a correlated event as in Descartes. Specifically concerning vision he stated, "The retina feels its own extension and position. . . . in vision we perceive merely certain states of the retina and that the retina is itself the field of vision. . . . On each visual globe the retina sees itself only as it is extended in space in the state of stimulation" (1843, p. 351; 1848, p. 1163; 1826, p. 54). Because the retinal state of excitation is physically extended in only two dimensions, visual sensations have only two dimensions. Müller though, due to this physiological explanation of visual extension, was thought to be a nativist (Ribot, 1886). Empiricists, such as J. Mill and J. S. Mill, would not attribute any spatial structure to sensations, and instead argued that perceptual space developed through association and memory.

The conceptual connection between the simulative assumption and the view that visual awareness is *of something in the observer* is quite explicit in Müller. If visual consciousness is a type of inner observation (the homunculus hypothesis), then it is not of the external physical world, and it must be limited to the dimensions of the inner representation (e.g., the states of nerves), because the inner representation is what is observed. Müller's "specific energies of nerves" hypothesis incorporates all these ideas, viz., the homunculus hypothesis, the simulative assumption and the denial of outer observation. Lastly, Müller's description of the qualitative dimensions of sensations in terms of Locke's secondary qualities, e.g., color, accentuated the separation between the perceiver and the physical world.

Gibson, in his criticisms of indirect or mediational conceptions of vision, has been especially concerned with Müller's view of the ontological and epistemological status of perception. Gibson viewed a major point of difference between himself and Müller over whether visual perception is based upon cognizance of the states of nerves, viz., sensations, or based on information in the optic array. Müller's view leads to an ontological separation of the physical world and perceptual consciousness. The idea that the brain "observes" itself in perception or that perception takes *place* in the brain is extremely entrenched in modern psychology and physiology. Müller's ontology, like Berkeley's psychology, persists in modern traditional thought. Gibson makes perception an ecological event (not localized in the brain), specific to ecological rather than neurological conditions.

Basically, the specific energies of nerves hypothesis identifies specific sensory qualities (e.g., color) with specific neurological areas. Color has a distinct place, sound a distinct place, and so on for smell, taste, and touch. Sensory qualities are clearly separated, thus reinforcing Berkeley's heterogeneity of senses hypothesis, and segregated to specific areas of the nervous system, both providing a modern interpretation of Galen's specific pneuma as well as initiating the modern neurological tradition of analyzing the nervous system, including the brain, into anatomically and functionally independent units or areas. Gibson's theory of perceptual systems would offer an alternative to both the physiological and psychological segmentation of the senses proposed in Müller's "specific energies" hypothesis.

The projection hypothesis first proposed in Descartes became the prevalent neurophysiological explanation of visual sensations during the latter half of the nineteenth century through the work of such persons as J. Meynert, (Polyack, 1957), and D. Ferrier (1874). This hypothesis provided an anatomical and physiological basis for the view that visual sensations are specific to the pattern of excitation at the retina, as implied by the simulative assumption, as well as further articulating the analytic treatment of the sensory nervous system found in Müller.

Since the Greeks, perceptual consciousness has been thought to be directly dependent upon some area in the brain. Because the brain was spatially separated from the retina, if visual sensations were copies of retinal patterns, the effect on the retina must somehow be transmitted unaltered to the brain. The projection hypothesis is simply the postulate that the neurological pathways between the retina and the brain transmit retinal patterns of excitation (see Diagram 12).

Referring to the diagram, if A, B, D and E are excited simultaneously, the pattern of excitation (Sr) will be square. The connection fibers in Z will produce the cerebral pattern A', B', D', E' (marked Sc) which is also a square. If the visual sensation (Ss) is identified with Sc, then Ss $\equiv$ Sc (as for Müller) or Ss can be thought of as a correlate of Sc (as for Descartes).

The projection hypothesis is conceptually connected with the theory of localization of the brain. During the 19th century the view developed that each psychological function was localized in some specific area of the brain; consequently, there was supposedly some delimited portion of the brain that contained the "visual sensorium" where optical pathways terminated (Flourens, 1824; Gratiolet, 1854; Polyak, 1957). Both the projection and localization theories became objects of criticism in Gib-

DIAGRAM 12

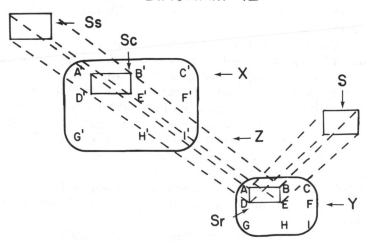

Points A, B, C . . . I are sensitive units on the retinal surface marked Y. Each point on the retinal surface is connected to a corresponding point in the brain marked X. These points in the brain are designated A', B', C', . . . I'. The physical connection between retinal and cerebral points is a set of independent and mutually isolated nerves in the optic pathway marked Z.

son's "perceptual system" approach to visual physiology. A clear expression of the projection-localization view is contained in the following quote by Munk. Note should be made that these ideas assume a physiological elementism corresponding with empiricism's mental elementism (Pastore, 1971).

> The central elements of the visual area, where the optic pathway terminates and where perception takes place, are arranged in an orderly manner and continuously, as are the receptors in the retina where the fibers arise, viz., that the adjoining retinal units remain close to the same units in the cortex. (Munk, 1879)

As mentioned before, the projection hypothesis presupposes a unidirectional causal chain model of visual perception. In terms of Diagram 12, S causes Sr, which causes Sc (and any associated neural units), which finally causes or parallels Ss. A mechanistic causal chain of discrete and segregated events flows from the external world "inwardly." Perception is causally separated from the external physical world.

Not everyone accepted the projection hypothesis as a sufficient explanation for sensitivity to the pattern of retinal excitation. The German philosopher Rudolf Hermann Lötze (1817–1881) formulated his "local sign" hypothesis (Boring, 1950; Ribot, 1886) in opposition to one implication of the simulative assumption, viz., that a pattern in retinal excitation was a sufficient condition for a corresponding pattern in visual sensation. Lötze sees Müller's physiological approach as a modern version of the homunculus hypothesis. Ribot summarizes Lötze's position.

> The grossest form of this mistaken solution is the old hypothesis of idea images. . . . Small copies of objects enter the "soul" from without. . . . This doctrine, in a much more refined and subtle form, indeed, meets us still everywhere. All the theories of space, in fact, admit more or less that the form under which a quality of simultaneous excitations of the nervous system follow one another in space, affords immediately the reason for a similar disposition of sensations in space. (Ribot, 1886, p. 78)

Instead, Lötze supposed that visual sensations originally corresponded to independent points of stimulation on the retina; hence, they were extensionless and spatially unrelated.

Before describing Lötze's "local sign" hypothesis, an important similarity between it and the projection hypothesis should be noted. Both hypotheses sought to explain sensitivity to the anatomical pattern of retinal excitation. The projection hypothesis implies that this sensitivity is physiologically innate, whereas the local sign hypothesis suggests that this anatomical sensitivity involves memory. Hence either position involved its adherents in supposing that visual perception was contingent upon the anatomical pattern of retinal excitation. Consequently, though Lötze rejects both the homunculus hypothesis and simulative assumption, he ends up in the same place, viz., how do we go from an awareness of inner spatial states to an awareness of outer spatial relations.

Inspired by Kant, Lötze included in his "local sign hypothesis" the assumption of an innate idea of space. Each local sign is not spatial but is interpreted as spatial, given this innate concept. Any visual sensation and corresponding point of retinal stimulation produces a muscular reflex in the eye that moves the point of stimulation to the fovea of the eye. The muscular sensations that accompany this ocular movement will be specific ("local sign") to the point stimulated on the retina. The extensionless visual sensations become associated with these muscular sensations, and this complex is interpreted in terms of the innate idea of space. The result is that the mind locates visual sensations with respect to the anatomical locations of points of stimulation on the retina, viz., their distance from the fovea. This localization of sensations is therefore only two dimensional.

Lötze's local sign hypothesis underwent modifications in the hands of Bain, Helmholtz, Wundt, Kulpe, and Titchener, among others. What it provided was an alternative to the projection hypothesis within psychology because it was a substitute explanation of how visual sensations corresponded to retinal patterns of excitation. Resultantly, it fitted adequately into Berkeley's theory of depth cues or signs. Berkeley had described the various distance signs of visible ideas, e.g., faintness, interposition, etc., as proportional to the retinal image. The local sign hypothesis furnished an alternate means by which the perceiver could be aware of these visual depth cues or signs.

FECHNER'S PSYCHOPHYSICS OF SENSATION

Gustav Fechner's (1801–1887) psychophysics reflects the general conception of science prevalent during the 18th and 19th centuries. His psychophysical model is the view Gibson adopted in his initial psychophysical theory of perception. Central to Fechner's psychophysics is the concept of mechanistic scientific laws and unidirectional causality. Gibson's psychophysics followed these principles. Where Gibson initially differed from Fechner was in rejecting Fechner's elementism, emphasizing instead the wholistic attributes of perceptual consciousness and stimulation.

Though Hume's epistemological critique of the logical necessity of scientific laws was extremely difficult to philosophically dispute, scientists continued to pursue the goal of finding necessary and universal relations between natural facts or "variables." Fechner aspired to metaphysical a identity between body and mind (Boring, 1942, 1950), and he saw this ontological thesis as demonstrable by showing that lawful relations existed between stimulus variables and conscious sensations. If the wavelength of light (a physical stimulus) is varied, the corresponding sensation of color should vary in a lawful and predictable way. Fechner believed scientific laws existed between mental and physical facts, where the physical fact is the cause of the mental fact. Where Descartes and Müller had proposed that lawful relations exist between mental and physiological (bodily) facts, Fechner went further, arguing that precise lawful relations exist between mental facts and external (to the body) physical facts. The external physical fact causes an internal physiological fact which in turn causes a mental fact, thus exhibiting a unidirectional lawful causal chain (intromission theory) beginning in the material world and terminating in sensory consciousness.

Whereas Fechner saw sensations as causal effects of stimulation, Gibson later would propose that perceptions were also causal effects of stimulation. If lawful relations exist between physical and mental facts, the mental facts will have a *veridical* correspondence (in some manner) with the physical world. Descartes' adoption of the principle of causality between mind and matter both insured the existence of a physical world and gave consciousness a real (or veridical) correspondence to this external world of matter. Gibson's psychophysics of perception was developed to demonstrate veridicality in perception and was based on the idea of a lawful correspondence between perceptual consciousness and the external physical world.

Fechner's psychophysics adopted the analytic emphasis on Newtonian science. Following the line of thought from Locke, Berkeley, Hume, and other empiricists, Fechner reduced sensory consciousness to sensations corresponding to simple, localized physical facts. Structuralist psychologists would incorporate Fechner's psychophysics because it was consistent with the analytic and elementaristic traditions. Sensations, the basic building blocks of consciousness, are lawfully connected with simple physiological and physical facts. Structuralists would analyze and describe these elements, and Fechner's psychophysics connected these mental elements with corresponding physical "elements."

The psychophysical approach, though it was applied to simple, elemental facts of sensory consciousness, was generally not extended to the level of perception prior to Gibson. (One exception to be discussed later was Leonard Troland, who was to influence Gibson in his formulation of a psychophysics of perception.) Perceptual consciousness involved global and structural features that, according to most empiricists and nativists, were a product of higher mental processes. Sensations were simple and connected with the elemental and discrete pathways and receptors of the senses. Further, the physical world of stimuli was presumably simple and elementary; consequently, there was no structurally complex description of physical stimuli commensurate with the structure of perception. In his psychophysics of perception, Gibson, had to develop a structural description of physical stimuli that was sufficiently global and complex to be commensurate with the facts of perception. Gibson's description of physical order in stimuli, such as light, involved an abandonment of the Platonic theory that global order and structure was a fact solely attributable to the mind.

WUNDT, TITCHENER, HELMHOLTZ, AND STRUCTURALIST PSYCHOLOGY

A major implication of Lötze's "local sign" hypothesis was that all spatial determination of visual sensations involves mental supplementation. Within Bain, Helmholtz and Wundt, the local sign hypothesis was made more consonant with empiricist physiology by eliminating the innate idea of space Lotze had postulated. For example, in Bain the spatial determination of visual sensations is totally a function of muscular ideas; no innate ideas of space were thought to be required.

Alexander Bain (1818–1903) and Hermann von Helmholtz's (1821–1894) treatment of visual perception best exemplified this emphasis on the muscular meaning of visual sensations. According to Bain and Helmholtz, visual sensations correspond to points of retinal stimulation; consequently, they are originally without extension and location. Muscular ideas are associated with visual sensations furnishing all the spatial meaning to vision (Bain, 1868, 1872, 1873; Helmholtz, 1866, 1873, 1878, 1894). This motor approach to visual perception is even carried to their discussions of binocular disparity. The disparity of "pictures" is not fused physiologically into single image in depth, but is interpreted as a sign of distance only after association with muscular ideas of distance (Bain, 1868, pp. 243–245; Helmholtz, 1873, pp. 113–125).

This increased emphasis within empiricist psychology on associated muscular meanings, has, if anything, become more pronounced and pervasive in psychological thought in the 20th century. Jumping ahead approximately 50 years to the advent of behaviorism (Watson, 1919, 1930), many psychologists no longer used the terminology of "visual sensations" and "muscular ideas." In spite of the metaphysical and terminological changes that occurred in empiricist psychology, the general form of explanations remained much the same. Instead of "muscular sensations," the accepted phrase became "muscular responses." Association now occurred between physical stimuli and associated or conditioned responses. Visual perception, as understood by many eminent behaviorists and neo-behaviorists (e.g., Hull, 1952; Pavlov, 1927, 1955), was the associated supplementation of visual stimuli with behavioral responses. Association naturally fits with elementism and building block psychology, and behaviorism carried over these principles from structuralism, attempting to construct behavioral habits rather than perceptions using these same empiricist ideas. Even with the loosening of behavioristic restrictions in post-1960 American psychology, the motor theory of perceptual enrichment has remained popular (Gyr, 1972, VonHolst & Mittelstadt 1950) The underlying thesis, going back to Berkeley and even Alhazen, is that spatial vision requires movement for its structure and order.

Hermann Ludvig Helmholtz (1821–1894) typifies much more so than anyone else before him a convergence of the philosophical, psychological, and physiological traditions in empiricist explanations of perception. His *Treatise on Physiological Optics* (1866), though extremely rich in detail and expansive in scope, is fundamentally an integration relying upon Berkeley, J. Müller, Lötze, and J. S. Mill while bringing in optics to give a complete picture of vision. He accepts the "specific energies of nerves" hypothesis, the associative depth cue theory and the local sign hypothesis and theoretically builds perceptions out of sensations and memories. In general theoretical approach and range of interests, Helmholtz is Alhazen reincarnated in 19th century mechanistic science.

Various affinities in approach can be found in comparing Helmholtz's views with those of Wilhelm Wundt (1832–1920), the founder of structuralist psychology. Wundt assumed that visual sensations were unextended, each corresponding to an individual point of neural excitation in the brain. Accordingly, Wundt adopted a version of Lötze's "local sign" hypothesis to explain how visual sensations become spatially determinate. Also, he utilized Berkeley's distance signs (cues) to explain how the depth, solid shape, and size of physical objects are apprehended through vision (Wundt, 1902). On both points he agreed with Helmholtz.

Beyond these similarities between Wundt and Helmhotz, there is a significant difference in approach. This disagreement exists in Helmholt's reliance upon the hypothesis of "unconscious inference" and Wundt's alternative process of "fusion." Helmholtz considered visual sensations to be signs or "tokens" (1866, p. 533) for ideas of spatiality. Spatial ideas after association with sensations were "unconsciously inferred" from experiences of sensations. Helmholtz compared this process of unconscious inference to John Stuart Mill's (1874) notion of inductive conclusions. Helmholtz's motivation in employing the term *inference* was functional. Given visual sensations and the final visual perceptions, it was as if an unconscious inductive inference had occurred from the former to the latter. He states, "while it is true that there has been, and probably always will be, a measure of doubt as to the similarity of the psychic activity in the two cases, there can be no doubt as to the similarity between the results of such unconscious conclusions and those of conscious conclusions" (1866, III, p. 4). As was the case with Berkeley and James Mill before him, for Helmholtz perceptions were basically combinations of sensations and ideas. Further, he borrows a concept (induction) from traditional empiricist epistemology (Bacon and Hume), with all its connected assumptions (e.g., knowledge begins with uninterpreted and indubitable particulars), and applies it to perceptual theory.

Though an empiricist in his psychology and epistemology, Helmholtz included the innate idea of causality to complete his explanation of perception. As with Descartes, Helmholtz supposed that the mind infers external causes for its sensations. Berkeley had inferred an immaterial God from the "visual language" (signs) of sensations. Helmholtz goes in the opposite direction, supposing the mind infers an external physical world from sensations. When the world is not directly revealed through sensory or perceptual consciousness and only "signified" as in indirect realist theories, such as Descartes' and Helmholtz's, some additional principle seems required to get to the external world. Helmholtz and Descartes invoked an innate idea of causality (Helmholtz, 1866, Vol. III sec. 16; 1873, sec. III; 1878; 1894). Essentially, Helmholtz accepts two basic ideas found in Ancient Greece. Through the senses, the perceiver is only acquainted with internal states, and it requires intellectualization to know the true world.

Wundt argued for a mental chemistry instead of an inference process. Spatial ideas were not obtained through muscular sensations, but were an emergent result of a fusion or "synthesis" of visual and muscular sensations. This is similar to, although, according to Wundt, not borrowed from, John Stuart Mill's concept of mental chemistry. The emergent properties of a synthesized "compound" are not reducible to properties of individual sensations or ideas. Wundt remarked, "Every psychic compound has characteristics which are by no means the mere sum of the characteristics of the elements" (1902, p. 375).

Granting this difference between Helmholtz, and Wundt, the general fact still remains that for both approaches visual perception is mediated or indirect. Secondly, the concept of elements is applicable to either Helmholtz's phenomenal concatenations or Wundt's phenomenal syntheses. It is just that in the latter case the perceptual "whole is more than the sum of its parts," but there is still a coming together, a "compound," or a "chemical fusion" of elements in visual perception. Perception begins with simple elements.

Wundt had argued, as had Lötze before, that muscular sensations per se do not provide the mind with ideas of space. In particular, muscular sensations produced by ocular movements do not furnish unextended visual sensations with bidimensional extent, location, and form. Instead, for Wundt these properties emerge in fusion. The incomprehensibility of this jump implied to some (for example, Titchener) that visual sensations must originally have extent if only in a primitive and undifferentiated state. How else could spatial extent arise? Titchener, contra Wundt, declared, "Nowhere . . . over the whole range of psychology, does the concurrence of attributes give rise to any absolutely new form of consciousness" (1910, p. 338).

Edward Titchener (1867–1927) exemplified, in his refusal to assume that visual sensations are originally without extent, a general growing discontent with this Wundtian-Helmholtzian position. On the other hand, Titchener's "context theory of meaning" is similar to Helmholtz's position. Specifically concerning the visual perception of the distance and solid dimensions of object, Titchener's views generally followed Helmholtz and Berkeley. The spatial meaning, excluding bare extent of visual sensations, is in the form of a supplementation of a non-visual (kinesthetic) context. Consequently, Titchener's position more closely resembled a pure building block description than Wundt's.

Titchener (1896, 1909, 1910, 1929) is best remembered for his context theory of meaning (Boring, 1950), but this idea basically derives from Berkeley. In many respects Titchener's system of psychology represents the culmination of the associative, elementaristic, and mentalistic line of thought initiated by Locke and Berkeley 2 centuries earlier. Structuralist psychology, championed by Wundt and Titchener, set out to analyze consciousness into its irreducible elements, including sensations, ideas, and feelings. These elements were connected through association and psychophysically correlated with simple properties and units of stimulation. Various challenges developed to this form of psychology around the turn of the century, and it was out of these newer views that Gibson's psychology emerged. The Gibsonian heritage goes back to Aristotle, but in more modern times it develops out of continental-German traditions and evolutionary-functional psychology. It is to these latter traditions that we now turn.

Chapter 8 _____

EVOLUTION
and FUNCTIONAL PSYCHOLOGY

NATIVISM, RATIONALISM, AND ACT PSYCHOLOGY

The rationalist triad of Benedictus Spinoza (1632–1677), Gottfried Wilhelm Leibnitz (1646–1716), and Immanuel Kant (1724–1804) stands in opposition to the empiricist triad of Locke, Berkeley, and Hume. Though Newtonian science clearly influenced at least Spinoza and Kant in some positive respects, the continental trio was in many ways in disagreement with Newton. Because Newton was British, the empiricist philosophers have more in common with him than do Spinoza, Leibnitz, and Kant. In the context of Gibson's development, the continental philosophers, though historically identified as rationalists and nativists, are connected with Gibson via Gestalt psychology and act psychology. Whereas Newton and the British empiricists emphasized analysis and the primacy of simple, independent elements (a building block universe), the continental philosophers emphasized organization and interdependence. Further, in the rationalist culmination of Kant and Hegel, process became a fundamental ontological concept replacing the more static concept of nature embodied in Newton and British empiricism. In general, it is through continental rationalism that the philosophical concepts of wholism (interdependency of nature) and dynamism (the primacy of process and charge) initially come to the forefront in modern western philosophy.

Perhaps the most pristine exponent of ontological unity and organization was Spinoza. Spinoza was an arch-rationalist in methodology and

Parmenidian in ontology. Spinoza believed in an eternal unifying substance in which all natural individuals or particulars subsist (1677). All individuals are understood and integrated within this naturalistic and wholistic theism. The first significant aspect of Spinoza's ontology is his extreme *wholism* where everything in nature is understood relative to the whole. The whole "holds" everything together, thus the universe is totally unified. There is one eternal and infinite substance; all particulars are determinate modifications of this all subsuming continuum. Spinoza uses the expression "through the eyes of eternity" to signify this wholistic, cosmological perspective on individuals. A particular is described relative to the Eternal One. This contrasts with the elementism and atomism of British empiricism and Newtonian physics and historically connects (as we will see) with Leibnitz's theory of monads and the Gestalt approach in psychology.

Equally, Spinoza was an arch-determinist and appears to be the first modern philosopher to unequivocally apply mechanistic determinism to the human mind. Where Descartes hedged on applying determinism to all aspects of the mind, Spinoza saw all aspects of the mind falling under a naturalistic determinism. The eventual application of a deterministic model to psychology in the 19th and 20th centuries was anticipated by Spinoza. Yet Spinoza's determinism, unlike the atomistic determinism of Newton, follows from Spinoza's wholism where all of nature is seen unified through an underlying God. Consistent with the mechanistic model of causality, Spinoza saw nature as a causal sequence, the past precisely determining the future. Underneath the plurality of observable nature stands God as the primary substance within which all individuals are interconnected. In fundamental reality, it is God that is totally determinate—there is no free will in the cosmos.

Though the historical contrast of rationalism and empiricism has popularly been interpreted as an epistemological difference regarding the source of knowledge, rationalists, such as Spinoza, following in the tradition of Parmenides and Plato, emphasized the primacy of a unifying order over the temporal plurality. But empiricists, using analysis as their starting point, saw the temporal plurality as primary and order and unity as derivative. In general, structuralist and behaviorist psychologies took an analytic approach, whereas Gestalt psychology, reacting to these elementaristic theoretical systems, emphasized wholism at the levels of behavior, neurophysiology, and consciousness. Influenced by more modern representatives on both sides of this theoretical dichotomy, one of Gibson's strongest and unique contributions was a reconciliation of whole-part dualism, without attempting to relegate to a derivative status either wholes or parts.

It is appropriate to comment here on the interdisciplinary connectivity exhibited throughout history. Though the focus of this history is psychology, in particular visual perception, a variety of other disciplines and ideas have already been historically inter-related, e.g., physics, geometry, art, biology, and philosophy. Since the Scientific Revolution, disciplines have tended to specialize and differentiate, yet there have always existed cross-disciplinary influences. Spinoza is the second philosopher noted (Berkeley was the first) who has had theological or spiritual concerns at the forefront of his psychological thinking. It could be argued that a significant portion of creative and influential ideas within one discipline come through cross-fertilization from other disciplines (Koestler, 1964). Spinoza's main philosophical theme is his naturalistic wholism, whereby all individuals are ultimately united within one immanent God. With a thorough rationalistic methodology (deductions based on abstract principles), Spinoza offered a monistic theory of organization. This rationalist passion for organization contra empiricist analysis is carried over and developed further in Leibnitz and Kant. Though the theme of cosmological unity has theological, as well as scientific roots, it would influence perceptual theory.

Locke depicted the mind as a tabula rasa in which complex ideas of visual perception were compounds of simple ideas. By the time of James Mill, empiricists had further developed this general view that the mind was nothing but an empty receptacle in which elements concatenated together. Descartes, on the other hand, believed the mind had innate dispositions. Leibnitz followed Descartes in this nativistic approach to the mind. Where Locke had stated there was nothing in the intellect that was not first in the senses, Leibnitz had replied, nothing except the intellect itself. According to Leibnitz, the mind has innate "ideas," "inclinations or dispositions" (1765, Bk. 1–2). Prior to what comes to the intellect through the senses, the intellect possesses an order or structure not derived from the senses. He opposed the *tabula rasa* view of the mind; ideas do not just combine or connect together. The mind in "apperception" (perception) is active in perceiving the world in terms of its innate capacities or constitution. Leibnitz's position is that the mind is neither empty nor passive in perception. The mind actively gives order to perception.

The nativism-empiricism issue in the history of psychology is to some degree a pseudo-issue. Though Locke, Berkeley, Hume and their many followers in the 19th century are labeled *empiricists,* to the best of my knowledge no theorist ever eliminated all possible innate characteristics to the mind. Locke and Berkeley supposed that the mind possessed various powers, and even James Mill, an arch-empiricist, still gave the mind the powers to remember and associate. Helmholtz and Lötze gave the mind innate ideas of causality and space, respectively. J. S. Mill and Wundt gave the mind the creative power to synthesize elements into perceptions. Leibnitz's point is that active powers must exist in the mind for perception to occur. Though Gibson would reject Locke's idea that the mind is a *tabula rasa,* Gibson did not believe, as did the rationalists and nativists, that mental order is needed to give perception order. Though Gibson did invoke the concept of activity in his description of perception, for him, order is actively discovered rather than actively synthesized.

Though Leibnitz historically falls within the rationalist tradition, a lineage that goes back to Plato and Parmenides, he is in many respects Aristotelian in his philosophy. Leibnitz's conception of the mind as activity is an early form of act psychology providing an historical link between Aristotle's process psychology and Brentano's nineteenth century act psychology (which also followed Aristotle). Leibnitz's emphasis on the mind's active nature is in contrast with Locke's passive view. It was the contention of Leibnitz that the mind does not receive or have painted on it impressions or sensations. Aristotle had distinguished between active and passive descriptions of perception, and the intromission (passive) and extromission (active) theories of perception in Ancient Greece reflect these alternate perspectives. Gibson in his psychophysical program appears to have described perception as passive (caused from the outside), whereas in his ecological approach he switched to an active theory of perception, rejecting the causal theory of perception. Perception is an active selection process. For Leibnitz, the mind does not passively receive impressions (causal-intromission models); rather, the mind actively synthesizes perception.

Leibnitz rejected the causal theory of perception in opposing Newtonian mechanistic causality as a model of nature. Starting from certain Aristotelian concepts, Leibnitz formulated a developmental model of natural processes based on the idea of "monads." Where Newton had analyzed the world into simple, inert elements of matter that were moved about by external forces, Leibnitz analyzed the world into complex "spirits" that were intrinsically complex, dynamic, and developmental. Leibnitz once said, in arguing against Newton's theory of atoms, "Always many, never one, therefore never many." Leibnitz believed there were no simple (unanalyzable) elements on which more complex entities were built. Everything was complex. Leibnitz rejected the elementism of Newton and empiricist philosophy and psychology. Secondly, Leibnitz rejected the "inert" or passive view of natural entities. Everything is intrinsically active. Monads are not "moved about" by external forces nor by each other because there is no such thing as mechanistic causality. Monads behave in "harmony," a harmony pre-established through a creative God. Monads are like synchronized "clocks" set in harmony by a master timekeeper.

Again, we see the naturalistic ontology of a philosophical system having a metaphysical and theological core. It would be naive to suppose that Newton's system did not have such an ingredient as well. Science cannot be divorced from metaphysics. For Newton, God created the eternal laws of nature. In believing that fundamental order derives from an eternal creator, Newton stands together with Leibnitz, reflecting a dualism stretching back to Plato. Leibnitz and Newton differ regarding the natural embodiment of order. For Newton, particulars (elements of matter) possess no intrinsic order; for Leibnitz monads possess intrinsic order. Leibnitz's system is clearly scientific in content and implications for it represents a definite challenge to the elementism that served as the theoretical building block of both Newtonian physical science and empiricist psychological science. Leibnitz adopts Aristotle's process ontology, treating the world as a multiplicity of active forms that develop according to an inner *telos*. Second, Leibnitz follows Aristotle's Gestalt view of nature where organization or complexity is inherent in all natural forms. Leibnitz's emphasis on mental activity is carried over into act psychology and functional psychology. The emphasis on organization is carried over into phenomenology and Gestalt psychology; and the emphasis on harmony, rather than mechanistic causation, is carried over into Gibson's ecological concepts of "attunement," "resonance," and "reciprocity."

Leibnitz appears to have used Spinoza's concept of particulars in developing his idea of monads. Though Leibnitz is a naturalistic pluralist, whereas Spinoza is a monist, Leibnitz has more in common with Spinoza than with a pluralist such as Hume. (Strictly speaking, Leibnitz adopted a dual-perspective on the cosmos. From within nature, the universe appears as a plurality of particulars, but from God's perpective, standing outside of time, the cosmos is unified.) For Spinoza, a true understanding of any individual comes through seeing how it fits within the whole ("the eyes of eternity"). A monad for Leibnitz embodies the total set of actual relationships with all other monads. A monad internally *reflects* the universe; it is a particular convergence of a set of relationships. A monad is a mirror. Consequently, the universe is embodied in each and every monad, where each monad is a unique perspective on the universe. Recall that this idea is similar to da Vinci's view of nature. For Hume and other empiricists, particulars (impressions or sensations) are intrinsically simple and independent. Gibson's treatment of order within nature falls more on the side of da Vinci and Leibnitz. Instead of describing stimulation as a set of discrete, simple elements of light (Alhazen, Kepler, Helmholtz), Gibson, in his ecological approach describes the optic array as an intrinsically complex convergence of energy differences.

Leibnitz also anticipates Gibson regarding space and time. Newton had proposed that space and time were absolute containments in which matter and motion existed. Leibnitz proposed relative and realistic theories of space and time. Quite simply, there is no space independent and transcendent of real arrangements and no time independent of real successions (Leibnitz, 1717). This theory anticipates Gibson's view that neither empty space nor empty time (Newtonian or Platonic abstractions) are ecologically real or perceived. Gibson substitutes surfaces for empty space and events for empty time. For both Leibnitz and Gibson, space and time refer to relationships or structures embodied in particulars. Leibnitz, therefore, rejects Newton's ontology of discrete inert elements contained in absolute empty voids (note this is also Locke's theory of the mind), replacing it with active structured processes connected together through a preestablished harmony. There are no atoms and there is no void.

The developmental view of monads contained in Leibnitz also has a modern ring. Newton saw change as rearrangement, but in the nineteenth century a new, more expansive view of change emerged. Evolution implied the development of novel species or natural kinds, thus undercutting the tradition of static (or eternal) forms initiated by Plato. Though Leibnitz's philosophy of monads, at first glance, seems strange and unusual, it actually stands much closer to modern scientific thought than Newton.

Whereas Leibnitz was critical of Newton, Immanuel Kant attempted to vindicate Newtonian science against the epistemological critique of Hume. Hume had attempted to show that experience can be analyzed into a plurality of distinct impressions. Hume's phenomenalism implied a world of absolute unrelated elements. According to Hume, at an epistemological level no logically necessary relationship could ever be established regarding regular sequences of facts. Kant tried to demonstrate that the individual elements of sensory experience are inherently organized in terms of the intuitions (or forms) of space and time. Secondly, Kant introduced a set of conceptual categories that the mind uses to meaningfully organize its experiences. In essence, according to Kant, experience is necessarily organized in terms of categorical abstractions and principled relationships and this general form of experience cannot be derived from sensory experience, in other words it is not learned or derived from the stream of particulars. Kantian philosophy consequently became a source of inspiration for nativistic psychologies of perception.

Kant (1724–1804) in his *Critique of Pure Reason* (1781) emphasized the active and integrative qualities of the mind. Sensations are not given to the mind without any spatial determination or organization—the mind organizes the "phenomenal world" in terms of the form of space. Kant distinguished between the phenomenal and noumenal worlds ("things-in-themselves") and argued that space only applies to the phenomenal (experiential) world. Nativist psychology would follow Kant in assuming that space was not acquired through association but rather was an inherited principle of organization in the mind (or brain). In both cases, whether it was nativism or Berkeleian empiricism, the mind imposed space upon visual experience. Gibson in both his psychophysics and his ecology of perception would attempt to explain "visual space" in terms of environmental and stimulus factors without recourse to contributions from the mind.

In summary, in several significant respects Kant stands at odds with Gibson. Kant accepted Newton's theory of absolute space and time. Further, on an historical level Kant falls into Platonic rationalism where the abstract and universal is used to explain the particular and transcient. Kant's abstract categories and intuitions of space and time order the particular sensations. In general, subsequent nativist psychologists would hypothesize abstract, ordering principles as the inherited features of the mind—stimulus input and unembellished sensory experience provided particulars. From an epistemological perspective, for Kant, the world beyond experience (noumena) cannot be described in any meaningful sense. All knowledge, including science, is limited to experience—noumena is unknowable. Kantian philosophy is therefore one modern source of subjectivism. Kant hypothesizes an independent "reality" but makes it beyond the reaches of the human mind. The mind is literally trapped within itself. Gibson's ecological realism, where mind and nature do interface, was developed to avoid subjectivism. In spite of all its subtleties, Kant's philosophy still accepted an absolute dualism of mind (phenomena) and matter (noumena). Kant's conceptual subjectivism as well as inflencing theories of perception also provided a foundation for subjectivism in the philosophy of science. In the late nineteenth century one popular interpretation of scientific theory was to view scientific concepts as possessing only instrumental utility rather than any true reference to objective reality (Poincaire, 1905). This "conventionalistic" interpretation was one Kantian inspired form of subjectivistic philosophy of science in the 20th century.

Two later psychologists who developed nativistic theories of space perception were Ewald Hering (1834–1918) and P. L. Panum. In contrast to Berkeley, for both Hering and Panum visual awareness was originally of both bi-dimensional extent and distance. Panum (Mach, 1906) contended that visual perception of depth was innate and depended on binocular disparity. The Helmholtzian interpretation of binocular disparity (also in Bain) implied that disparity is nothing but a sign of distance (in the Berkeleian sense) and must be associated with muscular sensations before it signifies the depth of an object. Panum believed that association was unnecessary and disparity produced a visual experience of depth. There was an inmate connection between retinal binocular disparity and visual depth.

Hering (1861–1864), influenced by Panum (Boring, 1942, p. 288), proposed a related explanation of visual perception of depth that also involved innate connections. According to Hering, each retinal point on both eyes has a depth value and through innate psychological connections produces a visual sensation of depth. Depth was seen not because the retinal mosaic simulated distance, which it obviously doesn't, but because each point on the retina produced, through innate connections, the sensation of depth. Despite being contemporary adversaries, both Hering and Helmholtz viewed visual perception of depth as depending on a contributory process. Hering thought it was physiological and innate, while Helmholtz contrarily supposed it was a process that depended on learned associations. In the 19th century, both nativistic and empiricist theories saw perception as involving a contribution (addition) from the perceiver. For a nativist, order does not have to be built up from particulars; it is imposed through inherited psychophysiological integration. Either way, through nativism or empiricism, the input from the world was conceived in elementaristic terms.

Hering's assignment of depth values to points of stimulation is made in accordance with their anatomical location on the retina. Each point on a retina has a depth value as a function of its position on this surface relative to the fovea. In addition, points on the retina have height and breadth values that serve, in conjunction with innate connections, to locate the direction of visual sensations. The optical basis for visual perception of direction and depth is described in terms of anatomical location. Similarly, it should be recalled that the "local sign" hypothesis implied that visual sensations were located (through associations) with respect to the retinal position of the corresponding points of stimulation. Gibson, in arguing against the hypothesis that visual perception is based upon the anatomical retinal image, developed the concept of the ordinal retinal image, and later in abandoning the retinal image entirely in favor of the optic array, moved even farther away from the anatomical retinal image. The theoretical significance of this difference is that an anatomical description of stimulation makes the basis of perception relative to the pecularities of anatomy, whereas Gibson's theory of the optic array explained vision in terms of ecological information. As was mentioned earlier, the anatomical retinal image theory grounds vision in a form of inner observation. We see that the anatomical retinal image implicated both nativist and empiricist theories in the homunculus hypothesis.

Although Hering often described the retinal image as a set of points, he did relinquish pointillism in his explanation of color contrast. Hering believed contrast was understandable if it was assumed that a visual sensation is not specific to excitation at any one point on the retina, but also depends on activity in surrounding locations on the retina. For Helmholtz, among others, visual sensations were specific to individual points of excitation; hence the quality (color) of a particular sensation was a function of only one point of excitation. Nativists followed the rationalist tradition in seeing the significance of "relationships." Classic empiricists such as Berkeley, Hume, and James Mill analyzed the world into independent particulars. For someone like Helmholtz, stimulation was described as independent particulars (points). Hering, in his theory of contrast effects, was proposing that stimulus relations (differences) effect what is perceived. This approach to stimulation anticipates Gibson's relational description of stimulation, in particular, his theory of the ambient optic array. For traditional analytic empiricists, stimulation was described as segregated absolute values. The theoretical significance of rationalists and nativists was to shift the emphasis to relational and wholistic considerations. Though most nativist psychologists (including Gestalt theoreticians) still treated stimulation in elementaristic terms, Hering in his contrast theory was moving in the direction of a Gibsonian description of stimulation.

Nativistic psychology, rationalism, and process ontology existed alongside Newtonian science and empiricist psychology throughout the 18th and 19th centuries, but these former approaches remained less popular. Early science emphasized analysis and elements. What turned the tide against the likes of Berkeley, Hume, and Newton was a second revolution in science that occurred in the years 1860–1910. Both biology and physics were transformed, and the effects of this scientific transformation began to seep down into psychology toward the end of the nineteenth century. The "new" ideas brought in by Darwin and Einstein were the primacy of change and the primacy of the field, viz., process and organization. The movements in psychology which took up these themes were functionalism and Gestalt psychology respectively. Almost 2 centuries later, Leibnitz triumphed over Newton and Locke.

THE THEORY OF EVOLUTION
AND EVOLUTIONARY PSYCHOLOGY

One crucial difference between Berkeleian theories and Gibson's ecological approach is in the powerful impact that evolution and functionalism have had on Gibson. Gibson's emphasis on explaining the veridicality of perception, his concern with the environment, his functional understanding of perceptual systems, his interest in how the senses evolved to afford

adaptation, and his ecological theory of perception all reflect the central-
ity of evolutionary and functional considerations in his thinking. His
central theoretical concept of the ecological reciprocity of the animal and
the environment emerges in the context of evolutionary and functionalistic discussions.

Prior to Darwin's theory of evolution, the prevailing explanation of the
relation between living forms and the environment was "static creationism." God created the cosmos as it presently exists. Newton believed
matter, space, time, and the laws of nature were all created "instantaneously" (at least within six days). Species or forms of nature did not
change. John Ray (1627–1705), an early naturalist who subscribed to such
a view, supposed organisms were created perfectly adapted to their
environment. There was no process of adaptation to the world because it
was a "divine contrivance" (Greene, 1959; Ray, 1701). (Compare this idea
to Leibnitz's idea of preestablished harmony.) Basically what predomi-
nated in science was a cyclical theory of natural time. Forms did not
transform; they did not emerge; they did not become extinct, they simply
passed through a cyclical process of birth, growth, deterioration, and
death.

The theory of evolution by natural selection effected the intellectual
and scientific worlds with a comparable influence to Newton's mechanics
a century and a half earlier. (Mead, 1936). In its simplicity and broad
implications, it quickly became known worldwide. It was often misrepre-
sented or misunderstood on some essential point, but it worked its way
into popular culture creating a scientific—religious controversy not seen
since the time of Copernicus and Galileo. In one stroke it considerably
undermined the classic separation of the human mind and physical nature
and underscored the ubiquitousness of change throughout the geological,
environmental, biological, and psychological realms. In essence, Darwin
argued that progeny are produced in an over abundance with sufficient
variation to necessitate competition for resources and the elimination of
certain variations, thus producing, over generations, a gradual change in
species. Through "survival of the fittest" living forms have evolved
(Greene 1959, 1981; Reed, 1978).

The hypothesis that species develop through a continuing process of
adaptation to their environment did not originate with Darwin's (1809–
1882) *The Origin of Species* (1859). The idea is found in Jean Lamarck's
(1744–1829) *Philosophie Zoologigue* (1809) and James Prichard's (1786–
1848) *Researches into the Physical History of Man* (1813), but the impact
of the complementary ideas of evolution and adaptation upon psychology
derived primarily from Darwin's works (1859, 1871, 1872). What did
originate with Darwin was the concept of natural selection as the explanation of evolution. Alfred Wallace arrived at the same idea at about the

same time, but it was Darwin who historically received credit for the theory and influenced the scientific world. Darwin marshalled enough facts and provided a scientifically acceptable explanation for evolution, providing a theory that could be applied to related sciences such as psychology (Boring, 1950; Gruber, 1981).

Before Darwin, the reasoning behind comparative psychology and physiology was quite different than after him in one important respect. The idea of evolution provided the basis for the belief in continuity of species, both physiologically and psychologically. Comparative psychology, in this sense, began with Darwin's *Expression of the Emotions in Man and Animals* (1872) and Romanes' (1848–1894) *Animal Intelligence* (1882). Herbert Spencer, for one, had presupposed species continuity by arguing that the mind could not be understood unless it was considered in the context of its phylogenetic development (1855, pp. 181–182). The assumption of functional continuity in organisms also played an important role in Gibson's (1958a, 1966a) treatment of visual perception. Those extremely basic or general characteristics of psychological processes across species become apparent by examining many different species. Conversely, those peculiarities of some selected portion of the total phylogenetic scale may be thought fundamental to a psychological process until a more complete sample of species is considered; for example, the retinal image had been an *idee fixe* in explanations of visual perception, when actually, according to Gibson, what is universally basic in vision is the optic array. Gibson's working hypothesis that visual perception in humans could be better understood through comparative considerations (best exemplified in 1966a, Chapter IX) played little, if any, role in the work of such individuals as Alhazen, Kepler, Berkeley or Helmholtz. The inspirational source for Gibson's concern with comparative visual perception was Walls and his encyclopedic work *The Vertebrate Eye* (1942).

Prior to the *Origin of Species* (1859), Herbert Spencer (1829–1903) in his *Principles of Psychology* (1855), had argued that "mental life" could be defined as an "adjustment of internal relations to external relations" (1855, p. 182). Through Darwin, this emphasis on the adaptive dimension of mind blossomed into functionalism. Psychological functions constitute the *modus operandi* of animal adaptation to the physical environment. Characterizing psychology in terms of the study of adaptative processes is quite apparent in the following statement by James Angell. "We shall adopt the biological point-of-view. . . . We shall regard all the operations of consciousness—all our sensations, all our emotions, and all our acts of will—as so many expressions of organic adaptations to our environment" (1904, pp. 6–7).

The psychological significance in evolution and adaptation led individuals such as Angell and Spencer to define "mental life" or "operations of consciousness" *ecologically,* i.e., in terms of a relationship to the environment. This novel abstract approach to the subject matter of psychology will momentarily be contrasted with Titchener's views. It is a contention of this inquiry that a functional and ecological explanation of visual perception is at odds with mind-matter dualism.

If the idea of adaptation becomes central in a functionalistic psychology, a connected issue emerges with significant force. "Adaptation" refers to a relationship between the organism and the environment. Organisms adapt with respect to a physical environment that possesses the necessities of life and the continuous tests of survival. Resultantly, the functionalistic psychologist, who characterizes psychological processes in terms of adaptation, needs to systematically investigate those adaptively significant features of the physical environment. It was Egon Brunswik and to a greater degree, Gibson who first took this problem seriously. How should we describe the physical environment in which animal perceptual capabilities have evolved? An important implication of the study of the environment, realized by Gibson and others, is that its structure and properties do not coincide with the description of the world offered by physicists. The environment of animals is functionally tied to animal existence and is at a different level of analysis and order than the world of traditional physics.

The concepts of interdependency and process were discussed in the context of modern rationalistic philosophy. The same themes arise again in our discussion of evolutionary theory. According to the static creationism theory, living species and other natural forms are independent, each created separately onto itself. Darwinian theory introduces two connected concepts of natural "relatedness." Though members within a species in some respects compete (e.g., for resources), there exists both intra-species and inter-species interdependency. Second, life forms are dependent upon the environment for resources and survival. Though these two points were acknowledged and studied by Pre-Darwinian naturalists, Darwin emphasizes the integrative nature of life much more than earlier biologists. It could be argued that in Pre-Darwinian times, nature was seen as integrated through some type of eternal being (e.g., Plato or Spinoza), yet this idea of a transcendent unifying being is replaced in Darwin's theory by inherant interdependency within nature. Thus a pre-Darwinian rationalist or Platonist would argue that particulars are ordered by imposed abstract principles. With post-Darwinian thinking the particulars of nature are not seen as discrete and unrelated, but related and interdependent. Though rationalists emphasized order, organization, and relatedness more so than analytic empiricists, they followed Platonic dualism in placing such features in the mental and/or eternal realm. Gibson's concepts of natural order and relatedness are clearly post-Darwinian.

Recall our discussion of the philosophical conflict between Parmenides and Heraclitus. Darwin's dynamic picture of nature is relevant to this issue and would subsequently effect Gibson's view of nature in a deep, pervasive sense. For Heraclitus, reality was flux, but it was the Parmenidian view that generally held sway over philosophy and science through the time of Newton. Newton's world did not change. Natural forms were eternal and separate. Within the Darwinian or evolutionary world view, order became more deeply embedded in the flux of transforming particulars. Where order had been separated from particulars and from change, order in nature was now more closely related to inherant organization between particulars and changes among particulars. For Newton, stellar objects went through motions but everything just kept repeating itself, and the laws and forms of nature were constant. Recall the cyclical theory of time. For Newton, cosmological bodies moved through the heavens in cyclical, ever repeating pathways. Darwin radically changes this world view (Fraser, 1978, 1982; Sherover, 1975; Whitrow, 1975). Using a distinction developed by Prigogine, Newton's dynamics described reversible processes (repeating cycles) of constant forms, whereas nineteenth century science uncovered a variety of irreversible processes (Prigogine, 1984) coupled with transforming forms.

Descartes had proposed that natural forms develop, and in the following two centuries Kant and LaPlace developed "evolutionary" theories of the cosmos. In the nineteenth century, Hegel, from a philosophical viewpoint, applied the concept of linear change to ontology and epistemology. Geological and paleontological evidence began to accumulate that seemed to indicate the earth and life had a changing history. The time was ripe for a radical shift further away from a Parmenidian perspective (Desmond, 1975; Greene, 1981; Sherover, 1975). The formulation of the second law of thermodynamics and its implied "arrow of time" further reinforced this new intellectual image. Nature showed fundamental change. New species emerged, other species became extinct. Even the cycles of the heavenly bodies, it would soon be discovered, were not constant.

The dynamic picture of nature would very quickly effect psychology as well as other sciences. Structuralism treated the mind as a concatenation of *inert elements;* functionalism and behaviorism described psychology's subject matter in terms of activities. In his psychophysical approach, Gibson treated the perceiver as a passive observer affected by the world. In his ecological approach, Gibson treats the perceiver as an explorer that "searches out" information about the world. In the 1950s, stimulation is fundamentally static; in the 1960s and 1970s visual stimulation, for

Gibson, becomes a flow of optical transformations with relative invariants (nothing is absolutely permanent). In general, Gibson became increasingly concerned with philosophical, mathematical, and scientific ideas about change. Change became a significant feature in his description of the environment and the ecosystem of a moving observer. Not that Gibson did not see constancy in nature any more—far from it. Gibson attempted to relate change to order and constancy, rather than treat them dualistically. In stimulation, invariants were related to transformations; in the environment persistance was related to change. By the time of Darwin, a scientific-philosophical movement began to emerge which saw more change in nature, yet attempted to reevaluate and redefine the relationship between changing particulars and order and constancy. Gibson's ecological approach in many ways reflects the dynamic view of reality introduced in the 19th century through Darwin and other philosophers and scientists. Order and lawfulness are not found within static and independent particulars, but rather across transforming and interdependent particulars.

PHENOMENOLOGICAL PSYCHOLOGY

The form of act psychology initiated by Franz Brentano (1838–1917) had an ancient heritage dating back to Leibnitz and Aristotle. Act psychology, as developed by Brentano, distinguished between activities of the mind and objects of these activities. It was based, fundamentally on Aristotle's subject-object distinction. Knowing, as an act(ivity) of a living form, is logically and functionally related to its "correlative objects." Following Aristotle's functional classification scheme for the *psyche,* Brentano treated the mind as a set of basic activities each with a different type of object (Aristotle's correlative object). Brentano rejected the structuralist view that the mind consisted of "thing-like" elements standing in mere juxtaposition with its correlated causes. Brentano (1874) understood perception as an act of the mind. This view opposed Wundt who followed Locke's notion of the mind as a passive *tabula rasa* for sensations. Sensations exist only as the (intentional) object of a mental act. Brentano objected to the idea that sensations first exist in the mind independent of any mental process. An object always involves an act. There is no "datum" simply received or "placed" within the mind. In fact, it is misleading to say that the mind "contains" its object. The objects of perceptual activity are not within the mind. Following Aristotle, Brentano is a realist where the objects of perception are within the physical world.

In explaining the relationship between act and object, Brentano used the principle of "intentionality." The relation between the perceptual act and its object is not causal. The act "refers to" an object. It is not an absolutely distinct event and is not caused by the object of its intention. The idea that perception "refers to" something and is not *caused* by something is found also in Dewey. A mental act is not a reaction. A mental act is active rather than passive. When Gibson moved from psychophysical to an ecological theoretical framework, there was a categorical change from treating perception as "passive" to treating it as "active." Further, for Gibson, perceptual activity is understood as intentional.

Brentano's act psychology constituted one of the major sources of the functionalistic approach in psychology. Brentano's basic acts are functional since each type of mental act is distinguished in terms of its particular function (e.g., sensing, feeling, judging). Further, a basic similarity in meaning between "function" and "act" is apparent, since for Brentano psychological phenomena ("acts") are examined and understood in terms of their "intentional objects" (compare to Aristotle's "correlative objects"). Correspondingly for functionalists such as Angell, James, and Dewey, the concern is with investigating relationships ("functions") of psychological processes to the physical world. Not unexpectedly, the German words *akt* and *funktion* were often used interchangeably (Carl Stumpf, 1873).

Structurlism offered a methodology for describing the content of consciousness based on an empiricist philosophy that emphasized analysis and simple elements. An alternative perspective on describing consciousness developed through Edmund Husserl (1859–1938), a student of Brentano. This new approach was named *phenomenology*. Husserl's central goal was a presuppositionless description of consciousness, thus providing a theoretically uncontaminated starting point for philosophical and scientific inquiries. There were as many forms of phenomenology as people who practiced it, but there was a general emphasis on describing consciousness wholistically, rejecting structuralism's obsession with analysis. Second, the subject-object distinction and the concept of intentionally usually occupied positions of importance in phenomenological studies, giving consciousness a more dynamic nature than in structuralism and empiricist philosophy. (For the history and philosophy of phenomenology from Brentano and Husserl to Maurice Merleau-Ponty, see Farber, 1966; Husserl, 1931, 1965; Kockelmans, 1967; Spiegelberg, 1965).

Two of the most influential psychologists in this tradition were James Ward (1843–1925) and Carl Stumpf (1848–1936). Both assumed that extension was an original property of visual sensations (Boring, 1950; Ward, 1918). Ward and Stumpf also disagreed with the Berkeleian-Wundtian concept of sensations in arguing that an active subject is always involved in sensations; hence, "pure sensations" are a fiction.

Stumpf, according to Boring, brought phenomenology into psychology (Boring, 1950, p. 369). For Stumpf, as well as his illustrious students, the Gestalt psychologists Wertheimer, Köhler and Koffka, phenomenology was understood as propaedeutic to psychological investigation. In developing his psychophysical approach early in his career, Gibson accepted his colleague Koffka's belief in the methodological priority of phenomenology. Both the desirability and possibility of a presuppositionless, naive description of experience can be questioned. Yet the ideal to start afresh in describing perceptual consciousness had a positive effect on both Koffka and Gibson.

Before explaining the relation between Gibson and Koffka's phenomenology, it should be mentioned that the type of phenomenology Gibson and Koffka believed in was symptomatic of mind-matter dualism. Supposedly, consciousness should be described intrinsically without consideration of related physical conditions. Further, phenomenology should describe perceptual experience in some sense independently of possible explanations of perception. It assumed a clear distinction between description and explanation that is epistemologically suspect.

Phenomenology is important in the history of visual perception because it offered an alternate method of describing perceptual consciousness to that of the various analytical introspective methods of Wundt, Titchener, etc. The view that Husserl had of phenomenology as a more naive or presuppositionless description of consciousness was decidedly antagonistic in spirit to the introspective method of directed analysis into elements. Phenomenological description presented consciousness not as a concatenation of elements, but in terms of more global and relational properties. Both Gestalt psychology and Gibson in his early development adopted a phenomenological attitude in describing perceptual consciousness. The phenomenology of Gestalt psychologists and Gibson was rather unsophisticated and actually latent with theoretical presuppositions but it was decidedly in contrast to the approach of introspective analysis and assuredly not unfruitful. Though not atheoretical, it did not accept the theoretical assumptions of introspection. This rejection of elementism and analysis was significant for it pointed out that such structuralist ideas were based on theory, viz., the ontology and epistemology of early science. Structuralism was not a "pure" description of consciousness. Further, in reconsidering Bacon, Berkeley, and Hume's empiricist ideal to simply describe what is observed, it becomes more apparent that what is an observable depends on what theory of observables one accepts. Recall that Berkeley's belief that distance is not a visual idea was founded upon the simulative assumption. In subscribing to a different view of what constitutes a valid description of perceptual consciousness, emphasis was shifted from mental elements to more global dimensions of consciousness. In turn, this phenomenological redescription provided different aspects of perceptual consciousness that required explanation, either physiologically or optically.

The hypothesis of "imageless thought," developed in the Wurzburg school under the direction of Osward Külpe (1862–1915) occupies a place in the history of the psychology of visual perception. It was "found" that in thinking there are certain contents of consciousness (*unanschauliche bewusstheiten*) which are not describable in terms of sensory attributes (Ach, 1905). These results, of course, were specific to thinking and not perception, but the general realization that consciousness is not completely portrayable in terms of traditionally listed set of attributes or qualities of sensations is significant. It preceded a similar theory developed concerning perception by Gestalt psychologists and Gibson. Two examples of nonsensational dimensions of perceptual consciousness can be found in Wertheimer's (1912) famous article on perceived movement in the phi-phenomenon and Gibson's (1966a) treatment of perceived occlusion. Again, within the context of this issue regarding imageless thought, the content of consciousness becomes a theoretical problem. The sensation, in fact, is a theoretical construct. In a mental chemistry approach (J. S. Mill or Wundt) it actually disappears from conscious content.

Another avenue of opposition to the Wundtian description of visual consciousness developed in the work of Christian von Ehrenfels (1859–1932). The hypothesis of "form qualities" proposed by Ehrenfels (Boring, 1950) represented a step in the direction of the Gestalt theory of consciousness. "Form qualities," according to Ehrenfels, were elementary constituents of visual awareness. This hypothesis was presented in contrast to the Helmholtizian view that visual consciousness consisted only of extensionless and formless sensations, and the Titchenerian view that visual consciousness had primitive extent but no determinate form.

Ehrenfels'disagreement with the introspectionist position was only partial. Proponents of the "form quality" hypothesis, such as Ehrenfels, Meinong and Cornelius (Boring, 1950) supposed that "form qualities" were "founded contents" constructed upon *fundamente* (sensations). Although the same form quality (e.g., squareness) existed across changes in sensations (e.g., from red to green dots), it was built upon these more fundamental constituents of consciousness. Visual forms were thought, in effect, to consist of more fundamental visual elements, viz., visual sensations. Secondly, Ehrenfels thought of form qualities as just a new type of mental element. He was still within the theoretical framework of phenomenal elementarism, where conscious content is thought to be built up from component parts. The form-quality psychologists followed Locke in continuing to characterize visual consciousness in terms of elements and the concatenation of elements. Gestalt psychology produced the actual break with the theory that visual consciousness consists of elements in any sense.

GIBSON AND FUNCTIONAL PSYCHOLOGY

Edwin Boring (1950) has argued that American functionalism was born in a meeting of Wundtian psychology and evolutionary biology. Furthermore, according to Boring, functionalism owes its emphasis upon utility and mental capacity to the "pioneer spirit" atmosphere of America. The origin and thematic structure of functionalism is more complex and has been examined and described by both historians and theoreticians of psychology (Angell, 1904, 1907; Carr, 1925, 1930; Dewey, 1896; Heidbredder, 1933; Marx & Hillix, 1973; Watson, 1968). The theoretical structure of functionalism owes a great deal to Aristotle and European act psychologists. From one perspective, it could be argued that Aristotle's emphasis on process, purpose, ecology, and wholism was put simply in the modern context of evolutionary science. Functionalism should also be seen as an antagonistic reaction to structuralism with its emphasis on static elements, Lockean psychology, and Newtonian science. The central spokesmen for functionalism, James, Angell, and Dewey all attacked traditional psychology in developing the functionalistic themes just mentioned.

It is interesting from an historical perspective to note that many functional psychologists who on one hand emphasized process and mental activity also emphasized an wholistic approach to consciousness and psychology. This connection between wholism and dynamism can be historically contrasted with the theoretically opposite pair of themes of elementarism and staticism that also are frequently connected together. To a degree this contrast should be taken as both historically and conceptually relative, for both functionalists and Gestalt psychologists were reacting against certain features of structuralism and analytic empiricism. As stated before, Gibson attempted through the concept of reciprocity to avoid the one-sidedness of either side of the dichotomy. Yet it is important to note that the wholistic-dynamic themes of functionalism, evolution, act psychology, and Gestalt psychology did have an impact on Gibson and he would criticize the limitations of elementaristic and static theories in natural science and psychology.

The "father" of American psychology, William James, also embraced the themes of wholism and dynamism. William James (1842–1910) in his *Principles of Psychology* (1890) contested the view that visual sensations are without extent. More fundamentally, his general concept of the relation between sensation and perception differed greatly from

Helmholtz, Bain, and even Berkeley. James agreed with Hering in that a sensation is not specific to just one point of stimulation on the retina. Each point will yield different sensations when in combination with different levels of surrounding activity at other points (1890, II, pp. 28, 30). James also argued that retinal points will produce different sensations as a function of experience (1890, II, p. 219), i.e., sensations are actually modified through learning. Recall that according to Berkeley, sensations do not change with perceptual learning. Instead, for Berkeley, more ideas are just associated or added onto the original and fixed sensations. James, in his psychophysiology, moves toward a Gestalt perspective. Also, James was moving toward a new conception of stimulation beyond the pointillism of earlier psychologists and other scientists.

In his theory of consciousness, James again sounds like a Gestalt psychologist. Perception was considered to be a "figured" unit and not in any sense a concatenation of elements (1890, II, pp. 80–82). There is global organization and integration within perceptual consciousness; it is not analyzable into independent elements in the sense developed by Locke, Berkeley, and James Mill.

For James, sensations are those aspects of consciousness involving direct acquaintance, whereas perception is knowledge about something. Despite the fact that perception developed ontogenetically from sensation, perception no longer contains sensations. Interestingly, this is a functional distinction and not a distinction based on basic elements and combinations of elements.

In disagreement with Berkeleians again, James suggested that visual sensations are originally undifferentiated and unordered, becoming directionally and relationally localized and differentiated through eye movements and associations (1890, II, pp. 153–176). Without going into the details, one significant fact regarding this view is that localization occurs through a process of differentiation and not, as in Lötze or Helmholtz, through a process of enrichment. Likewise, Gibson has thought of perceptual learning not as a process of supplantation, but of differentiation.

James supposed that visual sensations have "voluminousness" (1890, II, pp. 134–135). Although this original spatial dimension of visual awareness postulated by James is "crude" and "unordered," it still entailed a basic disagreement with Berkeley's position. Specific localization in depth is explained as a process of gradual differentiation based upon association (1890, II, p. 215). As was the case with bidimensional extent, the third dimension is not added to visual sensations but given in sensations from the beginning, and perceptual learning is once more not described as a process of enrichment of a dimension, but as a differentiation of a dimension. This again anticipates Gibson.

James' exposition lacked an optical explanation of visual depth. He did not believe any of the traditionally listed monocular or binocular conditions as both a necessary and sufficient condition for visual depth (1890, II, p. 220). The rationale for James' contention that visual sensations have the property of "voluminousness" was primarily "introspective" (1890, II, pp. 212–213). James' introspection though evidently differed from the methods of structuralists.

James' discussion of visual localization, both of direction and distance, contains another hypothesis of interest. Rather than describing localization as a process in which each sensation is placed individually and independently of other sensations, James argued that all visual sensations are localized and ordered within a global spatial framework (1890, II, p. 147). Berkeley had supposed that objects were localized at various distances independently of each other. And Lötze described directional placement of sensations in terms of individual local signs being associated with each visual sensation. Similarly, Hering and Helmholtz's positions implied a process in which sensations are individually localized. The hypothesis of a spatial framework is a radical departure from the point by point localization concept of Berkeley, Lötze and others. Though James speaks of the relative localization of sensations, it is the idea that localization is relational that anticipates both Gestalt and Gibsonian psychology. Gibson would provide a different explanation of how perceived objects are relationally placed than either James or Gestalt psychologists, but James' wholistic idea of explaining localization in terms of spatial relationships moves away from the elementaristic theory of Berkeley and other analytic empiricists.

James' general treatment of space perception contrasts sharply with the elementism of Berkeley and Newton. Perceptual and physical variables are not treated in isolation of each other and are therefore not seen as combining together as concatenations. Going back to Democritus' atomism and in modern times Francis Bacon's inductive epistemology, one view of reality has been to see it as built up out of independent elements, either in the physical or mental realms (witness Newton and Locke). An alternative theory would be to see reality differentiating out of what is simple but global, e.g., a fertilized cell subdividing into an embryo or a gaseous nebula coalescing into stars. What is initially an undifferentiated whole becomes increasingly segmented internally. In the same vein, James attacked the Newtonian concepts of absolute space and absolute time. Within consciousness there is neither empty space nor empty time (contra Kant). Both duration and extent are always filled, viz., space and time do not exist independent of particulars. Recall that Leibnitz had criticized the Newtonian concepts of absolute space and time, arguing instead for a relational approach. James at the psychological level is similarly arguing for a relational theory, where space and time are embodied in relationships between particulars. Gibson, at the ecological level, would attack both empty absolute space and empty absolute time. In fact, Gibson would avoid the terms *space* and *time* because they denote absolute empty dimensions. Ecologically, temporal relationships are embodied in particular events and spatial relationships are embodied in relationships between particular surfaces.

Ernst Mach (1838–1916), a contemporary of James, is not historically associated with functional psychology, but Mach's view also emphasize wholistic and functional considerations and attack various structuralist ideas. In his *Analysis of Sensations* (1906), Mach followed Hering in supposing that there are visual sensations of "space" due to hypothetical depth values of retinal points (1906, pp. 128–133). He opposed the judgment or inference theories of Helmholtz and Berkeley that entailed that depth is judged and not seen. Mach, through his investigation of "Mach rings" (Koffka, 1935), concluded that visual sensations are not a function of local retinal points of excitation but depend upon relations between points of excitation on the retina. As was also the case in Hering and James, this represented a departure from pointillism.

Influenced by the theory of evolution, Mach attempted to understand sensations (1906, Chapter IX) in terms of the adaptive necessities imposed upon the animal. Structuralism's treatment of sensations is fundamentally divorced from environmental relevancy. Though sensations and perceptions are described in terms of a model borrowed from the physical science, consciousness (or mind) is described and understood as an ontologically distinct and merely correlative realm. Functionalism involves the hypothesis that consciousness or psychological facts cannot be adequately understood as a distinct realm from the world. The scientific model of the universe that structuralism adopted was Newtonian and dualistic. Functionalism, due to the influence of evolutionary theory, rejects Descartes' absolute dualism. There exists a unity of the knowing mind and the known world.

Mach's position concerning the similarity of visual and tactual space should be noted as another deviation from Berkeley's theory and an anticipation of an important idea in Gibson. Mach stated that "optical and tactual space" are "homogeneous" in that the "relations of tactual space" are "similar to those of visual sensations" (1906, p. 187). Berkeley had argued for complete heterogeneity between vision and touch. Conversely, Mach argued for a higher order identity; a hypothesis anticipative of Gibson's views. What naturally follows from this idea of homogeneity is that spatial relations are not specific to any one type of sensory quality, but are higher order relational properties of all sensations. Berkeley's theory implied that spatial relations were dimensions of (i.e., intrinsic to) the qualities of any one type of sensory quality, hence they had to be dissimilar across the different senses.

In another significant departure from 18th century science and philosophy, Mach attacked (1960) the Newtonian concepts of absolute space and time in his *Science of Mechanics*. The relative theories of space and time conceptually connect with the "framework" hypothesis noted already in James and developed in Gestalt and Gibsonian psychology. Where space and time are absolutes, each physical and/or perceptual entity is given an intrinsic fix in both space and time. If space and time are treated relativistically, the spatial and temporal fixations are not independent and intrinsic to each entity. To give each element a spatial and temporal value based upon an absolute and distinct dimension is to construct a dualistic model of order. This dualistic approach can be traced back through Newton and Plato. Conversely, to give each element a spatial and temporal value relative to other elements is to construct a wholistic model of order based on relationships between elements. The concept of a framework of reference will be shown as based on wholistic relationships within the distribution of elements rather than some absolute framework independent of elements. Though James, Mach, and Gestalt psychologists moved in this direction, it is with Gibson that a non-dualistic, relational theory is most consistently and thoroughly developed.

In general, it is the theme of interconnectivity that pervades the late nineteenth century and provides a similar underlying theme in both functional and Gestalt psychology. Aristotle's ecological psychology related together the psyche and the environment, and American functionalism, viewing life as an evolutionary process of forms adapting to an environment, treated psychological facts as functions that involved the world in order to insure survival in the world. Darwin's theory of evolution, though it primarily attacked the static view of nature, also rejected the dualistic view of mental and physical entities. Darwin's concept of adaptation functionally connects mind with the environment.

The concept of a psychological function goes back to Aristotle, but the idea also has a more modern origin. Dallenbach (1915) traced the development of the term *function* in modern psychological literature. The psychological usage of the term first appeared in English in Thomas Brown (1820) who referred to "functions of mind." According to Dallenbach, Brown's concept of function was influenced by the phrenological notions of "faculties" and "functions" in the writings of Gall and Spurzheim (1808) (Dallenbach, 1915, pp. 478–479). *Function,* in this sense, has an analytical purpose, viz., to divide the mind into distinguishable parts. Using the term to refer to adaptive capacities comes in with James (1890).

If psychology's goal is no longer just to describe the mind per se, but rather with understanding how the mind is involved within adaption and adjustment to the environment, considerations naturally turn to the utility of mental processes. James exemplified this functional attitude. For James, consciousness is understood in terms of its utility or function (1890, Vol. I, Chapter 5). Describing the mind independently of its functions (which is essentially Wundt and Titchener's approach) was considered inadequate by James. Beginning with Descartes, one basic approach toward understanding the mind is to describe it in absolute or intrinsic terms. This approach should be connected with the dualistic notion of treating the mind as a separate substance or thing. Functionalism offers a relational theory of the mind connecting it with the environment. Further, because the mind is tied to questions of utility, mental processes are related to consequences (What is accomplished?). "Purpose" which appears in Aristotle's concept of function, also becomes a theme in functional psychology.

James Roland Angell (1869–1949), one of the cofounders of functional psychology (Hernstein & Boring, 1965, p. 500), was influenced chiefly by William James and John Dewey. In his "Functional Psychology" article of 1907, he sought to delineate some of the more important differences between functional psychology and Titchener's structural psychology.

He first pointed out that functional psychology is concerned more with describing mental operations than mental elements; hence functional psychology is closely affiliated with act psychology. Angell saw Titchener and Wundt as more involved with mental elements (sensations and ideas), whereas functionalists were more inclined to study mental activities. This first contrast is between active and static models of the mind.

According to Angell, a second major difference between functional and structural psychology was that for the former, mental activities are studied in their relation with the environment. The functional questions of mental processes revolve around ascertaining how these activities preserve adaptation with respect to the environment. This second contrast is between dualistic and integrative models of the mind and the physical world.

From Angell's discussion, it can be gathered that there are two separate meanings of the word *function* in psychological literature. Woodworth (1948) later attempted to clarify this distinction. Functional psychologists may study a mental function, meaning a mental operation or process or they may investigate a function in the sense of the *use* of some activity of the organism. In the former sense, individuals such as Wundt, Titchener and Berkeley were concerned with functional questions. For example, they all were interested in describing the processes through which sensations were combined or fused (Woodworth, 1948).

The starting point and emphasis though for a structuralist or association-ist was elements.

Titchener (1898, 1899), aware of a "functional" aspect to his studies, still argued that descriptive analysis of consciousness in terms of attributes of sensations should precede the "how they are combined" questions. The "what for," or utility question, was not considered by Titchener as part of psychology, but part of biology (1929). Psychology, according to him, dealt with the relation between conscious experience and the physical organism, in particular the nervous system. Biology was concerned with the relation of organisms and the environment. The epistemic dimension to perception, viz., perceptual knowledge of the environment, fell outside of psychology (1929, Chapter II). Consequently, Titchener conceived of much of functional psychology as either biology or epistemology.

If Titchener were alive today, he would undoubtedly think that the subject matter of Gibson's ecological program falls outside of psychology. The demarcation proposed by Titchener between psychology and biology methodologically separates the perceiver and its environment. Psychology, as a science, studies "consciousness" without bringing the environment into the inquiry at all. Conversely for Gibson, visual perception cannot even be defined independently of the environment. As Gibson views visual perception as a veridical cognizance of the environment, questions regarding the nature of knowledge (perceptual) necessarily enter into his inquiry.

Related to the connected notions of adaptation and function is the *normative* idea of accomplishment. Function and adaptation involve the idea of accomplishment for some criteria of success is intrinsic to both of these concepts. Gibson has been impressed with the degree of *functional excellence* in visual perception, and his theories have been directed primarily toward explaining the veridicality of visual perception. Unless this functional emphasis is kept in mind, neither Gibson's ecological program nor his earlier psychophysical program can be understood.

Gibson's student education emphasized functionalist and empiricist themes. The most significant direct source for these theoretical themes was one of Gibson's teachers at Princeton, Edwin Bissell Holt. The relation between Gibson and Holt (1873–1946) is many-faceted. Although Gibson has named Holt as one of the past individuals to whom he owed the greatest intellectual debt (1966a, p. viii), Gibson in many ways is more indebted to Koffka or Troland, and there are irreconcilable differences between Gibson and Holt. However, Gibson learned functionalism first hand from Holt.

Holt was a behaviorist and opposed to the inclusion of an entity of consciousness within the subject matter of psychology (Holt, 1915, p. 172). Instead, cognition, which would include perception, was described as a response to the distal environment. Holt rejected consciousness as an intervening entity between the environment and responses. Holt's behaviorism is consequently a functional behaviorism emphasizing the environmental significance of psychological variables. The mind as an ontological construct independent of the physical world seemed superfluous. (James though, recall, felt that the mind did have an adaptive or functional significance relative to the environment.) Holt abandons an absolute dualism of mind and body (matter), because in this sense, the mind is disconnected from the environment, yet the functional significance of behavior is apparent. Gibson sought to avoid a Cartesian dualism of mind and body within his ecological theory. Also, his attempt to explain veridical perception in terms of environmental-stimulus variables without recourse to mental contributions can be interpreted as a form of behaviorism. Yet Gibson's theory of perceiver-environment reciprocity, while involving a rejection of Descartes' absolute dualism, is not a materialistic or functional behaviorism. Secondly, his rejection of mental contributions in perception does not involve a reduction of perception to behavior; perception, for Gibson, is clearly distinguished from behavior. Where Gibson does side with the behaviorists is in their rejection of a dualist theory of mind that separates and isolates the mind in a second ontological realm.

Gibson labeled himself a behaviorist and named Holt as the individual most responsible for this outlook in him. Yet Gibson has never been a behaviorist in the sense in which Holt was one. The psychophysical approach Gibson expounded through the 1950s could be interpreted as a type of behaviorism, but it was clearly different from Holt's. The psychophysical approach involved a phenomenology of perceptual experience and as previously mentioned, Gibson's psychophysics and phenomenology had a dualistic dimension. Both Holt and Gibson described perception as a function of the environment, but Gibson in the 1950s was motivated toward finding functional relations between stimulation and perception. Holt had thought this impossible. Gibson, even in the 1950s, assumed that relationships existed between the environment and stimulation and between stimulation and perception. In summary, what Gibson shared with Holt's behaviorism was an attempt to free psychology of dualism. They both believed that dualism could be avoided by functionally relating psychological variables to the environment. Where Gibson differed from Holt was in rejecting Holt's idea that all psychological variables were behavioral.

The view that consciousness consisted of elements was paralleled in the 1900s by the belief that behavior consisted of nothing more than a set of reflexes. Holt (1915, pp. 153–157), on the contrary, had argued that behavior could not be adequately described as a set of reflexes. At the molar level there are emergent functions in behavior that are nonexistent in individual reflex-arcs, because behavior exhibits organization and coordination. Behavior is coordinated relative to the environment; reflexes can be described without reference to the environment. Behavior is organized into relational patterns (e.g., walking, talking, eating, etc.), where a description of the individual movements would not be equivalent to a description of the molar behavior. Analogously, a description of individual notes is not equivalent to a description of a melody. Holt's critical attitude toward behaviorial reductionism corresponded to the Gestalt attack upon the Lockean notion of phenomenal elementarism.

In his commentary on the reflex-arc hypothesis, Holt introduced what he designated as the "bead-theory of causation" (1915, pp. 157–162). According to Holt, this view of causation entailed that a causal process is a series of successive states, and each state is caused by the immediate previous state and is predictable from it. Basically, the "bead-theory of causation" is the mechanistic theory of causation. Holt argued that this concept of causation was assumed in the reflex-arc hypothesis. The reflex arc hypothesis describes reflexes as muscular movements causally instigated by stimuli. Behavior is not, Holt contended, a function of the immediate stimulus, but of the environment. By this he means you can predict from the environment what behavior will occur, but behavior cannot be predicted from stimulation. Behavior is coordinated relative to the environment. Holt assumes in this argument a lack of correspondence between stimulation and the environment. Oppositely, Gibson did believe there were correspondences between stimulation and the environment. Consequently, Gibson in his early development supposed that perception is a function of the proximal stimulus. (After 1960, Gibson dropped this "formula" for visual perception.) Although Gibson never subscribed to the reflex-arc hypothesis, he did assume a mechanistic theory of causation in his psycho-physical explanation of perception. Though Gibson dropped the psychophysical idea that perception is a function of stimulation, he never abandoned the idea of environment-stimulation correspondence. What he substituted for his psychophysical theory was more clearly anticipated by Dewey than Holt.

One of the most influential and philosophically sophisticated functionalists was John Dewey (1859–1952). Although nowhere in his writings does Gibson acknowledge any special significance to it, Dewey's article "The Reflex-Arc Concept in Psychology" (1896) anticipates several fundamental ideas in Gibson's ecological psychology. The article though was a classic within functionalist literature, as also was James' *Principles of Psychology,* and it is not surprising that Gibson's ideas show affinity to both Dewey's and James' views.

For Dewey, behavior should be thought of in terms of molar or higher-order co-ordinations and not as a set of elementaristic reflexes at the molecular level, and behavior or psychological processes in general should be depicted as adjustments. Dewey would say that the response is *to* the stimulus—it is coordinated with respect to proximal stimulation and the distal environment. Dewey was influenced by German act psychology and philosophy and gave behavior an intentional rather than causative interpretation. Psychological activity should be depicted functionally (i.e., in terms of adaptations to the environment).

As was described in the discussion of Descartes, the reflex-arc hypothesis depicted perception and behavior as a series of stages (e.g., stimulus, neural activity and response) that are unidirectional in causal dependency. Dewey in criticizing the reflex-arc hypothesis singled out the ideas discrete stages and unidirectional psychological causation as extremely misleading. Psychological activity is not a set of discrete stages (i.e., stimulation, neural activity and responses) are not separate processes. According to Dewey, they form an "organic unity" and not a mere "mechanical conjunction." The argument that perception is not a series of separate stages would become central within Gibson's conception of perceptual activity in the 1960s. For Gibson, perception involved circular interdependencies rather than mechanistic chains. Similarly, for Dewey, the integrative and nonconcatenative nature of psychological activity entailed an interdependency between all aspects of sensori-motor coordination. The reflex-arc hypothesis implied that the motor response is dependent upon the sensory stimulus, while for Dewey, sensori-motor coordination is "virtually a circuit." Perception involves muscular adjustments to stimulation, in that stimulation is contingent upon "movements of body, head and eye muscles" (1896, p. 355–356); responses are contingent upon stimulation, but stimulation is just as much contingent on responses. In more modern terminology, this would amount to saying that stimulation is not an independent variable with respect to perception or the animal's ongoing activities. Gibson would eventually assert that stimulation is obtained by and not imposed upon the perceptual systems. One of the main reasons Gibson moved beyond his psychophysical approach was his rejection of a unidirectional model of causation. Further, viewing psychological activity and stimulation as interdependent is a step toward a reciprocal theory of the perceiver and the environment.

Dewey contended that perception primarily was an "act," i.e., a continuing process of motor adjustment to the physical world. Sensation ("the sensory quale") is a dual function of stimulation and the act of perceiving, hence stimulation is not a sufficient condition for conscious sensations. There is no passive *tabula rasa,* inasmuch as there must be an "act of seeing . . . looking" accomplished through the motor mechanisms of the organism in order for there to be a visual "sensory quale." Dewey was consequently speaking as an act psychologist in the tradition of Brentano and Leibnitz contra Locke. Likewise, Gibson after 1960 no longer saw perception as a causal effect of stimulation upon the mind, but rather as necessarily involving activities of the perceiver for there to be any type of effective stimulation. The gist of both Brentano's and Dewey's act psychology is that act and object are interdependent. All acts of knowing have objects of knowledge and all objects of knowledge (however impoverished) have concommitant acts. Perception cannot be understood as a subjective creation or an effect of external causes.

With the development of act psychology, evolutionary theory, and functionalism in the 19th century, several significant themes emerge that would positively influence Gibson. One philosophical starting point for these scientific developments was continental rationalism with its emphasis on organization and wholism. Continental philosophy also provided a basis for process or act psychology. An essential idea in late 19th century psychology was dynamism—mind was a process rather than a substance. The concept of mental activity provided a means by which to relate the mind to the world. In a similar vein, evolutionary theory treated life (including mind) as a process of adaptation to the environment. Dynamically relating the mind to the environment sets the stage for a theory of ecological psychology. Dualism separates and isolates mind and matter. Wholism as a philosophical-scientific principle enters psychology from two sources, viz., the concept of structural organization where integrated entities are not seen as mere concatenations of parts and the concept of dynamic relationships where psychological processes or activities have a functional/intentional/adaptive relation to the environment. Gibson did not simply accept the above ideas as they were initially articulated. Rather, he extended them and attempted to integrate them with an empiricist psychology.

I believe that mind-matter dualism, in the sense of two distinct substances, best characterizes the line of thought running from Plato to Descartes and Newton. With the advent of evolutionary theory and functionalism, mind-matter dualism comes under attack. Yet it would be simplistic to state that what replaces mind-matter dualism in Gibson is a theory of mind-matter reciprocity, for the very terms *mind* and *matter* denote substances, and Gibson alternatively uses *animal* and *environment,* which do not carry the ontological meaning of self-sufficient absolutes. Recall that Gibson would also avoid the terms *space* and *time* with their absolute denotations.

Where Gibson goes beyond both functionalism and Darwinian evolution specifically relates to the concept of the environment. The term *adaptation* carries with it the idea that psychological and biological processes (progressively) conform to the conditions of the environment; thus the environment has the status of an independent standard relative to which life is to be understood. Darwin has been interpreted as a materialist, for life and mind owe their existence and nature to the environment. For Gibson, it is a mistake to conceptualize the environment as a self-sufficient substrate or given; the existence of the environment is reciprocally interdependent with the existence of life. Darwinian evolution and the related concept of functional adaptation, indeed, do assume a materialistic (monistic) ontology, at least in the sense that the environment is thought of as primary and biological-psychological processes as secondary or derivative.

Considering Gibson's theory of animal-environment reciprocity, we can see in a general sense why Gibson's ecological psychology rejected the unidirectional model of causality in explaining perception. Reciprocity entails interdependency. Unidirectional causality entails independent causes and dependent effects. Reciprocity entails integration. Unidirectional causality entails discrete events. As Dewey noted the stimulus-response reflex arc hypothesis misses the dependency of stimuli upon responses and ends up with successions rather than coordinations. Relatedly, Brentano criticizes structuralists' sensations, for the objects of knowing do not exist without acts of knowing. We can carry this concept of interdependency back to Aristotle's treatment of psychological activities and correlative objects. What we see both historically and theoretically is that the concept of reciprocity not only stands in opposition to dualism and monism but also to the unidirectional causal theory of perception.

Chapter 9 _____

GESTALT PSYCHOLOGY

Wholism as a theme in modern psychology is primarily associated with the Gestalt movement as formulated and developed by the German psychologists Wertheimer, Köhler and Koffka. Max Wertheimer's (1880–1943) well known study of perceived movement (1912) provided the experimental ground work and inspiration of several major ideas in Gestalt psychology. Wertheimer interpreted the "phi-phenomena" as demonstrating that visual consciousness could not be described in terms of the qualities of visual sensations postulated by the introspectionists. In this particular case, perceived movement was neither an attribute of sensations nor a property of combinations of sensations. According to Wertheimer, it was a fact of consciousness as immediate and irreducible as sensations. Just as it had been with Ach's studies (1905), consciousness did not seem describable solely in terms of the qualities of sensations.

In a later article (1921), Wertheimer contested the validity of the general hypothesis of conscious elements. For him, perceptual experience was not *"sinnlose undverbindung"* (a meaningless combination) in character. Consequently, any attempt to describe consciousness in terms of mere combinations of elements is based on a misconception concering the nature of consciousness. Further, global or higher order facts of perceptual consciousness are not based upon elements in the sense of mental chemistry. Wertheimer's disagreement with phenomenal elementarism was unqualified and complete. Visual form is not a concatenation of elements, (e.g., Helmholtz); an emergent property of elements in fusion (e.g., Wundt); or a second level structural element built upon first level elements (e.g., von Ehrenfels). It does not have more basic constituents in any of these senses. The global relationship is primary.

The three main figures of Gestalt psychology, viz., Wertheimer, Wolfgang Köhler (1887–1967), and Kurt Koffka (1886–1914), all approached perceptual consciousness from a different viewpoint than individuals within the empiricst tradition. Instead of attempting to analyze experience into elements, they endeavored to represent it in an unanalytical, nonelemental way under the banner of phemonenology. Resultantly, there was more freedom of description with the constraints of Wundtian introspective terminology removed. More importantly, Gestalt psychologists accused the introspectionists of distorting experience in their analysis. In adopting this attitude, additional terms were accepted as descriptively valid concerning perceptual consciousness. What Titchener (1909, 1910) thought was a "stimulus error" in introspective description (attributing a property to a sensation that was actually a property of the world) was a phenomenal given for Gestalt psychologists. Of special significance in Gestalt psychology were form, figure-ground, objects, and segregated "whole characters" as phenomenally immediate features of perceptual consciousness. The aforementioned were facts of consciousness not psychologically mediated by inference, association, or suggestions. Since they were supposedly "irreducible" and "immediate" in experience and relational in character, explanations of them as such were required. They could not be explained in terms of more primitive elements either phenomenally or physiologically. These facts of consciousness are not elements. Consciousness is a Gestalt—a whole—possessing an integration. There are no absolute independent elements in consciousness. In essence, the Gestalt psychologists were arguing that relationships and relational properties are as primary as the supposed elements of consciousness. Consequently, there are no units or entities independent of relationships.

In the 1950s and 1960s, Gibson argued for "a direct realist theory" of visual perception. One meaning of "direct" often employed by Gibson, viz., the absence of psychological mediation based upon sensations, is clearly implied in the Gestalt view of the *phenomenal* immediacy of perception. Traditionally, perception is described as complex experiences, and sensation is described in terms of simple elements. Gestalt psychology rejected the building block theory of consciousness, stating that the simple and elementary does not precede the complex and wholistic. As early as his psychophysics of perception, Gibson followed the Gestalt theory of perceptual consciousness.

If Gestalt psychology headed in a new direction concerning perceptual consciousness, the opposite was true concerning their treatment of the visual stimulus. For example, Köhler (1947, pp. 162–163) argued that the visual stimulus must be described as a mosaic of points on the retina. The rationale for this decision is identical with that of Heider's (1927) and will be commented upon in the later discussion of Heider. What should be stressed is that the general form of all Gestalt explanations of perceptual consciousness included the assumption of optical pointillism. Hence, the Gestalt position is totally at odds with Gibson's anti-elementarisitc conception of visual stimulation.

Köhler's 1913 article includes the first mention of the "constancy hypothesis," of which he accused many past perceptual psychologists of presupposing. The constancy hypothesis entailed that a visual sensation is totally determined by one local point of stimulation both qualitatively and quantitatively. Stated differently, the phenomenal effect (or correlate) of any receptor unit is independent of the activity in other units. A simpler statement of what Köhler meant by the "constancy hypothesis" would be that sensations are a strict function of stimulation, but since for Köhler the visual stimulus was pointillistic, the former characterizations of the "constancy hypothesis" are more precise and explicit. In particular, the "constancy hypothesis" assumes that activity around a local point on the retina does not effect in any way the visual sensation that corresponds to that point of excitation. Köhler argued that the "machine theory" of physiology (which he identified with Descartes' projection hypothesis of independent transmission pathways from the eye to the brain) was assumed in the "constancy hypothesis." Köhler believed that the perceptual nervous system has organization and is not a set of independent units. During visual perception, physiological interaction occurs between impulses transmitted to the brain from the eyes. Correspondingly, the effect of one point of stimulation upon perceptual consciousness is not independent of other points, since there is neural interaction and organizational processes in the brain (Köhler, 1941, p. 492; 1947, pp. 100–135). It should be noted that Köhler's general hypothesis of neural interaction parallels Hering's explanation of perceptual contrast.

Organizational processes of the brain are postulated to explain the facts of experience uncovered through phenomenological description. Perceptual consciousness exhibits organized and "segregated wholes" from the phenomenological view point, whereas visual stimulation conceived of as a set of independent points contains none of these characteristics. The dynamic principles of neural organization transform this mosaic into physiological field relations that correspond with perceptual consciousness. The process runs from simple elements without order to ordered wholes.

Because this transformation from a mosaic to a segregated whole does not depend on "learned" connections, Gestalt explanations of the various facts of perception (e.g., form, solid, shape, size, and distance of objects) do not involve an associative mediational process comparable to that within Berkeley's theory. On the other hand, the Gestalt presupposition that the visual stimulus is a mosaic necessitates a constructive process in visual perception. Similarly, the Berkeleian conception of the retinal image implied the necessity of a constructive process in visual perception; in the latter case it was a function of learning, whereas in the former it was physiologically innate.

Although Köhler adopted a pointillistic conception of the visual stimulus, visual perception for him involved cognizance of higher order relations. What determines the constancies of perception are physiological relations in the brain. For example, perceptual size constancy depends on a constant physiological relation over various transpositions conditioned by changes in the object's distance (Allport, 1955, p. 113; Boring, 1950, p. 612). The general hypothesis that visual perception is determined by relationships and not absolute values is carried out in Gibson, but for Kohler, these relationships were physiological and not optical. If the Gestalt psychologists were wholistic at the physiological and phenomenological levels, they remained elementaristic at the stimulus level. This last point they shared with empiricists. Where Gibson differed from both traditional empiricists and Gestalt psychologists was in arguing that wholistic-relational order existed in stimulation. Further, because both empiricists and Gestalt psychologists postulated a constructive step in perception, they both ended up believing that perception is indirect (Shaw and Turvey, 1981).

The Gestalt concept of organization involved the idea of interdependency. Instead of independent elements being ordered from "above," "elements," or "parts" exist in a state of dynamic interdependency. The term *dynamic* is given an interactional interpretation whereby parts of a Gestalt are interdependent because they effect each other. Further, a Gestalt is understood as complex yet unified, meaning that a Gestalt has interdependent parts yet, relative to its context, it has a segregated integrity, e.g., a figure segregated but related to its ground. Regarding these ideas on organization the Gestalt psychologists rejected the dualistic contrast of order and elements. Of particular note, the Gestalt psychologists further articulated the hypothesis of a spatial framework (James) in terms of their theory of interdependent organization (see Koffka and Gibson on the spatial framework).

HEIDER AND ECOLOGICAL PSYCHOLOGY

In many important respects, the work of Fritz Heider (e.g., 1927, 1930) more closely resembles the ideas of Gibson than any other psychologist associated with the Gestalt tradition. Heider pointed out (1927, p. 35) that serious investigation into describing the physical environment, which the "perceptual system" (a terminological anticipation of Gibson) has adapted to had been slighted in the psychology of perception. His article "Thing and Medium" (1927) represented a first step in remedying this situation. As Heider argued in a clearly functionalistic tone, perception cannot be considered independently of the environment, because perception is defined as an evolved adaptive relation between the organism and the environment. The environment, within such an evolutionary-functional perspective, is part of a functional Gestalt. Psychological functions are related to features of the environment.

According to Heider, concern should be with the "macroscopic" structure or "macroreality" of the physical surroundings. Just as there are different levels of analysis in describing the organism, there are different levels of units and organization in the physical world. This macro-level of reality is just as scientifically real as the microlevel studied by atomic physics. More importantly, it is the level of physical organization with respect to which perception is adaptive. This ontological claim undercuts the elementaristic theory that physical reality is nothing but atoms in a void. If indeed there are multiple levels of physical reality then one of the basic arguments for an indirect theory of perception is thrown open to question. Recall the previous discussions of Descartes, Locke, and Newton in which perception could not be of the "real" physical world because that world as described within Newtonian ontology was significantly different from what is perceived.

Heider's overall discussion of the environment is noteworthy in at least two respects. First, his observation that perceptual psychologists had slighted investigating the environment is historically correct. Little was ever said, except for the constant assertion that the environment consisted of objects in space. This neglect of systematic examination of the environment and its relation to the animal reflects the mind-matter dualism of Newtonian science. Heider's change of stance reflects an evolutionary and ecological perspective. Secondly, Heider was anticipating an ever growing concern of Gibson with the environment of perception and behavior. Since the 1960s, Gibson began his treatments of visual perception with a description of those aspects or constituents of the environment that visual perception is specific to epistemically. This is quite revolutionary in approach, since previously most psychologists and philosophers interested in visual perception jumped right into describing perceptual consciousness or the process of visual perception per se with little or no mention of the environment, and only superficial and mechanical remarks concerning the visual stimulus. Newton and Kepler's views on matter and energy were accepted without question.

In conjunction with his discussions of the environment, Heider (1927, 1930) gave comparable effort to describing stimulation and its relationship with the physical environment. Noting once again an investigative blind spot, this time regarding the "mediators" of visual perception, Heider, in stressing the degree of specificity between stimulation and the environment, sought to develop descriptions of both general and specific stimulus-environment relations. Such considerations on Heider's part paralleled Gibson's future discipline of ecological optics. Ecological optics, for Gibson, is not the study of optics *per se,* but of specific relations between invariants and transformations of the optical array and persisting and changing properties of the environment.

Heider argued that stimulation can and should be independently considered from the process of visual perception. In fact, Heider did not think the "mediator" of visual perception to be an image in the eye, but the light rays in the medium reflected from the environment. This attempt to describe the optical basis of vision independently of the animal anticipated a similar goal in Gibson's ecological optics. This is not to say that for Gibson or Heider stimulation was described independently of considerations pertaining to the perceiver because this would be nonecological. Rather stimulation was not localized within the perceiver. The retinal image is within the perceiver. Reflected light or the optic array lies in the medium between the perceiver and environment.

According to Heider, light rays coming from an object form "spurious units." Because each light ray is causally independent of each other ray, Heider contended that there was no actual organization (interdependency) of rays, and therefore an eye must receive nothing but a set of unrelated points (assuming that organization entails causal interdependency). Consequently, a process of organization is required to transform this concatenation of points into organized and segregated wholes. This same reasoning was behind both Köhler's (1947) and Koffka's (1935) acceptance of optical pointillism and their contention that a process of physiological organization was necessary in visual perception.

Interestingly, the Gestalt psychologists accepted Kepler's elementaristic treatment of light. They rejected the idea that there could exist levels of reality within light. Their reasoning was that relationships exist only where there is interaction among those entities within the relationship. Yet there is a circularity in this reasoning for in accepting Kepler-Newton's theory of light, they accepted an elementaristic theory of light where light is defined as independent elements.

KOFFKA AND VISUAL SPACE PERCEPTION

Though differences exist between Gestalt psychology and Gibsonian psychology, in particular over the Gestalt contention that physiological organization is necessary for phenomenal organization, Gibson found many ideas and experiments in the Gestalt tradition significant. As an introduction to a comparison of Koffka and Gibson, two studies within the Gestalt tradition of particular relevance should be described. These studies by Ternus (1926) and Duncker (1929) are of particular significance to the concept of perceptual organization (see Ellis, 1938). Given their experimental results, the Gestalt psychologists and Gibson would offer two different theoretical explanations.

Ternus (1926) was concerned with investigating the conditions of phenomenal identity. He found that the phenomenal identity of a point over time was not contingent upon a corresponding excitated point on the retina remaining anatomically identical. Complementarily, the same anatomical point of excitation could yield two nonidentical phenomenal points. Ternus ascertained that phenomenal identity was determined by an excited point's relative location within a group of excited points on the retina. (See Diagram 13) Ternus presented this conclusion in Gestalt terminology: "Phenomenal identity depends upon Gestalt identity; homologous points in two Gestalten will exhibit phenomenal identity" (1926, p. 154).

The temporally successive points OB and OC are not seen as identical with XB and XC, but identical with XA and XB, where XA $\equiv$ OB and XB $\equiv$ OC. Ternus concluded from this and similar demonstrations that phenomenal identity of two temporally successive points is a function of identical location, not on the retina, but within the relative configuration of points per se. Since XB and OC occupy the same relative positions within XA $-$ XB $-$ XC and OB $-$ OC $-$ OD, respectively, they are seen as the same point. If two successive points were seen as identical because of identical retinal position, it should then be that XB = OB and XC = OC, but this did not occur.

DIAGRAM 13

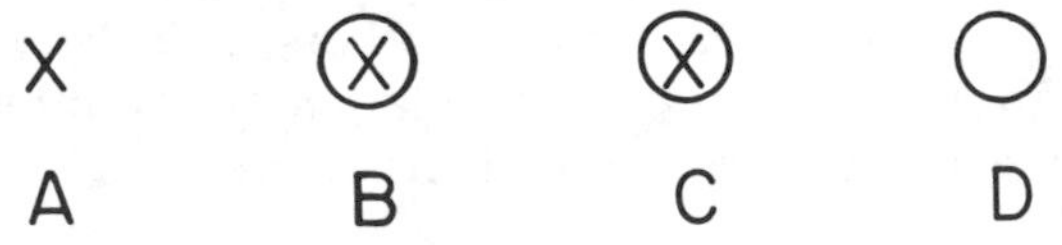

X   Ⓧ   Ⓧ   O

A   B   C   D

A, B, C, and D are four adjacent retinal locations. At time X, retinal locations A, B, and C are excited; at successive time O, retinal locations, B, C, and D are excited.

The importance of Ternus' study in Gibson's development was that Gibson interpreted these results to imply that the perceiver is not normally sensitive to the specific anatomical locations of excitation points on the retina, but to the relative locations of points (or patterns) in the retinal image. Simply stated, the perceiver is sensitive to the ordinal retinal image and not the anatomical retinal image. This hypothesis, it should be recalled, was involved in Berkeley's resolution of the problem of the inverted image. It is to be contrasted with the "local sign" hypothesis of Lötze, Helmholtz, Hering, and others, that entailed anatomical sensitivity. Generally, it is an experimental demonstration of the concept of an intrinsic spatial framework.

In a series of experiments, Duncker (1929) discovered that perceived movement depended on a "phenomenal frame of reference." As mentioned, most psychologists supposed that sensed location was a function of retinal location; placement of sensations occurred through anatomically specific local signs (Hering, Lötze, Helmholtz, etc.). In order to explain why a retinally fixed point sometimes is perceived as moving (e.g., when a perceiver's gaze follows a moving object) or why a moving point on the retina yields no perceived movement (e.g., when an object remains stationary, but the eyes move), it was supposed that the perceiver compensated for these nonveridical sensations through unconscious registration of eye movements. In both cases, the general implication was that movement or nonmovement of physical objects was not seen, but only mediated (or inferred, e.g., Helmholtz) via muscular sensations of eye movements and sensed anatomical locations of excitation. This type of explanation goes back to Alhazen. Further, it assumes that spatial location and movement is fixed relative to a mental frame of reference that stands distinct from physical stimuli. Embodied in this assumption is the dualism of mental order and physical particulars as well as the Newtonian concept of absolute space.

If seen movement and location were a function of location or movement of stimulus points relative to anatomical points on the retina, it should follow that with only one excited point anywhere on the retina there should still be perceived location (Witasek, 1910). The "local sign" hypothesis entailed that each visual point was localized independently of all others by anatomical "local signs." Contrarily, it was found by Guilford and Dallenbach (1928), among others, that there was no exact localization with just one point of stimulation on the retina; in fact the perceived point actually moved around erratically. This is the well known auto-kinetic effect.

Duncker's study attempted to demonstrate, in part, that the auto-kinetic effect occurred because seen movement and location were not contingent upon anatomical movement and location of corresponding stimulus points, but depended on a visual spatial framework. With only one retinal point of excitation, this visual spatial framework is missing; hence, seen movement and location become indefinite. In general, the location and movement of objects (or points) were not seen with respect to retinal location or movement, but were seen with respect to one another. "The phenomenal motions of separating objects is determined by the kind and degree of mutual "localization" of these objects, and this whether one of them is localized relative to the other or both are localized with regard to each other respectively" (Duncker, 1929, p. 170).

In Duncker's experiments, some point(s) serve(s) as a visual frame of reference for localization of other points. For cases in which only two points are presented, each may serve as the reference point for localization of the other. Again, as in Ternus' study, it is not the relations between the points in the retinal image and points on the retina, but relations within the image that are perceptually significant. Another historical-theoretical feature highlighted through Duncker's study is the elementarism embodied in the local sign hypothesis. Duncker argued for a wholistic, interdependent theory of spatial location. The local sign hypothesis assumed that locations are independently fixed for each "element" of stimulation.

One qualification that is required concerning the above studies is that the Gestalt interpretation of these results implied that the image per se, if only conceived of as a set of independent points, did not contain these spatial relations. It was cerebral physiological organization that supported such relationships. Gibson (1950a), on the contrary, considered the retinal image as including such "ordinal" relations. When Gibson shifted from a psychophysical theory (1950a) to an ecological theory (1966a), such stimulus relationships were ascribed to the optic array.

The single work within Gestalt psychology that had the most pronounced effect upon Gibson's thinking was Koffka's *Principles of Gestalt Psychology* (1935). Throughout his articles and books, Gibson cited this work more than any other publication generated within the Gestalt tradition. Gibson and Koffka were colleagues at Smith College for over ten years and although Gibson never accepted the Gestalt principles of physiological organization, Gibson clearly took seriously many of the points raised by Koffka. Before meeting Koffka, from whom he learned Gestalt psychology first hand, Gibson, as a devout empiricist, was intent on refuting through traditional learning principles the nativistic and nonanalytical features of Gestalt psychology. The direction of Gibson's theorizing and experimentation significantly changed after his interactions with Koffka.

Inspired by the work of Köhler (1920), Koffka (1935, Chapters I-II) explained how the concept of order was applicable to nature as well as mind. For Koffka, organization existed at the molar or macrolevel of the physical world, in the brain, and in perceptual experience. At the macro-level, the physical environment does not just consist of "lines and points" but "things" (1935, pp. 215, 69–72). Furthermore, experience at the molar level is not describable in terms of sensations of color or forms of color (1935, p. 178). Koffka clearly went beyond structuralism and analytic empiricism in applying the concept of interdependency to sensory physiology and perceptual consciousness. Yet there were still some dualistic limitations in Koffka's thinking. One of the major differences between Koffka and Gibson is that the latter saw order in all spheres relevant to visual perception, whereas Koffka did not believe that the visual proximal stimulus at the retina exhibited any organization. Koffka and Köhler did move beyond Platonic dualism in believing that the physical environment was not built up from independent elements; rather it possessed an intrinsic order of interdependency. On the other hand, though Koffka did ascribe order to the physical world, he did not believe it possessed meaning. Meaning was given through psycho-physiological processes.

In his discussion of possible explanations of perception, Koffka rejected the hypothesis that it is specifically a function of proximate stimulation, which following Köhler (1913), he labeled as the "constancy hypothesis" (Koffka, 1935, pp. 80-86). He presented many examples to show that perception was not a function of stimulation (e.g., Koffka, 1935, pp., 83, 84, 145, 170; Mach, 1906), but what he always meant by stimulation was a mosaic of energy units. For example, Mach rings demonstrate that local stimulation at one point on the retina may have several distinct phenomenal results depending upon stimulation at other positions on the retina. Koffka concluded from this that the specifics of the phenomenal "looks" of things are not determined by the specifics of proximal stimulation. These results could also be interpreted to mean that the optical support for vision should not be thought of as merely a set of points.

The rationale for Koffka's belief that stimulation is a mosaic of independent points (1935, pp. 75, 84, 98, 175), was identical with that of Heider (1927) and Köhler (1947), viz., where there is no causal interaction there is no organization. Since light rays do not interact, they are not organized. Because perception is not a function of stimulation, (i.e., the "constancy hypothesis"). organizational processes in the brain are required. This constitutes a major difference between him and Gibson, since for Gibson the brain does not organize an unorganized input. To develop this comparison further, at the simplest level an energy relationship or ratio would be an example of stimulus order for Gibson. For the

Gestalt psychologists a difference or relationship of energy values in adjacent light rays would not be considered to be a physical "reality."

Koffka and Gibson (1950a) approached perceptual consciousness through phenomenological description. Koffka, though, wished to explain "why things look as they do" as revealed through phenomenology, whereas Gibson (1950a) was concerned with "why things look as they are." The question of the veridicality of visual perception Koffka considered secondary to the more general problem of explaining "the looks of things," whether they were veridical or not (1935, pp. 76, 79). Contrarily, given his functionalistic attitude, Gibson was concerned primarily with explaining "veridical looks" and not so much with "looks" in general. As mentioned earlier, Gibson and the Gestalt psychologists were together in introducing relational and global features into their descriptions of consciousness, yet Gibson attempts to relate such features of perception to features in stimulation and in environment.

Koffka's discussion of phenomenal identity betrays another assumption concerning the visual stimulus that was a carry-over from earlier theory. In referring to the study of Ternus (1926) and a similar one by Metzger (Koffka, 1935), Koffka argued that a process of fusion in the brain was required for perceived identity. Two successive points at two different locations on the retina are, according to Koffka, separate stimulus events, because they are anatomically and temporally distinct. Physiological fusion transforms distinct events into a perception of one point moving (Koffka, 1935, pp. 285–287). What is persupposed in this argument is that successive stimulus points are different if they are anatomically and temporally distinct in location on the retina. Again, this represents another clear and important difference between Gibson and Koffka, insofar as Gibson from 1950 onward did not describe the visual stimulus in terms of instantaneous anatomical values.

Koffka considered the *Ganzfeld* condition studied by Metzger (1930) as representing the simplest case of stimulation. The *Ganzfeld* condition is homogeneous optical stimulation to the total field of view. Perceived depth, albeit of an indeterminate nature, resulted in most cases in a *Ganzfeld* condition. Koffka concluded that perceived depth was not dependent on any of the traditionally listed depth cues, because they were all missing in this situation. (Phenomenological descriptions were not always very explicit or uniform across subjects.) For Koffka, perceived depth was contingent upon a tridimensional process in brain that can result from purely homogeneous stimulation (Koffka, 1930, 1935, pp. 115, 159–164). Although Koffka did not accept the simulative assumption regarding the visual stimulus, he did, in this explanation, assume simulation in the processes of the brain. If three dimensions are seen, the supporting physiological field must be three dimensional. Secondly, Koffka was arguing that perceived depth does not have as a necessary condition heterogeneity in the proximal stimulus. Conversely for Gibson, distance is seen only in conditions of heterogeneous stimulation. Because the initial presentation of homogeneous stimulation is different from the immediately preceding stimulus conditions, the onset of homogeneous stimulation is only homogeneous in space, and not in time. From a phenomenological perspective, the question arises over what, if anything, is experienced in the *Ganzfeld* condition, especially after a period of time. For Gibson, the perception of distance involves the perception of surfaces and in the *Ganzfeld* condition there are no perceptible surfaces.

The studies of Metzger (1930) and Katz (1935) led Koffka to suppose that visual perception of a surface required heterogeneity (microstructure) in the proximal stimulus. Heterogeneous stimulation involves variations in either light intensity or wave-length across the field of view. Visual perception of a clearly defined and solid surface, as opposed to either a dense fog appearance in Metzger's results, or the "film color" of Katz's experiments, occurred only when micro-heterogeneity in light was presented to subjects (Katz, 1935; Metzger, 1930). Again Koffka thought it was necessary to postulate an organizational process in the brain in addition to the stimulus conditions (1935, p. 117). Given microstructure in stimulation, a perceived surface is articulated and maintained only because of dynamic forces in the brain. Gibson, who also derived much significance from the studies of Katz (1935) and Metzger (1930) did not draw the same conclusion. For Gibson, visual depth requires visual surfaces and the perception of surfaces involves heterogeniety in stimulation. The property of optical microstructure or "optical texture" was a real property for Gibson. Spatial variations or differences in light are relationships within optical energy. The term "heterogeniety" and its opposite, "homogeniety," do not, in this context, designate properties of individual light rays but rather of the extended stimulus display. Gibson applied Gestalt principles to stimulation though Gestalt psychologists were unwilling to do so. Understanding the *Ganzfeld* experiment and its implications for surface and distance perception became one of the first situations in which Gibson would apply his relational thinking about stimulation.

Although Koffka did not consider depth cues as a necessary condition for the general phenomena of visual perception of depth, he did suppose that they were involved in visual perception of specific distances of objects. His interpretation of how they functioned was that instead of binocular parallax or convergence yielding corresponding sensations that suggest distance as signs (Berkeley), these various stimulus conditions produce perception of distance without any learning or mediating sensations (Koffka, 1935, pp. 123–124, 160–161). In spite of this dissimilarity between Koffka's and Berkeley's views on perceived depth, both individuals postulated contributory and mediational processes in their explanations. Koffka suggested an organizational activity in the brain, while Berkeley proposed associated "tangible ideas"; hence, both stand in opposition to Gibson's contention that visual perception of depth is direct.

In comparing the theories of Berkeley and Gestalt psychologists a distinction can be made between the type of indirect theory that postulates a mental (conscious) mediational step (Berkeley's view) and a physiological mediational step (Gestalt view). At the conscious or phenomenological level, perception is immediate for the Gestalt psychologists. The Gestalt psychologists argued that phenomenologically there is no experience of elements being organized. Yet since they basically agreed with the analytic empiricists in describing stimulation in an elemental fashion, they were required to postulate an organizational process somewhere to account for the organization apparent in perceptual experience. Further, both the Gestalt psychologists and the analytic empiricists were conceptually bound up in a unidirectional causal chain model of perception, thus they both end up with causally indirect theories of perception.

In disagreement with Hering's (1861–1864) and Helmholtz's (1866) "point by point" explanations of seen location and movement, Koffka (1935, Chapter V, VII) hypothesized that location and movement of objects are seen with respect to a visual spatial framework. Drawing upon the general phenomena of figure-ground relations and the studies of Brown, Metzger, Duncker (1929), and Wertheimer (1912), Koffka (1935, Chapter VII) concluded that the figure-ground relation demonstrated that a figure's orientation was seen with respect to its surrounding ground. The figure-ground phenomena is the fact of forms being segregated from context or background within perceptual consciousness. Though perceived as distinct ("segregated"), a form or figure will be perceived relative to its surroundings. From Wertheimer's study (1912), he concluded that the spatial orientation of objects were seen with respect to a framework, for example, the orientation of objects within a room are perceived relative to the "mainlines" of the room which anchor the visual vertical and horizontal axes. Koffka also inferred from this study that the spatial framework for vision is visual and not tactual, and corresponded to the "mainlines" within visual perception. This last hypothesis represented another important difference between Koffka and Berkeley in that spacial determination for Berkeley was primarily, or exclusively, tactual or muscular in derivation. Gibson, in adopting Koffka's idea of a visual spatial framework, would also argue against the Berkeleian view that spatial determination does not arise through vision per se. Lastly, Koffka hypothesized that perceived movement is always relative to some visual reference point or framework. In all of the above experimental conditions, Koffka without exception, incorporated into his explanations a process of physiological organization that actually provided the framework, never supposing that the spatial framework could be furnished through the proximal visual stimulus.

Throughout this discussion of Gestalt psychology, the idea of a spatial framework has been a significant theme. Gibson would explain space perception in terms of the concept of a spatial framework and one of his main sources of inspiration for this was Koffka. This type of explanation of distance, depth, or space was also developed by William James. It is both wholistic and nondualistic. Individual locations are seen relative to the whole and this wholistic framework is not a frame of reference that exists distinct from those perceptual objects localized, e.g., a Newtonian frame of reference is distinct and dualistic and the Berkeleian theory of tactual-muscular space is also treated as distinct from those visual objects localized. Furthermore, the Berkeleian theory sees localization as a point-by-point process where each visual element is localized separately. At the other end of the theoretical continuum, experience is not built up from below (individual elements), but rather is ordered from above as in Plato's dualistic theory. At least at the level of experience, the Gestalt psychologists saw wholes and parts and entities and relationships as interdependent. They did emphasize wholes and relationships in their criticisms of analytic psychologists, but I believe that overall they held a more balanced view of interdependency. I believe that Wertheimer's critique of phenomenal elementarism, viz., that an unrelated presence of elements is meaningless should be interpreted as an expression of whole-part interdependency. The figure-ground demonstrations should likewise be interpreted as an expression of entity-relationship interdependency.

Throughout Koffka's *Principles* (1935, pp. 218, 228, 229, 234, 236) the term *invariant* can be frequently found. The word was employed by Koffka to refer to postulated relationships between perceived size and distance for a given retinal form's size and between perceived shape and slant for a given retinal form's shape. According to Koffka, neither variable of either pair is first perceived and then the other, but both size and distance, or shape and slant, occur simultaneously in visual perception.

These explanations deviated from those offered by most individuals in the empiricist tradition. For example, in Helmholtz (1866, Vol. III), visual perception of size was mediated by first "inferring" the distance of an object, and visual perception of the solid shape of an object depended on a prior "inference" of its slant. The classic empiricist explanations of distance and slant invoked mediational processes. Consequently, because size and solid shape are derived from distance and slant plus retinal size and form, size and solid shape involve a two-step mediational process. Koffka believed that size and shape, as well as distance and slant were phenomenologically immediate. Further in coupling together size and distance and slant and shape he was arguing for a process of interdependent determination of perceptual facts. The empiricist explanation, assuming an elementarism of perceptual units, proposed that each of the four perceptual facts noted above (distance, size, slant, and shape) involved a distinct computational process.

Koffka's contention that there existed invariant relations between these perceptual facts has become known as the "size-distance" and "shape-slant" invariance hypotheses (Hochberg, 1971). Within the period of his psychophysical program, Gibson (Gibson, 1950a; Gibson and Beck, 1955) did suppose that type of invariance between size and distance, or shape and slant, but his more recent usage of *invariance* (1966a) is not similar in meaning to Koffka's. In the 1960s, Gibson employed the term *invariance* to refer to the fact of persistence in the transforming optic array, a concept of order applied to stimulation that Koffka would have in principle rejected.

The related concepts of order and organization were a primary focus of attention for Gestalt psychologists, and their critiques of both structuralism and behaviorism emphasized the problems of a one-sided analytic, elementaristic psychology. Order and organization were seen everywhere by the Gestalt psychologists, except regarding stimulation. A significant difficulty with their traditional (elementaristic) treatment of stimulation can be noted using those very wholistic principles they invoked to criticize the analytic empiricists. The Gestalt psychologists contended that perceptual units (e.g., a figure) are segregated relative to their context (ground). Units (or entities) and their relationships emerge (or exist) together. Order and organization designate facts about relationships. Though the analytic empiricists divested particulars of order and organization, in a dualistic philosophy they included ordering principles in a second or separate realm. For the analytic empiricists, order is derived from the mental processes of memory and association. It makes no sense for Gestalt psychologists to talk about units or particular entities independent of relationships or wholistic organization of such entities. For example, they refer to points of stimulation as "spurious" units. At least regarding consciousness, physiology, and the environment, they saw units and organization bound together. In effect they rejected the ontological dualism of order and particulars. But how then can the physiological dynamics that give rise to phenomenological organization and segregation be applied to stimulus energy which lacks both order and particular determination? Though the Gestalt psychologists speak as if stimulation consisted of unrelated particular elements, according to their nondualistic philosophy of order and particulars, it could only be consistently thought of as a chaos possessing neither organization nor individuation. Consequently, a chaotic input would provide no basis for any particular perceptual experience, let alone a veridical experience. Those psychologists and other scientists who treated stimulation as a set of independent elements, with each element possessing certain intrinsic determinate values (e.g., wavelength or intensity), hypothesized that the mind related together and gave order to (spatially and temporally) such particulars. The Gestalt psychologists rejected this building block or two-stage process. The Gestalt psychologists end up with a dualistic picture for they do not relate together the environment and perceptual consciousness. In fact, the Gestalt psychologists end up in a subjectivistic quagmire reminiscent of Kant's problem of relating phenomena with noumena. If it is in principle impossible to sytematically and determinately relate perceptual experience to what is the presumed basis of such experience then a correspondence of experience and the world becomes meaningless. They interpose between mind and matter a chaos of energy and though they had interesting ideas regarding "Why do things look as they do?" (e.g., the relationship between individuated units and organization), they do not get at the question of "Why do things look as they are?"

Where the Gestalt psychologists make an advance over previous theories of perception is in their powerful critique of pure elementarism. What constitutes a unit? Elementarism advocates the idea that units are a given and exist prior to relationships. In fact, for pure elementarism relationships have only a derivative status. The Gestalt psychologists point out that at the phenomenological level, units exist within a context, viz., a field-ground or a framework. The empiricist's idea (which basically is also the atomists idea) of an absolute, fundamental starting point of elements is impossible.

With an understanding of the insights and limitations of Gestalt psychology, we have reached a point in our history where some basic theoretical conclusions can be drawn. Explanations of perception can be roughly divided into dualistic, materialistic monistic, and idealistic monistic. There are, of course, other divisions that could be used, for instance, nativistic-rationalist and empiricist, but I believe the dualistic-monistic division is more useful in understanding Gibson's significance in the history of perceptual theory. Dualistic theories inevitably face the problem of relating together incommensurable domains (e.g., mind and matter), stability and change, reality and appearance, or order and particulars. Monistic theories attempt to derive one domain from the other, inevitably finding this an impossible task, unless the presumed derivative domain is slipped in at the starting point. In fact, it may be impossible to conceptualize a monistic theory that is meaningful, for instance, elements without relationships or order without particulars. Aristotle's critique of both Plato's dualism and Democritus' materialism is founded upon the insight that although form and matter and the other conceptual distinctions of philosophy and science are meaningful, in reality one half of a duality cannot exist without the other.

Gibson's answer to the question regarding the veridicality of perception did not involve a return to the elementaristic and dualistic empiricism of the 18th and 19th centuries. Gibson, in fact, took ideas the Gestalt psychologists had developed regarding perceptual consciousness, e.g., the spatial framework and interdependent determination, and applied them to stimulation as well as the ecosystem as a whole. By describing stimulation in terms of concepts of spatial and temporal order, and relating this structured and ordered stimulus "array" to both the perceiver and the environment (the concept of information), Gibson was able to relate together "perceptual looks" with environmental reality. The theme of reciprocity runs through Gibson's development, becoming increasingly central in the ecological period (1960–1980). The concept of reciprocity is an extension and elaboration of Aristotle's approach, providing an alternative to both dualism and momism and their inherant limitations. Reciprocity provides the conceptual tool necessary for relating together the knowing subject (the perceiver) and the known world (the environment).

Chapter 10

THE ANTECEDENTS
of GIBSON'S PSYCHOPHYSICS

BORING'S PHENOMENOLOGY

There are many 20th century psychologists who influenced Gibson in different ways. In developing his ideas Gibson was eclectic and sometimes incorporated into his thinking ideas from a very diversified group of individuals. Though it may sound paradoxical, the novelty of Gibson's ideas in part derives from the diversity of influences on his development. The functionalist William James, the behaviorist Holt, and the Gestalt psychologist Koffka can be included as significant influences as already discussed but there are many others yet to be examined. They include the historian Edwin Boring, the psychophysical systematist Leonard Troland, the functionalist Egon Brunswik, the philosopher Ernest Cassirer, the biologist Walls, and the automotive engineer L. Crooks. Arthur Koestler (1964) argued that creative thought arises through a cross-fertilization of diverse and seemingly unrelated ideas. If we add to our list of influences the indirect but strong effects of evolutionary theory, Aristotelian philosophy, act psychology, and the input of Gibson's wife, the developmental psychologist, Eleanor Gibson, we then get an approximate picture of how varied were the themes and concepts that Gibson pulled together in his theories. In approaching the historical beginnings of Gibson's work, three of the aforementioned psychologists are examined. At this point in our history, Boring, Troland, and Brunswik are significant for they would effect Gibson's growth especially during his earlier psychophysical period, which we turn to in the next chapter.

The hypothesis that consciousness consisted of elements dominated psychological thought through the end of the 19th century, but phenomenal elementarism soon lost its almost exclusive stronghold in psychology. Titchener (1915) eventually moved from the hypothesis of elements to the hypothesis of attributes of consciousness, which he listed as quality, intensity, extensity, protensity, and attensity. In conjunction with Titchener's abandonment of conscious elements was the assault levied by Gestalt psychologists against the phenomenological validity of phenomenal elementarism. Elementarism, though, moved over into behavioristic psychology. Dewey, Holt, and later Tolman all thought it appropriate to continue and further refine the Gestalt attack on elementarism, but the focus shifted from consciousness to behavior. The idea taken from Newtonian science, that nature was built up from a set of basic elements continued to attract systematic and theoretical psychologists.

The great historian of psychology, Edwin Boring, who would later engage Gibson in a debate over the phenomenology of perception (1951, 1952b), developed a theory of consciousness that integrated features of both structuralism and Gestalt psychology. This theory would influence early Gibson. It seemed reasonable to Boring (1933) to hypothetically characterize consciousness neither in terms of attributes nor Gestalten, but in terms of dimensions. Portraying consciousness as consisting of dimensions appeared to Boring to be free of the narrow descriptive restrictions associated with introspection and structuralism. But at the same time, it provided a general systematic concept that, according to Boring, was missing in the phenomenology utilized by many Gestalt psychologists.

The four fundamental dimensions of consciousness which Boring proposed were quality, intensity, extensity, and protensity (1933, p. 23). These dimensions in turn may contain dimensions within themselves, for example, extensity in vision has at least two dimensions, viz., breadth and height. The term *dimension* implied the idea of a continuum of variation. For example, the qualitative dimension of hue is understood as the continuous series of variations red-orange-yellow-green-blue-purple-red. In this way, consciousness was not depicted as an immensely large list (443,544) of distinct qualities of elementary sensations as in Titchener (1896, p. 74).

The idea that perceptual consciousness can be described in terms of continuums of various dimensions impressed Gibson in his early development and he used it as early as 1937. When Gibson first began to describe perceptual consciousness in a systematic way in the 1930s, he adopted Boring's term "dimension" instead of sensations, elements, or segregated wholes. The elements of introspective psychology were illogical and too restrictive in scope for Gibson, whereas the phenomenological terms of Gestalt psychology were not systematic or analytical enough. Result-antly, Gibson's type of phenomenology differed in certain respects from that employed by Gestalt psychologists. The phenomenology of distance perception employed in Gibson's psychophysics is a noteworthy example of Boring's concept of conscious dimensions. Earlier, in the 1930s Gibson used the dimension concept to categorize and describe form perception.

For Gibson, the hypothesis of dimensions was a step away from sensory elements, yet it was only a step. A complete catalogue of consciousness assumes an elementaristic theory and Gibson would by the 1960s end up very close to the Gestalt psychologists in arguing that a complete catalogue in principle was impossible. From the 1960s onward Gibson proposed various systematic lists of environmental features per-ceived, but he invariably qualified such lists by adding that they were not intended to be exhaustive.

TROLAND'S "PSYCHOPHYSIOLOGY" AND GIBSON'S PSYCHOPHYSICS

The idea of a psychophysics of both sensation and perception was implicit in Descartes' theory of lawful causality between mind and matter, but in the 19th century, only a psychophysics of sensation developed. The complementary proposal of a psychophysics of perception is basic to the innovative character of Gibson's approach in his early period. Naturally, the question should arise as to whether the explicit suggestion, that there are corresponding complex features of stimulation and perception, origi-nated with Gibson. It seems that Gibson procured the basic idea of a psychophysics of perception from Leonard Troland. Gibson from the 1930s was quite familiar and sympathetic with the writings of Troland and there are numerous parallels between Gibson and Troland.

Leonard Troland's most comprehensive statement on the nature and problems of psychology is his three-volume, 1,200 page *Principles of Psychophysiology* (1929, 1930, 1932). Reflecting both a contemporary and historical scholarship rarely achieved, it aspires to be an integration of the facts and theories of psychology, past and present. But in spite of (or maybe because of) the author's eclectic aspirations, what emerges is not simply an encyclopedia of information, but a truly individual conceptuali-zation of psychology. *Principles of Psychophysiology,* at a systematic and meta-theoretical level, is similar to Boring's *Dimensions of Conscious-ness* (1933). During the turbulant 20s and early 30s, these works stand out as attempted syntheses of the principles of Titchener's structuralism, Gestalt psychology, and early behaviorism.

Troland's treatment of sensation and perception is a fine example of both his eclectism and uniqueness; though it is founded upon an integration of appropriated concepts it exhibits certain distinctive features. Troland's aim is to extract a common set of assumptions, shared by both structuralists and Gestalt psychologists, that would provide a conceptual scheme for systematically categorizing and interpreting the facts of sensory psychology. He transforms these presumably common assumptions, hitherto considered secondary, into explicit and central principles eliminating from his definitions those criteria invariably professed as crucial in distinguishing between sensation and perception.

Troland's philosophical starting point is a dualistic ontology similar to Descartes'. Prevalent at this time was the Machian inspired phenomenalism of Titchener (1910, 1929) which reduced the subject matter of all sciences to sensation, with the terms *physical* and *psychological* designating different functional groupings of the same sensations. But equally monistic, and also objectionable, was Watson's (1913, 1919) public-physicalistic phenomenalism; again we find the theory that all sciences, including psychology, are exclusively about observables. Only in Watson's case, these observables are facts of a physical world (Troland, 1929, pp. 36–42).

As an alternative to these views of science, Troland proposed a dualistic ontology. The physical sciences are empirical since they use observations as evidence for the hypotheses they test, but these hypotheses are not about experience; they deal with a physical world that is an inference from experience; the subject matter of the physical sciences is not to be identified with experience (1929, pp. 69–81). Consequently, experience becomes the sole province of psychology. Troland divides this science into introspective psychology, defined as the systematic description of immediate experiences, and psychophysiology which studies the physical conditions of experience (1929, pp. 82–84).

For Troland, experience encompasses as its constituents sensible qualities, their arrangement, "inner" feelings and thoughts, and relations or changes pertaining to any of these components. This is an introspective definition, but experience could also be defined psychophysiologically as a "system of elements and processes" precisely correlated "with the higher coordinate phases of nervous action in a waking, living organism." Consciousness is a "cross-section" or "snapshot" of experience at an instant in time; it consists of all the facts of an individual experience existing in the present (1929, pp. 85–90).

Concerning Troland's introspective position on the wholism-elementism controversy, in some respects he appears sympathetic with Gestalt psychology. For example, he argues that consciousness consists of complex wholes or configurations which contain parts. The properties of configurations, e.g., spatial forms, are wholistic in that they are not introspectively equivalent to the properties of their parts. An exhaustive listing of the parts of configuration and those parts' attributes does not yield a complete description of the configuration. But complementarily Troland believes that the parts of configuration need to be included in introspective description; introspection also involves analysis, and here he sides with the structuralists.

Koffka and Köhler never rejected the role of analysis in science; they only opposed the extreme elementaristic interpretation of scientific analysis advocated by many structuralist psychologists. Yet, the Gestalt emphasis was on wholes rather than parts. Troland wished to strike a balance between wholism and elementarism. If every complex configuration was simply given a separate designation, ignoring its possible analysis, then the number of phenomenological names would become too numerous and unmanageable. According to Troland, this tendency toward an undesirable proliferation of terms can be found in Gestalt psychology. Through the analysis of complex facts, descriptions achieve a simplicity and precision necessary in science (1929, pp. 40, 70, 106–112; 1932, pp. 134–135).

Although Troland distinguishes between complex wholes and their parts, he does not believe that either precedes the other in consciousness. In simply considering consciousness per se the experiences of parts and configurations are equally immediate. Consequently, it is imperative in correctly describing Troland's view that the idea that wholes have parts be clearly distinguished from three other hypotheses that could be confused with it. First, he rejected the idea that the complex whole is formed through a combining together of elements. He also rejected the idea that such building-block elements are the actual *parts* of the completed whole. Also, he did not believe that a complete description of the complex whole is achievable through a listing of parts. (These three hypotheses are usually associated with structuralist psychology, though Wundt definitely rejected the second). Troland was not so foolhardy as to deny that an experienced square contained parts, but he rejected these other hypotheses. These other hypotheses, as a group, summarize some of the essentials of the theory of elements of consciousness or elementarism (Boring, 1950, pp. 221–222, 329, 333, 384–386). Troland's treatment of wholes and parts moves away from the monistic extremes of wholism and elementarism. He views wholes and parts, at least at the level of consciousness, as equal in status. In this regard, he is close to Gibson's treatment of wholes and parts.

Troland cannot distinguish sensation from perception on the grounds that sensation is immediate and perception is a mediated product of sensation. Troland, in discussing the neurophysiology of processes that yield sensory consciousness, describes it as a synergistic activity. Numerous sensory pathways converge and are integrated into one unified, complex state in the brain that correlates with immediate consciousness. So he does speak in terms of parts combining to yield wholes, but this is a hypothesized fact of neurophysiology, and not a fact of consciousness. In consciousness, no such combining of parts into wholes reveals itself in introspection. Both are just as immediate (1932, pp. 20–137). We could ask, does he simply distinguish sensation and perception in terms of parts and wholes, i.e., does he refer to the parts of configurations as sensations and the configurations taken as a whole as perceptions? As we will see, he does not.

Determining the conditions of consciousness constitutes the remaining half of psychology. For Troland, these conditions lie in the hypothetical physical world. The term *psychophysics* refers to the study of relations between this physical world and consciousness, whereas the more restricted term *psychophysiology* designates the science of relations between consciousness and the physical organism. In either case, the goal is to discover *functional* relations or correlations between variations in consciousness and in the physical world. What is achieved in approaching this goal is increasing interpredictability, given one specific physical variable and its value, the correlated conscious variable and its value is predictable and vice versa (1929, pp. 139–144, 148–149).

Troland introduces the concept of the response arc in explaining his meaning of phychophysical correspondence. Beginning with objects in the environment, we find a sequence of causally dependent stages (i.e., a unidirectional causal chain of events) proceeding from objects to stimulation, to sense-organ processes and so forth, that terminates in effects produced upon the environment by movements of the organism. Each succeeding stage in the response arc is causally dependent upon the previous one and causally determinate of the next stage (1929, pp. 156–160). Basically, this is Descartes' chain model (see Diagram 14).

The problem of psychophysics and psychophysiology is defined as the ascertainment of functional relations bctween consciousness and variables of the response arc. Although Troland presumes that the "adjustor phrase" cerebral processes are the immediate correlates of consciousness, this does not preclude for him the possibility of functional relations between consciousness and earlier stages in the response arc. Since the environment is causally related to stimulation, which in turn is causally related to sense organ processes, etc., earlier stages in the response arc are causally related to the immediate determinant of consciousness. If this is the case, earlier stages should then show degrees of correlations, at least in some respects, with consciousness, the immediate conditions of consciousness in the brain supposedly showing perfect correlation with experience (1929, pp. 161–165).

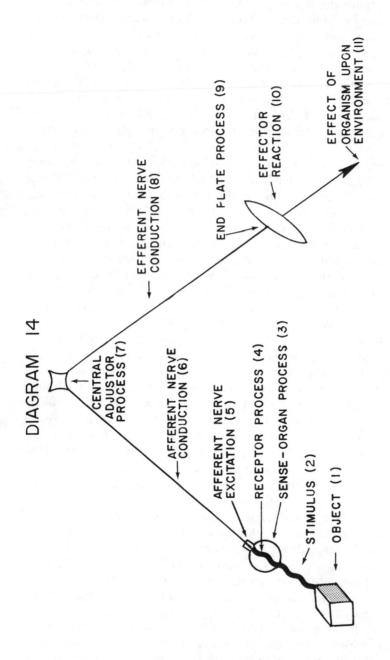

DIAGRAM 14

The phrase *psychophysical correspondence* was used by Gibson to designate correlations between experience and proximal stimulation (Gibson, 1950a). Troland uses the term "psychophysical" more generally to designate relationships between experience and anything physically outside of the organism's skin. Depending on how "proximal stimulus" is understood, stimulus-experience correlation may or may not be an example of "psychophysical correspondence." For example, if we agree that the retinal image is the visual proximal stimulus, then discovered correlations between it and visual experience would be psychophysiological; whereas if the visual stimulus is identified as the sheaf or array of light adjacent with the eye's outer surface, viz., the cornea, then correlations found between this optical array and experience would be psychophysical.

Gibson in his psychophysics followed Troland on the general model of the response arc. During the 1940s and 1950s, Gibson saw perception as caused by physical variables earlier in the response arc and lawfully correlated with them because of the causal connections. In the 1960s, Gibson dropped Troland's psychophysical model in favor of a view of psychophysical coordination similar to Dewey.

Troland's concept of psychophysical causation, though unidirectional and mechanistic, is not as simple as Helmholtz or Fechner. According to most structuralists the phenomenal results of excitation of any particular neural unit was unchanging. Regarding sensations of color, any one excited neural unit will have a specific sensation of color corresponding to it when the intensity and spectral composition of light stimulating it remains the same. Conversely, Troland supposed that for any stage in the response arc, the reaction at stage $X + 1$ is a dual function of the reaction at the previous stage X and the momentary state of $X + 1$. Because the state of stage $X + 1$ varies as a function of its previous reactions, there is no simple functional relation between the states of stages X and $X + 1$ (1929, p. 160). Gibson in his adaptation study experiments adopted a similar view of psychophysical correlation incorporating Boring's dimensions of consciousness and Troland's "flexible" interpretation of psychophysical relationships.

Having defined his concepts of psychophysiological explanation and the response arc, Troland provides psychophysical definitions of the basic psychological processes such as sensations, perception, and volition. Each psychological concept will refer to a relationship between experience and some stage of the response arc. Different psychological terms do not refer to different kinds of experience; they refer to relations (correlations) experience shows with different stages in the response arc (1929, p. 215).

For many, perception is thought of as a synthetic process, often involving the combining of sensations and memory elements. Though Gestalt psychologists reject the ideas of elements and a synthesizing process in consciousness, perception involves a synthetic process that occurs neurologically. Though Troland accepts as almost a truism that a synthetic process occurs neurologically, he not only rejects, as did the Gestalt psychologists, that such a process is introspectively available, but also rejects the notion that we should use this presumed neurological fact of synthesis in arriving at a definition of perception (1929, pp. 215–216, 228–229, 233).

For Troland, the fundamental fact of what psychologists and laymen call perception is that it is awareness of the objective environment or world. If either Gestalt or structuralist psychologists classify illusions or hallucinations as examples of perception, they would then object to Troland's suggested criteria. But Troland apparently believes they would not, and would be willing to accept his characterization of common opinion as valid.

Because Troland distinguishes between experience and the physical world, he must say that experience, when it is perceptual, is correlated with or representative of the physical world and not that the physical world is ever part of the actual content of experience. If there is a synthetic or reintegrative neurological process in perception, we should take this fact as instrumental and secondary to the basic characteristic of perception, viz., objective correspondence. Using this objective feature of perception as his starting point, Troland proposes both a psychophysiological definition of perception and a description of the science of perception.

All stages in the response arc are hypothesized as correlated with features of experience, including what Troland designates as the objective stage. The objective stage of the response arc is that set of conditions outside the skin or sense-organs that effect the response sequence in the organism; it includes the environment and stimulation (1929, p. 229). Because the basic fact of perception is its objective correspondence we can define the science of perception as the investigation and ascertainment of correlations between experience and the objective stages of the response arc. For example, concerning vision we find correspondences between perceived size and objective size, or perceived depth and objective distance. In defining the visual stimulus as an optical projection to an eye, we find correlations between the arrangement of patterns in this optical projection and the arrangement of colored forms in visual experience (1929, pp. 324–326).

So what exactly is perception? It is not a particular kind of experience, but rather a particular kind of *relationship* between experience and the response arc. It is that set of relationships—more precisely psychophysical correlations—between experience and the objective response arc. If we treat the objective response arc as the independent variable and experience as the dependent variable, then insofar as experience is *functionally dependent* on the objective response arc, it is perceptual. So in saying that a feature of the environment is perceived, Troland means that there is a representation of it in experience that varies concomitantly and lawfully with changes in that feature; hallucinations are consequently excluded as instance of perception. The important parallel between Troland and Gibson is that they both take veridicality as a basic criteria of perception. Gibson excludes illusions and hallucinations as examples of perception.

Defining perception in this manner cuts across the dichotomy of wholes and parts, as well as ignoring the supposed synthetic nature of perception. Troland distinguishes between elements, attributes, configurations, and forms in experience (1929, pp. 113–138; 1932, pp. 20–21); more generally, he speaks of the component (parts and attributes) and composite (compounds) facts of experience. In investigating perception, we find psychophysical relations for both component and composite facts of experience (1929, pp. 126–129).

Troland's concept of perception is functional rather than structural and necessarily includes an epistemological criterion of objective veridicality. Similarly, Gibson, even in his psychophysics of perception, understood perception as having an objective reference. This identification of perception with objective knowledge is functionalistic and avoids the structuralist-Gestalt pitfall of defining perception intrinsically without reference to the environment.

For structuralists, sensations were thought of as the elements of consciousness, but Troland argues that the criterion actually used was not mentalistic or introspective. We can ask why structuralists included in their list of sensations certain items and not others or why Titchener (1929) believed the so-called sensations have certain attributes and not others. According to Troland, the answer that defenders of the concept of sensation offer is to view sensations as the conscious correlates of the receptor process. The receptor process can be thought to include activity in the receptor cells of the sense organs and the connecting sensory nerves, but not any transforming processes of the cerebrum (1930, pp. 1–4).

If Köhler's and Koffka's critique of the "constancy hypothesis" is compared with Troland's interpretation of the structuralist's concept of sensation, one finds a noticeable similarity. The Gestalt psychologists argued that structuralists allowed as sensations and their attributes only what was predictable from the "constancy hypothesis." Because this hypothesis is psychophysiological, Troland and the Gestalt psychologists agree that the structuralist's real basis for listing sensations and their attributes was not introspective (Koffka, 1935, pp. 80–98; Köhler, 1913, 1941, 1947, pp. 67–99). In fact, what we observe is that judgments regarding the "immediate" objects of a sense invariably involve theoretical assumptions about the total receptive process including cerebral and stimulus factors. If Gestalt, Gibsonian, and Berkeleian descriptions of sensory-perceptual consciousness were compared, the differences are significant and correspond with basic differences in theoretical vocabulary and ideas.

In his history of perceptual theory, Pastore (1971) has followed the Gestalt psychologists in arguing that empiricist theories include under sensation (or immediate experience) those features predictable by the constancy hypothesis. The problem with this interpretation is in understanding how retinal stimulation should be described. Berkeley's rationale for rejecting distance perception was based on restricting vision to the number of physical dimensions of the retinal image. Therefore, Berkeley did not consider visual stimulation restricted to localized individual points in his distance perception argument and the Köhler-Pastore interpretation is invalid. Yet although Berkeley was an idealist and most later empiricists who followed him, strict phenomenalists, Troland is correct in noting that empiricist decisions regarding immediate sensory experiences were not primarily based on introspection. Empiricist decisions had physiological and physical assumptions behind their descriptions of experience derived from Newtonian science and Cartesian physiology. Gestalt phenomenological descriptions presupposed field organization concepts, and Gibson's early phenomenology used dimensional (Boring), functionalistic, and relational concepts. Theory and fact are not independent of each other. The professed ideal of a pure description of experience was never in reality achieved.

Troland foregoes the professed elementaristic definition of sensation, replacing it with a psychophysiological one. Under the topic of sensation he treats all those facts of consciousness which show correlation with the afferent portion of the response arc. Sensation, like perception, is not a particular kind of experience; the science of sensation studies correlations between consciousness and afferent processes; hence the sensation of red, for example, refers to the psychophysiological relation between a certain variable quality of experience and certain variations in the afferent processes. Strictly speaking, sensation, like perception, has no introspection or mentalistic meaning per se. It is a relational concept (1930, pp. 5–8). Yet Troland is in the same position as the structuralists and Gestalt psychologists at least in that he does assume a particular theory of sensory processes.

Troland is able to retain the concept of sensation without having to suppose the elementaristic or building-block theory of consciousness. Complex consciousness is not built up out of simple elements; rather it is structured and integrated immediately, as the Gestalt psychologists argued. But this does not imply that the complex cannot be introspectively analyzed or that the complex does not consist of parts. Simply, we should not commit the kind of error that Empedocles once did, when he hypothesized that since the human body consists of parts (e.g., arms, legs, head, etc.), it was originally formed by these parts coming together. Although sensory consciousness contains forms like squares, the square is not put together from four lines.

Troland's functional distinction between sensation and perception seems very similar to Gibson's corresponding distinction in his *Senses Considered as Perceptual Systems* (1966a). For Gibson, perception is objective, whereas sensation is experience correlated with physiological activity. Gibson also follows Troland in rejecting the idea that perceptions are built up from sensations. Sensation and perception are understood as different types of functional relations of experience to the physical world. Where Gibson differs from Troland is in rejecting in his ecological approach the ontological dualism of Troland's psychophysics and psychophysiology.

The physical energy adjacent to the surface of a sense-organ is referred to by Troland as the stimulus. For vision, accordingly, the retinal image is not the stimulus for visual perception, but rather the light entering the cornea (1930, p. 10). Consequently, Troland's psychophysics of perception was simply the general working hypothesis that objective experience is a function of stimulation. In his early development Gibson thought of visual perception as a function of stimulation, but he considered the retinal image to be the visual stimulus (1950a). Only later did Gibson abandon this view in favor of the optic array.

Troland's general description of the, visual stimulus (1929, pp. 325–326) exhibits some important resemblances with Gibson's depiction of the optic array. Several are worth noting. Troland described the visual stimulus in terms of natural perspective and not pictorial perspective. Secondly, the optical basis for vision was depicted as "two cones having their apices at the respective pupils and having common bases on the reflecting surfaces" (1929, p. 325). Optically it consists of a "sheaf of rays converging to a point" (1929, p. 325). In addition, this "ocular ray sheaf" contains angular subdivisions. Troland remarked, "If we consider a group of lines which correspond with the natural subdivisions of the reflective surfaces before the eye, each component of the surface will be represented by a definite solid angle" (1929, p. 326). Troland falls into the line of thought stretching from Euclid to da Vinci. More generally, the emphasis is placed on optical structure in the physical medium rather than on a "thing-like" image that is viewed by the perceiver (homunculus).

One last connection between Troland and Gibson concerns Gibson's idea of perceptual systems as functional and not anatomical in delimitation. Troland suggested that receptors should be classified according to their functions and not their anatomical characteristics (1930, pp. 13–14), but his resulting classification showed almost total overlap with a categorization based on anatomical differences. Aristotle's original classification of the senses had been primarily functional, based on the "correlative objects" of sensory awareness. Where Gibson more dramatically moves toward a functional clasification of the senses is in his inclusion of exploratory (muscular-skeletal) structures in a perceptual system.

If Boring provided early Gibson with a systematic concept for describing perceptual consciousness, Troland offered a way to scientifically conceptualize the relationship between perceptual consciousness and stimulus variables. In effect, Troland suggested there were laws of perception as well as laws of sensation. Gibson's approach in the 1930s and 1940s was to study lawful relations between perceptual dimensions and corresponding stimulus dimensions, for example, inclination and curvature of lines. Such perceptual and stimulus variables were more complex than those mental and physical elements examined in structuralism and the psychophysics of sensations. To complete the explanatory picture, there is another significant relationship that Gibson would increasingly address. What is the relationship between stimulation and the environment? This question was a concern of Egon Brunswik.

BRUNSWIK AND PROBABILISTIC FUNCTIONALISM

The effect of Brunswik's (1903–1955) approach to visual perception upon Gibson's thinking was both positive and negative. Although Brunswik's (1935, 1943, 1944, 1952, 1955a, 1955b, 1956) position was in many respects nothing but a sophisticated version of Berkeley's views, there are certain noteworthy variations. In some respects, Brunswik's substantive and methodological views closely resemble Heider's ecological psychology. Knowledge of Brunswik's individualized modification of empiricist psychology is requisite in understanding Gibson's thinking in his 1950 book, because Gibson's historical understanding and criticism of depth cues and Berkeley's theory relied heavily upon Brunswik's own particular explication. Because of Gibson's Brunswikian influenced depiction of Berkeley's theory, Gibson in 1950 was not fully cognizant of the actual and crucial disagreements between his psychophysics of visual perception and Berkeley's position.

In distinguishing between the proximal and distal stimulus, Brunswik emphasized the lack of "univocality" between such "causal couplings" (Brunswik 1935, 1943, 1944). For Brunswik, the "distal stimulus" was the environment. The retinal depth cues, described by Brunswik, were only probabilistically correlated in variation with variations in the distance of objects. Recall that Berkeley formulated and advocated the role of signs of distance independently of this fact of probable correlations. Gibson in 1950 continuously spoke as if proximal stimuli were thought of as cues, i.e., requiring association and inference, because they were only probabilistically related to distal events, but this was only an addendum offered by Brunswik. Gibson (1950a) contrasted his view that there are univocal relations between the environment and the proximal stimulus with Brunswik's belief in probable relations. This comparison was valid, but Gibson mistakenly took this to be the essential difference between his concept of stimulation and the core meaning of distance signs.

Boring and Harper in 1948 proposed a demarcation in meaning between the terms *clue* and *cue,* both of which had been employed in referring to signs of distance. They suggested that when *clue* is used a process analogous to reasoning was implied, e.g., in Helmholtz and Locke. Conversely, cue should denote an automatic or mechanical process, e.g., in Berkeley and James Mill.

The term *clue* is more applicable than *cue* in Brunswik's idea of visual perception. Brunswik adopted what he referred to as a "ratio-morphic model" of visual perception (1952). The intervening process between depth clues and the final perception was characterized as a "strategy" or "reasoning type inference" (1952). It was from Helmholtz's notion of "unconscious inference" that Brunswik drew his historical inspiration, but inasmuch as clues were now thought of as probabilistic, the mediational process for Brunswik was more analogous to reasoning then for Helmholtz. When Gibson disputed the "Theory of Clues" and the hypothesis of inference in perception (Gibson, 1950a, pp. 19–22), his depiction of the position he was criticizing was derived primarily from Helmholtz and Brunswik who were actually "clue theorists." Gibson, because of his one-sided historical perspective on this point, overintellectualized the intervening step suggested by most Berkeleians.

This historical misrepresentation is mentioned because it is the contention of the author contra Gibson *circa* 1950 that the important difference between Gibson in 1950 and Berkeley that afforded Gibson a way of avoiding psychological mediation in either sense ("clue or cue") was not just Gibson's belief in optical-environmental univocal specificity, but

Gibson's rejection of the simulative assumption and the homunculus hypothesis. Though Berkeley did not believe in a homunculus, as Armstrong (1956, 1960) correctly points out, Berkeley's theory contains conclusions (the necessity of simulation) that only follow if a homunculus was assumed.

In contrast, there are some similarities between Brunswik and Gibson. Brunswik (1956) maintained that research in visual perception involved representative studies of the "ecological validities" of depth cues. This type of investigation would consist of ascertaining in normal situations the correlation coefficients between proximal stimuli and such distal facts as the sizes and distances of objects. The correlation coefficients discovered would be the ecological validities of cues in proximal stimulation. Although Brunswik thought of ecological validities as probabilistic, i.e., less than 1.0, the general idea of a systematic and representative study of the relations between proximal stimuli and the environment was anticipative of Gibson's ecological optics. In fact, it was Brunswik's exposition of this ecological aspect of research in visual perception and his conviction that proximal-distal relations were correlational and probabilistic that instigated Gibson's ecological optics. Brunswik raised the issue of stimulus-environment relations to the forefront of perceptual theory. Except for Heider, the issue had not received much systematic attention. Gibson, in his ecological optics, accepted the challenge and in fairness to Gibson's 1950 interpretation of depth cue theory, psychologists, in theory and research, did not express themselves as if they believed there existed a detailed and rich set of exact relationships between stimulation and the environment.

As a function of representative samplings, a systematic description of the normal environment became necessary. Brunswik's concern with characterizing the typical naturalistic surroundings of human activity reflected both his interest in ascertaining the ecological validities of proximal stimuli and his overall functionalistic approach to visual perception. Somewhat identical factors in Gibson's thinking motivated him in the same direction, but Brunswik never developed to any comparable extent the ecology of perception implicit in his proposals. This is assuredly due, in part, to his early death, but Brunswik's ecology, to the degree to which it was formulated, was severely handicapped. His descriptions of the environment and various optical signs were limited to the traditional terminology of "objects" and "depth cues." On the other hand, evolutionary and post-Newtonian concepts have played a much greater role in guiding the development of Gibson's ecology and ecological optics.

Part III

THE PSYCHOPHYSICS
of PERCEPTION

Chapter 11_____

THE GENESIS
of GIBSON'S PSYCHOPHYSICS

ADAPTATION AND PSYCHOPHYSICAL CORRESPONDENCE

While Gibson was a graduate student at Princeton, Holt arrived from Harvard to join the faculty at Princeton. Holt, as previously mentioned, was a behaviorist, attempting to redescribe all of the supposed facts of consciousness, such as perception, attention, intention, and so on, in terms of behavior. Gibson, already enthusiastic about the ongoing behavioristic movement, was naturally sympathetic toward Holt's "motor theory of consciousness." Holt's behaviorism undoubtedly reinforced Gibson's functionalistic philosophy, because one noteworthy feature of early behaviorism was its emphasis on a psychology that had practical applications and tied the animal more closely to the environment. Further, behaviorism was monistic, attempting to avoid the dualism of body and mind.

Another feature of early behaviorism that Holt and most others within this movement supported, was an emphasis on learning. Behaviorism was empiricistic. Gibson emerged as a "radical empiricist" (as he says, 1967a, p. 129) through his contact with Holt. Due to its origin in Locke, Berkeley, and Hume, empiricism tended to be both associative and elementaristic in theory. Gibson began his postdoctoral research in visual perception within the Berkeleian tradition. He initially believed that visual perception of form, distance, and so on, depended on visual signs being associated with muscular responses. Gibson was, in part, shocked out of his Berkeleian view of perceptual learning in his research in visual adaptation (Gibson, 1933, 1937a, 1937b; Gibson and Radner, 1937). On the other hand, one leftover from Gibson's "Berkeleian" days is his stated opposition to the hypothesis that innate ideas are involved in visual perception. Gibson is not a nativist in the sense of Kant, Descartes, or Hering, but there are certain themes in nativism and rationalism that Gibson at least tries to address. Gibson stayed a radical empiricist in believing that all knowledge comes through the senses, but he rejected associationism and the building block view of perception, putting much more weight on natural structure and organization as had the nativists and rationalists.

Gibson's 1928 doctoral thesis attempted to refute a recently published study by Wulf (1922), and reflected his early Berkeleian background. Wulf had interpreted the results of his study concerning the reproduction of visually perceived forms in a manner that appeared to Gibson definitely antagonistic to an empiricist view of visual perception. After receiving his Ph.D., Gibson joined the faculty at Smith College, where his first publication "The Reproduction of Visually Perceived Forms" (1929) reported the results of his thesis work. On the other hand, the majority of Gibson's (Gibson, 1929, 1934a, 1935, 1936a, 1936b, 1939a, 1939b, 1950c; Gibson and Gibson, 1934, 1950; Gibson, Jack & Raffell, 1932; Gibson & Hudson, 1935; Gibson & Raffell, 1936) earliest published studies did not deal specifically with visual perception but with conditioning, memory, and related topics. His focal interest in perception emerged gradually during the 1930s and 1940s.

Wulf (1922) studied how outline forms were reproduced by subjects after a temporal delay during which the forms could no longer be inspected by the subjects. He attempted to systematically describe the changes in the reproduced forms relative to the actual forms in terms of Gestalt dynamical principles of neural organization.

Gibson oppositely argued from his results (1929) that changes in the reproduced forms were explainable in terms of the effect of past perception or memory. At one point in his paper he stated,

> The types of change here observed may all be explained, it is believed, by the supposition that the experience of the individual has brought into existence certain habitual modes of perception, and that these perceptual habits, rather than the laws of configurations, condition the changes observed. (1929, p. 35)

Gibson was proposing, without much further explication, that past experience with often encountered forms effects ongoing visual perception. A few pages later, he suggested, "(These) phenomena might be explained by the hypothesis that new perceptual activity in the observer takes place in terms of old perceptual habits" (1929, p. 38). This conclusion of Gibson concerning the determinants of visual perception could be interpreted as significantly different from his later belief (1950a) that past experience doesn't contribute to visual perception. The dissimilarity is, though, not clear cut, since what Gibson meant by visual perception in this early article was not exactly what he later meant by it. What is apparent is that Gibson sounds like a Berkeleian to the degree that he does make explicit his explanation of his experimental results.

Within this study, Gibson was actually investigating determinants of misperception and not perception. The changes in reproduction described in his study represented divergencies from the actual forms on the cards. Accordingly, the effect of perceptual habits is postulated to explain mistakes or errors, for example, differences between the form and its reproduction. Gibson, therefore, in stating that his experimental results could imply that perceptual habits affect ongoing perception, was not drawing his later emphasized distinction between perception and misperception. In the future, Gibson without exception or qualification thought of perception as *veridical perception,* and was primarily concerned with explaining the veridicality of perception.

There are two further divergencies in approach between this early study and Gibson's later work that are worth mentioning. First, Gibson used rather ambiguous figures in this study; something he later sought to totally avoid. Secondly, his stimuli were two-dimensional outline forms. Gibson would later argue against the ecological appropriateness of employing outline forms in research directed towards understanding perception in natural surroundings. Such forms are not very representative of the most basic facts of the environment. Neither the environment nor stimulation is as structurally impoverished as two-dimensional outline forms. Both are richer. In turn, ambiguity and misperception can be tied to such nonrepresentative, impoverished experimental conditions.

On the other hand, Gibson supposed that his expressions "perceptual activity" and "perceptual habits" were "functionalistic" (1929, p. 38). He intentionally avoided, in using these phrases, any reference to "memory images" or "perceptual images"; this choice was apparently motivated by a wish to circumvent an explanation stated in mental terms. This terminological preference of Gibson does seem to reflect the influence of Holt's behaviorism and functionalism, but the precise nature of these relationships cannot be uncovered from his remarks in this publication.

From Berkeley's perspective, spatial emplacement of visual sensations was a function of associated nonvisual (tactual-motor) sensations. One hypothesis connected with this basic theory was that an altering of the normal visual-motor connections would eventually produce different spatial meanings for each visual sensation. Such a modification was possible through the wearing of prism spectacles (Helmholtz, 1866; Stratton, 1896, 1897). Distorting prism spectacles could be constructed that would reinvert the retinal image, curve optical lines to the right or the left, or in some other manner alter the incoming light. Upon first wearing distorting prism spectacles, the visual world appeared spatially altered from normal analogous to the way the spectacle-produce-retinal image differed from the normal retinal image. Both Helmholtz (1866) and Stratton (1896, 1897) discovered that after a sufficient duration of wearing spectacles, the visually perceived world became relatively normal again. This normalization, according to them, took place because new associations had been formed between visual sensations and muscular sensations. Insofar as visual sensations were merely signs of spatial relations, they could, in principle, yield visual perceptions of any given spatial value depending upon the spatial value of the muscular sensations associated with them.

In 1929, Gibson followed in the tradition of the investigations of Stratton and Helmholtz and began a series of experiments to determine the effects of prism spectacles that produced curvature of straight vertical lines. As he much later (1967a, pp. 132–133) remarked, he initiated these experiments to "verify" the interpretation of Stratton that prism adaptation eventuated because visual experience was corrected by "tactual" experience. Upon first approaching these studies he accepted "Bishop Berkeley's theory of visual perception" (1967a, p. 133).

The results that Gibson obtained, reported in 1931 and published in 1933, had a negative effect on his Berkeleian convictions. Initially, Gibson had his spectacle-wearing subjects sit motionless, but visual adaptation and the predictable negative after-effect still occurred. Phenomenally curved lines became straight and upon removing the spectacles, physically straight lines appeared proportionally curved in the opposite direction. Supposing that the source of visual adaptation and correction could be eye movements, he attempted to have his subjects fixate without moving their eyes, but he obtained the same results. Adaptation was of comparable strength to subjects who were allowed to move their eyes.

At this point, an ingenious idea occurred to Gibson. Why not have subjects look at physically curved lines without spectacles? If adaptation to curvature was a consequence of new associations between vision and muscular-tactual factors, then no new associations should form where there was no alteration of normal associations, and there should be no adaptation. Instead, Gibson found both adaptation (inspected curved lines gradually appeared straighter) and negative after-effects (in post-adaptation conditions physically straight lines were phenomenally curved in the opposite direction). The amount of adaptation and negative after-effect were slight but they occurred in most subjects. Also, Gibson observed comparable effects with physically bent lines. In addition, when curved lines were traced tactually, unaccompanied by visual inspection, there were kinesthetic adaptation effects and negative after-effects.

It should be noted that from this point onward, Gibson's view of perceptual learning in vision began to diverge from the Berkeleian view of associations of visual and tactual-motor sensations. The experimental results of this 1933 study appeared to demonstrate that whatever the basis of visually perceived spatial relations it could not, in all cases, be associated tactual-muscular ideas (or responses). As for an alternative explanation, Gibson did not present a clear one until much later.

In attempting to systematically describe and explain these results, Gibson came to some general conclusions concerning visual perception that are historically significant. Several fundamental topics of continuing importance in Gibson's approach such as psychophysical correspondence, visual experience, and the sensation-perception distinction can be discussed in the contexts of the implications he drew from these studies. The series of adaptation studies that Gibson would conduct became a "crucial experiment" in how it effected his theoretical perspective.

Given this varying relation between phenomenally curved lines and curved lines on the retina, what conclusions did Gibson draw concerning the relation of stimulation and perception? First, a curved line on the retina is not a necessary condition for a corresponding phenomenally curved line. This, of course, is in conflict with the simulative assumption. Seventy years before, Helmholtz had noted this fact of nonsimulative correspondence between retinal forms and perceived forms after wearing prism spectacles. As such, Helmholtz believed that form was not determined visually but muscularly, i.e., form was not a visual sensation caused by the forms in the retinal image, but was added by associated muscular (motor) memories. Gibson would not accept this explanation of visually perceived curvature after adaptation, since his nonprism conditions excluded possible new muscular associations. (But, as will be shown subsequently, in a later article (Gibson & Mowrer, 1938) Gibson was still confident, contra-Koffka and pro-Berkeleian, that spatiality in visual perception was fundamentally a function of nonvisual factors.) Furthermore, Gibson rejected a possible Gestalt explanation that implied a lack of exact stimulus-phenomenal correspondence and a process of internal organization (1933, p. 30).

Although any one degree of curvature of a line in the retinal image can be correlated with different curvatures of phenomenal lines, Gibson contended that there existed a flexible psychophysical correspondence of the phenomenal and physical *continuums* of curvature. It is flexible because changes can occur between specific physical values of curvature and correlated phenomenal values. Even after adaptation, there is still psychophysical correspondence. It is just that the specific physical correlate values of individual phenomenal values have changed. Also the psychophysical shift is describable in terms of continuums and not individual elements, because if any one retinal-phenomenal correspondence is altered, all other relations of commensurate phenomenal-physical correspondence change proportionally. (This shift only happens between phenomenal values and the local area of the retina upon which the curved line was presented during adaptation.) The phenomenal shift even occurred for physical values of curvature not presented during the adaptation condition. Hence, it was phenomenal curvature conceived of as a set, system, or continuum, that shifted in physical correlates, and not independent phemonenal elements. For example, he stated, "When a retinal curved line is correlated with a phenomenal less curved line, then for the area in question a retinal straight line is correlated with a phenomenal oppositely—curved line" (1933, p. 31).

Expanding on this idea of phenomenal continuums, Gibson suggested a possible analogy between perception of a line and perception of color. "For both types of perception, experiences may be classified into a continuous series with two opposed kinds at the ends and a definite and unique neutral experience in the middle, into which they both merge" (1933, p. 28).

Gibson's proposal of phenomenal continuums was strikingly similar to Boring's (1933) hypothesis that perceptual experience, in general, can be described in terms of continuous dimensions. Although by this point it had only limited application, Gibson did not owe his initial proposal to Boring, because Gibson's 1933 article was submitted for publication October 9, 1931, while Boring's book was not published until 1933. On the other hand, by 1936 Gibson had read Boring's book (cited in Gibson 1937a). Gibson remarked much later (1967a, p. 130) that Boring's hypothesis of dimensions of consciousness had a great effect on him. What Boring's book furnished Gibson was a systematic and general term for characterizing perceptual consciousness that was close in meaning to his own idea of continuums and avoided elementarism.

Gibson's hypothesis of flexible psychophysical correspondence ran counter to a long tradition in the psychology of visual sensation. In the Berkeleian tradition of the nineteenth century, it was assumed by Helmholtz, among others, that psychophysical correspondence was rigid. A elemental stimulus produces a corresponding elemental sensation. For Helmholtz, there was psychophysical correspondence between intensity and wavelength values of points of retinal stimulation and the brightness of hue of visual sensations. In 1933, Gibson discovered a flexible psychophysical correspondence for curvature values, and was convinced of a similar type of alterability concerning the psychophsics of color sensations. By 1936 he had become familiar with and impressed by Troland's (1930) suggestion that this flexibility of psychophysical correspondence applied to numerous other cases. In 1937, Gibson, following Troland, proposed an extension in the scope of application of the hypothesis of flexible psychophysical correspondence.

In 1933 Gibson had noted that at least color exhibited the same kind of adaptation and negative after-effects as curved lines. Because of this similarity in behavior, Gibson suggested (1933, p. 29) that the usual distinction between lines as "perceptual" and color as "sensory" may not be as definite as usually thought. By 1937 (1937a, p. 232), he was arguing that the sensation-perception distinction was a "false dichotomy." On the other hand, he never actually rid himself of some kind of distinction (1950a, 1966a) although he has sought to avoid what usually goes along with this demarcation, viz., that sensations are the basic building blocks of perception. As early as 1933 (p. 29) he argued, citing James (1890), that perception of a line is "basic," as if Gibson meant to imply that visually perceived lines are not inferred from sensations of color, but rather caused without psychological mediation by retinal lines.

Concerning Gibson's eventual opposition to mediational explanations of visual perception, his discovery of a psychophysical relation of retinal-phenomenal curvature was one instigating force in the genesis of his general psychophysics of visual perception. Gibson's psychophysics involved causal mediation, but the inferential step between stimulation and visual perception was missing. Hence, the bare beginnings of Gibson's psychophysics of perception and his attack on indirect realism are found in his complementary 1933 remarks that there is psychophysical correspondence in perception of lines and that phenomenal lines are as basic as phenomenal colors.

In 1936 Gibson submitted for publication three articles (Gibson, 1937a, 1937b; Gibson & Radner, 1937) in which his conceptual and experimental analyses of adaptation, sensory after-effects, and psychophysical correspondence were more sophisticated and general in scope. He described various conscious dimensions, such as color, brightness, and temperature, that undergo a shift in physical correlates and exhibit predictable after-effects.

Boring's term *dimension* was now employed and defended by Gibson. Of particular relevance was what Gibson referred to as an oppositional dimension (1937a, p. 224) in which one value at the midpoint is neutral (or the norm) and values at the end points are complementary or oppositional dimensions, e.g., hot-cold, right-left curvature in lines, etc. For oppositional dimensions, Gibson noted that, "during prolonged perception the correspondence between the sensory series and the stimulus series has been altered throughout in such a way as to reduce the discrepancy between the norm and the perception" (1937b, p. 566).

Diagram 15 is an explication of the previous quote. It is based on Gibson's improved discussions (1937a, 1937b) of shifts in psychophysical correspondence. The example used is curvature of lines.

Referring to the diagram, if, for example, F is the adaptation figure, it will eventually yield E' instead of F' (signified by dashed line). In turn, there will be a negative after-effect for E, such that it now produces D'. All other correspondences are shifted one letter to the left. Gibson sought to extend the applicability of the above type of shift effect to other oppositional dimensions in kinesthesis, taste, and touch (1937a). This dependency of all specific physical-phenomenal correlations upon one instance of an adaptation shift was the main reason for Gibson's rejection of the ideas of independent elements and his acceptance of phenomenal dimensions. Secondly, note that in the above example, the adapted physical line looks more straight, hence more neutral in curvature, than prior to adaptation.

In two of these three studies (Gibson, 1937b; Gibson & Radner 1937), Gibson investigated visual adaptation to tilted lines. Besides finding adaptation, negative after-effects, and a shift in psychophysical correspondence, Gibson observed an interesting new phenomenon. He ascertained that if a line titled 5 degrees from vertical (e.g., to the left) was looked at for a sufficient period of time, not only would a vertical line appear slightly tilted to the right, but a horizontal line would also appear slightly tilted to the right. The negative after-effect for both a vertical and

DIAGRAM 15

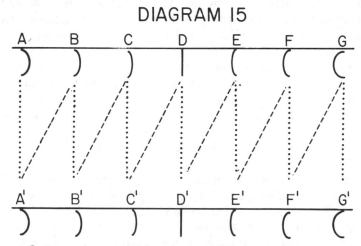

A, B, . . . G are seven values of physical curvature. A', B', . . . G' are seven corresponding values of phenomenal curvature. In normal conditions (without any adaptation) the psychophysical correspondences are as signified by the connecting dotted lines. Lastly D and D' are the neutral values of the two series.

horizontal line was in the same direction away from its actual orientation, viz., in this example a slight clockwise rotation. A comparable effect occurred if the test figure was tilted 5 degress from horizontal. In the postadaptation condition, a physically nontilted vertical line was perceived with a slight tilt in the same direction of rotation as a physically nontilted horizontal line. Gibson concluded from these results that, "Perceptually the horizontal and vertical directions do behave as if they were aspects of a single system for visual orientation, or a single *spatial framework*" (Gibson & Radner, 1937, p. 464)

The relationship between the phenomenal vertical and the phenomenal horizontal, as revealed in the aforementioned study, plus Gibson's close exposure at Smith to Koffka and the Gestalt psychologist's hypothesis of a visual spatial framework seem to be the main determining factors involved in Gibson's adoption of this hypothesis. Though Gibson steered clear of innate organizing processes, he began to show signs of being influenced by Gestalt psychology. Yet Gibson's concern with establishing psychophysical relations was indeed a radical empiricism, even more so than Berkeley or Helmholtz, for Gibson was moving toward eliminating any type of mental contributions in perception above and beyond stimulation per se. His psychophysics followed Troland.

One final remark concerning these articles on adaptation is that Gibson's major focus was describing and explaining a general instance of noncorrespondence between perception and the physical world. A fundamental fact about adaptation in these studies was that it resulted in misperception, in both adaptation and negative after-effect conditions. Except for one passing remark (1937a, p. 242) Gibson directed little attention toward indicating the relevance of these studies toward an understanding of veridical perception. This orientation would change drastically in the next 10 years. (For Gibson's later views on adaptation see Gibson, 1958d, 1962d, and Gibson & Backlund, 1963).

THE VISUAL FRAMEWORK AND THE RETINAL IMAGE

In a series of articles, Gibson (Gibson 1934b; Gibson & Mowrer, 1938; Gibson & Radner, 1935, Gibson & Robinson, 1935) initially approached the general problem of visual perception of orientation. In one limited respect, he followed Koffka (1935), but overall Gibson remained Berkeleian notwithstanding the previously mentioned criticisms of traditional empiricist psychology connected with his adaptation studies (viz., Gibson's opposition to phenomenal elementarism, the sensation-perception distinction, and the "local-sign" muscular explanation of adaptation effects).

The major point of disagreement between Gibson and traditional empiricist psychology within the just cited publications was Gibson's employment of the hypothesis of a spatial framework. This hypothesis represented the key similarity between Gibson and Koffka, from whom Gibson apparently took the idea. Although he did not acknowledge any particular debt to Koffka, Gibson introduced the spatial framework hypothesis through citing Koffka's *Principles* (1935), (e.g., Gibson and Mowrer, 1938, p. 300; Gibson and Radner, 1935, p. 48; Gibson and Robinson, 1935, p. 46). On the other hand, Gibson could have first come in contact with the idea in James' *Principles* (1890) which he read prior to the appearance of Koffka's book.

In a *Psychological Monograph* edited by Gibson (1935), he reported how well subjects were able to recognize titled forms and recall the amount of tilt in these forms. There are several historically interesting aspects to these experiments. First, Gibson was employing rather artificial stimulus conditions (outline forms) in studying visual perception. Secondly, in interpreting the results of the research reported in these studies, Gibson first utilized the concept of a spatial framework in arguing that the identity of a form is, in some cases, a function of its orientation in a framework, and that the orientation of a form is seen with respect to a framework (Gibson & Radner, 1935, p. 63; Gibson, Robinson, 1935, p. 46). Consequently, he appeared to be contesting the Berkeleian view that spatial location of a figure is a self-contained process independent of other localizations.

A very rough but decided anticipation of a later hypothesis of Gibson's is found in one of these early articles (Gibson & Robinson, 1935, p. 45). In discussing the recognition of geographical outlines in different orientations, Gibson contended that the fact of recognition of these forms over transpositions must mean that in some sense their perceived characteristics are independent of orientation. That nothing but an inkling of the idea of invariance over transformation is contained in this argument can be agreed upon, but it is a step, albeit barely, in that future direction.

In examining Gibson's views on the visual spatial framework, two of his adaptation articles containing some relevant material need to be further discussed. The data Gibson obtained (Gibson, 1937b; Gibson & Radner, 1937) on adaptation to tilted lines did not appear to him to be consistent with Koffka's contention that the visual spatial framework is totally determined visually. The adaptation effect of a vertically tilted line becoming more phenomenally vertical was never complete in any of Gibson's subjects. Koffka (1935) and Wertheimer (1912) had earlier suggested that if all visual lines were tilted along the vertical axis, they eventually would appear vertical, since the main lines in vision determine the vertical and horizontal axes of visual perception. Gibson never observed complete adaptation (normalization) for even one tilted line. Also, Gibson noted a negative after-effect only for the area of the retina stimulated in the adaptation condition and the corresponding area in the other retina. The whole "visual field" did not exhibit a shift in its physical correlates of vertical and horizontal.

During conditions of simultaneous contrast (Gibson, 1937b), where a physically tilted grille of parallel lines was superimposed on a vertical straight line, the latter did not appear to subjects as tilted in the opposite direction to that of the physical tilt of the grille. Besides, the grille was never perceived by Gibson's subjects as becoming perfectly vertical. Because of these facts and other considerations, Gibson in the following year (Gibson & Mowrer, 1938) argued that although the hypothesis of a spatial framework was valid, its ultimate determinants were postural and not visual contra Koffka and Wertheimer.

Gibson summarized his views in the following,

> Both the visual and the postural vertical are determined by visual factors and gravitational factors acting jointly, with orientation to gravity, however, as the more decisive factor in cases of real conflict between the two types of sensory data and the primary factor genetically. (Gibson & Mowrer, 1938, p. 303)

Some examples of main orientation lines supplied through vision would be the horizon line, the vertical and horizontal outlines of erect objects (building or trees), and the walls of most rooms. According to Koffka (1935, Chapter 6), such lines determine the vertical and horizontal axes for vision, in that the orientations of all objects are seen with respect to this framework. Gibson (Gibson & Mowrer, 1938) repeated Wertheimer's (1912) experiment in which the main lines of a room were tilted, in this case, 45 degrees counter clockwise (p. 308). He found that the floor of this tilted room never came to appear horizontal or its walls vertical. The explanation Gibson offered was that when the main visual lines were in conflict with the postural feel of the direction of gravity, the latter would be dominant. Gibson also cited evidence (p. 311) that subjects placed in a completely dark room excepting for one luminous line were able to adjust this line to vertical quite accurately. His general conclusion from these facts and those previously mentioned was that visual perception of orientation does not necessarily involve a visually determined spatial framework. In this article, Gibson adopted an anatomically relative conception of visual stimulation and accepted a mediational step in visual perception. Both of these ideas were subsequently abandoned by Gibson in the 1950s.

When the head is tilted, the visual world does not appear to rotate, but the horizon line on the retina rotates with respect to the retina. Gibson suggested that the postural feeling of head tilt compensates for this horizon line tilt on the retina (Gibson & Mowrer, 1938, p. 303). In another passage, he remarked in a more general vein (p. 319) that a vertical line on the retina could correspond with any physical orientation of a line depending on head or eye tilt. Because there is no specificity between orientation lines on the retina and in the world, Gibson argued that the perceiver must be aware of the physical orientation of the eyes with respect to the line of gravity to correctly see the orientation of lines.

Insofar as lines projected onto the retinal image from stationary physical configurations only rotate with respect to the retina when the eyes are rotated around their own axes or that of the head, Gibson was consequently presupposing in the above argument that the purely visual sense of orientation is sensitivity to the orientation of lines in the retinal image with respect to the retina. Actually the image per se does not rotate with respect to the physical world. Since he accepted the anatomical retinal image regarding seen orientation, the visual vertical and horizontal axes for Gibson were the axes of the retina. Through vision, all localizations are made with respect to these anatomical axes.

Accordingly, Gibson at this time believed that the "skeleton" of a veridical spatial framework must be provided through postural determinants, which he listed as excitations from the labyrinth or inner ear, "tactual pressure on the soles of feet," the "muscle sense," and "internal visceral pressures," and so on (Gibson & Mowrer, 1938, pp. 301, 319). Via anatomically oriented visual sensitivity and a muscular postural "skeleton," visual perception of spatial relations in the physical world is mediated. With respect to visual perception of spatial location and orientation along the horizontal and vertical axes, Gibson was following Berkeley.

Recall that in an earlier article (1933, pp. 29–30), Gibson had argued that muscular local signs of retinal movement and position do not account for adaptation to visual curvature. The same argument would also apply to tilted lines, as studied in two later articles (Gibson, 1937b, Gibson & Radner, 1937). In the present article (Gibson & Mowrer, 1938) Gibson contended that visual perception of tilt (i.e., orientation of lines) must ultimately depend upon non-visual determinants. Gibson, in the following passage, endeavored to resolve this apparent contradiction.

> although the normal retinal-phenomenal correspondence for perception of the vertical may apparently be shifted under the influence of a process similar to sensory adaptation with negative after-effect without any postural determinants being involved the maximum change is slight and is confined

to the stimulated area. The framework *as a whole* manifests great stability
and resistance to such a change in correspondence. (Gibson & Mowrer,
1938a, p. 312)

In conclusion, Gibson at this time accepted the Berkeleian hypothesis
that visual perception of spatial relations is contingent upon tactual-
muscular mediation. It was only after his aviation studies (1947) that
Gibson really moved away from Berkeley concerning space perception.

Interestingly, Gibson was not cognizant of the degree of similarity
between his view and "older theories" that emphasized the role of
"cues" in perception. Although no specific references of such "older
theories" are given, he must have had in mind individuals within the
Berkeleian tradition. Gibson argued that his position differed from such
"older theories" in that space-perception, for him, is a "motor phenomenon" intrinsically tied to "spatial behavior." He accused previous "theories" of attempting to explain spatial behavior in terms of cue-mediated
spatial perception. The difference, as Gibson saw it, was that "older
theories" explained spatial perception and behavior through "cues,"
whereas he accounted for spatial perception and cues through behavior
(Gibson & Mowrer, 1938, p. 319). Yet for Berkeley "cues" or signs derive
their perceptual meaning from tactual and muscular factors (these sources
being in the form of sensations). If there is any valid difference between
explanations it may be in Gibson's behavioristic emphasis over the
mentalistic approach embodied in Berkeley and structural psychology.

One historical-epistemological lesson to be derived from Gibson's
adaptation and spatial framework studies is the tenacity of the standard
empiricist theory in his own mind in spite of difficulties in "fitting"
hypotheses with "facts." In the 1930s Gibson had no real alternative
theory to Berkeley's views excepting for Gestalt psychology which also
appeared to have problems in accounting for the facts. Gibson was
introducing a variety of changes ("patchwork theorizing") into the standard empiricist views, yet still holding to the main lines of these ideas.
The empiricist theory, in his mind, had not been "falsified," yet there is a
general discontent evident in Gibson's writings. In retrospect, it appears
that Gibson was being pushed off in a new direction, though in the 1930s
this new direction had not crystalized.

FUNCTIONALISM AND PERCEPTION

Gibson's thinking and research thus far described revolve around ecologically atypical situations. His stimuli have been outline forms and simple
lines, in many cases ambiguous or nonsensical. Conditions included

fixating at lines, through prisms or without them. In general, little attention was directed toward studying uninhibited perception in natural surroundings, and his research was mainly concerned with cases of misperception rather than perception.

By the end of World War II, Gibson's whole approach to investigating visual perception had drastically changed. This transformation of attitude occurred when he had to deal with practical problems that involved *perceptual proficiency* in nonlaboratory conditions. The origins of such functionalistic concerns, though, occurred prior to his war research in a jointly published article (Gibson & Crooks, 1938) with an automotive engineer named Laurence Crooks.

When Gibson faced the question of how individuals are able to drive automobiles, the problem was explaining a specific type of perceptual-motor *skill*. His attention was directed away from cases where misperception and perception were investigated without distinction, to a situation in which the primary problem was understanding the conditions of veridicality in visual perception.

A related problem involved presenting a characterization of this skill that had practical applications. In his own judgment, the "theory" that emerged must prove its worth, in part, pragmatically. Resultantly, the concepts he adopted were a function of such considerations. Henceforth, Gibson continued to emphasize this dimension of the validity of explanations, i.e., what practical implications does it have? One major reason for his general discontent with traditional empiricist theory was its lack of utility in investigating the practical problem of characterizing airplane navigation and its paucity of implied suggestions for instruction.

Being able to see where you are going and being able to see where you can translocate safely without collision are uses of perception. Gibson was obliged to conceive of perception in terms of some of its functions. Approaching perception as a function or capacity and not merely as an internal state requires inclusion of a description of the environment to which perception is related functionally. Perception is taken out of a dualistic context and placed in an ecological context.

This points to a significant difference between a functionalistic conception of perception and Wundt and Titchener's structuralism, or Köhler and Koffka's Gestalt psychology. If perception is depicted primarily in terms of its functions, it is described in relation with the environment. Conversely, if "perception" is understood independent of its functions, it is primarily described with respect to activity in the brain. This, of course, is not an "either-or" situation, but a difference in emphasis that is quite evident in comparing functionalists, such as James and Angell with psychologists such as Wundt, Titchener, Köhler, or Koffka.

Functionalism leads away from mind-matter dualism, because in considerations of psychological phenomena the environment is brought into the general definition of psychology. Contrarily, Berkeleians and Gestalt psychologists alike usually described psychological facts merely as a conscious state dependent upon activity in the brain and sense-organs. As a more delimited case of mind-matter dualism, perception is epistemologically divorced from the world (environment) leading to perceiver-world dualism. A functional approach, such as in Aristotle, logically connects the knower with the known, and the knowing "mind" cannot be in reality defined independent (e.g., as a brain state) of what is known. Mind-matter dualism as an ontological thesis is connected with subject-object dualism, an epistemological thesis. To separate the perceiver (and perceiving) from the world involves both ontological and epistemological separations, e.g., in Plato. (Plato connects the rational mind with eternal forms.) The functional approach, in conjunction with evolutionary theory, brought the knowing ("adaptive") mind together with the known world and redirected the focus of research in perception and related areas of cognition.

In the Crooks study Gibson attempted to characterize the most relevant environmental features specific to several functions of visual perception. No longer was the concern with lines or outline forms, but instead the focus was on representative conditions of a type of perceptual-motor adjustment. In proceeding in this direction, Gibson introduced such terms as *terrain, destination, obstacle, collision,* and *path* (Gibson & Crooks, 1938, p. 454), words quite different in meaning from the usual ones such as *objects, depth,* or *form.* The concept of terrain is especially important, because it gradually evolved into the concept of surface layout.

In describing the "field of safe travel" (Gibson & Crooks, 1938, p. 455), Gibson introduced the concept of valences that he borrowed from Lewin (1936). Features of the environment have meanings with respect to locomotion or other human activities, e.g., obstacles may hinder movement or terminate it completely; an open road can be driven across; a wet or icy road is dangerous at high speeds. Eventually, Gibson substituted the term *affordances* for valences in describing such adaptively significant factors of the environment.

In one particularly interesting footnote (1938b, p. 465), Gibson remarked that when a person in one car is passing another car while there is a third oncoming car, the first driver's degree of "constancy" or veridicality in perceiving the relative speeds of three cars is "striking." Gibson thought it was so "extraordinary" because of the supposed lack of correspondence between the visual stimulus (the retinal image) and many aspects of the physical surroundings. At this time it was considered amazing that this transformation between deficient stimulation and perception did occur; later (1947), Gibson supposed it was amazing that this transformation could be believed by anyone to occur. He eventually concluded that the veridicality of visual perception in such complicated situations as automobile driving and navigation is usually so pronounced that it must be based upon something more complex and more specific to the world than point stimuli or depth cues, as traditionally conceived. The hypothesis that visual perception is supported by stimulation specific to the environment constituted the beginnings of Gibson's concept of stimulus information.

CARR'S GROUND THEORY

Gibson's work with Crooks in characterizing the environmental context of automobile driving and his interest and knowledge regarding the concept of a spatial framework are two of the main sources for his "ground theory" of space perception. A third source comes from Harvey Carr. Gibson's ground theory provided both an ecologically representative and wholistic approach to space perception, as well as being the first fully developed example of a perceptual psychophysics based upon a complex, wholistic description of stimulation.

Harvey Carr's (1873–1954) *An Introduction to Space Perception* appeared in 1935 and for many years thereafter was used by Gibson as a text for the perception courses he taught at Smith College. (This information was personally communicated to the author from Gibson.) Consequently, Gibson was very familiar with this work prior to his research in the armed forces during World War II. This fact is significant because it implies that the general idea of a "ground theory of space perception" is not Gibson's own creation It is in Carr's book. It is not my contention that Gibson's belief in the validity of a "ground theory" was founded upon Carr's work, but only that the idea was in Gibson's mind before his aviation research. Exactly what Gibson could have procured from Carr can be best ascertained through an examination of the following key excerpts from Carr's book:

> The visual world . . ., is a sensory continuum—a continuum of sensed objects. An object is always seen as distinct from an environing background of objects. Any two separated objects are seen against an intervening background consisting of a part of some other object such as a wall, a forest, a lake, the ground, or the sky. When we speak of seeing the distance between two objects, we are merely referring to the magnitude of this intervening visible background. (1935, p. 1)

> In viewing a landscape scene, the observer not only sees the object whose distance he is judging, but he sees himself in contact with the earth, the ground between his feet and the object, and the ground between the base of

the object and the distant sky line. The amount of ground between the object and himself relative to that between the object and the sky line varies with the distance of the object, and hence judgments of the distance of an object may be based upon this relation . . . (hence) judgments of a distant object projected against the sky . . . are much more indefinite and unreliable than if these objects were located on the ground. (1935, pp. 270–271) .

The hypothesis that perceived distance is variable across surfaces and not between them is apparent in the preceding quotations. Because the prevalent historical characterization inherited from the ancient Greeks and continued in Newton's physics represented the perceived world as consisting of a set of physical objects each separated from the perceiver by "empty" space, Carr's "sensory continuum" constituted a drastic reconceptualization of the environment perceived through vision. For Carr, the distances of objects are specific amounts of intervening background.

Secondly, insofar as the problem was reformulated in this way, the hypothesized optical basis for perceiving distance contained a totally new type of construct. Before, the "signs" or "cues" for seeing the distance of objects were correlates of the *specific distances of objects*. Carr introduced an optical correlate for the "ground" or *continuous distance in all directions* that is involved in seeing the distances of objects. Both of these innovative ideas (environmental and optical) are essential aspects to Gibson's 1950 explanation of distance perception.

Carr's theory of distance perception is founded upon a functionalistic psychology and an ecologically more valid description of the environment of animals. It is noteworthy that 3 years after the publication of Carr's book, Gibson published his automotive study article in which "ground" concepts enter the scene and functional issues become of central importance. From an evolutionary-functional perspective, it is quite obvious that terrestrial animals live their lives moving across a ground rather than flying through space like Kepler's and Newton's solar bodies. What may seem obvious ("the facts") in retrospect is not necessarily what seems obvious at the time—such is the power of a theoretical framework on scientists' minds.

In spite of Carr's proposals of an environmental continuum and an optical correlate of this continuum, his sole utilization of these concepts was to account for how the distances of objects are visually perceived and not how the physical continuum of distance per se is perceived. This focus of Carr reflected previous thinking on depth perception and is not anticipatory of Gibson's 1950 approach, in which the facts of the distance continuum and the perception of the continuum were stressed.

Another difference between Carr and Gibson involved Carr's failure to consider the fact that the amount of retinal distance from the image of one's feet to the image of an object is not proportionately related to the object's actual distance. Another type of scale was required for the continuous distance of the ground that would be specific to actual physical distances. Gibson's hypothesis of stimulus gradients provided such a scale.

THE CONCEPTS OF INVARIANCE AND TRANSFORMATION

The reciprocal concepts of invariance and transformation are central to Gibson's treatment of stimulus structure within his perceptual psychophysics circa 1950. Toward the end of the 1940s, the concept of invariance entered into visual perception literature. Two well-known articles containing this idea were Wallach (1948) and Pitts and McCulloch (1947). These publications are cited because they antedated Gibson's inclusion of the idea in his 1950 book, but it must be stressed that the eventual scope of application of invariance in Gibson's writings was in no measure foreseen by either Wallach or Pitts and McCulloch. Secondly, Gibson's major sources of intellectual debt for an understanding of this concept and its potential worth in visual perception were neither Wallach nor Pitts and McCulloch, but the philosopher Ernst Cassierer (1944), the naturalist D'Arcy Thompson (1942), and the mathematicians Richard Courant and Herbert Robbins (1941). Gibson was familiar with all three publications prior to 1950.

In his *Science and Hypothesis,* Henri Poincaré (1905) presented the following problem: How do we distinguish between changes of state in an object and changes of position? (Recall Ternus' study) The answer Poincare (1905, pp. 57–60) gave was that if an alteration in our sense impressions corresponds to a change in position of an object, there exists some movement of the eyes, head, or body that will restore the original impression, whereas this is not the case if there transpires a modification in the state of an object. Cassirer (1944) took this to be a clear example of the relevance of the concept of group to the problems of visual perception. Changes of position can be perceived as such, because the corresponding sense-impressions are conceivable as variations in a group of transformations that, quite significantly, contains an inverse transformation for any transformation. Since the transformations are reversible, the class of variations constitutes a group.

Cassirer's general position, as expressed in this article, was that sense-impressions, which appear to correspond to pointillistic stimulation, are ordered by the perceiving subject into groups of transformations. Although Cassirer contested the "constancy hypothesis" (pp. 12, 19), he understood this proposal to be a hypothesized relation between stimulation and perceptual content. Almost no one ever held such a position (excepting for Gibson in his later perceptual psychophysics); the type of constancy most often presumed was between stimulation and sensations, and this assumption Cassirer himself seemed to hold but he was not very explicit on this point. According to Cassirer, the subject searches for the *possibility* of invariants by conceiving of various sets of sense-impressions as belonging to groups of transformations. Or stated differently, Cassirer followed Poincare in arguing that sense-impressions serve as the "occasion," but not the basis for the formation of invariants by the perceiving organism. For Cassirer, the invariant is not embodied in the transforming sense-impressions but is provided by the mind as a way of organizing sense-impressions together as a transformational group. Given the aforementioned view concerning the origin of invariants in perception, it can be concluded that Cassirer differed markedly from Gibson. The similarity between Gibson and Cassirer was their employment of the notion of invariants of groups of transformations to account for the constancy of the perceived physical world. But for Cassirer, invariance is supplied by the mind whereas for Gibson, groups of transformations of the visual stimuli contain invariants.

The applicability of the concept of transformations to so many diverse structures in nature appears to have impressed Gibson considerably upon reading D'Arcy Thompson's *Growth and Form* (1942). That seemingly quite distinct forms, such as the skulls of man, chimpanzee, and baboon, could be depicted as particular variations along some continuous and simple transformation suggested to Gibson the likelihood of a similar fruitful enterprise in describing projected forms on the retina. And more importantly, given the above possibility, there should exist invariants within the groups of continuous transformations that would provide an optical basis for perception of a clearly differentiated and relatively invariant physical environment. As Thompson (1942) noted, there are "discriminant characters" within continuous transformations that "remain invariant" for that group. Following this lead, Gibson, would argue that invariants across optical transformations provide the basis for seeing an object's physical dimensions as constant, and that perceptual discrimination of objects is supported by groups of projective transformations that exhibit distinct invariants, i.e., different "discriminant characters" (Gibson, 1950a, pp. 152–154).

The general direction assumed in the Cassirer-Thompson discussions is that order is embodied in change. Following Plato's separation of order and change, science and philosophy tended to see order as transcendent to the flux of particulars. Heraclitus and Aristotle attempted to show how order and persistence could be embodied in change, but as reflected in perceptual theories in modern times, order and persistence were usually thought of as impositions upon flux. Gibson's belief that constancy and order could exist within a transforming flow of stimulation represented a true Aristotelian perspective.

According to Courant and Robbins, "Any mapping of one figure onto another by a central or parallel projection, or by a finite succession of such projections, is called a projective transformation" (1941, p. 169). As such, there exists a mathematically well-defined relation between a figure and a projective transformation of it. By 1950, Gibson realized the implications for the psychology of visual perception of this concept in projective geometry (p. 9). Conceived of as a projective transformation of the physical world, the retinal image should contain "ordinal variables" that are mathematically related to the three-dimensional physical world (1950a, p. 8).

Assuming this relationship, a new answer could be given to a question quite ancient in origin. What is the relationship between properties of the retinal image and the three-dimensional spatial properties of the physical world? Berkeley's answer was *covariation in only certain instances*. As Berkeley would have expressed it, although some variations in the retinal image do covary with some variations in the physical world, the two properties in question are *distinct* in nature, for instance, distance of an object and faintness of its corresponding image. But Courant and Robbins, presented a different answer to this problem.

> The image made by a painter can be regarded as a projection of the original onto the canvas, with the center of projection at the eye of the painter. In this process lengths and angles are necessarily distorted, in a way that depends on the relative positions of the various objects depicted. Still, the geometrical structure of the original can usually be recognized on the canvas. How is this possible? It must be because there exist geometrical properties "invariant under projection"—properties which appear unchanged in the image and make the identification possible. (Courant & Robbins, 1941, p. 167)

Notwithstanding that this statement was made with respect to recognizing the world represented in a painting, an analogous argument is relevant to how the physical world is perceived given the properties of the retinal image. Gibson, (1950a, pp. 8–9), in drawing upon Courant and Robbins, was to take this important step. Although Gibson first hypothesized a preservation of invariant properties of the physical environment in its projective transformations at the eye in the framework of a retinal image psychophysics, the same idea was carried over in his ecological optics. There is a new sense, in which this hypothesis constituted a return to Democritus' view that the physical world is simulated at the eye of the observer.

The simulative assumption in the *eidola* theory pertained to replication of individual objects in a concrete literal sense. Courant and Robbins are arguing that the set of geometrical (spatial) relations within the total scene are preserved in an abstract (mathematical form), for example, a series of "different" projective transformations of the same environment situation may differ in literal perspective outlines but the total series will possess certain invariant features. These invariants of a series of projective transformations are relational and abstract. The projective transformation is not seen (the homunculus hypothesis) but it contains "information specific" (Gibson's later terminology) to the environment, and a set of projective transformations will embody relational invariants specific to the persistant features of the environment.

Chapter 12 _____

GIBSON'S "PERCEPTION of the VISUAL WORLD"

THE CONCEPT OF PERCEPTION

In three successive and increasingly more systematic formulations of his "psychophysical theory" of visual perception, Gibson (1947, 1948, 1950a) outlined the beginnings of a truly independent and ubiquitous approach to visual perception. The third work in this series was Gibson's first book, *The Perception of the Visual World*. Previously, Gibson had been concerned with issues limited in scope, but after World War II, in a more generalistic vein, Gibson stated his problem as "How do we see the world around us?" (1950a, p. vii). Secondly, he emerged after World War II as a thinker and investigator decidedly on his own. In the 1930s, Gibson's approach to visual perception was mainly derivative, but by 1950 he had explicated a program for investigation that was fundamentally in disagreement with Berkeley's empiricism, nativism, and Gestalt psychology (compare Gibson, 1950a with Gibson & Fernberger, 1941).

The uniqueness of Gibson's psychophysical program in 1950 was not so much a function of its various constituent concepts and hypotheses being really new; many of them individually were anticipated by previous writers. It was the unique constellation of ideas, the development of hypotheses that previously had been given limited application, and the implications he drew from such hypotheses that made Gibson's psychophysical approach a novel one.

Immediately after World War II, Gibson's general approach to visual perception was guided by a mixture of phenomenology and functionalism (1947, 1948, 1950a). He introduced the problem of visual perception (1950a, Chapter 1) with the Koffkian-phenomenological question, "Why do things look as they do?" but he was actually concerned with a functionalistic variation of this question, "Why do things look as they are?" His major interest was not describing and explaining phenomenal experience in general, but with a phenomenological characterization and psychophysical explanation of *veridical* perceptual experience.

From the Gestalt psychologists, Gibson (1950a, pp. 23, 26; 1948, p. 161) took the belief that an unprejudiced description of perceptual experience is both possible and a necessary propaedeutic for explanations of visual perception. What Gibson assumed was that if the general problem is to explain the "looks" of things, first you must first have a description of these "looks" (1950a, p. 26). This is a common empiricist ideal (description should precede explanation) associated with the Baconian-inductivistic philosophy of science. But of greater relevance, if any method whether it be phenomenology or introspection, has as its stated goal the characterization of perceptual experience disconnected from the physical environment, then it is a manifestation of perceiver-world dualism. What is historically noteworthy in light of the above discussion is that Gibson circa 1950 subscribed to one form of mind-matter dualism, in spite of the fact that he did not consistently practice it. It was only toward the end of the 1960s that Gibson became sufficiently cognizant of the fact that the animal as perceiver and its commensurate physical environment could neither be understood nor investigated independently of one another. In coming to this realization, Gibson's approach has become clearly ecological and opposed to mind-matter dualism.

Gibson's characterization of perceptual experience was intended to be phenomenological in the sense that no attempt comparable to introspection would be made to unnaturally analyze experience. Of course, this begs the question of what is "natural," but neither Gibson nor the Gestalt psychologists appeared to be aware of this difficulty. What matters in an historical sense is that Gibson's acceptance of Koffka's argument for the necessity of an atheoretical and unprejudiced phenomenology led him to describe perceptual experience at a more global level than were Titchener's or Wundt's introspective analyses of experience.

Gibson (1950a, pp. 8, 133–134, 187) suggested that the "elementary" or "fundamental impressions" are not "color bits" but surfaces, edges, motion, distance, depth, and so on. These basic phenomenal facts were obtained by Gibson through a *selective* phenomenology. Perceptual experience, as understood by Koffka, would include both veridical and nonveridical experience, because his initial concern was with describing experience independently of any relation it may have to the world. This would be "pure" phenomenology, but Gibson (1947, pp. 199, 205–206, 211; 1948, p. 176; 1950a, p. 43) often stated that his primary interest was with veridical visual perceptual experience or "objective seeing." (Another synonymous term frequently employed by Gibson was the "visual world.") In order to make this distinction, Gibson was required to go beyond just describing experience, because it is only when the relationship between perceptual experience and the physical world is considered that the concept of veridicality has any meaningful application. Hence, as soon as Gibson considered the subject matter of his psychophysical program, the concept of perceptual experience per se disappeared, as did perceiver-world dualism.

The emphasis on the visual world in Gibson's approach derived mainly from his aviation studies (1944, 1947). He became extremely impressed with the extent and degree of veridicality in size perception, recognition of various aircrafts at far distances, and distance perception in aircraft pilots. As he later stated (1950a), the "real mystery" in perception is not that there are discrepancies between what is perceived and the physical world, but that there are so "few discrepancies." One of the most ubiquitous facts about perception is its veracity in natural conditions. (This realization is reminiscent of Einstein's remark, "The most incomprehensible thing about the universe is that it is comprehensible.") The question Gibson attempted to answer was how this was possible, or why do things (almost always) look as they are?

It cannot truthfully be stated that previous individuals were not enagaged in the study of the veridicality of visual perception (functionalists assuredly were), but the chief motivation for many, Koffka being one, was to describe and account for the look of things, where both veridical and nonveridical "looks" were of equal significance. Secondly, excepting maybe for Brunswik, the verity of visual perception did not occupy the status of an *idee fixe* within any of the various forms of Berkeley's theory as it did in Gibson's psychophysical theory. Gibson in the 1950s was interested almost exclusively in experimentally isolating the factors involved in veridical visual perception, (i.e., the visual world.)

What accounts for this shift in emphasis from pure phenomenology to veridical perceptual experience? The influence of functionalism upon Gibson is one reason. But at this historical point, a key catalyst for Gibson's shift would have to be his aviation work. In fact, in several respects, the aviation work was significant in moving Gibson toward his perceptual psychophysics. Having to adopt a different perspective on perception contributed to the novelty of his perceptual psychophysics. Pragmatic and functional concerns are of paramount importance in aircraft landing.

Inasmuch as characterizing veridical perceptual experience involves a description of the physical environment that corresponds with the visual world, Gibson in *The Perception of the Visual World* was obliged to seriously consider the question: What are the features of the physical environment that experience is specific to in visual perception? The next section deals with how he answered this question.

THE ENVIRONMENT

Gibson's (1950a) explanation of distance perception involved a reconceptualization of the nature of environmental space that animals visually perceive. This particular revision was just one instance, albeit an important one, of the more general endeavor initiated by Gibson in the 1940s toward describing the physical environment of human activity and perception. Insofar as this interest, instigated by Gibson's concern with veridical perception, brought the environment into the psychology of visual perception, Gibson's psychophysical program was not consonant with perceiver-world dualism. Ultimately, the intermittent discussions of the environment in the 1950s developed into one of the three major aspects of Gibson's ecological program of the 1960s.

The representation of the environment of visual perception offered by Gibson in 1950 differed from both depictions proposed by physical scientists and those suggested by psychologists and philosophers interested in visual perception (1950a, Chapters 1 and 3). Gibson's physical environment was at a different level of macro-organization and segmentation than descriptions offered by physicists. This level of physical structure was neither of atoms and molecules nor of planets and galaxies, but of physical units and arrangements measured in centimeters and meters. He noted (1950a, p. 78) the investigation of the physical world at this level was not a major enterprise of physical scientists. Physics especially, which is taken to provide a "true" description of the physical world, does not deal with the level of size and organization Gibson found relevant to perception and behavior. Consequently this level is often thought of as "chimera" of the mind, though, as Gibson repeatedly pointed out, it is just as real as atoms or planets.

Anticipated by Gestalt psychologists (Heider in particular) Gibson's argument is simply that there exist multiple levels of reality. A level of reality involves both units and relationships. Elementarism in physics and psychology identifies reality with a set of independent, irreducible units having an absolute character. In elementarism there exists only one level of reality. Elementarism assumes that there exists a primary set of entities independent of relationships. This is dualistic. Within Gestalt psychology, there are no intrinsic units for all units are set in relations. What makes any one set of units more real than any other set? Can all of reality be conceived as concatenations of ultimate units? Following Gibson, there is no basis for identifying units at any one level of analysis as more real than any other.

For Gibson, the environment did not consist of objects separated from the perceiver by empty space, but of a ground or terrain that is structured in terms of hills, edges, valleys, surface texture, etc., and upon which are scattered objects in various arrangements. (At the level of analysis of solar-galactic bodies "objects in space" is more valid.) Recall that Carr (1935) had proposed that the seen distance of objects was a dimension across the surfaces that objects rest upon. During his armed forces research, Gibson arrived at a similar conclusion. In flying a plane a continuous terrain lies below the pilot and not just a set of discrete objects. Gibson (1947, p. 185) contended that it was the space of this physical continuum that was of primary importance for the pilot, and individual distances of objects were perceived with respect to this continuum. Perceived distance for the airplane pilot, according to him, becomes indeterminate without the presence of this continuous terrain.

Later, Gibson (1950a, pp. 60–61) argued that this fact of a continuous terrain or ground is not just a basic environmental fact for pilots, but for all terrestrial life. The physical environment that land animals have evolved within does not consist of objects in empty space, but of a continuous terrain or ground upon which objects are located. (Note the employment of an argument based on evolutionary considerations.) Interestingly, Gibson had to go up into space to see the ground.

Previously, psychologists had sought to explain how a human perceives the individual distances of discrete objects—the distance of each object conceived of as the length of "a line directed endwise to the eye." For Gibson, the problem was how the continuum of distance across the ground in all directions away from the perceiver is visually perceived. The distance of each individual object is perceived as a specific amount of distance across this continuum or ground. Gibson presented a diagram that represented these two divergent conceptions of perceived physical distance. (From 1947, p. 187; 1950a, p. 62—with slight modification)

Referring to Diagram 16, if the line that bisects WXYZ is the ground, the problems for Gibson were how the continual increase of distance across the ground is visually perceived, and secondarily, how the particular distances of W, X, Y, or Z across this surface are seen. For Berkeley, the problem was how the length of an imaginary line through space, for example IA, is perceived. The physical space that is perceived for Gibson is a dimension *across* surfaces, whereas for Berkeley it is a dimension *between* two surfaces, viz., the eye and an object.

Observe that in Gibson's formulation something varies with a change

DIAGRAM 16

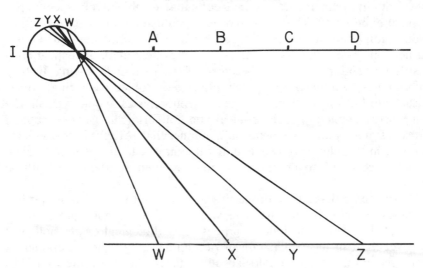

in the distance of an object, while for Berkeley A, B, C, and D all project to the same point I on the retina. Due to the fact that perceived physical distance was depicted in a novel way, a new retinal "correlate" of physical space was uncovered. (Although Gibson used the word *correlate*, it was too weak a term for what he actually meant.) The concept of stimulus gradients resulted from this reinterpretation of distance. Before turning to the concept of gradients, Gibson's basic psychophysical theory needs to be discussed.

PSYCHOPHYSICAL CORRESPONDENCE, SIMULATION, AND BERKELEY'S THEORY OF PERCEPTION

In 1950, Gibson thought of the process of visual perception as a unidirectional causal chain or sequence of events proceeding from the physical environment to the eyes up through the optic nerves and eventually terminating in the brain (1950a, pp. 44–50). Consequently, for Gibson, the visual proximal stimulus viz., the retinal image, was an indirect cause of perceptual experience, and the concomitant activity in the brain was the immediate cause. This representation of visual perception, which stems from Descartes, was eventually abandoned by Gibson in the 1960s.

Gibson's general psychophysics of perception, almost undoubtedly derived from Troland (1929, 1930), incorporated within it the aforementioned causal model. Troland had supposed that functional relationships could be discovered between the proximal stimulus and perceptual experience, since the proximal stimulus, which was correlated with the physical environment, was an indirect cause of objectively specific perceptual experience. These discovered stimulus-phenomenal correlations would constitute a psychophysical *explanation* of perception. Gibson turned this proposal into a fundamental principle for investigation in visual perception. It should be emphasized that in following Troland, Gibson was hypothesizing a psychophysics of "objective seeing," or the visual world. The rationale of the psychophysics would vanish if it supposedly applied to both veridical and nonveridical visual perception. Gibson stated almost in an axiomatic manner that, "There is always some variable in stimulation (however difficult it may be to discover and isolate) which corresponds to a property of the (perceived) spatial world" (1950a, p. 8).

In assuming that all the properties of the visual world, no matter how complex, subtle, or global, have specific stimulus correlates, Gibson concluded that no contributory process (psychological or physiological) was required in an explanation of perceptual experience. Berkeleians, nativists and Gestalt psychologists all assumed that the optical basis for visual perception was deficient in some sense and therefore required either organization or supplementation or both. Instead, Gibson contended that the visual stimulus was not impoverished; hence, his psychophysics involved correlations analogous to the type between wavelength and color where no contributory mediational step was commonly thought to be required. In a psychophysics of perception both variables of the mathematical functions may be more complex, but they would nonetheless be straightforward functions—in fact, causal laws.

In order to more thoroughly understand the nature of Gibson's psychophysics of perception, how it avoided postulating an intervening constructive step and why the visual proximal stimulus was no longer considered inadequate, three questions are considered and answered. First, what other factors were involved in Gibson's acceptance of a psychophysics of perception besides Troland's proposals? Second, how does Gibson's explanation of visual perception differ from explanations founded upon the concept of signs or simulation? Third, how did Gibson's concept of visual stimulation differ from pointillism and the picture model of the retinal image?

Concerning the first question, it has already been remarked that Gibson questioned a clear sensation-perception distinction after his adaptation studies. Because it was the popular opinion that sensations have specific stimulus correlates, there was no reason to think differently regarding perception if the demarcation between the two types of experience was abandoned. This appeared to Gibson a reasonable possibility given the success of the psychophysics of sensation.

Second, Gibson's adaptation studies did seem to reveal psychophysi-

cal correspondence for degrees of phenomenal curvature, tilt, and bent-
ness in lines. The psychophysical correspondence uncovered was not a
rigid coupling of specific conscious and retinal values, but there was
always a discoverable specific correspondence of conscious and retinal
values.

Third, Gibson no longer believed in the hypothesis of conscious
elements. Rather, for Gibson, perceptual consciousness could be described in terms of dimensions (1950a, p. 11) in the sense defined by
Boring (1933). Hence, complex perceptions could not be explained in
terms of more basic phenomenal elements (Gibson 1948, p. 160). Given
our previous discussion of Gibson's rejection of physical elementarism, it
is clear that in general Gibson was moving away from an elementaristic
theory of reality.

Fourth, Gibson was very impressed by the extent of veridicality in
perception and the degree of consensus across individuals' reports of
what they perceived. He reasoned from these facts that visual perception
could not be primarily determined by subjective factors, such as cerebral
organization or past experiences, but must be based on more objective
factors (1950a, p. 14).

Gibson slighted physiological and psychological processes in the 1950s
because he believed that such factors could not account for the veridicality of visual perception. Because individual variations in such physiological or psychological processes are initiated by specific variations in
proximal stimulation, unless the latter is specifically correlated with the
physical environment, perception would not be correlated. There would
be no way to explain how the "visual world" corresponded with the
physical environment except if it was assumed that visual perception was
psychophysically correlated with objectively specific stimulation. This
incredibly consequential, but simple insight that visual perception must
be correlated with proximal stimulation if it is to be veridical eventually
evolved, after several noteworthy modifications, into Gibson's hypothesis that visual perception is based on stimulus information. Consequently,
Gibson in 1950 concluded that the primary avenue for explaining veridicality in perception was isolating the stimulus variables with which the
visual world was correlated (Gibson, 1948, p. 160; 1950a, p. 14).

During his aviation studies, Gibson (1947) discovered that the perception of continuous distance appeared to be correlated with a yet unnoticed
stimulus variable, viz., the gradient of texture density. This raised for
Gibson an intriguing possibility. If a reconceptualization of the environment had resulted in the uncovering of an apparent example of psychophysical correspondence in perception, might not there be many other
similar cases that had been overlooked because the common representations of the environment were faulty or misleading?

What Gibson noted in experiments dealing with so-called "reversible figures," the effects of set or attitude upon perception, and two-dimensional outline forms, also reinforced his conviction in a psychophysics of visual perception. All of the aforementioned types of studies seemed to provide ample evidence for a lack of correspondence between stimulation and perception. For any given proximal stimulus, the resulting perception supposedly varied as a function of set, past experience, etc. Gibson (1941, pp. 794–795; 1948, pp. 167, 169) observed that in such cases the stimulus conditions were invariably impoverished or ambiguous (i.e., stimulation was not specific to one environmental fact). They did not demonstrate that where there was a lawful relationship between the stimulus and the world, perception was not a function of the stimulus. In general, the aforementioned studies yielded nonveridical or unstable "perceptions." Such ambiguous and impoverished conditions were not representative of natural conditions.

Turning to the second question, what major incompatibilities existed between Gibson's psychophysics and the simulative assumption and Berkeley's sign hypothesis? Although Gibson did not use the phrase *simulative assumption*, he clearly opposed the idea. In the following quote, he was quite definite in this respect. (Similar remarks can be found in Gibson, 1948, p. 180; 1950a, pp. 5, 116, 134, 190.) "The stimulus-variable within the retinal image to which a property of visual space corresponds need be only a correlate of that property, not a copy of it" (1950a, p. 8). The assumption disputed in the previous passage is that in order to *see* (not just infer) some property in the world, that property must be simulated in the retinal image. (The one common exception to this rule was color.) A phenomenal effect in the psychophysical relation was always, excluding color, a simulation of the optical image. Conversely, Gibson asserted that a stimulus correlate of a property of the physical world was sufficient to produce a perception of that property. And correspondingly, a perception, which is a function of some specific stimulus, need not be a simulation of that stimulus. One of the major reasons why various historical figures hypothesized a process of supplementation in visual perception was their adoption of the simulative assumption. (For example, distance needed to be added to visual sensations since it wasn't simulated in the retinal image.) Avoiding this supposition would eliminate one major obstacle toward believing in a psychophysics of perception. Since there were 2,000 years working against him, why did Gibson suppose the possibility of nonsimulative psychophysical relations? There are at least three answers that can be offered to this question.

One answer lies in Gibson noting that the original rationale for the simulative assumption was the homunculus hypothesis, and later the picture concept of the retinal image (Gibson, 1950a, pp. 54, 62). Both of these ideas had long since lost any credibility in their original forms, but the simulative assumption did not succumb to the same fate. It continued in importance in spite of the fact that there was no longer any apparent justification for holding it. Descartes and Lötze, in particular, were aware of the relationship between the simulative assumption and the ideas of a homunculus and retinal picture. It can be concluded that one reason for Gibson's rejection of the simulative assumption was simply realizing that there was no reason to hold it, if one reliquished belief in a homunculus and a retinal picture. Gibson gave up these ideas. For him the perceiver was not aware of the visual world because there occurred an internal observation of the retinal image. Rather, the retinal image was thought of by Gibson as the proximal stimulus for the visual world, that is, as a *cause* of perceptual experience.

What led Gibson to see that the rationale behind the simulative assumption was the homunculus hypothesis? Troland had suggested a psychophysics of perception in which perceptual experiences could be considered a direct function of the proximal stimulus without there being an intervening step of sensations. Although Troland was well aware of the fact that the proximal stimulus did not simulate its physical sources in all respects he contended that perceptual experience of the physical world was the immediate phenomenal effect of the proximal stimulus. This would entail a rejection of the simulative assumption in psychophysical correspondences. Because the literary source for Gibson's psychophysics of perception was Troland's writings, Gibson's rejection of the simulative assumption could have been based, in part, on Troland's views.

Also, Gibson had studied at least one case of a nonsimulative psychophysical relation between proximal stimulation and perceptual experience. In his adaptation studies, the subjects' experiences in the negative after-effect condition were not simulations of the proximal stimulus. This occurred without any apparent intervening effect that was a simulation of the stimulus, and there was still a specific stimulus value correlated with each experienced degree of curvature or tilt.

It is highly probable that the apparent contradiction between the simulative assumption and both Troland's psychophysics and the results of Gibson's adaptation studies motivated Gibson to consider the rationale of the simulative assumption. By the end of the 1940s, he had done just this and realized that it was based on the homunculus hypothesis and the picture concept of the optical image.

Before leaving this discussion of how Gibson's psychophysics differed from the simulative assumption, an apparent paradox needs to be introduced. Recall that after Alhazen and Kepler, the hypothesis that the optical image does simulate all the spatial properties and relations of the world was relinquished. Followers of the *eidola* hypothesis, such as Democritus, believed in complete simulation of the world in the *eidolae,* but it was thought from the Middle Ages onward that all that reached the eye was a two-dimensional physical configuration. In 1950, Gibson proposed that although it is true that a literal replica of the world does not reach the eye (i.e., a simulation of the physical world), there is a different sense in which the physical world that is perceived is simulated in the optical image at the retina; or as he said, "in a special sense, the outer world *does* get into the eye" (1950a, p. 9).

When an observer looks at some specific area in the physical world, his retinal image can be considered a mathematical (projective) transformation of that given area. Regarding this mathematical transformation, Gibson remarked that he was "borrowing" an "assumption" from geometry that implied that there are invariants not "lost" in this transformation (1950a, pp. 9, 153). The specific source Gibson had in mind was probably Courant and Robbins (1941, Chapter IV). (Gibson did not cite them on p. 9, 1950a, where the idea was first expressed, but he did so on p. 153, 1950a, where it was further developed.)

Within Gibson's *Perception of the Visual World,* there is further development of this general hypothesis that the spatial properties of the physical world are mathematically preserved in the retinal projection. He gave some specific examples (1950a, p. 153 ff) that are mentioned later. The important fact to be kept in mind at this point is that although Gibson referred to the proximal stimulus as a "correlate" of the physical world, he actually meant something stronger. When he argued that "correlates" of the physical world in the retinal image were the stimuli for the visual world, he was using this word to emphasize the difference between his concept of mathematical preservation and the prevalent notion of physical replication.

Gibson's psychophysics of perception explicitly attacked the sign hypothesis proposed by Berkeley. When Gibson originally proposed a general psychophysics of visual perception (1947, 1948), he was not always definite that there was any difference in meaning between perceiving via cues and perceiving via stimuli. The terms were often used interchangeably (e.g., 1947, pp. 177, 223; 1948, pp. 177–179), but in one instance he did distinguish their meanings (1947, p. 191). In this last cited passage he stated that perceiving by means of a cue involved inference or a mediational process, whereas an inference was not required if the perception was based on stimulation. This demarcation was carried over in his 1950 book. The question that needs to be answered is why perception via cues involved inference, while perception via stimulation in Gibson's psychophysics did not require this kind of intervening step.

Recall that Berkeley's reason for supposing that an intervening step was necessary in visual depth perception was that the retinal image did not simulate physical distance. The visible ideas that were "proportional" to the retinal image were, for Berkeley, limited to the dimensions of the image. They could not be of distance; the idea of distance could only be suggested from the mental sign. Berkeley hypothesized that the basis of this suggestion was association between "visible" and "tangible ideas." Gibson avoided the mediating psychological step because he believed that the proximal stimulus could produce a perception of distance without having to simulate (in Berkeley's sense) physical distance. Hence, because Gibson's psychophysics was an alternative to the proposed simulative relation between visible ideas and the retinal image that Berkeley accepted, no process of suggestion via cues was required.

This contrast is the crucial sense in which Gibson's concept of stimuli for perception (i.e., perceptual psychophysics) differed from Berkeley's hypothesis of sign mediated perception. Gibson, though, did not fully realize that this was the important disparity between his view and Berkeley's. He supposed that the concept of a cue implied a probabilistic relation between variations in the retinal image and in the physical world. The idea that cues are probablistically correlated with distal relations was taken by Gibson from Brunswik (1944). Oppositely, Gibson thought his proposed higher-order properties of the retinal image were "exact correlates." Gibson believed that the reason an inference was necessary with cues was that cues are probable correlates of distal relations (1950a, pp. 115, 116, 137). But this idea is only first stressed by Brunswik and was not a necessary assumption in Berkeley's original formulation. In fact, contrary to Gibson (1950a, p. 61), Berkeley actually believed that the various signs of distance were reliable correlates of the distance of an object. It is true that the correlates of spatial properties and relations in the world listed by Berkeleians are limited both in scope and number relative to Gibson's proposed "correlates." Secondly, it is also true that most of the traditional cues were not thought of as geometrically related to distal spatial properties and relations. But it certainly was not the case that Berkeleians believed these cues were cues because they were equivocal.

Because the relationship between Berkeley and Gibson is crucial in understanding both the history of visual perception and Gibson's own development, this comparison needs to be further discussed. Berkeley was an extremely astute and influential theorist and it is important not to oversimplify and casually dismiss his theory. If Gibson in his psychophysics of perception was providing a real alternative to Berkeley, then Gibson's psychophysics was accomplishing a huge theoretical step because Berkeley is the eponym of a theoretical perspective in psychology as significant as Newton's theory was in physics.

Gibson states that depth cue theorists suppose a judgment-like process is involved in depth perception (1950a, pp. 13–24, 69, 108, 129, 138). When Berkeley is careful, he also opposes the "judgment" theory (1709, sec. 4–7, 10, 24, 42; 1732, sec. 8–10; 1733, sec. 14, 427). Mediation, for Berkeley, means one idea eliciting a second idea—there is nothing quasi-logical about this process. The best analogy would be that it is an associative "reflex." Because visible and tangible ideas bear no resemblance to each other, there cannot be any logical process connecting them. The judgment metaphor comes later with J. S. Mill, Helmholtz, and Brunswik. When Gibson suggests that perception is immediate, he is saying more than just that it does not involve judgment-like processes. He is saying it is as immediate as seeing color. "Immediate process . . . implies that the impression of distance may have a definable stimulus just as the so-called sensations have" (1950a, p. 69).

Gibson repeatedly states that his psychophysical theory is concerned with explaining the "visual world" (objective seeing) (1950a, pp. 14, 20, 42–43, 54–58). This functionalistic-epistemological emphasis in Gibson is significant, and although theorists like Koffka emphasized experience per se, as well as showing a great interest in illusions, Berkeley was also concerned with objective seeing. In fact, Berkeley emphasizes at times the "proportional," "uniform," "constant," and "regular connexion" between ideas of vision and touch (1709, sec. 144–145, 152, 1732, sec. 8, 12; 1733, sec. 40, 66, 68). For Berkeley the ideas of touch constitute the objective world. His idealistic metaphysics turns the objective world of matter into tangible ideas contained in the universal mind of God. Speaking of visual ideas as the "language of the Author of Nature," he goes so far as to state that the major point of his theory is how we learn this "universal language," thus perceiving the world veridically. Berkeley, defending the common man's view of the world, attacked the supposed reality of Newton's *inferred* world of colorless atoms. Similarly, Gibson was concerned with the objective reality of perception, though he has not gone to the metaphysical extreme of Berkeley in rejecting the world of atoms. For Gibson, there are equally objective levels of physical reality. To be fair to Gibson, though, Berkeley and, more importantly, his followers did not define perception epistemologically as a form of knowledge; rather, it was defined as an experience. Secondly, Berkeley and his followers never devoted much attention to either the objective conditions of perception (stimulation) or the objective environment that is perceived.

As stated earlier, Berkeley's theory of distance perception did not follow from his idealism; hence, it was not Gibson's realism contra Berkeley's idealism that separated the two on depth perception. In fact, many followers of Berkeley were realists, albeit indirect realists, and Gibson, in his psychophysics of perception was still an indirect realist in at least one important sense. Though Gibson rejected psychological mediation in any sense and also rejected the homunculus hypothesis ("inner observation"), he *ontologically* separated perceptual experience and the physical environment. Experience *corresponded* with the environment. In Gibson's ecological approach, perception was *of* the environment. In the 1950s Gibson, still following Berkeley and other empiricists, saw perception as a state rather than an activity; consequently Gibson was not giving perception as thorough a functional interpretation as he would later. Even if Gibson had believed in the 1950's that what is seen is the physical environment, it would not follow that if the environment possessed three dimensions then all three dimensions would be seen (Armstrong, 1960, pp. 8, 26–31). Realism does not imply a complete or total awareness of all properties of reality.

The problem with using descriptions of consciousness as an arbitrar in theoretical disputes can be illustrated through a comparison of Berkeley and Gibson. Berkeley does not initially use assertions based on introspection in arguing that distance is not seen (1709, sec. 2–11; 1732, sec. 8–9), though he does invoke introspection to refute the natural geometry approach of Descartes and Kepler. Only as an afterthought does he use introspection to support his views (1709, sec. 45; 1732, sec. 8). Berkeley, though, does believe that introspection reveals that ideas of distance are tactual-muscular. Recall that James held to the opposite view where introspection reveals a visual experience of three-dimensional spatial volume. Gibson, in turn, described the experience of distance as something different than James—as an experience across surfaces. Historically, there have been as many different descriptions of perceptual consciousness as explanations. Theoretical explanations do not seem to be applied to preexistent perceptual facts—the facts come together with the theories. The idea of a pure description of perceptual consciousness does not hold water, and any theoretical difference, such as explanations of distance perception between Gibson and Berkeley, cannot be accounted for in terms of different conscious descriptions. The different descriptions presuppose the theoretical differences.

It could be argued that the significant difference between Gibson and Berkeley is in their conceptions of distance. If distance is a line (length) through space, how could it be seen for *what* is there to see? Conversely, if Gibson defines distance as the continuum across the ground then there is *something* to see. The conclusion could be drawn that Gibson rejected the depth cue explanation because he defined distance differently. As mentioned earlier, this interpretation is not correct, but there are certain additional remarks that will further clarify the issue.

If Berkeley is thought of as an "air" (empty space) theorist, then we are glancing over a very important critical hypothesis in his philosophy. Berkeley attacked the very conceivability of absolute empty space assumed in Newton's physics (1707–1708, No. 35; 1709, sec. 43, 122–127; 1710, sec. 115–116; Luce, 1944, pp. 323, 328). (Kant would support Newton.) When Berkeley does speak of perceiving *empty* space, he reduces it to sensations of exertion without feelings of resistance. Perception of extension, in accordance with his empiricism, is always in terms of some sensory quality. Berkeley states, "No extension but surface perceivable by sight" (1707–1708, No. 35).

It is noteworthy that in spite of this view, Berkeley still rejects slant and solidity as visual ideas—they must be obtained through touch and muscular effort. The unquestioned assumption of Berkeley's era was that all features or aspects of three-dimensionality were beyond vision. When Berkeley states that only surface extent can be seen he was not only arguing against Newton's empty space but he was tacitly suscribing to the idea that vision is limited to two-dimensional extent. Berkeley's real problem is in explaining how the distances of objects are perceived and not how empty space could be perceived. And when it comes to the distances of objects, Berkeley does believe there are visual correlates. These additional considerations bring us back to the conclusion that Berkeley accepted literal simulation as a necessary condition for spatial vision, whereas Gibson did not, and in spite of whatever other theoretical differences separated them, it was this difference of opinion that unequivocably separated them.

VISUAL STIMULATION

One of the most important factors behind Gibson's basic assertion that there existed psychophysical correspondences for the totality of perceptual dimensions was his reformulation of the concept of the proximal stimulus. He reasoned that psychologists had accepted the necessity of contributory processes and the impossibility of psychophysical correspondences in visual perception because they had described the retinal image at the wrong level of analysis. Koffka (1935), for example, argued against specific correspondences between the proximal stimulus and perception and had disparagingly referred to this view as the constancy hypothesis, but Koffka considered the proximal stimulus only as a set of points. Gibson's psychophysical proposal in 1950 was in actuality a reassertion of the constancy hypothesis founded upon "a broader conception of stimulation" (1950a, p. 62), except now the constancy postulated was between perception and the proximal stimulus. It could be the case that nothing needed to be added to a redescribed proximal stimulus in order to make perception what it is, viz., organized and specific to the physical environment (1950a, pp. 24–25).

The general hypothesis involved in Gibson's psychophysics, taken from Troland, was that mathematical functions could be discovered between variations in a dimension of perceptual consciousness and variations in stimulation. The retinal image was thought by Gibson to be the visual stimulus and was considered the necessary condition for all vision (1950a, p. 44). The retinal image was the visual stimulus because it was the immediate cause of physiological activity and, indirectly, visual perception (Gibson, 1950a, p. 63). Consequently, in two noteworthy respects, Gibson's conception of the optical basis of vision in 1950 still followed traditional views. First, he thought at this time that the stimulus for vision was the retinal image. Secondly, he continued to characterize the optical basis for vision as a stimulus, viz., as a cause. Six years subsequent to the publication of *The Perception of the Visual World,* he substituted the optic array for the retinal image and soon thereafter dropped the general supposition that the optical basis for vision caused visual perception. Both these rather drastic modifications marked the decline and eventual relinquishment of his psychophysical theory and the beginning of his ecological approach.

On the other hand, Gibson (1947, 1948, 1950a), in his initial development of a psychophysics of perception, broke with several historically prevalent views of the retinal image. First, the retinal image was no longer depicted as functionally analogous to a picture. Second, when considering the retinal image as the stimulus for vision, he did not characterize it as merely a set of points. Instead, Gibson introduced the concept of adjacent order in describing the stimulus for vision. Third, retinal patterns as stimuli for the visual world were depicted independently of their relations with the anatomical units in the retina.

The latter two hypotheses of Gibson are first introduced at an abstract level. A more thorough and concrete discussion of these proposals along with an examination of Gibson's concepts of the 360° retinal image and sequential stimulation is presented in the next section within the contexts of specific issues such as surface and distance percep'   ..

The stimulus for vision could be described in terms of a set of points of light energy, each causing excitation in one individual receptor unit in the retina. If the effect of the retinal image was described in this manner, the correlated (or caused) phenomenal experience was invariably thought of as a set of extensionless sensations. Toward the end of the 19th century, many Berkeleians and non-Berkeleians contested this implication. Gestalt psychologists later carried this revolt even further, but the problem was that if the peripheral visual nervous system initially reacted to just points of stimulation, then a process of either physiological organization or concatenation seemed necessary.

Contrary to this line of reasoning, Gibson suggested that "simultaneous variation over a set of receptors . . . and the order of such a variation" could be considered a stimulus for vision. He postulated that the stimuli discovered in a psychophysics of visual perception would be types of ordinal stimulation. If this was found to be the case, it could be concluded that eyes responded to order and variations of order as such and not the individual values of each point of stimulation (1950a, pp. 62–63, 151, 152). Characterizing the stimulus for vision differently than just a set of independent points was not completely new, but the historical alternative to pointillism had been to describe optical support in terms of two-dimensional forms, often as analogous to pictorial forms. Gibson's hypothesis that an ordinal relation in the retinal image (e.g., a texture gradient) was a visual stimulus was clearly incommensurable with the pictorial form representation of the retinal image. In effect, Gibson was arguing that relationships (e.g., ratio's, transitions, etc.) between energy values were stimuli.

Through Ternus (1926) and Koffka (1935), Gibson became acquainted with the idea of the "transposable Gestalt." The major negative implication of Ternus' study was that anatomical identity of a point of stimulation over time was not a necessary condition for a phenomenally identical point. Instead, a phenomenally identical point corresponded to the stimulus point that occupied the same position relative to other stimulus points over time. In explaining this fact, Koffka (1935) argued that a physiological process of organization was required.

In contrast to Koffka's view, Gibson proposed a distinction between the anatomical pattern of retinal stimulation and the ordinal pattern of retinal stimulation (1950a, pp. 55–58). In the former case, identities of stimulus points, positions of patterns within the image, and movement of points and patterns in the image are described with respect to an anatomical locus. Conversely, all of the above may be depicted independently of the anatomical retina; this was for Gibson the "ordinal" concept of stimulation. Such facts of the image are described relative to the arrangement in the image per se, for example, the same stimulus point over time is defined as that point that occupies the same relative position with respect to other points. The stimulus for visual direction is not anatomical position, but relative position within the patterns of the retinal image, and movement is defined as a change in position of a point or pattern relative to other patterns in the retinal image. In visual perception, the eyes directly react to these ordinal features of the retinal image and not the specific loci of excitation on the retina. This ordinal theory is relational, whereas the anatomical theory gives stimulus points absolute values. In the anatomical view, the position of any stimulus point or pattern can be ascertained independently without reference to other points of stimulation. Gibson's concept of ordinal stimulation applies the relational theory of organization to stimulation. The relational theory was discussed as it applied to the spatial framework hypotheses of the Gestalt psychologists and James, but Gibson took the theory as a way in which to describe order in stimulation. Previous history has shown that the only real principle of visual stimulus order was Kepler's camera image. Gibson was proposing that relations (e.g., identities or differences in light energy) offered a basic ordering principle of visual stimulation.

If, as Gibson suggested, the eye reacts to "ordinal patterns," no process of organization or allowance for eye movements is required to explain why an object retains its identity and constant position when its projected retinal pattern moves over the retina during eye, head, or body movement (Gibson, 1950a, pp. 55–56, see Diagram 17).

In Gibson's (1950a, pp. 1–7, 26–43) phenomenology of visual perception a distinction between the "visual world" and the "visual field" was proposed. The visual world corresponded to the physical world in that it is veridical experience of the world. In his discussion of the visual stimulus, Gibson (1950a, Chapter 4) proposed that ordinal patterns of the retinal image were the stimuli for the visual world, i.e., the visual world is in psychophysical correspondence with ordinal stimulation (1950a, p. 57). Conversely, Gibson suggested that the visual field was a function of the anatomical pattern of stimulation. Gibson also argued that the visual world was not dependent on the visual field. Consequently, this demarcation was not the usual sensation-perception distinction since traditionally visual perception was derived via contributory processes from visual sensations. Gibson's visual world-visual field dichotomy, though, is analogous because the visual world is objective experience, whereas the

DIAGRAM 17

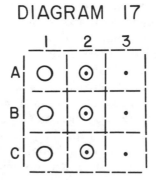

A1, A2, A3, B1, . . . C3 are nine locations on the retina. Locations stimulated at time X have a circle in them. Locations stimulated at time X + Y have dots in them. If the stimulus is anatomically defined, A2○ = A2·, etc. and A2○ has the same position as A2·, etc. Ordinally considered, A2○ = A3·, or C1○ = C2·, and A2○ has the same position as A3·, etc.

visual field is subjective experience. Second, Gibson's distinction is similar to Troland's sensation-perception distinction. By the mid 1960s, Gibson's visual world-visual field distinction had become somewhat transformed to greatly resemble Troland's (1929, 1930) understanding of the difference between sensation and perception. This movement toward Troland's views is quite significant since the basic theme of Gibson's *Senses* (1966a) was very close in meaning to Troland's demarcation between sensation and perception.

SURFACE AND DISTANCE PERCEPTION

Three factors that undoubtedly played an instigating role in Gibson's initial formulation of his "ground theory" of space perception were his aviation research (Gibson, 1947), Carr's thoughts on the perception of distance (1935), and the ecological universality and functional significance of the terrain in evolution and animal activity. Of comparable importance regarding the genesis of Gibson's "ground theory" were the studies of Metzger (1930) and Katz (1935). According to Gibson, a major implication of these studies was that perceived space became at best indeterminate when the stimulus condition for surface perception was eliminated (Gibson, 1947, p. 289; 1950a, pp. 4–5, 53, 66–67). Metzger (1930) had proposed the term *microstructure* to designate this requisite stimulus feature, but in 1947 Gibson, drawing his inspiration from Metzger, substituted the more general term *texture* to refer to this essential stimulus condition for surface perception.

Recall that Koffka (1935) saw in Metzger's (1930) study a demonstration that visual perception of three dimensions occurs with totally homogeneous stimulation. Contesting Koffka's interpretation of the *Ganzfeld* experiments, Gibson argued that spatial perception vanished with homogeneous stimulation and the absence of a perceived surface. Simply stated, without a visual surface supported by optical texture, there was no visual space; hence, stimulus heterogeneity was a necessary condition for a visual surface and visual space. The results of Metzger's experiments, if construed in this manner, are in conflict, as Gibson noted (1950a, p. 64), with the local sign hypothesis of spatial emplacement. Perceptual localization of position does not occur even though all the individual anatomical units in the retina are stimulated. If each unit produced a sensation that had a local sign associated with it, subjects should perceive in the *Ganzfeld* situation a determinate two-dimensional plane, each point on this plane having a specific location.

In conjunction with Gibson's growing conviction during the 1940s that space (distance) was perceived across a continuous terrain or surface, he developed an explanation to account for this hypothesized perceptual fact. Gibson suggested that various types of stimulus gradients were the optical basis for perceiving continuous distance in all directions across the terrain. He defined the term *gradient* as an "increase or decrease of something along a given axis or dimension" (1950a, p. 73). These included the gradients of texture, objects' projected sizes, binocular disparity, width of inlines, and probably most significantly, deformation of the retinal image. Although all of the stimulus gradients were proposed by Gibson in 1947, his discussion of each of them was cursory; only in 1950 were they all thoroughly described and explicated. Due to the limitations of space, neither the gradient of binocular disparity (Gibson, 1947, pp. 193–194; 1950a, pp. 100–106 nor the gradient of aerial perspective (Gibson, 1950a, pp. 86–90) are considered.

First let us examine how Gibson sought to account for visual perception of distance across a surface when the observer is stationary. He began his explanation by making two assumptions about the physical environment. Solid surfaces in the environment, in particular the ground, invariably are not perfectly smooth or chemically homogeneous. Secondly, the grain or small structural irregularities of surfaces are, on the average, evenly distributed—this being especially true for the granular structure of the ground (Gibson, 1950a, p. 77). To initiate an explanation with environmental considerations is noteworthy insofar as it is historically unusual and indicative of Gibson's future ecological approach to problems in visual perception. Corresponding to these environmental conditions, the retinal image of a projected surface will have texture if such surfaces are illuminated and the eye is correctly focused. Due to the granular surface of the ground, the sides of each "grain" facing the source of illumination will reflect more light than the sides facing away. This produces on the retina an alteration of areas of higher and lower levels of light energy or *optical texture*. A texture unit can be defined as a circumscribed area of homogeneous light intensity.

Consider a hypothetical situation in which an observer is facing a surface with a stochastically even distribution of granular irregularities. Geometrically, it can be demonstrated that the relative density of texture units for any given area of the retinal image is a function of the distance of its projective area on the surface. The longitudinal separation of texture units decreases as a linear function of distance, whereas decrease in vertical separation is a negatively accelerated function of distance (see Diagram 18).

There will be a specific gradient of increasing density of texture units on the retina from top to bottom when an observer is standing on level

DIAGRAM 18

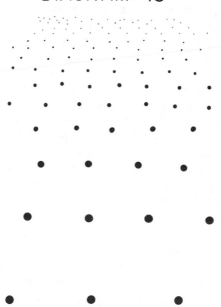

ground. According to Gibson, this gradient should produce a perception of continuous distance in all directions across a longitudinal surface (1947, pp. 188–191; 1950a, pp. 77–86).

If the gradient is eliminated, the corresponding perception should be of a frontal surface, a frontal surface being defined as a surface which intersects a longitudinal surface at a 90° angle (see Diagram 20).

In most cases, there will be objects of various sizes scattered over the ground. If for any given area of the ground the average size of objects is approximatly equal, there will exist a gradient of decreasing average projected size of objects from the top to the bottom of the retinal image (1947, p. 191; 1950a, pp. 77–86).

A third type of gradient can be observed in cases in which a physical surface is composed of parts with rectilinear "inlines," such as floors or sidewalk pavement. For example, the boards of a floor an observer is standing on project upon the retina a gradient of decreasing longitudinal separation of inlines that is a linear function of distance, and a gradient of decreasing vertical separation of inlines that is a negatively accelerated function of distance (1950a, pp. 86–90; (see Diagrams 21 and 22).

The depth of individual objects on the ground are, contrary to the Berkeleian explanation, perceived within a spatial framework, viz., the continuum of distance across the ground provided by the retinal gradients (1950a, pp. 176–183). Because the top of a projected form of an object

DIAGRAM 19

When the gradient is reversed, the receding longitudinal surface will be perceived above one's head, i.e., a ceiling effect.

(this corresponds to the base of the object because the image is inverted) is located somewhere along the retinal gradient, the scale of distance provided by the retinal gradients fixes the particular distances of objects. As mentioned earlier, this explanation is "similar" to Carr's account of object depth perception.

For Gibson, retinal gradients were conceived of as stimuli for the visual perception of distance and not as signs. Perceived distance across a surface was hypothesized to be a psychophysical function of a stimulus gradient (i.e., no process of inference or associative mediation was thought to be required). Gibson's major reason for maintaining that a stimulus gradient produces perception of continuous distance without a contributory intervening process was the fact that a specific value of a gradient is a precise (not probabilistic) mathematical function of the rate of increasing physical distance of an evenly structured surface (1950a, p. 92). Gibson's basic assumption that if there is a psychophysical correspondence in vision, then the visual stimulus in this retinal-phenomenal relationship is environmentally univocal, anticipates his later contention (1966a) that visual perception is contingent upon optical information (i.e., invariants and transformations in the optic array are ecologically specific to features of the environment).

DIAGRAM 20

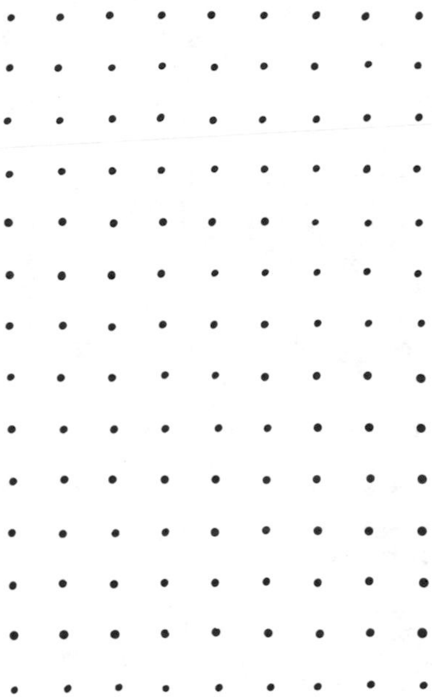

Though in Gibson's *Visual World* the hypothesis of ecological corre-spondence is not emphasized nor independently developed apart from the hypothesis of psychophysical correspondence, as it is in his later book, *The Senses,* it is clearly contained within the earlier work. The retinal image is thought of as a geometrical projection of the surrounding environment (1950a, pp. 47–48); this geometrical relationship is "pre-cise," "lawful," and "specific" (1950a, pp. 8–9, 52–53, 80–86). Regarding distance, according to Gibson there exists a correspondence between variations in the rate of recession of surfaces (changes in slant) and the gradient of texture density (1950a, pp. 67, 70–71, 80–86, 88, 92). Similar statements are made regarding the relationship of the gradient of deforma-tion and distance (1950a, pp. 119, 190, 126, 127, 138, 143). Finally Gibson explicitly argues that veridical visual perception has as a necessary condition ecological correspondences (1950a, p. 54). As a functionalist, Gibson was looking for an objective basis for veridical perception.

Looking ahead, Gibson eventually de-emphasized the significance of retinal gradients with a stationary observer. A major reason for the lessening of importance of these stimulus gradients was the experimental fact (Gibson, Purdy, & Lawrence, 1955) that in isolation they did not yield stable and veridical perception of continuous distance. As Gibson real-ized, the explanation for this negative result was that although for a given

DIAGRAM 21   DIAGRAM 22

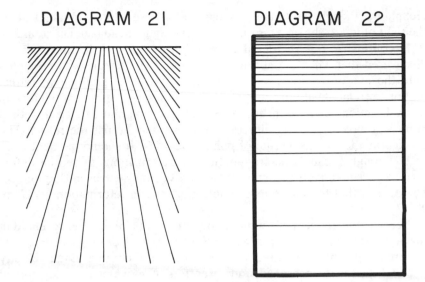

surface slant, there will be a specific stimulus gradient, if one drops the assumption that the surface must be stochastically evenly textured, a retinal gradient is projectively specific to an infinite number of surface slants. This lack of ecological specificity for gradients with a stationary observer and the apparent fact that visual perception based upon these stimulus variables was not specific to one surface slant led Gibson in the late 1950s to place more stress on a type of visual stimulation that was ecologically specific, viz., sequential order. The origins of Gibson's understanding of this type of stimulation date from 1947 to 1950.

When Gibson initially approached the problem of how airplane pilots perceive distance, the normal condition encountered was obviously not a stationary observer, but a continuously moving one. In such circumstances, the gradients of texture density, object size, inline width, etc., still persist, but there will now be a new stimulus gradient that was not present when the observer was stationary. Gibson referred to this stimulus variable as the "velocity gradient" (1947, pp. 192–193), 219–226), "retinal motion perspective" (1948, pp. 182–184) or the "gradient of deformation" (1950a, pp. 117–131).

For the moment, consider cases in which a moving observer fixates upon the point in the environment toward which he is moving. It had been known, at least since the time of Helmholtz (1866), that the relative velocity of an optical point in the retinal image across the retina is inversely proportional to the distance of its projective physical source. Awareness of such retinal velocities (motion parallax) was thought of as a depth cue for the distances of objects (Helmholtz, 1866, III, pp. 295–297).

Helmholtz, though, limited his discussion to those retinal velocities off to the right or left as the observer is moving straight ahead (see Diagram 23).

In contrast to this restricted conception of retinal velocities, Gibson discovered that when the surface structure of the terrain was projected onto the eye of a moving observer, there existed a gradient of retinal motion correlated with the continuously increasing distance of the terrain in all directions away from the observer (see Diagram 24). Each retinal point will have a rate and direction of movement across the retina. The gradient is the increasing rate of point velocities. It should be mentioned that although Gibson's diagrammatic characterizations of retinal deformation were invariably in terms of velocity vectors such as in Diagram 24, he stressed that the image as a whole underwent deformation (1947, p. 222).

Because the gradient of retinal deformation was initially represented in the aforementioned manner, it was an instance of describing a property of the proximal stimulus relative to the anatomy of the retina. Each velocity vector is actually the speed and direction of movement of an optical texture unit over the retinal surface. Yet so far in this discussion of retinal deformation, it has been assumed that the observer fixates at the point on the horizon toward which he is moving. What happens to the retinal velocity vectors when the observer moves his eyes or head? The result is that a constant velocity vector (anatomically defined) is added to every velocity vector. Gibson realized this meant that although the individual anatomical values of velocity vectors will vary as a function of eye movement, the gradient of relative velocity vectors remains invariant. Inasmuch as this gradient is totally independent of image movement over the retina, it is a gradient of ordinal stimulation rather than anatomical stimulation (1950a, p. 125–127).

What is of considerable historical interest in Gibson's gradient of deformation hypothesis is that it is a variable definable only over time. Because the analogy between the retinal image and a static picture

DIAGRAM 23

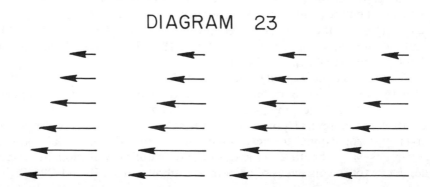

DIAGRAM 24

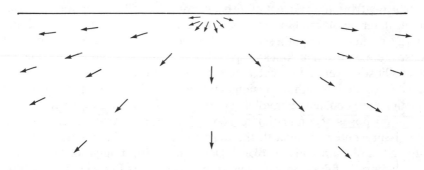

became popularized, the perceiver was not thought to be sensitive to optical change, a property of optical change, or an invariant of optical change as such. Only those instantaneous properties of one given retinal image were thought of as stimuli. Perceived change, such as movement, always required memory images, integration, inference, or some process of meta-temporal organization. For Gibson, memory images of immediately preceding retinal images were not thought necessary; the eyes of an observer were directly sensitive to change and the gradient of change.

It is historically interesting that, given the above fact, Gibson continued to refer to the proximal stimulus as the retinal image. The gradient of optical deformation on the retina is not, strictly speaking, a property of the retinal image as it was traditionally understood. Relative flow velocity only emerges with temporal variations in retinal stimulation. Gibson later abandoned the view that the retinal image was the visual stimulus, and one of his main reasons behind this change was that a temporal transformation is not a property of a static momentary image. Temporal or sequential order became for Gibson his second basic ordering principle of stimulation. Gibson would become increasingly interested in the dynamic or temporal dimension of stimulation, something he first noticed in his aviation studies. Not only did Gibson discover the ground up in an airplane, he also "discovered" motion and time.

Gibson also noted that besides retinal flow being environmentally specific to continuous distance, it was also correlated with the direction of locomotion of the observer. When the head and eyes are motionless, the point in the retinal image that all deformation radiates from was referred to as the focus of expansion. Significantly, the projective source of the focus of expansion is that physical point in the environment towards which the observer is moving. Thus, the focus of expansion could yield accurate visual sensitivity to direction of locomotion (1947, pp. 226–230; 1950a, pp. 124–128, 135, 224). This hypothesis represented another im-

portant departure from traditional psychology in that it had been generally thought that bodily movement could not be sensed through vision.

Starting from the concept of visual stimuli for self-perception, Gibson,
in his later ecological psychology, would challenge Müller's specific
energy of nerves hypothesis. Proprioception is not specific to certain
senses (e.g., muscular kinesthesis). But perhaps at a more fundamental
level, Gibson eventually treated perception and proprioception as continuously coupled together. Vision, audition, and all the other sensory
functions are ecological, involving both perception and proprioception.

For purposes of summation and comparison, the standard list of depth
cues is presented along with the four basic types of stimulus gradients
outlined in Gibson's *Visual World*. Depth cues are thought of as "signs"
or "elicitors" of depth perception—the perceiver is first cognizant of the
cue and then derivatively, distance. Secondly, distance perception is of
independent objects separately. Regarding stimulus gradients, the perceiver is not normally aware of the gradients. The gradients cause an
immediate awareness of distance, primarily as a global continuum, and
secondarily of individual objects against this background (the spatial
framework hypothesis).

The Depth Cues
1. *Accomodation:* In focusing, the degree of muscular tension in the
   lens is inversely correlated with the distance of the fixated object.
2. *Convergence:* Degree of muscular strain in eye muscles is inversely
   correlated with the distance of the fixated object.
3. *Binocular Disparity:* The degree of disparity is correlated (inversely) with the distance of an object.
4. *Motion Parallax:* The relative speed of an image moving across the
   retina correlates (inversely) with the object's distance.
5. *Size:* The father away an object is, the smaller its image on the
   retina.
6. *Interposition:* One object blocking a complete view of a second
   object indicates that the first object is closer.
7. *Aerial Perspective:* Objects farther away look less clear, whereas
   objects closer show more detail and sharper definition.
8. *Geometrical Perspective:* Convergence of lines indicates (increasing) distance.

It should be noted that some depth cues appear similar to Gibson's
stimulus gradients. Gibson thought of some of the depth cues as special or
limiting cases of stimulus gradients, though how a depth cue is theoretically interpreted is different than how stimulus gradients are conceived. A

gradient is a wholistic property of stimulation, mathematically or abstractly identical with the recession of the ground away from the observer.

The Simulus Gradients

1. *Texture Density Gradient:* The optical projection to an eye contains a gradient of increasing texture density for surfaces receding in distance from the observer.

2. *Size Gradient:* The optical projection to an eye contains a gradient of decreasing sizes of structures from objects at increasing distances from the observer.

3. *Line Gradient:* The optical projection to an eye contains vertical lines converging to a point at the horizon and horizontal lines becoming increasingly closer together with increasing distance from the observer.

4. *Gradient of Movement (Deformation):* As an observer moves across a surface the projected figures of environmental structures closest to the observer exhibit maximum relative speed across the retina, as well as maximum rate of expansion, whereas for structures farthest away the projected figures show minimum relative speed and rate of expansion. If an observer is moving away from an environmental structure, the projected size decreases—the farther away, the slower the optical contraction.

OBJECT PERCEPTION

The surface of the physical terrain is normally not only structured with small irregularities at the scale of millimeters and centimeters, but also at the level of meters and miles, i.e., the terrain consists of hills, mountains, valleys, canyons, etc. This macrostructure can be analyzed into inclines and declines of specific rates. A maximum rate of decline would be a 90° dropoff, whereas a maximum rate of incline would be the side of a mountain or plateau at a 90° angle to the ground. The rate of incline and decline may in addition be relatively constant, for example, when a dropoff is straight down, or the rate may vary as in the surface curvature of hills and valleys. Gibson used the expression "surface slant" to refer to this macrostructure feature of the terrain.

Any surface slant can be characterized in terms of its optical slant, the angle between the surface and the line of regard of the eyes of the observer (Gibson, 1950a, pp. 99, 143, 172). For example, a frontal surface that has no optical slant produces a 90° angle if interesected with the line of regard. Gibson believed that the rate of a stimulus gradient is specifically correlated with the degree of optical slant of a surface. Any permanent, transient, gradual, or abrupt alteration in the optical slant of the ground (or an object) will have a specific correlate in a change in the rate of the stimulus gradient (Gibson, 1950a, pp. 91–99). (See Diagram 25 for a gradient of a surface that curves away from the observer and Diagram 26 for a surface that abruptly changes slant more toward the observer.)

Although the following implication was not fully developed by Gibson in his 1950 book, it is worth noting that the rate of increasing distance of the ground away from the eyes of the observer (degree of optical slant), across any given extent of ground, is a gradient, i.e., the amount of change in distance from the observer between two points on a surface divided by the surface extent between those two points yields a value from 0 to 1.0. A drop-off straight down yields a value approaching 1.0, whereas a frontal surface approaches a value of 0. Since the projected stimulus gradient of retinal deformation is a precise mathematical function of it, the constancies and variations of the physical gradient of the surface layout are not lost, but preserved, in the stimulus gradient. In this sense, at least certain features of the environment are mathematically retained in the retinal image. The relationship between the changing stimulus gradient and the variations in surface slants extending outward around the perceiver is not merely correlative in the Berkeleian sense.

In explaining the visual perception of the solid (three-dimensional) shape of an object, Gibson, following Koffka (1935), assumed that it is never perceived independently of the object's slant. In 1947 (pp. 171–172), Gibson spoke as if there existed a mediational step between first

DIAGRAM 25

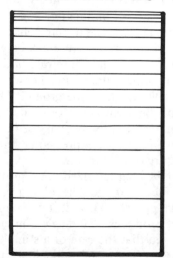

DIAGRAM 26

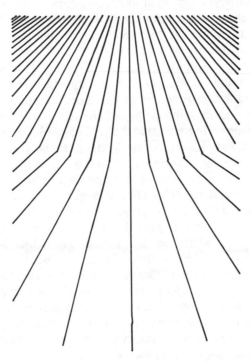

perceiving the slant of an object and its projected form, and then perceiving its solid shape. This account of perceived solidity was similar to the explanation, originating with Alhazen, that was proposed by Berkeleians. One year later Gibson still believed that the shape and slant of an object were linked in visual perception (he continued to hold this belief in the 1950s), but he no longer described the process of perceiving solid shape as mediational (1948, p. 181). As an object rotates, its projected form undergoes (except for a perfect sphere) compression or expansion. Secondly, there occurs texture densification or rarefaction. For a given projected side of an object, if there is retinal form compression there is concomitant texture densification, whereas retinal form expansion is coupled with texture rarefaction. Hence, there is a reciprocal variation in texture density and projected form. Gibson suggested that the "sum or product" (he appeared to be unsure) of these "reciprocal stimulus variables" is constant and is the visual stimulus for solid shape (1948, p. 181). In 1950 he pointed out that the gross number of texture units in a retinal form is constant and specific to the surface area of the facing side of an object. When an object is rotated, its sides would not appear changed in area or form if the stimuli for perception of solid shape are the previously listed ones. Perceiving the solid shape of an object is not mediational, but instead a direct psychophysical function between stimulation and visual perception. Later in the 1950s, Gibson attempted to verify the above psychophysical hypothesis. Eventually, in the late 1950s, Gibson formulated an alternative account of the stimulus basis of perceived shape founded upon the concept of invariants of optical transformations, but he was clearly moving in this direction in arguing that there is something constant in stimulation even though perspectives on an object change.

In his war research, Gibson studied the accuracy of size perception in outdoor conditions. He found that the size of an object could be perceived veridically even for objects extremely distant (784 yards) (1947, pp. 205–211). At this time, Gibson contended, citing the evidence of Holway and Boring (1941), that size perception depended upon distance perception (1947, pp. 197–199). In 1950, Gibson argued that size perception was contingent upon distance perception in the sense that the stimulus gradients for continuous distance provided a scale for perceiving the extent of a physical area anywhere on the ground. An object's size will remain constant in visual perception because it is a function of this scale for extent of surface (Gibson, 1950a, pp. 174–186). As was also the case with Gibson's account of an object's relative position and distance, the idea of a visual spatial framework (that provides a scale for area of extent) was employed by Gibson in explaining the perception of an object's size. The ground is the environmental framework and the corresponding stimulus gradients are the stimulus framework.

One difference between Gibson's understanding of size perception and Boring's was that Gibson supposed size should become perceptually indeterminate when distance became indeterminate. Conversely, Boring (Holway & Boring, 1941) contended that their results demonstrated that size perception approached relative retinal size when distance became indeterminable. The reason for this disagreement was that Boring believed objective size was mediated via retinal size and depth cues, whereas for Gibson the perceived size of an object was not mediated by prior registration of retinal size. Gibson soon thereafter clashed with Boring on this difference of opinion (Boring, 1952a, 1952b; Gibson, 1952b).

Berkeleians (e.g., Helmholtz, 1866, Chapter 30 and Brunswik, 1944) invariably have supposed that perceived objective size was based upon retinal size, distance perception, and a psychological process analogous to inference. Boring (1942, pp. 288–299) presented some of the history but he erred (pp. 223, 298) in stating that Berkeley argued for this type of mediation. For Berkeley, size perception was *not* mediated by distance perception, but by visible signs of size (Berkeley, 1709, sections 59–78).

The hypothesis of distance-mediated size perception should really be related to Alhazen.

In the last few sections, Gibson's wholistic approach to stimulation has been a central theme. Not only did Gibson suggest that both spatial and temporal relationships should be considered as visual stimuli, providing stimulation with inherant principles of order, but Gibson treated the ordinal retinal image as a complex, organized whole. Features (parts) within the image are described relative to the overall configuration (the whole). This wholistic stimulus configuration was the set of gradients. Gibson in the future would work this wholistic theory out in more detail and scope, such that distance, location, movement, size, shape, and slant all would be incorporated into this basic scheme.

THE VISUAL FRAMEWORK

The perceived constancy of an object's size and shape were for Gibson actually just individual cases of the more general perceptual phenomena of a stable visual world (1947, p. 227; 1950a, p. 166). Visually perceived objects retain their position, size, shape and identity over time when in physical fact they do not move, change size, alter in shape, or disappear. What is the stimulus basis for this perceived stability and constancy of the environment? Previously Gibson (1938a) had argued that the spatial stability of the visually perceived world was based on "postural stimuli," an answer that was quite similar to the Berkeleian explanation of this phenomenon. In 1950, the answer Gibson offered differed radically from his previous one in many respects. His change in position concerning the solution to this problem, to a great extent, reflected his overall abandonment of Berkeley's theory.

According to Gibson (1950a, pp. 145–162), neither visual nor gravitational sensitivity is primary in determining the spatial framework of perception. Instead, he viewed them as concomitant determinants, either one being a sufficient condition for providing stable spatial axes in perception. One factor responsible for Gibson's relinquishment of his old solution was the work of Asch and Witkin (1948a, 1948b, 1948c). They had found that instead of the postural sense of direction dominating the visual axes, when an artifical conflict was introduced between visual and postural stimuli for orientation, there usually occurred a "compromise." Gibson thought these results implied that neither vision nor postural sensitivity was dominant in determining the spatial framework for vision (1950a, p. 150). But even if this were true, the real problem for Gibson was finding an explanation of how vision can have an independent stable spatial framework. The explanations provided by Gibson to this problem and the related issue of the boundlessness of the visual world are of incomparable historical interest. First, as mentioned earlier, Gibson's abandonment of Berkeley's theory is most evident in his resolution of these problems. Consequently it is here that Gibson's originality at this stage in his development was most apparent and striking. Secondly, Gibson's later concept of an optic array is, within limits, anticipated in his 1950 explanation of the stable and boundless visual world. What follows is a summary of Gibson's explanation of the stable and boundless visual world (Gibson, 1950a, pp. 160–162).

If the visual stimulus is described ordinally instead of anatomically, arrangement and relative position of stimulus patterns remain invariant when the eyes are rotated. Of particular significance, the stimulus "correlate" of the total terrain does not rotate around when the eyes are turned. Consequently, there exist invariant ordinal relations between the projection of the ground and stationary objects, even when the eyes are rotated. The stimulus "correlate" of the ground yields a stable spatial frame of reference for all the objects on the terrain, providing a basis for the perception of the constant size, shape, orientation, and position of unchanging physical objects.

When the observer moves his eyes and body, the visual stimulus could be described as a sequence of discrete retinal images. What actually occurs on the retina is not a sequence of separate images, but continuous optical transformations during locomotion and interspersed ordinally overlapping images during eye movements. There are within these transformations, relatively persisting ordinal patterns and relations. This relative ordinal permanence exists because for any two successive points in time (between shifts in eye position or body position) there is a varying amount of overlap of ordinal patterns and relations. Because of this overlap, the retinal transformations occurring as an observer turns his eyes will have a set of ordinal patterns all of which will be ordinally related to one another. Likewise during locomotion the total set of ordinal patterns and relations is never instantaneously interchanged with another set. Note that Gibson is looking for order and permanence embodied in change.

This hypothesis of an unbounded potential image of ordinal relations is conceptually halfway between the traditional retinal image and Gibson's later idea of an optic array. Gibson suggested describing the toal set of ordinal retinal relations of a hypothetical complete rotation of an eye around any one point in space as a 360° potential "image in time." This hypothetical image, which at any one instant in time is only partially on the retina, is boundless and ordinally unitary. When the observer moves across a surface, there will be various samples of a *continuous* series of these 360° images. Because there are hypothesized ordinal invariants over a continuous series of images, e.g., the continual projection of the terrain, the ordinal patterns of the series are related to one another. Gibson contended that the invariants of such continuous transformations are the stimuli for the stable properties of the visual world when the observer is locomoting. This would explain why the visual world has identity, permanence, and boundlessness over time, instead of being composed of bounded, transient and separate impressions. In this explanation, Gibson is reuniting the dual ontological realms of Plato. Unity, order, and permanence in stimulation emerge when time and transformations are brought into a description of stimulation. The hypothesis of a series of static, separate retinal images is rejected.

Gibson, in postulating that this 360° potential image is the visual stimulus, was suggesting that the permanence, stability, and boundlessness of the physical environment is actually preserved in the optical basis for vision. This would constitute another example of Gibson's general contention that the environment "in a special sense does get into the eye." The historical problem, conditioned by Kepler's analytic treatment of stimulation, was that an inappropriate level of analysis of stimulation was assumed. Further, because the traditional description was elementaristic, stimulus values were absolute values, e.g., wavelength, intensity, and anatomical location. As we will see in later chapters, Gibson becomes increasingly concerned with "stimulus structure," i.e., relationships within stimulation. Absolute localized values of energy are rejected as the stimulus basis of perception. It is wholistic and relational stimulus structure which preserves the environment.

Chapter 13 _____

GIBSON'S PSYCHOPHYSICS

THE CONCEPT OF PERCEPTION

The period 1950–1956 can best be thought of as a time when Gibson attempted to experimentally carry through and further explicate the approach he expressed in *The Perception of the Visual World*. But this period should also be recognized as the period in which problems and ideas emerged that later instigated Gibson's abandonment of the psychophysical approach. (Some of these motivating factors are evident in the psychophysical theory of Gibson in 1950.)

Gibson's psychophysical theory was founded upon the simple hypothesis that if perception is veridical, there must then be a causal basis for it in stimulation. In attempting to outline such psychophysical relations, Gibson described stimulation at a level of analysis (or order) commensurate with a phenomenology of perception. Because he thought that veridicality must be accounted for through stimulation, he viewed possible physiological or psychophysical factors as having a negative or negligible effect upon perceptual veridicality. Consequently, Gibson contended that the hypothesis of non-stimulus determiners in perception was experimentally supported by studies in which perception tended toward nonveridicality. In such experiments, stimulation was impoverished and non-stimulus factors became more dominant. Following Troland, it is the objective conditions (including stimulation) that account for the veridicality (objectivity) of perception (Gibson, 1951b, pp. 94–96, 105; 1953, p.

121; 1954a). Because Gibson (circa 1950) thought of the retinal image as the *cause* of veridical visual perception, and viewed the process of vision as a causal series of events beginning in the eye and terminating in the brain, any non-stimulus factors could not have a positive effect on perceptual veridicality. This follows because the basis of veridicality, viz., the stimulus, is independent of processes in the perceiver in a unidirectional causal chain. The problem Gibson eventually faced regarding this unidirectional causal model was that environmental specificity in visual stimulation appeared to be only necessary and not sufficient for perceptual veridicality; Gibson's ecological hypothesis (1961a) of the optic array *was that it was not a cause of visual perception.* Gibson's concept of stimulation changed from a cause of perception to an opportunity for perception. Gibson took this approach when it became apparent to him that various psycho-physiological factors were essential in visual perception. Gibson did not view these psychological and physiological processes in the usual contributory and mediational sense. One line of thought that led Gibson in this new direction was his literal world-schematic world distinction.

The demarcation between the literal visual world and the schematic visual world was introduced by Gibson in *The Perception of the Visual World* (1950a, pp. 210–212); a year later, he further developed the distinction and its implications (1951b, pp. 98–109). According to Gibson, the degree to which visual perception is stimulus determined, it is correspondingly "literal"; conversely as visual perception becomes less a function of stimulation and more a function of subjective factors, it is progressively more "schematic." That is, though Gibson's primary concern as a functionalist was to explain the veridicality of perception, he acknowledged the reality of misperception and accounted for it through non-stimulus factors. The question is why visual perception should vary to the degree to which it is stimulus determined. The answer Gibson offered, although he did not realize it at the time, was inconsistent with his psychophysical program.

Gibson maintained that visual perception was literal (stimulus determined) when the observer attended to and explored the physical environment thoroughly and meticulously. Perception is more schematic as exploration and attention become more cursory and under the influence of momentary needs, emotional states, social stereotypes, and mental set (1950a, pp. 210–212; 1951b, pp. 98–109).

It was also suggested by Gibson that corresponding to these two types of determinants of perception there should be two semi-distinct theories of perception. Explaining why perception is literal involves a psychophysics (Gibson's goal), while accounting for its divergence involves studying personality and social factors (1951b, p. 104). The former theory was considered primary and most important (1951b, 1953, p. 126); Gibson's paramount investigative concern was with perception's function and not its dysfunction.

The difficulty inherent in the ideal that a psychophysical "theory" will explain veridicality derives from the fact that stimulation is not a sufficient condition for visual perception, i.e., optical support is *not* a cause inasmuch as literal perception depends on the facts of attention and exploration (by Gibson's own admission). A correlate of a physical fact in the retinal image *as such* does not necessarily cause a veridical perception of this fact. Therefore, veridicality can never be accounted for by merely discovering which environmentally specific optical invariants are concomitant with the visual perception of the environment. Without the fact of attention there would not be perceptual-optical or perceptual-environmental correspondence; hence, it is essential to include its role in an explanation of veridical visual perception. Secondly, attention is actually involved in determining which "potential" images do become actual on the retina. The retinal image per se is not an independent variable; it is contingent on what the animal looks at in the environment. This is not to say that psycho-physiological factors add to the structure in stimulation or even "copy" it, but rather that stimulus structure is not a sufficient condition for perceptual veridicality. The perceiver must do something. Further, the retinal image can not be treated as independent of subsequent psycho-physiological processes, for its existence depends on such processes.

The relation proposed by Gibson (1950a) between the visual field and the visual world was immediately attacked by E. G. Boring (1952a, 1952b). For Gibson, the latter was not dependent on the former. Oppositely, Boring believed the visual world was contingent on the visual field. Boring thought of Gibson (1950a) as a phenomenologist in the tradition of Gestalt phenomenology (Boring, 1951, 1952a, 1952b). This was paritally correct. Boring drew an analogy between Gibson's belief in the phenomenal immediacy of the visual world and the Gestalt hypothesis that perceptual experience is immediate and not built up out of elemental sensations. Alternatively, Boring suggested that Gibson's visual field is actually the "reduced" visual world (1952a, 1952b). Although Boring's arguments may be unsound, the possibility of his making them existed because of a weakness in Gibson's argument for the phenomenal primacy of the visual world.

Consider the following. An ordinal relation can be derived from anatomical retinal relations through a cancellation of eye and head movements. For example, a stimulus point from a stationary source moves across the retina when the eyes rotate. Its ordinal location does not change but its anatomical location does. If the amount of eye movement was unconsciously registered and substracted from the anatomically relative stimulus point movement, the result would be a perception of stationary location. The perception based upon anatomical relations and "computation" would therefore be identical with an ordinal-based perception. (This computation hypothesis can be found from Alhazen onward through Helmholtz and structuralists.) Because Gibson's visual field roughly corresponded to the anatomical retinal image, it could be argued that the visual world is a dual function of the visual field and unconscious (or physiological) allowance for eye and head movements. This account would imply that the visual world was mediated and not psychophysically direct.

Gibson's (1952b) rebuttal to Boring suffered because Gibson could not refute the hypothesis that the visual world was actually based upon the visual field (assuming sufficient mental acrobatics on the part of the perceiver). Much later, Gibson, noting the weakness of his former argument, was able to avoid this alternative explanation of the visual world (1966a, p. 237). If visual perception is not explained in terms of the retinal image (ordinal or otherwise), there is no possibility of its derivability from the visual field (or the anatomical retinal image). Gibson's concept of the optic array provided just such an alternative in an explanation of visual perception; the optic array is independent of eye, head, and body movements. It should be noted though that the ordinal retinal image provided a simpler explanation than the anatomical retinal image at least in not requiring the registration and cancellation of eye-head-body movements. Further, in order to explain the boundless and integrative nature of the visual world through the visual field, memory and constructive processes would also have to be introduced.

A second topic of importance in Gibson's phenomenology of visual perception during this period was his position concerning phenomenal surfaces. Although Boring's hypothesis (1933) of dimensions of consciousness was influential in Gibson's thinking, Gibson, in one noteworthy instance, still adhered to the hypothesis of conscious elements in 1950, suggesting (1950a, p. 8; 1950b) that one of the elementary impressions of spatial experience was a visual surface; visual space was composed of and reducible to visual surfaces. He later decided that surfaceness was not an "elementary experience" but a value along a conscious dimension (Gibson and Dibble, 1952, p. 418). This dimension varies from one extreme of determinate surface quality to the other extreme of indeterminate voluminous fog. There are degrees of surface quality. This switch in Gibson's phenomenology of visual surfaces represented an even further move in the direction of Boring than in 1950.

VISUAL STIMULATION AND OPTICAL INFORMATION

The development of the optic array in Gibson's psychophysical approach, as an alternative to the retinal image, was gradual. As mentioned earlier, the potential 360° retinal image by Gibson (1950a) was a partial step in the direction of the optic array. In 1955, (Gibson, Olum, and Rosenblatt, 1955; Gibson, Purdy and Lawrence, 1955) Gibson made the explicit switch from the retinal image to the optic array. It should be emphasized that originally Gibson referred to the optic array as the visual stimulus, as if to imply that it was the cause of visual perception.

In the introductory discussion of his optical tunnel article (Gibson, Purdy, & Lawrence, 1955) Gibson stated that "The stimulus for visual perception is focusable light, that is, light which is capable of forming a pair of images in the two eyes." This "optical stimulus" is the sheaf of rays entering each eye, and, quite significantly, Gibson proposed that "the rays," in terms of which the optical stimulus is described, should be concevied of as points of change and not as absolute values of energy (pp. 1–2).

In this article, Gibson's reason for suggesting that the optical sheaf was the visual stimulus was based on his Ganzfeld study (Gibson & Waddell, 1952) and Metzger's (1930). A differentiated retinal image was necessary for visual perception, and this type of image was contingent upon accomodation and a sheaf of rays entering the eye that has transitions. Therefore, a sheaf of rays containing transitions is the necessary condition for visual perception, and it is the independent variable in a psychophysical relation.

Two additional reasons for Gibson's substitution of the optic array for the retinal image can be uncovered in a 1955 article dealing with "motion perspective" (Gibson, Olum, & Rosenblatt, 1955). Gibson, in describing the vector velocities of a deforming retinal image, previously had defined velocity relative to the surface of the retina (1950a, pp. 117–124). In 1955, Gibson avoided the idea of retinal velocity vectors by representing the gradient of deformation in the sheaf of rays entering the eye. If the gradient of deformation is understood as a global transformation of the sheaf of rays, there is no need to postulate the addition of a constant velocity to all retinal velocities when the eyes move. Deformation in the sheaf of rays is independent of eye movements.

A second factor that motivated Gibson to substitute the sheaf of rays for the retinal image in this publication (Gibson, Olum, & Rosenblatt, 1955) was the fact that the complete pattern of deformation could not be depicted on the retinal image. Instead, the total gradient could be conveniently represented on the projection of light from the ground to an abstract point.

Even if the aforementioned considerations constituted the original incentive for Gibson's renunciation of the time-honored belief that the optical basis of vision was the retinal image, what was Gibson's source for the idea of the optic array? In all probability, Gibson is indebted to Troland and perhaps Heider. Gibson was very familiar with their publications many years prior to 1955 and, as far as the author can ascertain, sympathetic with their views. On the other hand, the concept of the optic array in Gibson's thinking has over the last 18 years undergone various modifications and refinements that were not inspired by either Troland or Heider. More generally, the concept of a convergent array of light (or light energy) can be found in some form down through the ages from Greeks to da Vinci. Given Gibson's views on stimulus structure, the optic array concept more satisfactorily fits these ideas than does the retinal image.

Gibson had argued (1950a) that previous perceptual theorists assumed only probabilistic relations between variables of the visual stimulus and properties of the environment. Rather, what had been the usual historical case was that very few environmental correlates were thought to exist in visual stimulation. In contrast to this historical fact, Gibson in 1950 had hypothesized that there were univocal or specific stimulus correlates for all features of the visually perceived environment. This concept of environmental specification is what Gibson eventually meant by the assertion that there is information in the optic array. Gibson began to use the term *information* (Gibson, Olum & Rosenblatt, 1955, p. 383; 1956, p. 206) to denote the fact that stimulation was specific to the properties of the environment. In conjunction with the aforementioned ecological hypothesis, Gibson assumed that the perceiver would (if he is attentive, sophisticated, etc.) see what the stimulus was specific to in the physical world. Or stated differently, visual perception is objectively specific to the environment up to the degree to which its stimulus conditions are objectively specific to the environment.

Earlier the phrases "ambiguous stimulation" and "conflicting stimulation" were introduced. A related concept not yet mentioned, but often employed by Gibson, is "redundant stimulation" (1950a, 1952a, 1956). In the case of vision, "ambiguous stimulation" meant for Gibson circa 1950–1955 a value of a variable of stimulation that was projectively related to more than one environmental fact. For example, a retinal form may result from a whole family of shape-slants. Or a texture density gradient may result from an evenly microstructured surface slanting away from the perceiver or an unevenly microstructured surface at 0° optical slant. Gibson believed that perception resulting from such cases of ambiguous stimulation would be unstable, i.e., not consistently specific to any one environment fact. In the 1960s, Gibson substituted "equivocal information" for "ambiguous stimulation" (1966a, pp. 246–249).

For Gibson, "conflicting stimulation" meant two values of different stimulus variables that were specific to contradictory environmental facts. For example, a longitudinal surface could be constructed where texture irregularities became increasingly less dense such that it projected to the eye of an observer a zero texture density gradient. As the observer approached the surface the gradient of deformation would be specific to extended surface distance but the texture gradient would be specific to a frontal surface, hence the stimulus conflict. If visual stimulation "conflicted" with postural stimulation (Asch & Witkin, 1948a, 1948b, 1948c) with respect to the directions of up and down, each would be correlated to a different direction; hence, the corresponding perception of the vertical and horizontal axes should oscillate or reach a compromise. Similarly, later Gibson dropped the phrase "conflicting stimulation" in favor of "conflicting or contradictory information" (1966a, p. 296).

Normally, stimulation is not only specific to just one set of environmental facts, but "redundant." During close observation, the gradients of binocular disparity and retinal deformation in visual stimulation are specific to the same facts concerning the distances of objects across the ground (see also Gibson & Carel, 1952; Gibson, Olum & Rosenblatt, 1955). Therefore, the objective veridicality of visual perception is doubly supported through stimulation. "Redundant information" replaced "redundant stimulation" in Gibson's ecological approach (1966a, pp. 287–304). All of the previous ideas revolving around the notion of optical specificity (to the environment) were absorbed into the concept of visual information and the general hypothesis that visual perception could be veridical to the extent to which there was information about the environment in the optic array.

In summary, during the early 1950s, Gibson was clarifying and developing the idea of ecological correspondence between stimulation and the environment. What is the structure of stimulation? What is meant by correspondence and a lack of correspondence? What happens when there is a lack of univocality? And what are the pros and cons regarding identifying the retinal image as the visual stimulus? One central theme of this period, supporting and further clarifying his functional approach to perception, was that where information becomes equivocal or conflicting, perception becomes indeterminate and subject to individual variations. Stimulus specificity to the environment is a necessary condition for veridical perception.

SURFACE AND DISTANCE PERCEPTION

The hypothesis that a gradient of density of texture units was the stimulus for visual perception of continuous distance across a surface underwent various modifications during the period 1950–1956. The hypothesis that optical texture in the retinal image was the stimulus for a perceived surface was altered. Gibson's postulated psychophysical relation between the degree of phenomenal surface slant and the gradient of texture unit density suffered a negative fate for both experimental and conceptual reasons. Thirdly, Gibson moved further away from the idea of velocity vectors being defined relative to the retinal surface.

In defining the visual stimulus for a perceived surface, Gibson in 1950 meant by a texture unit a delimited area of homogeneous intensity and wavelength. If an eye was sensitive to texture units in the above sense, it would be responding to absolute values for each given area of the retinal image. When Gibson argued (1950a) that a perceived surface was a function of retinal texture, he did not mean to imply that the eye initially responded to the absolute value of each unit and derivatively the heterogeneity across units. But his definition of texture units in the above sense was not commensurate with the hypothesis that an eye reacts directly to heterogeneity. A new definition of optical texture was necessary.

Gibson proposed such an alternative by defining retinal texture in terms of transitions and not units of absolute values (Gibson, Purdy, & Lawrence, 1955, p. 2). Transitions could be described in terms of the rate of change of intensity or wavelength across the image and the change in the rate of change of intensity or wavelength. Gibson's hypothesis that the eye was sensitive to texture entailed a direct reaction to transitions without a mediating step of responding to absolute values at each location. In offering this new definition of texture, Gibson moved further away from the hypothesis that the visual stimulus was describable in terms of absolute localized values of energy, viz., pointillism. This new definition of optical texture was relational and was a specific application of his 1950 concepts of stimulus structure and order.

In 1950, Gibson opposed Koffka's contention that homogeneity in visual stimulation was a sufficient stimulus condition for perceived space, maintaining that retinal texture (hence a phenomenal surface) was essential for visually perceived space. In order to more convincingly demonstrate his position, Gibson conducted a series of experiments (Gibson, 1950b; Gibson and Dibble, 1952; Gibson, Purdy, and Lawrence, 1955; Gibson and Waddell, 1952) to investigate more thoroughly the stimulus conditions for a perceived surface.

One of Gibson's major hypotheses tested in these studies was that the stimulus for a visual surface was "gradients of luminous intensity in the image between small regions of different intensity (that) are maximally steep" (Gibson & Dibble, 1952, p. 414). Because of the results obtained in these experiments, Gibson saw a problem with the above statement's implication that a phenomenal surface is an all-or-nothing affair. In these articles he came to the different conclusion that surfaceness was a variable dimension. What led Gibson in this new direction?

Although Gibson found that complete stimulus homogeneity yielded, at best, a phenomenal space that was "indefinite," "indeterminate," or "ambiguous" (Gibson and Waddell, 1952, pp. 267, 269), a maximally differentiated texture was discovered not to be necessary for a phenomenal surface. A homogeneous area of stimulation that is sufficiently large in angular extent and is surrounded by a region of different intensity yielded a degree of phenomenal surfaceness "with respect to hardness" (Gibson and Dibble, 1952, p. 417). The bounded homogeneous area had no texture, so this result contradicted the simple formulation of the texture hypothesis. It appeared to Gibson that the contour of the bounded area was an adequate stimulus condition for a relatively "hard" phenomenal surface.

In general, Gibson found that a phenomenal surface was not an all-or-nothing affair, but depended upon several stimulus factors, e.g., degree of texture differentiation, angular size of a contoured region, density of transitions (number per unit area). It varied from indefinite fog, to film color (Katz, 1935), to a soft surface and a hard surface (Gibson & Dibble, 1952). At best, his hypothesis of maximally small and steep transitions was necessary for the last case. Because of these psychophysical relations for various grades of surfaceness, Gibson abandoned the idea that a surface was a phenomenal element and the simple texture hypothesis proposed to explain this elementary experience. Surfaceness was hereafter thought of as a dimension of consciousness, in the tradition of Boring's (1933) view of consciousness.

Gibson's gradient of texture density hypothesis underwent substantial revision in his studies with the "optical tunnel"; see Diagram 27.

It was found that as more elements (number of transitions) were added to a retinal density gradient, visual perception of continuous distance through the tunnel became more probable and perceived distance of the "pseudo tunnel" more accurate (Gibson, Purdy & Lawrence, 1955, pp. 5–8). The simple fact of a texture gradient being correlated with continuous physical distance was not sufficient for perceived distance, as such, or the veridical perception of the magnitude of distance. The degree of retinal density (number of transitions) must be great enough or distance perception becomes increasingly indeterminate and less veridical.

Another fact revealed in the optical tunnel experiment was even more significant. In one situation, the tunnel was arranged to project a zero gradient and the subject viewed the tunnel monocularly and without head movement. According to Gibson's texture density gradient hypothesis, this situation should have produced a phenomenal flat (frontal) surface, but on the contrary, subjects' reports varied. Sometimes the tunnel appeared flat, but more often it was seen as having some depth. Gibson was forced to conclude that the texture density gradient in isolation was

DIAGRAM 27

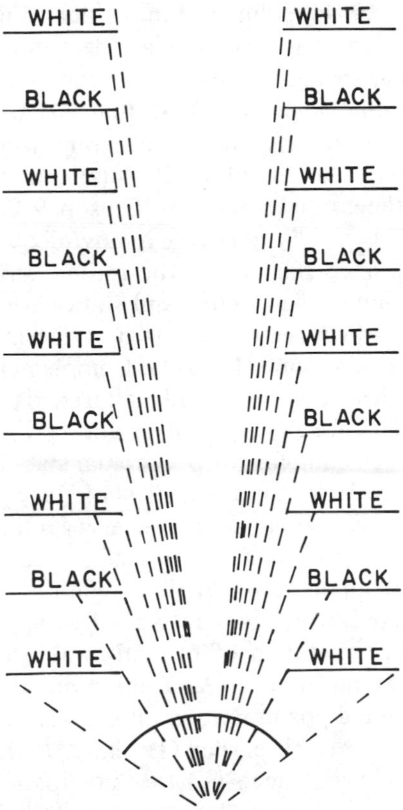

A longitudinal section of one arrangement of nine elements (transitions) projecting a density gradient from peripheral to center. The tunnel is a series of alternating black and white surfaces with circular holes (from Gibson, Purdy, and Lawrence, 1955, p. 3)

not in psychophysical correspondence with a definite and accurate perception of the degree of surface slant (Gibson, Purdy & Lawrence, 1955, p. 10–12). Why shouldn't there be a psychophysical correspondence between the gradient of texture density and perceived slant and surface distance? In answering this question, Gibson introduced the idea of ambiguous stimulation. This concept is historically important because it is related to Gibson's later idea that veridical perception is based on stimulus information. The gradient of texture density in isolation is not projectively specific to one possible environmental condition. Where there is lack of univocality between stimulation and the environment, there is a corresponding lack in veridicality and determinateness in perception. The concept of information entails ecological specificity.

SPACE AND MOTION

In two articles (1952a, 1954c) published in the period under examination, Gibson returned once again to one of his oldest interests: the stimulus condition for the visual spatial framework. In the latter cited publication Gibson argued, following Duncker (1929), that visual motion was determined by a visual frame of reference. This framework for Gibson was supplied by the ordinal relations of visual stimulation, in particular the optical projection of the ground. (See also Gibson & Smith, 1955).

When an observer is visually pursuing a moving object, the projection of the object remains fixed relative to the retinal surface, but it moves relative to the projection of the ground and stationary objects. This type of transformation of ordinal relations was hypothesized as the stimulus for perceived motion (1954c, pp. 310–311). Complementarily, Gibson did not think that motionlessness of optical patterns relative to the retinal surface was the stimulus for perceptually stationary objects. Instead he contended that the visual stimulus for perceptual stability was a preservation of ordinal relations. When an object is stationary its projected image on the retinal surface moves about as the observer rotates his eyes, but no change occurs in relative positions of patterns on the retina. If the visual spatial framework is supported by ordinal relations, the object should remain perceptually fixed, which is what actually happens.

Gibson's (1952a) interpretation of recently published data in studies (e.g., Noble, 1949; Mann, Berry, & Dauterive, 1949; Passey, 1950) dealing with the visual and postural determinants of phenomenal vertical and horizontal was similar to his earlier (1950a, p. 150) explanation of the Asch studies. Again, Gibson suggested that in situations where postural and visual stimulation are in conflict, phenomenal results may, quite naturally, be contradicotry across different studies and unstable for any one subject. Gibson had originally introduced the phrase "conflicting stimulation" in 1950, but was indefinite as to its meaning. Secondly, it was not clearly explained in 1950 why conflicting stimulation should produce unstable and varying perception. Besides an analogous elucidation regarding ambiguous stimulation, the clarification of the concept of conflicting stimulation was also involved in Gibson's development of the idea of information.

FORM, SLANT, AND SHAPE

The psychophysical correspondence proposed by Gibson (1950a) between the gradient of texture density and the degree of phenomenal slant was not corroborated in his optical tunnel study. Earlier, Gibson had attempted to test this hypothesis utilizing different stimulus conditions (1950b, pp. 375–378), viz., an irregular pattern and a regular grid pattern. The projected gradients were varied and subjects reported perceived slant. Generally, a correlation was found between degree of perceived slant and the texture gradient, but subjects underestimated the actual optical slant; hence, the psychophysical correspondence was not exact.

In a later experiment, Gibson (Gibson & Cornsweet, 1952) sought to experimentally separate optical slant from what he referred to as geographical slant. Geographical slant was the slant of a surface relative to the line of gravity, whereas optical slant was defined relative to the line of sight. Both, according to Gibson, are perceivable, but Gibson had emphasized (1950a, 1950b) optical slant, thinking it was "simpler" (1950b, p. 369) or "determined by fewer variables of stimulation" (Gibson & Cornsweet, 1952, p. 12).

Gibson stated that in his earlier study (1950b), he had not controlled for the possibility that subjects were reporting geographical slant instead of the desired optical slant. In this later experiment (Gibson and Cornsweet, 1952) he had subjects judge and report each type of slant separately. It was once again found that the perception of optical slant was not a strict function of the texture density gradient. Ultimately, Gibson lost both conviction and interest in his hypothesis of a psychophysical correspondence between the texture density gradient and perceived optical slant. This change of heart was due in part to the negative data in the above studies, but an important conceptual realization was also involved.

What is historically noteworthy in Gibson's 1950–1955 understanding of geographical and optical slant is the fact that he did not employ the idea of a visual spatial framework to explain either kind of phenomenal slant. The optical slant of any surface was supposedly perceived independently of the average gradient projected from the overall terrain or ground. In ecologically normal situations this average gradient should be specific to the perpendicular of the line of gravity. Likewise, Gibson, in endeavoring to account for the perception of geographical slant, assumed that it was a dual function of perceived optical slant and postural stimulation resulting from the eye-head position relative to the line of gravity (Gibson & Cornsweet, 1952, p. 14). Gibson believed perceived geographical slant was mediated and not just a function of visual stimulation. Also, presupposing the above explanation, perceived geographical slant would not be dependent on a visual spatial framework.

This approach to perceived slant was not in harmony with his almost universal utilization of the visual spatial framework in dealing with other problems in visual perception such as position, distance, size, and motion. If, according to Gibson, the stimulus correlate of the physical ground provides a visual frame of reference for most geometrical features of environment, should not the perceived slant of any surface also be relative to this framework? But which kind of slant (geographical or optical) could be explained in terms of a visual framework?

In noting that the ratio of a texture gradient projected from a delimited surface and the surrounding average gradient projected from the ground is specific to a surface's geographical slant, Gibson later provided a hypothesis for surface slant perception consonant with this idea of a visual framework. Optical slant is not perceived very accurately because the perceiver is normally, primarily, and directly sensitive to geographical slant via this ratio of gradients. From an ecological and evolutionary point of view, this perceptual fact makes sense because it is hills and cliffs that need to be perceived in order for animals to survive and locomote efficiently. As was the case with his redefinition of optical texture, Gibson changed a specific idea making it consistent with a general principle, viz., in this case he was extending the application of the spatial framework hypothesis to perceptual slant.

From the time of Alhazen onward, depicting the optical basis for vision in terms of pictorial forms was a common practice. Gibson (1950a) had proposed an alternative characterization of stimulation in disagreement with this view. The observer was not aware of his retinal image (pictorial concept) nor were gradients, in any sense, forms. This was especially true for the gradient of retinal deformation which definitely was not a property of a static picture. In the article dealing specifically with the problem of visual form (1951a), Gibson amplified his previous arguments against the pictorial form-retinal image analogy. In particular, he challenged the Berkeleian position that awareness of two-dimensional forms was more immediate than perception of solid shapes. Explanations of solid shape perception, since Alhazen, involved postulating sensitivity to two-dimensional forms in the retinal image (via a homunculus, simulation, or a local sign mechanism) as a mediating step. This awareness of retinal form plus signs (depth cues) produced solid shape perception. Gibson, on the other hand, argued that if just outline forms were presented to subjects, the resulting perception would not in all cases be of a form without slant and distance. Instead, Gibson believed that the effect would be unstable perceptions of physical surfaces at varying slants (1951b, pp. 410–411). Visual perception of a perspective form without a slant is not any more direct than an outline form perceived at a slant.

In a later publication (Gibson & Beck, 1955), Gibson further developed the above thinking and attempted to experimentally ascertain its validity. Consider first that any projected form on the retina can result from an infinite set of physical surfaces at varying slants. A particular projected triangular form on the retina may arise from any member of a family of triangles at different slants (see Diagram 28).

DIAGRAM 28

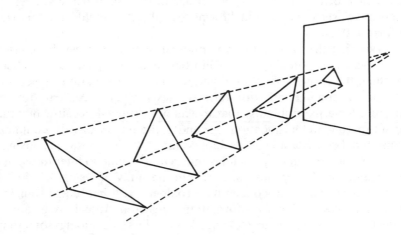

Gibson argued that the perception resulting from an isolated retinal form would be of a member of its family of shape-slants; hence, there will be a perceived form at a specific slant and not always a form at zero slant and distance. Furthermore, because each member of this family is a unique coupling of a particular physical form at a particular slant, Gibson supposed that these form-slant couplings would be preserved in perception; this was the shape-slant invariance hypothesis of Koffka (1935). In disagreement with most Berkeleians, Gibson contended that retinal form was not a stimulus for perceived form, but for a family of form-slant couplings. Why did Gibson maintain this position?

Insofar as a retinal form is not projectively specific to any one shape-slant, Gibson concluded that the perceptions should vary. Any visual perception produced by a retinal form should be of some member of its family of shape-slants. What Gibson was presupposing in this argument was that the environmental univocality of a stimulus determines the degree of specificity of the resulting perception. Lack of a one-to-one psychophysical correspondence is a consequence of a lack of one-to-one stimulus-environment correspondence. Second he was assuming that a perception corresponds to the environmental correlate of its stimulus and not the physical dimensions of the stimulus per se. (This latter view would be the simulative assumption.) This type of reasoning was anticipative of his thinking regarding optical information, viz., the projective specificity of the optic array to the environment sets the limits for the veridicality of visual perception.

The shape-slant invariance hypothesis had been previously tested by Stavrianos (1945) with negative results. A perceived shape was not uniquely coupled with one particular slant. Gibson obtained similar results (Gibson & Beck, 1955, pp. 126–130), but he did find that for a given retinal form there was no one singular form-slant perceived. If the perceiver was sensitive to retinal form, the subjects should have reported that form at 0° slant.

Overviewing the variety of experimental tests of the psychophysical theory, there is no simple relationship between theory and fact. Gibson throughout the early 1950s altered and de-emphasized various aspects of his theory in conjunction with various "tests"; yet is is clear (for the theory did have its problems) that it was not dropped because of some crucial experimental falsification. Secondly, the theory of 1950 could not be considered consistent in all its applications for Gibson was proposing a new set of guiding general principles that required time to filter down into all the various problems and issues within the study of vision. The result of such experimental and conceptual problems was theoretical transformation and growth. This transformation reached a critical point later in the decade when the theory changed its colors, becoming something different than before. The ecological approach, though a new theoretical perspective, was related to the psychophysical theory and was not a complete turnabout. We can see, for example, how the concept of information (ecological correspondence) was connected to Gibson's idea of psychophysical correspondence. The ecological approach takes many of the ideas of the psychophysical approach, transforms them, and places them in the broader context of an ecological systems psychology. Even in the 1950s one area of concern where Gibson's thinking sounds ecological is perceptual learning.

PERCEPTUAL LEARNING

Within empiricist psychology in the 18th and 19th centuries, perceptual learning involved either the adding of ideas to sensations or a fusion of ideas with sensations. This theory is first clearly expressed by Berkeley in his associative explanation of perceptual development, and though various scientists and philosophers in the empiricist tradition introduced a variety of sophistications, the theory essentially stayed the same. This view of perceptual learning was supported by both theories of optical inadequacy in traditional psychophysiology, viz., the simulative assumption and pointillism. Visual sensations resulting from the retinal image were either limited to the simulative properties of the image (hence a phenomenal picture was produced) or they were restricted to the dimensions of points. Either type of psychophysical correspondence never changed, no matter how mature or experienced the perceiver became. The problem of visual perceptual learning for empiricists was therefore how visual sensations were supplemented and organized together, i.e., given the immutable raw material of sensory experience, the mind enriched it.

Gibson challenged this whole line of thinking because for him the visual stimulus was sufficiently organized and would cause (without extra-visual stimulation) all the basic perceptual facts (e.g., orientation, distance, solid shape and size) that traditional empiricists thought needed to be added to visual sensations. But if the causal result of visual stimulation did not require supplementation and organization what, for Gibson, did perceptual learning involve? In order to answer this question, we must look at Gibson's 1950–1955 concept of psychophysical correspondence more closely because his view is decidedly different from the view of Berkeley and his followers.

For empiricists such as Berkeley, psychophysical correspondences were innate and unchangeable. Oppositely, Gibson during the 1950's believed that psychophysical correspondence in perception developed through learning or maturation (1953, p. 128; Gibson & Gibson, 1955b, p. 448). For example, two slightly dissimilar patterns of stimulation produced by two objects of different shape may not, in an infant, yield a perceived difference in shape, but after learning and maturation, the stimulus difference may produce a perceived difference; or two different rectangles may not originally, via stimulation produce a perception of a similarity between them. But after perceptual development, what is invariant between the two stimulus patterns will cause a perception of their being something identical about the two rectangles, viz., that they are both rectangles.

Perceptual learning, as Gibson understood it during the 1950s, was increasing psychophysical correspondence (1953, p. 135). (A second complementary meaning of perceptual learning in Gibson's thinking will be described later.) This involved either increasing stimulus differentiation (the first example in the previous paragraph) or increasing stimulus abstraction (the second example), rather than stimulus supplementation or organization (1950a, pp. 129, 218–222). Given such a view, there may appear to be a problem with the scientific testability of Gibson's basic psychophysics, for if there does exist an organized and specific stimulus to an environmental fact, it does not follow that such an environmental fact will be perceived. Perceptual learning or development may be needed. How then can the psychophysical hypothesis of stimulus-perception correspondence be refuted? This indeed is a problem, and Gibson would eventually give up the psychophysical hypothesis as he originally proposed it, but Gibson's concern even as early as 1950 was in explaining the veridicality of perception and to the degree to which perception is veridical, he contended that there is specificity in stimulation to the environment with commensurate organization. Gibson rejects the traditional empiricist theory of perceptual learning (enrichment) because it simply does not explain how perception could be veridical. If two objects are correctly perceived at different distances, how else could this difference be seen unless there is a difference in stimulation? One cannot say the difference arises in the mind (through enrichment) for why does the correct difference (let alone any) get added? So, although a stimulus difference may not be a sufficient condition for a perceptual difference, it is a necessary difference for a veridical perceptual difference. Given Gibson's basic functionalist stance, what is becoming apparent is that the hypothesis of stimulus-environment correspondence is in actuality the more crucial and central idea, even as early as the 1950s—it simply had not been teased out and explicitly given the key position it held from 1960 onward.

What besides Gibson's insistence on the richness and specificity of visual stimulation led him in this new direction regarding perceptual learning? Regarding Gibson's hypothesis of modifiable psychophysical corerspondences, his initial experimental inspiration derived from his adaptation studies. Secondly, inasmuch as the general concept of flexible stimulus-perceptual correspondence along with numerous examples is contained in Troland's books, Gibson's early contention that psychophysical correspondences were mutable was greatly reinforced as well as further refined from his reading of Troland's books.

Gibson's hypothesis of increasing discrimination in perception had several sources; first was his work while in the armed services (1947). In particular, learning to recognize various aircraft impressed Gibson as not being a process of supplementation of sensations, but of increasing determinateness in perception. Second, Gibson was familiar with James' (1890) view that perceptual development was not a process of adding to visual sensations but of discrimination. For James, perception, as it developed in the child, went from indefiniteness and gross differentiations to determinateness and subtle differentiations. Further, Gibson believed that Gestalt theory had refuted the Berkeleian "theory" of perceptual learning (1953, p. 124). This could be interpreted to mean that Gestalt theory had shown that the analytic elements of perceptual consciousness were not a starting point for wholistic configurations but a consequence of such configurations. Finally, and perhaps of most immediate importance, was the contention of his wife Eleanor, a developmental psychologist (E. Gibson, 1940, 1953, 1969; Gibson and Gibson, 1953) that perceptual learning included a process of differentiation (Gibson, 1953, p. 130). One general conclusion of the aforementioned publications of Eleanor Gibson was that psychophysical correspondences are not fixed but become more differentiated through practice and learning. Eleanor Gibson's background included a strong behaviorist-learning element and she brought with her an understanding of the phenomena of stimulus discrimination in behavioral learning experiments (See also Gibson, 1979b). In summary, all these influences had an anti-elementaristic emphasis, rejecting the idea that psychological phenomena are built up out of independent immutable elements.

From an epistemological perspective, a major problem with the Berkeleian view of perceptual learning is that it does not, strictly speaking, involve a concept of learning at all. For a Berkeleian, "learning" was the adding or fusion of ideas with sensations. In the twentieth century it became the adding of responses to stimuli. Either way, the explanation offered did not address itself to the problem of perceptual learning and perceptual knowledge.

Simply, perceptual learning implies the acquisition of knowledge because learning is an epistemological conception. (For example, the appropriate definition of "learning" listed in *Webster's New World Dictionary* (1968, p. 833) is "the acquiring of knowledge"). Knowledge in turns denotes a particular kind of relationship between the knower and what exists as fact. A new idea or new response attached to either a sensation or a stimulus is not necessarily new knowledge, because the new relationship may be nonveridical. Perceptual learning can only be defined as a particular type of change in the relationship between the perceiver and facts of the world. It must become cognizant of some fact of the physical world where previously there was no awareness of this fact, such as the shape of a particular apple or a law of nature. For example, to see (to know) that one tree in your backyard is slightly more tilted than another tree next to it is perceptual knowledge if in fact the first tree is more tilted, and it is a case of perceptual learning if previously the difference in orientation was not noticed. Conversely, to acquire the idea that apples are cubical in shape would not be learning or new knowledge, because apples are not cubical in shape.

The concept of veridicality must be involved in a concept of perceptual learning. The mentalistic (sensations and ideas) version of a Berkeleian concept of perceptual learning does not include the idea of a world at all ("perceptual learning" goes on in the mind), whereas the behavioristic version at best (e.g., Hull, 1943; Pavlov, 1927; Postman, 1955) implies no distinction between veridical and nonveridical cases of stimulus-response associations. This argument assumes that knowledge has an objective, real reference and is not simply a set of beliefs or experiences that have more utility, consistency, or conventional acceptance. Embodied in the concept of knowledge is the idea of truth and a reality to be known.

This deficiency in the Berkeleian approach Gibson noted and stressed in his exchange with Postman (1955) over whether perceptual learning involved differentiation or enrichment (Gibson and Gibson, 1955a, 1955b). Postman had defined perceptual learning as a change in stimulus-response relationships, but such a definition would imply, for example, "that a progressive decrease in discriminative accuracy . . . should be considered learning" (Gibson & Gibson, 1955b, p. 449).

Turning to the Gibsonian position, if increased veridicality is a necessary component in a definition of perceptual learning, how did Gibson apply this criteria to his definition of perceptual learning in his psychophysical theory? For Gibson, perceptual learning involved increasing psychophysical correspondence. Within Gibson's psychophysical approach this hypothesis was intimately related to Gibson's contention that perceptual learning involved increasing differentiations of particular facts of the environment and increasing sensitivity of more similarities in the environment. The psychophysical hypothesis was an explanation of this ecological view of perceptual learning.

For Gibson, perception was a type of veridical cognizance of the physical environment. He assumed quite straightforwardly that this veridicality depended on stimulation being specific to the differences and similiarites in the environment; the objective specificity of perception was based upon the objective specificity of stimulation and the fact of psychophysical correspondence between perception and stimulation. Since visual stimulation is rich in "correlates" of the physical environment, increasing psychophysical correspondence (stimulus differentiation and abstraction) entailed increasing veridicality in perception of differences and similarities in the environment.

The phrase *ecological view of perceptual learning* was used in the previous discussion quite deliberately in order to stress the fact that Gibson's conception of perceptual learning denotes a type of change in the relationship between a perceiver and its environment and not merely a change in the perceiver. In this sense, it would be misleading to characterize it as a "psychological theory," if "psychology" is understood as a science of the animal per se. Gibson must explain how it is possible for the perceiver and environment to be related and given this relationship how is veridicality of perceptual knowledge possible. For Gibson, stimulus information (specificity) provides the connection between the perceiver and the environment, and psychophysical correspondence the explanation of veridicality. In the 1960s Gibson began to refer to himself as a realist, and, among other things, this designation meant that he believed in perceptual truth or veridicality.

Aristotle was a realist, for he believed that knowledge was of the world of nature and not some separate eternal (Platonic) realm. In order to provide a plausible explanation for a realist theory, the world of nature must be described in such a way as to be compatible with the mechanisms and nature of knowledge (Aristotle attempted this.) Gibson addressed the issue of what are indeed the facts of nature in the 1960s. His theory of the environment and his theory of information (e.g., ecological optics) provided a basis for understanding the conditions and reference of perceptual knowledge.

Chapter 14

THE GENESIS
of ECOLOGICAL PSYCHOLOGY

FUNCTIONALISM, EVOLUTION, AND ECOLOGY

The period 1957–1961 saw Gibson significantly alter his psychophysical theory, transforming it into an ecological approach to perception. Chronologically, the ecological accent developed in Gibson's mind before his ideal of a perceptual psychophysics lost its central significance. It was not until after the early 1960s that Gibson stopped characterizing his position as a "psychophysical theory" of perception. The ecological approach did not replace the psychophysical approach so much as absorb much of it into a broader, more fundamental context. Many significant themes of the 1950s remain in the 1960s and 1970s.

Two major topics to be discussed are the discipline of ecological optics and the concept of perceptual activity. The beginnings of both of these ideas were intimately tied to the academic year (1954–1955) Gibson spent as a visiting professor at the University of California at Berkeley. It was while he was at Berkeley that two of its professors, viz., Egon Brunswik and Gordon Walls, had a catalytic effect upon Gibson's thinking. During Gibson's stay at Berkeley, Brunswik was writing a systematic book on perception (Brunswik, 1956) that was decidedly at odds with Gibson's approach. Brunswik's book, which Gibson later reviewed (Gibson, 1957c), was an important instigating force in Gibson's development of ecological optics. At Berkeley, Gibson met Gordon Walls and became familiar with this noted physiologist's monumental work *The Vertebrate*

Eye and its Adaptive Radiation (1942). The general themes of investigation within Wall's book influenced Gibson strongly.

The major goal of Walls' work (1942) was to describe the anatomy of "eyes" and their function in terms of evolved adaptations to various types of environments and biological necessities of survival. The word "eyes" is in quotes because even across only vertebrate species, there are noteworthy anatomical and functional differences in visual organs. If one looks at visual organs in the course of evolution or simply across different species, many dissimilarities can be found. Interestingly, not all species have image-forming eyes, nor do all vertebrates have adjustable accomodation. Hence, neither a camera-like mechanism nor a retinal image are necessary for vision. This biological fact, impressed upon Gibson through Walls' book, was undoubtedly a factor in Gibson's dropping the hypothesis that the retinal image was the visual stimulus; the retinal image was not biologically universal. The optic array was the ubiquitous and necessary fact in the evolution of visually sensitive species (Gibson, 1958b, p. 140; 1959, p. 473; 1960a, p. 219; 1961a, pp. 254, 256; 1966a, pp. 154–155). If one's investigative concern was with explaining vision in all species, a goal that became increasingly clear in Gibson's writings (1958a; 1961a, 1966a, Chapter IX), the retinal image hypothesis just wasn't adequate, since it was not essential for vision.

In 1966, drawing heavily upon Walls' work, Gibson introduced the problem of visual perception via an examination of evolved adaptations (functions) of "eyes" to various environments (1966a). Simply, the central problem for Gibson by 1966 became "what are eyes good for?" (1966a, p. 154). This functional question was directed not just toward the visual organs of man but to all animal species. The functions of vision most discussed were those of adaptive consequence. This general theme in Gibson's exposition seems to have been inspired by Walls' concern with evolved adaptation in describing visual functions (1966a, p. 155). (See especially, Gibson, 1958a, which was written in 1955–1956.) Walls' work provided Gibson with numerous examples of how vision had evolved in different species to afford survival.

Looking at vision in terms of evolved adaptations led Gibson to consider the most general and biologically significant ecological facts across species. Through Walls, Gibson once again was turned in the direction of considering the environment of organisms. Previously he had looked at the environment because he was a functionalistic-phenomenologist concerned with the veridicality in perception. But the related concepts of evolution and adaptation in Walls' investigation of vision had a greater effect upon Gibson's thinking about the environment. Almost immediately after his contact with Walls, Gibson's publications showed an increasing stress on describing the biologically important facts of the environment of organisms. (Gibson, 1958a, 1958b, 1959, 1961b). Gibson gave more space and distinctive emphasis to the environment.

One of the numerous instigating forces in Gibson's development of ecological optics derived from Walls. Both the optic array and the environment have been relatively invariant throughout evolution. From an evolutionary viewpoint, visual perception could be understood as an adaptation to the invariant and lawful optic array-environment relations. Insofar as ecological optics is an attempt to study these invariant relations of the optic array and the environment, its development was motivated by Gibson's evolutionary examination of visual perception (1966a, Chapter IX).

Many examples of the functional integrity of visual anatomical structures and the functional identity of varied anatomical structures are found throughout Walls' book (e.g., 1942, pp. 225, 254, 301, 376–377). A function of vision is defined with respect to the environment, e.g., being able to perceive the total surounding terrain, or particularly well in one direction. Functional unity and coordination for a group of anatomical structures (e.g., eye, head, and torso), and functional identity in different structures (e.g., periscopy and no neck in one animal and frontal eyes with a flexible neck in another animal) are central ideas within Gibson's theory of perceptual systems.

As a consequence of Gibson treating vision as a psychophysicist, a phenomenologist and a functionalist, his general view of visual perception in 1950 involved the ideas of stimulation, experience and veridicality. Gibson's understanding of visual perception from the late 1950s onward reflected the increasing importance of ecological considerations. Resultantly, in some respects, Gibson's concept of visual perception in his ecological approach differed from his earlier (1950a) viewpoint. We begin with a brief examination of the definitions of perception Gibson provided during the period 1957–1961. These definitions are indicative of the overall goals of the ecological approach, and form a succinct introduction to the major topics treated in this chapter. The necessary inclusion of reference to the environment was an underlying theme of these new definitions of perception.

In an article dealing with reinforcement in perception, Woodworth suggested that perception could be understood as the "registration of objective facts" (1947, p. 119). In considering this definition of perception, Gibson stressed the fact that it avoided any "mentalistic connotations" (Gibson, 1958c, p. 39). Rather, Woodworth was exclusively emphasizing the functional fact of perception, viz., cognizance of the environment. Gibson was definitely sympathetic toward this characterization of perception. Several other remarks by Woodworth led Gibson to conclude that Woodworth thought of perceptual cognizance as a "process" or "activity" of "contact" with the "environment." The key terms in the sentences are *activity, contact,* and *environment* (or *objective facts*).

In the next two years, Gibson would provide several definitions of perception, all of which appear to reflect Woodworth's thinking. The following are three of these definitions which Gibson proposed.

> The word *perception* in this essay means the process by which an individual maintains contact with his environment. . . . Perception . . . (has therefore) not (been) defined in terms of either consciousness or of behavior. (1959, pp. 457–458)

> Perception is the process by which an individual is acquainted with his immediate surroundings. (1960d, p. 1)

> Perception is the having and achieving of knowledge about the world. . . . The essence of perception is selective attention to something important. (1960a, p. 220)

Note first that all the preceding definitions avoid any reference to experience or use of mentalistic terminology. This is not to say that Gibson had become a behaviorist; rather, the definitions are purely functional. (There are no behavior terms either.) More specifically, they refer to an ecological relation between the perceiver and the environment. Secondly, perception is understood as knowledge, that is to say, it is veridical. The definitions have an epistemological dimension. Thirdly, Gibson implied by "contact" direct perception in the sense of its being neither inferentially indirect nor causally mediated. Finally, perception is a directed activity and an achievement of the perceiver.

The general problem of explaining how the perceiver is in "contact" with its environment is partially investigated through ecological optics. Insofar as perception is tied to the environment, an explanation of the ecological conditions necessary for perceptual knowledge must be attempted. Because there was no comparable discipline in Gibson's psychophysics, one significant difference between his ecological and psychophysical theories is the existence of ecological optics in the former. The hypothesis of stimulus-environment correspondence, as previously argued, is contained in Gibson's psychophysical theory, but the idea of a disciplined study of such relationships had not been explicated. Stressing of the term *contact* was greatly a function of Gibson's new idea of optical support (in contrast to stimulus causation) that developed in ecological optics. In Gibson's definitions, the role of the perceiver also comes into prominence, where before it was of minimal concern in the psychophysical approach. Not that Gibson thought of the activity of perceiving as an intervening process, but it was now (circa 1960) in a different sense believed to be necessary in visual perception, requisite in the perceiver achieving "contact" with its environment. As stated in the previous section on perceptual learning, Gibson in the 1960s began to call himself a realist. In order to support this position, Gibson needed to redefine the perceiver and the environment in order to demonstrate their compatibility and consequently how contact (knowledge) is possible. Gibson's new definition of perception is both ecological and epistemological, relating an active perceiver with a informative environment.

THE ENVIRONMENT

In *The Perception of the Visual World,* Gibson (1950a) began his treatment of visual perception through a phenomenological description of perceptual experience. From 1957 onward, Gibson's approach to the problems of visual perception proceeded differently, in that, instead of offering and answering the question "how do things look?", Gibson initiated his discussion of issues (e.g., motion, shape, distance perception) by describing "what is there to see?" (e.g., 1957a, 1958a, 1960d, 1961b; Gibson & Bergmann, 1959). This constitutes another major difference between the ecological and psychophysical theories. A description of the environment to be perceived became Gibson's starting point replacing phenomenology.

What factors instigated Gibson's abandonment of phenomenology as his starting point in investigating visual perception? First, Gibson's concept of visual perception as revealed in the previously cited definitions was now extremely functional and ecological; hence, perception could not be described independently of the environment. This accentuation of the functional aspect of visual perception was coincident with Gibson taking seriously the concept of adaptation in characterizing vision.

Secondly, through the influence of Walls' evolutionary approach, the primacy of considering the environment in an investigation of visual perception was impressed upon Gibson. If vision is treated as an evolved adaptation to the environment, then ascertaining those most adaptively significant facts of the environment, to which perceptual capabilities are functionally related, is essential in understanding visual perception. Considered from the viewpoint of all species, such facts of the environment uncovered should have greater objectivity in the study of visual perception because of their extreme generality. *Surface layout* and *medium* became central terms in Gibson's description of the environment once he considered the necessary conditions of successful locomotion in all species (aquatic, terrestrial and aerial) (Gibson, 1958a, p. 183; 1958b, p.

140; 1960b, p. 26; 1960d, p. 5). The environment is understood relative to mobile rather than sedentary life forms (e.g., plants).

Gibson's shift from phenomenology to the environment could be seen as physicalistic and antimentalistic, but Gibson's approach to the environment was ecological. The investigation of the environment was not of a macrolevel physical world conceptually independent of animals because the environmental facts Gibson emphasized were those relevant to species adaptation (e.g., successful locomotion, 1958a), the prevention of injury and death (1961b), the conditions that support continued existence (air, stable terrain, food, shelter, the opposite sex, etc.) (1958a, 1966a, Chapter 1). Hence, Gibson's procedure of describing the environment to be perceived was also not some form of perceiver-world dualism. By the late 1960s and early 1970s, Gibson's investigation of the environment clearly presented itself as an ecology of animal-environment relations that methodologically affirmed the reciprocity of the perceiver and the environment, inasmuch as the environment to be perceived was invariably discussed in the contexts of the question: What does it afford the animal?

Brunswik's proposal for a representative methodology in psychological research was also involved in Gibson's amplified interest in the environment. It was suggested by Brunswik that experimental situations in a perceptual study should be ecologically normal (representative) for the species under study, or else the results obtained would probably have limited generality. In stressing the fact that perceptual capabilities evolved in the context in certain environmental conditions, Brunswik was led to the conviction that psychological functions must be studied in their evolved natural (for a given species) context (Brunswik, 1956).

The above methodological hypothesis was already important in Gibson's thinking (1947, 1950a). Evolution provided an explanation and conceptual framework for the compatibility (or reciprocal relation) of the animal and the environment. Why is there harmony? What Gibson concluded through his review of Brunswik's book (Gibson, 1957c) was the simple fact that discovering the normal conditions of evolved capacities was not a simple matter. A representative methodology, if desired, involved a directed scientific discipline of investigation—an ecology of psychological evolution. This ecology must be guided by considerations of what appears significant in the environment for behavior and continued existence. One cannot just assume the representativeness of an experimental situation. Because of Gibson's desire for a representative methodology, his attention turned toward developing an evolutionary ecology that would tell him what are representative situations. What is representative for a fish? A bird? A mammal? A primate? Man? This is a far cry from his 1930 studies involving lines and outline forms. Besides Gibson's ecology being relative to animal dynamics and evolution, it was in a general sense theoretical as opposed to merely descriptive. Phenomenology was intended to be purely descriptive. Further, it was of consciousness, considered independent of the physical world or environment. Gibson's studies of the environment are both theoretical and ecological.

The last and probably most crucial event involved in Gibson's development of an ecology of visual perception was the emergence of ecological optics. Before turning to Gibson's original formulation of ecological optics and the question of how its genesis was related to an increased concern with the environment, some of the early substantive results of Gibson's investigation of the environment are mentioned.

In 1950, Gibson argued for the importance of studying the physical world at a level of analysis appropriate for visual perception. The reductionistic contention that the physical world actually and only consisted of atomic particles was not, in 1950, convincing to Gibson. Instead of supposing that only the super-small was "real" or "objective," Gibson had argued for the validity of describing the physical world at a different level of analysis. "Validity" is understood not just as instrumental utility but as objective correctness (Smart, 1968, Chapter 5).

The argument for the scientific validity of describing the physical world at a molar level of analysis became, after 1956, a point of emphasis for Gibson (e.g., 1959, pp. 469–470). The strength of the argument compared to 1950 was amplified because it was now stated from an evolutionary viewpoint. The physical conditions of survival and adaptation are only, in a trivial sense, atoms and microscpace. Evolution is specific to the macroreality of a surface layout and a medium. One could add from an ontological viewpoint that the reason why we do not see atoms when we look at a tree (or some other macroreality) is that a tree as a macrostructure is not atoms.

During the period 1957–1961, surface layout emerged as a central idea in Gibson's ecology, taking the place of the older notion of ground. Surface layout took the place of the ground as the spatial framework for vision. One definition he provided of surface layout was the "geometrical properties of surfaces as edges, corners, slants, convexities, or concavities" (1960b, p. 26). Environmental spaces were now described in terms of surface layout.

In two articles of this period, Gibson offered two different three-fold classifications of the environment. Gibson, in the earlier of the two, divided the environment into the terrain of environmental spaces, permanent objects, and changes and events (1960d, p. 14). What is noteworthy in this proposal is the inclusion of the generic term "events"; its central significance in the environment had been slighted even by Gibson. Also of further interest was the citing of sequences of events as a perceivable environmental fact (1958c, p. 48). Breaking with the idea that visual perception is confined to the "instantaneous present" was responsible for Gibson's inclusion of the fact of change (events and sequences of events) in the perceivable environment.

In the later article (1961b) a second classification of the environment was suggested. The environment divided into the classes of natural geographic, artificial (manmade) and animate and social (1961b, p. 78). This schema is evidently not at odds with the former, but is only a different way of splitting up relevant facts. The category of special significance is animate and social. Although it had been previously discussed (1950a, Chapter 2), little attempt had been made to systematically study the perception of animate or social facts. This oversight began to disappear after 1957 (e.g., 1957a; 1959, p. 484; 1963; 1966a, pp. 22–26).

The general picture that emerges in Gibson's initial development of an ecology of perception is perception as an active epistemic accomplishment geared to survival in a structured and dynamic environment. The environment is ontologically relative to the perceiver and there is no absolute sepration of mind and matter or perceiver and world. Neither the perceiver (or perception) nor the environment is understood atheoretically, for each pair of the reciprocity is selectively investigated and described involving concepts or assumptions regarding the other member of the pair. This reciprocal relation of perceiver and environment will now be examined in more detail through the study of ecological optics and the theory of active perception.

ECOLOGICAL OPTICS

In 1950, Gibson opposed the hypothesis, associated mainly with Brunswik, that there existed only probabilistic relations between variables of stimulation and facts of the environment. According to Gibson, there was projective univocality between the retinal image and the environment. The discipline of ecological optics derived from this early belief in stimulus specificity. Additionally, Gibson carried over from his psychophysics his wholistic approach in describing stimulation. Yet some additional factors were necessary before ecological optics emerged in Gibson's mind in clear form. The first was Gibson's abandonment of a retinal image psychophysics. Also Gibson was taking Brunswik's hypothesis of stimulus equivocality much more seriously, by developing an explicated and systematic alternative to Brunswik's position. Finally, there was Brunswik's 1956 proposal of a potential avenue of inquiry to ascertain the specificity of stimuli to the environment.

The retinal image is a fact contingent upon the perceiver (e.g., accomodation is necessary). The optic array, on the other hand, is a fact independent of any perceiver. Consequently, although it is impossible to discuss the specific relations of the retinal image and the environment independently of a hypothetical perceiver, this is not the case concerning the relation between the optic array and the environment.

Recall that the optic array entered Gibson's investigative program in 1955. Gibson in 1956 read and reviewed Brunswik's final statement on perception (Gibson, 1957c), in which Brunswik suggested the investigation of the ecological validities of "cues." Brunswik, of course, supposed that ecological validities would always be probabilistic. Gibson (1957c) considered this a dilemma, since perception was invariably quite veridical. What is important in Brunswik's proposal was his distinction between the ecological validity of a cue and its "weight." The former was the actual degree of specificity between stimuli and environmental facts in representative situations, whereas the latter was the particular validity encountered by a perceiver. The former was a cue's *potential* validity (specificity) while the latter was the cue's *effective* value in perception. What Brunswik provided in his 1956 book was a clear challenge to the univocality-equivocality issue and a suggested methodology for resolving the question.

The challenge became extremely important to Gibson at this time (*circa* 1956) precisely because the successful adaptation and survival of organisms had recently become paramount in Gibson's thinking (through Walls). Likewise, Brunswik, inasmuch as he viewed the psychology of perception from the viewpoint of evolution and functionalism, treated psychological problems as questions dealing with the *modus operandi* of adaptation and survival. The dilemma Gibson saw in Brunswik's position was how could there be "survival in a world of probable objects"? (This quoted phrase was the title of Gibson's review, 1957c, of Brunswik's book, 1956.)

Brunswik's idea of objective ecological validities suggested the possibility of investigating the stimulus-environment specificities independently of their effective value for the perceiver. For Gibson, the optic array exists independently of a perceiver and potentially can be studied as such, with the primary interest being to discover the specific relationships between the optic array and the environment. (There is a more basic sense in which ecological optics is not independent of Gibson's understanding of the nature of animals, but this issue will be examined later.)

The historical hypothesis that the above events instigated the beginnings of ecological optics is supported by the fact that the idea of the discipline first appears in Gibson's writings immediately after his year at Berkeley. It was not until 1960 that the specific phrase "ecological optics" was used by Gibson (1960b, p. 25), but the idea was contained in earlier articles. For example, in 1957 he proposed the possibility of an "optical geometry . . . relevant to vision" (1957a, p. 294); or "a generalized geometry of perspective . . . a geometry of the ways in which light specifies the world of surfaces from which light is reflected" (Gibson, 1960a, p. 218). A second source of evidence comes from Gibson's acknowledgement that Brunswik (1956) realized the need for a discipline to study the relation of stimulation and environment (Gibson, 1960c, p. 699; 1961a, p. 260).

Ecological optics is concerned with discovering the specific projective relations between the environment and the optic array. Consequently, an ecology or description of the environment of animals is part of ecological optics. This explains why Gibson's development of an ecology of visual perception was tied to the emergence of ecological optics.

Given that veridical perception is contingent upon the specificity of the optic array to the environment, any discussion of a particular issue in perception, (e.g., distance, surface, or shape perception) should contain the relevant facts of ecological optics. From 1957 onward, Gibson began his treatments of perceptual problems by first considering the relevant environmental facts and their projective transformations in the optic array (e.g., Gibson & Gibson, 1957). (This procedure would also seem to indicate that, at least in practice, ecological optics was a component of Gibson's theoretical approach in 1957.) Only after noting the facts of ecological optics germane to the topic did his exposition turn to the perception of the environmental facts. This is in contrast to the traditional ideal that Gibson himself followed in 1950 of presenting a phenomenology of perception before providing an explanation of perception.

Ecological optics treated the optic array (in its first years) as a "potential" stimulus in the sense that it was considered independent of any effect it had upon a perceiver. It is the potential stimulus for veridical visual perception in that it is projectively related to the environment. The array could be "effective" if it is sampled, where "effective" means having a perceptual effect (Gibson, 1958a, p. 184; 1958c, p. 43; 1960c, p. 401; 1960d, p. 4; 1961a, p. 256–257; Gibson, Gibson, Smith, & Flock, 1959, p. 43). Hence, ecological optics does not include anything analogous to a psychophysics of visual perception.

After the two previously cited publications (Gibson, Purdy & Lawrence, 1955; Gibson, Olum, & Rosenblatt, 1955) appeared in which Gibson first hypothesized that the optic array was the visual stimulus, the older hypothesis of the ordinal retinal image vanished. In all subsequent articles, the optic array was the visual stimulus (e.g., Gibson, 1957a, p. 183; 1958a, pp. 183–184; 1961a, pp. 254–257; Gibson & Bergman, 1959, p. 129; Gibson, et al., 1959, p. 43).

The ordinal retinal image died in a second sense also. Thereafter, whenever Gibson compared the optic array to the "retinal image," he always meant the anatomical retinal image (e.g., 1958b, p. 129; 1960d, p. 17). He just gave up talking about the ordinal retinal image. One probable reason for this was Gibson's desire to contrast, in as pronounced a manner as possible, the optic array with the "retinal image." There are certain similarities between the 360° potential ordinal retinal image and the optic array that are missing between the anatomical retinal image and the optic array. In addition, historically, the retinal image was anatomically and not ordinally described. If Gibson wished to compare his hypothesis of the optic array with the most prevalent view, it was the anatomical image that he needed to critically juxtapose with his position.

In 1955, the optic array was described as the sheaf of rays (transitions) entering the eye. By 1961 all reference to the eye was avoided in defining the optic array, e.g., "An optic array is the light converging to any position in the transparent medium of an illuminated environment insofar as it has different intensities in different directions" (Gibson, 1961a, p. 255). An array is "ambient," meaning a convergent pencil of rays, as opposed to "radiant," meaning a divergent pencil of rays. Loosely speaking, ambient light surrounds a point in the medium. The optic array is not just ambient; it has transitions. For Gibson, a converging ray in an optic array is understood as a change in intensity (1960a, p. 217; 1961a, p. 257). The array should not be thought of as ambient light with different intensities in different directions, but as differences of intensity in different directions.

One of the first problems to face Gibson in describing the array led him back to Euclid's notion of natural perspective. In thinking of the retinal image as a picture, the appropriate way of geometrically characterizing its projective relation to the world was pictorial perspective, but Euclid, da Vinci, and Troland had described perspective in terms of geometrical projection to a point. Since the optic array was differences of light intensity convergent to a point, that is to say, from all directions (360°), it could not be represented in terms of pictorial perspective (Gibson, 1961a, p. 255). The optic array is unbounded whereas a picture is bounded. Consequently, Gibson turned toward natural perspective to describe the projective relation of the optic array and the environment. Because Troland's writings contained the idea of natural perspective and an "ocular ray sheaf" (1929, p. 325), it seems extremely improbable that the above considerations of Gibson were developed independently of Troland's views.

Since the optic array consists of transitions, it has "structure" (Gibson, 1960b, p. 27; 1961a, p. 257). There are minute transitions across seconds of arc, more global transitions at the level of minutes, and still more global differences at the level of degrees (1961a, p. 258). In referring to this fact of structure, Gibson used the words *form* and *pattern,* yet such terms were rather vague. Gibson, aware of this lack of precision in his terminology, suggested that "mathematical procedures" needed to be developed for describing the optic array (1959, p. 499). One thing Gibson was convinced of was that the terminology of physical optics was inappropriate (1961a).

For any given point in the medium there is an optic array. Each array is unique in specific structure, since each array is a different projective transformation of the environment. Just as important, the optic arrays of any two adjacent points in the medium are intrinsically related and therefore, are not discrete entities. The set of arrays for any line through the medium is a continuous projective transformation of the environment. Any continuous sequence of optic arrays will contain certain invariants (1958a, p. 193). Every optic array in the open air medium contains the horizon line—a sharp and permanent low-high intensity transition that approximately bisects an optic array. The basic hypothesis of the continuity and relatedness of sets of optic arrays is similar to the older Gibsonian concept of ordinal invariants across potential 360° retinal images (1950a). One obvious and significant difference is that in the latter case, Gibson was referring to something which *potentially* existed, whereas the set of optic arrays in the medium does in fact actually exist. Stated differently, the horizon line exists as an invariant across a temporal sequence of retinal images, whereas the horizon line exists simultaneously and continuously in all arrays in the medium.

Besides structure, the two other central concepts in Gibson's description of the optic array are invariants and transformations. The two major substantive hypotheses of ecological optics are that the invariants of a continuous series of optic arrays are projectively specific to the persistant features of the environment, and that optical transformations are projectively specific to the changes in the environment (Gibson, 1954b; 1959, p. 484; 1960a, p. 218; 1960d, p. 16; 1961a, p. 260).

What should be stressed is the logical connection between the general concepts of invariance and transformation. An invariant can only be defined over a change. The concept of invariance means something which remains the same. Conversely, where there is a transformation, there must also be something invariant. Simply stated, where there is change there is permanency, and where there is permanency there is change. Consistent with this general logical point, an optical invariant for Gibson meant what remained unchanged through an optical transformation. Note that at the levels of ecology and ecological optics, the concepts of stability and change are tied together and not ontologically separated as in Platonic philosophy or the Heraclitian-Parmenidian split.

Transformations can be subdivided into two general types. The first takes place when something changes, e.g., moves, in the environment. The second occurs across a continuous series of optic arrays when the observer moves about in the environment. Both types of transformations, as well as the invariants in such changes, were considered by Gibson as potential stimuli. In fact, Gibson from 1957 onward thought of invariants of transformations and transformations as primary in the visual perception of the environment. This view would have significant ramifications regarding Gibson's view of the role of the perceiver in visual perception.

What then happened to the retinal image (however defined) in Gibson's ecological program? The retinal image was now considered only to be the stimulus for the retina, while the optic array was the stimulus for the "ocular system" (Gibson, 1961a, p. 256). Understanding what Gibson was implying in this comparison between the retinal image and the optic array involves answering several questions. What did Gibson mean by the word *stimulus* in his initial formulation of ecological optics and especially how was this term related to the concept of information? What conditions were necessary in order for the potential stimulus (the optic array) to be effective? And what did Gibson mean by the term *ocular system?*

Why is the optic array a potential stimulus for visual perception? By 1961, Gibson's answer was simply that it "carried" information. In the last chapter it was stated that Gibson began (1955–1956) to use the term *information* to mean the projective specificity of the optic array to the environment. In the following years this definition became quite explicit in his writings (1960b, p. 25; 1960c, pp. 699–700; 1961a, p. 259). The stimulus for veridical visual perception was always by necessity an optical invariant or variant specific to what was perceived in the environment. The array consequently was a potential stimulus because it was projectively specific to the environment. This was equivalent to saying the optic array was the stimulus for visual perception because it contained information. One point to keep in mind is that the phrase "the optic array carries or contains information" is somewhat misleading. Information is not a fact intrinsic to the array or describable just in terms of the array. Information refers to a particular type of relationship between the array and the environment, viz., the relation of univocality. Because information means specificity of optical invariants and transformations to the environment, ecological optics could be thought of as the study of information in the aforementioned sense. (Eventually Gibson would emphasize that information was ecological, specifying both the environment and the animal.)

Gibson emphasized the fact of information in the optic array by saying that the array had meaning. The meaning of the optic array was its exterospecificity (1960b, p. 25; 1960c, pp. 699–700). This concept of meaning or information in the array was contrasted by Gibson with the hypothesis of signs in Brunswik. A sign has only probable meaning in that it is probabilistically correlated with environmental facts. Historically, this view of Gibson's is somewhat misleading since the extero-specific meaning of signs for Berkeleians (e.g., J. S. Mill, Berkeley, Helmholtz, and Titchener) was always associated phenomenal context. A sign did not have probable meaning, but rather no meaning.

A second contrast Gibson later (1966a) stressed was between his idea of information and Müller's specific energies of nerves hypothesis. Gibson thought that for Müller, stimulation has specificity only to the nerves excited. This interpretation of Müller's viewpoint is not completely correct, but there is still an element of truth in the contrast. For Müller, neural excitation had no direct extero-specificity, though it is mediationally connected through a causal chain with the external physical world.

Another noteworthy historical contrast is with the simulative assumption and the homunculus hypothesis. For Gibson, the perceiver was directly cognizant of what optical information specified, i.e., what it was univocally related to in the environment, whereas the simulative assumption entailed that sensory awareness corresponded to the properties of the retinal image. The crucial difference between Berkeley and Gibson circa 1950 was Gibson's rejection of the simulative assumption. Gibson's alternative to both the simulative assumption and the homunculus hypothesis was implicit in *The Perception of the Visual World* (1950a), but it was not until around 1955–1960 that he explicated sufficiently his information based theory of perception. Information possesses both commensurate structure and environmental specificity, but in contrast with the simulative assumption and homunculus hypothesis, we perceive the environment rather than the structure and properties of light.

PERCEPTUAL SYSTEMS AND THE PROCESS OF PERCEPTION

Information carried by the optic array is a necessary though not sufficient condition for visual perception. It is a potential stimulus. Consider one point in the medium of an illuminated environment. Such a locus in the medium is referred to as a *station point*. At this particular station point there will exist an optic array. If a perceiver is brought into the picture, so that the nodal point of one of its eyes occupies the station point in question, will the perceiver necessarily see anything specified by this optic array? The answer to this question that Gibson would provide from around 1960 onward was *no*.

The optic array is not a stimulus in Gibson's (1950a) older meaning of the term. The word "stimulus" then implied the fact of it being effective, causing a perceptual effect. The retinal image was thought of as a stimulus because Gibson believed it was a sufficient condition for visual perception. This difference in meaning between Gibson's "retinal image" in 1950 and the "optic array" in 1960 marks another crucial difference between his psychophysical and ecological theories.

Gibson believed that various perceptual activities were necessary for the optic array to be effective. In one passage he listed quite a few factors he thought were involved in the effectivity of the optic array.

> whether or not a potential stimulus becomes effective depends on the individual. It depends on the species to which he belongs, on the anatomy of the sense organs, the stage of maturation, the capacities for sense organ adjustment, the habits of attention, the activity in progress, and the possibilities of educating the attention of the individual. (Gibson, 1960c, p. 701)

Conceiving of visual perception as an activity of the perceiver has had two quite distinct historical meanings. For individuals such as Locke or Helmholtz, visual perception consisted of a passive and active element. The passive aspect was the effect of the retinal image on the organism resulting in sensations. This stage in visual perception is passive in that the presence of a retinal image is sufficient for an effect in the perceiver. Something is caused in the organism by the existence of an image produced on the retina. The active aspect involved those subsequent psychological or physiological processes that transformed the sensations (or excitations) into perceptions. In this case, the activity of perception intervened between the effect of the image and the final perception. This general characterization of visual perception has been the prevalent one.

In contrast, for Dewey and many act psychologists of the previous century, there was no independent passive element in perception at all. Some type of activity was thought requisite for any visual effect. The activity of visual perception in this case did not intervene between an effect upon the organism and the final perception, because there isn't any effect independent of the activity of perceiving. For act psychologists, visual perception was not a subsequent stage after the activity of perceiving. Visual perception simply is the activity. (Recall Dewey's position that there are not discrete stages in perception.) For Berkeleians and Gestalt psychologists alike, there are three conceptually distinct stages in visual perception (stimulation, physiology, experience), while for Dewey there is really just one event; stimulation, physiology, and experience are interdependent.

Where does Gibson fit into this historical dichotomy? Beginning in the period 1957–1961, Gibson referred to visual perception as an activity (e.g., Gibson, 1958c, p. 43). Further, he supposed that an optic array was effective in visual perception only given this activity. These two contentions were actually identical. The activity of perceiving was described by Gibson as the registering of information in the optic array (1958c, p. 51). This registration of information is the optic array being effective. The fact of an optic array being effective is not something caused by or mediated by the activity of perceiving. The activity of (veridical) perceiving involves an optic array (or series of arrays) becoming effective. As was also the case for act psychologists, there were not, for Gibson, discrete stages of stimulation, activity, and visual perception.

The historically dominant view of causation in visual perception, viz., the undirectional model, will be compared with Gibson's (1960d, pp. 6–7) feedback loop model in order to further clarify Gibson's concept of perceptual activity. The causal chain model of visual perception in its modern form originated with Descartes. Visual perception was thought to result from a unidirectional causal series of events. The retinal image and its immediate neurological effect are independent of later stages, whereas visual perception is the final stage in this series. Any activities (physiologically or psychologically conceived) intervene between these end points. Visual perception is a dual function of the effect of the image and intervening factors which modify this input.

Gibson proposed a different model in which the functional dependencies were characterized in terms of "feedback loops." Although Gibson's feedback loop hypothesis was definitely anticipated by Dewey, it does not appear that Gibson took it directly from Dewey (see Diagram 29).

Diagram 29   The Feedback Loops for Exploring or Enhancing Visual Information (adapted from Gibson, 1960d, p. 7)

One example of a feedback loop is the focusing of light. Ambient light that has structure needs to be focused by the eyes in order for it to be perceptually effective. Hence the effectiveness of the optic array involves an activity of variable focusing. This functional dependency is signified by the arrow going from the left to right in Diagram 29. Note that this dependency of stimulus effectiveness on a process of the perceiver is in contrast to the unidirectional causal chain model. Secondly, there is feedback from effective stimulation to the activity of focusing. The activity is a continuous process of adjustment to the feedback (e.g., degree of sharpness in contrast). There is a functional interdependency of perceptual search and adjustment with effective stimulation that is circular and reciprocal.

Perceptual activity does not *cause* effective stimulation nor does effective stimulation cause perceptual activity. Neither activity nor effective stimulation is a true independent variable or cause in the sense of the unidirectional model of causality. Each is functionally interrelated with the other. They are not actually distinct events but two aspects of the same process, viz., visual perception. The degree of determinateness in the accomodated optic array is continuously feeding back into the activity of accomodation, insofar as the latter varies as a function of loss of perceptual clarity.

A second, more general example of this circular and unitary process is visual perception of persistant features of the environment. Invariants in the optic array are a necessary condition in this case, but such invariants must be perceptually effective. How does this involve the activity of perception? Consider the transformations of structure across a continuous series of optic arrays. What remains invariant across this series is information for the permanent properties (surface layout) of the environment. Gibson stressed the importance of the invariants of a series of optic arrays as information for a perceiver because any one optic array is projectively nonspecific to an environmental layout. Gibson had found that one specific projection of a shape or retinal gradient of texture density in isolation did not yield consistent veridical perceptions (Gibson & Beck, 1955; Gibson, Purdy, & Lawrence, 1955). In neither of these cases was the optical projection specific to one environmental fact. Assuming that nothing is moving in the environment, the optically necessary condition for univocal environmental specificity involves the invariants of transformations across a series of optic arrays. The necessary stimulus condition for the perception of permanency is temporal change and multiple perspectives.

A continuous series of optic arrays only becomes effective by being sampled by the perceiver. The perceiver changes its head and body position in exploration of the environment. The condition of stimulus change is supplied through the process of changing viewing positions. This activity of overt attention must occur in order for the invariants of a series of optic arrays to become separated from what is just unique to any one given optic array. Also, this perceptual activity is selective in that it is a sampling of the infinite set of optic arrays in any medium. Consequently, the particular series of optic arrays and the specific subset of the total set of optical invariants in the medium that become perceptually effective are contingent upon the processes of perceptual exploration.

Conversely, the activity of exploration is directed toward the isolation of invariants (the perceiver looks to see what there is or what else there is). Hence, exploration involves sensitivity to which invariants remain over optical transformations. The effective invariants feed back into exploratory activity in the sense that the isolation of invariants is guided by what already has been perceived and what remains perceptually ambiguous.

In both of the previous examples, visual perception is not a causal chain with beginning, intervening, and final stages, but a continual circular process of functional interdependencies that does not contain discrete stages. In 1950, Gibson assumed the unidirectional model, but as of 1958–1960 he abandoned it. This significant modification in Gibson's thinking was coincident with his transition from a psychophysics to an ecology of visual perception. Psychophysics assumed a causal dependency of perception on stimulation.

Viewed as an activity, visual perception involves exploration, adjustment, and selective attention relative to the potential stimulus, viz., the optic array. The visual perceptual system was postulated by Gibson as the functionally integrated *modus operandi* of these perceptual activities. It was Gibson's new answer to the question "With what do we see?" From the infinite number of optic arrays in a medium, only a small set are ever sampled and even then only certain details of any sampled array ever become effective in visual perception. The retina construed as a passive receptor was not the appropriate mechanism for this activity. Additionally, the retina is not at the appropriate level of analysis for Gibson's description of the potential stimulus. To be understood functionally, visual perception must include both the sensitive retina and coordinating, exploratory, and selective mechanisms. The perceiver explores and adjusts to the environment through accomodation of the lens, moving of the eyes, head, and body, and fixating fine details within any sampled array. Gibson considered those anatomical structures necessary for these perceptual activities as the visual perceptual system. The visual system is at a different level of analysis than the retina, and is commensurate with Gibson's new description of the potential stimulus. The activities of these anatomical configurations are functionally organized through feedback loops and hence are a system. A system therefore includes both anatomical and dynamic features. It is not simply a spatial structure or arrangement. A perceptual system is a functional and dynamic unity containing anatomical parts, a clear Aristotelian idea.

The active system of visual perception was a necessary consequence of Gibson's understanding of the potential effectiveness of the optic array. If Gibson thought the optical basis of visual perception sufficient, the visual perceptual system would not have any function because the function of this system is to make the optical basis for vision perceptually effective. The visual perceptual system is the means by which the perceiver makes effective numerous types of conditions thought by Gibson to be necessary in order for optical invariants and transformations to be perceptually effective.

The idea of a visual perceptual system begins to appear in Gibson's writings around 1957 (e.g., Gibson, 1957a, p. 289; 1958c, pp. 42–43; 1959, pp. 467–471; 1960d, p. 3). Of particular interest is the following clear expression of the visual perceptual system by Gibson.

> The eyes react by exploring the array, fixing and converging on certain details, sharpening the contours by focusing the lens, and pursuing a moving bit of detail. . . . The receptive system . . . "tunes itself" by adjusting the apparatus for clear reception. The lens-retina-nerve-muscle system is not passive but active. It continually creates new stimuli for itself, searching out in an optic array the relations, ratios, grades, and invariants of pattern which specify facts of the world (Gibson, 1960a, p. 220).

Three points are worth emphasizing regarding this quote. The retinal image-unidirectional causal view implied that visual perception involved the retinal image producing excitation in the retina. On the contrary, for Gibson the visual perceptual system controls excitation at the retina. Secondly, Dewey's (1896) idea that a response does not occur because of a stimulus but rather is to the stimulus provides a succinct characterization of Gibson's new conception of visual perception. For Gibson, the stimulus was not given to the perceiver but discovered by the perceiver. Thirdly, the general function of the activities of the visual perceptual system is not to contribute to optical information. Instead the system obtains information insofar as it adjusts itself for the best "reception." (Although used by Gibson in the above quote, *reception* is not the best term to convey the actual meaning of this hypothesis. A better term, which Gibson favored since the middle 1960s, is *resonance*.) Given Gibson's description of potential stimulation as invariants across optic arrays the visual perceptual system provides a mechanism at the appropriate level of analysis and organization to explore and extract such information.

Though not explicitly used by Gibson at this point in his development, the concept of reciprocity captures many of the new ideas discussed in this chapter. Perceptual activity and effective stimulation are reciprocals, distinct, yet interdependent. Neither creates the other, yet they are not separate and absolute, as in dualism. The exploratory activities of the perceiver are embedded in the ecosystem, along with stimulation and the environment, thus visual perception is ecological. Though perceptual activities are activities of the perceiver, they are functionally related to information about the environment. The more encompassing concept of perception, involving and subsuming exploratory activities, is an epistemic relation of perceiver to an adaptively significant environment.

INVARIANTS AND TRANSFORMATIONS
OF THE OPTIC ARRAY

In 1957, Gibson offered an explanation of the visual perception of the shape of a surface that ran counter to traditional explanations. Previously (Gibson & Beck, 1955), Gibson attacked the view that retinal form produced a simulated perceived form. He did not develop an alternative explanation of surface shape to the view that it resulted from retinal form plus distance cues. Two years later (1957a; Gibson & Gibson, 1957), Gibson supplied this missing hypothesis.

There are six different types of transformations of a projected moving surface shape, viz., vertical translation, horizontal translation, size change, horizontal foreshortening, vertical foreshortening, and rotation of a pattern (1957a, p. 290). Correspondingly, rigid motion can be described in terms of six different types; there are three kinds of translocation and three kinds of rotation. Each of the aforementioned optical transformations is projectively specific to one of the six types of rigid motion of a surface. A surface moving toward a perceiver produces an expanding change in size of projected form. Vertical and horizontal motion produces vertical and horizontal translocation. Of particular significance are vertical and horizontal foreshortening. In these two cases the optical form does not remain invariant, but the form of the change of form is an invariant. If a cube is rotated around its vertical axis, its projected sides will undergo horizontal and vertical foreshortening. Only when a square surface is exactly frontal will it project a square form, but the total series of projected forms will be specific to a square surface. Furthermore, a repeating, invariant sequence of such transformational series will be specific to a cube. The invariant of the transformation is projectively specific to the shape of a surface, whereas any one projected form is not. The fundamental difference between this view and older views is that, for Gibson, the information for shape is an invariant of change, a "formless invariant." Traditionally, the basis of perceived shape was two instantaneous values (static retinal form and the momentary distance value of depth cues). Perceived shape (a relatively permanent property) is not based on a static property such as form but rather upon an invariant embedded in change.

In normal environmental situations the shapes of surfaces are often perceived veridically without the surfaces (of objects) necessarily moving. How then is veridicality insured in an environment of stationary objects? The answer is that the perceiver normally moves about and explores the environment. Either the transformation of vertical foreshortening or horizontal foreshortening of a projected pattern can be produced by a change in the observation point of the perceiver. The optical invariants specific to a surface shape can become effective through a sampling of optic arrays. There is a need for an active perceptual system in the veridical visual perception of surface shape.

The isolation of these invariants by the perceiver should not be construed as an all-or-nothing affair. Physical objects have more than one side and, correspondingly, there are invariants specific to each of these surface shapes. These invariants are not registered at once when the observer moves, but require for their isolation various exploratory activities. The perceiver may not look at every structural characteristic of an object and resultingly will not perceive all of them. The more the perceiver explores, the more invariants are isolated and the more of the object is perceived. Veridical perception of surface shape is a paramount example of how the activity of perceiving is involved in effective stimulation and how effective stimulation involves optical transformations. In fact, Gibson's investigation of shape perception was one of the prime motivating factors behind his increased emphasis on invariants of transformations as information about the permanent features of the environment. Permanency and change are tied together.

A problem related to the perception of surface shape was the perception of object identity. Why is a physical object seen as the same object over time even when it changes position? Similarly, how is one object distinguished from another object? These questions Gibson understood as falling under the general problem of the permanency of the perceived environment. The beginning of an explanation was proposed soon after his articles on shape perception and naturally followed from his explanation of the latter. He suggested (1958b, pp. 143–144) that the invariants for a set of stimulus transformations for one object are distinct from the invariants for another object. Also, a projection of one object is related to the projection of another object by a discontinuous transformation, whereas any two projections of one object are related by a continuous transformation. In accounting for the visual perception of object identity, the concepts of invariance and transformation were again fundamental in Gibson's thinking.

According to Gibson (1959, p. 481), visual perception of the continuance and permanence of the environment depends on the invariants of transformations of sampled series of optic arrays. By virtue of the fact that these invariants exist across optic arrays, optic arrays are united and not discrete. As the observer moves from one place to another, new vistas of the total environment open up and some existing vistas disappear. The permanent characteristics of the environment that are in view change. This implies that there is a continuous change of optical invariants as the observer moves from place to place. There is never a complete change of invariants between any two connected series of arrays; hence, all the arrays of the medium of the total environment are related to one another, and the environment is perceived as continuous. Although the aforementioned concept of the relatedness of optic arrays is somewhat developed in the period 1957–1961 (also see 1958a, p. 193), it was not until 1966 that Gibson presented a thorough formulation of it (1966a, pp. 206–208). What is noteworthy in Gibson's understanding of the visual spatial framework is the primacy of invariants *of* transformations. Gibson was attempting to extend the concept of invariants across transformations to the total range of perceptual problems.

In the period of 1957–1961, Gibson's understanding of the nature of the gradient of optical deformation underwent a significant conceptual development. As has already been mentioned, although Gibson used vector velocities to depict optical deformation, he did not mean to imply that the eye was sensitive to point velocities. In the period being discussed, Gibson provided the beginnings of an alternative description of the gradient of optical flow.

The optic array has structure at all levels of analysis. Its most global patterns consist of parts which, in turn, have pattern. These patterns of parts also have parts that have pattern, and so on, past the limits of visual acuity. Any region of the optic array, no matter how small, is never simply a point, but has shape and internal differences. Whenever the observer moves, any such region of structure does not move in just one direction, but undergoes a transformation of pattern in all directions (1958b, p. 140).

In another discussion of the gradient of deformation, Gibson proposed that the transformations of the optic array should be described in terms of differential velocities and not absolute velocity vectors (1958c, p. 46). How this suggestion fits together with the latter (in previous paragraph) requires explication, but one fact is evident: the gradient of deformation is not to be understood in terms of point velocity vectors or even in terms of velocities. Deformation in the optic array should be described in terms of the *relations* of transforming structures. The gradient of optical deformation the observer registers is a gradient of differences of structural transformations across the optic array.

When an observer moves about the environment, the transforming optic arrays sampled do not of course just contain invariants. The fact of transformation means that something is variant. Gibson, during the period 1957–1961, came to the general conclusion that while optical invariants are information about environmental permanency, optical variants are information for environmental change and changes in observer position relative to the environment. (1959, p. 484; 1961a, p. 261)

A perceiver's ability to know of where it is going and where it is presently located depend on certain variants in the series of sampled optic arrays. This idea was expressed in a less developed form in Gibson's 1950 book. What was novel in Gibson's attitude toward visual proprioception after 1955 was his belief in its ubiquitousness (1955, pp. 482–483; 1958a; 1959, p. 462; 1960d, p. 4). For Gibson, proprioception is an ongoing process of the visual perceptual system. It became important enough in Gibson's mind following his stay at Berkeley for him to develop a "theory" of it, in an attempt to explain the control of locomotion (1958a).

Gibson's growing interest in the adaptive significance of visual perception was, in all probability, partially responsible for his belief in the omnipresence of proprioception. The connection between survival and successful locomotion through the environment is evident, as well as the relation between accomplished locomotion and proprioception. Gibson, in presenting his systematic views of proprioception (1958a), introduced the topic through considerations of adaptation and locomotion.

A second reason for Gibson's thesis of the pervasiveness of visual proprioception was his realization (1958a) that any optic array is unique to its station point in the medium. Also, there is a unique difference between any two optic arrays that is projectively specific to the change of position of the perceiver relative to the environment. Consequently, the position and change of position of the observer in the environment is always specified in any sampled optic array. In the 1960s and 1970's, perception and proprioception were systematically tied together providing a description of ecological sensitivity.

An important advance beyond the concepts of Duncker occurred in the period 1957–1961. This development in Gibson's thinking was connected with the heightened significance he saw in the concept of transformation. When a physical surface was rotated and projected onto a screen, an observer not only perceived the surface shape as constant but as moving (rotating) (Gibson & Gibson, 1957). Gibson hypothesized that the types of transformations these projected patterns underwent could be considered optical information for rigid motion, i.e., a shape changing in position but not in shape. Gibson later argued that certain other types of transformations should yield perceptions of non-rigid motion, i.e., change in both position and shape (Gibson & von Fieandt, 1959). The general hypothesis tested and supported was that the types of transformations specific to non-rigid motion should yield perception of non-rigid motion. (See also Gibson & Smith, 1959; Gibson, Smith, Steinschneider, & Johnson, 1957 regarding Gibson's thinking on motion perception during this period.)

In all of the previous examples, Gibson's explanations relied on optical invariants and transformations that were projectively specific to features of the environment. This reliance was indicative of Gibson's general conviction after 1960 that veridical vision was primarily supported by sensitivity to optical change and invariants of optical change. As mentioned earlier, the basis of this general contention was Gibson's realization (1955–1960) that invariants and transformations of the transforming optic array are univocal, whereas structure in the static optic array is often equivocal. Gibson realized the importance of time (successive order) in stimulation.

It is noteworthy that invariance and transformation are reciprocal concepts. Taken together with his reciprocal understanding of perceptual activity and effective stimulation, as well as his emerging ecological treatment of the perceiver and the environment, we see that reciprocity becomes an important theoretical concept as his approach becomes increasingly ecological. Reciprocity also becomes important as his description of perception becomes more dynamic (e.g., optical transformations, exploratory perceptual activity, and motion and change in the ecosystem).

Part IV

ECOLOGICAL
PSYCHOLOGY
and PERCEPTUAL
EPISTEMOLOGY

Chapter 15 _____

GIBSON'S "SENSES CONSIDERED as PERCEPTUAL SYSTEMS"

THE ECOLOGICAL APPROACH TO THE ENVIRONMENT

In his review of Gibson's *The Senses Considered as Perceptual Systems*, Boring remarked "How James Angell and the Chicago group should have welcomed this book sixty years ago, the first truly functional psychology of sense perception that has ever been written" (Boring, 1967, p. 150).

Gibson's *Senses* (1966a) is a functional approach to perception, but equally, it is an evolutionary approach. Perhaps in its most basic form it is an ecological approach embracing both functional and evolutionary perspectives. Gibson, for the first time offers a general theory of perception, going beyond just vision, though over half the book concerns visual perception. After covering the basic triad of the environment, the perceptual systems, and the ecology of stimulation, Gibson treats each sense in more detail, and completes his survey with vision.

Gibson's starting point in the *Senses* is an ecological description of the environment; it is ecological because the environment is understood relative to animals. For Gibson in 1950, the primary function of phenomenology was to "lay bare" the "facts" of perception requiring explanation. After Gibson's year at Berkeley (1954–1955), an ecology or "science" of the environment was substituted for phenomenology now providing the "facts" that required explanation. By the 1960s Gibson identified the environment as "What is perceived?" (1966a, p. 7). Phenomology is both subjective in orientation and dualistic, whereas an ecology of the environment is objective and not based on an absolute dualism.

The environment is what is perceived, but it is also the "source of stimulation" necessary for perception (1966a, Chapter 1). An explanation of perception involves an understanding of how stimulation from the environment can "specify" the environment. Therefore, Gibson is attempting to scientifically explain why the environment is intelligeible– how it can be known. Such an explanation would support Aristotle's realism and "solve" Einstein's mystery, i.e., "The most incomprehensible fact of the universe is that it is comprehensible." Dualism ascribes the intelligibility of the world to the mind. In the *Senses*, Gibson shifts the emphasis over to the world, though ultimately his explanation of the world's "knowability" is ecological, involving both perceiver and environment. At this point in his development he attempts to convinvingly make the connection between the environment and stimulation as well as the perceiver and stimulation. In the *Visual World*, Gibson offered a new level of analysis for describing stimulation. In the *Senses* he relates this stimulus structure to a complementary level of analysis within the environment and the perceiver. A description of the environment is essential to ecological optics or ecological acoustics (1966a, pp. 79–81). The structure of the environment determines the structure of stimulation, and the ecology of stimulation, e.g., ecological optics, is the study of environment-stimulation relations. Complimentarily, perceptual systems and their activities are described at a level of analysis commensurate with the structure of stimulation and the structure of the environment.

Gibson conceives of the environment as those conditions in which life has evolved (1966a, pp. 8–9, 156–158). In considering the evolving structures and capabilities of living forms, it is the ways of life and opportunities of the environment that serve as the framework for discussion. A way of life involves various *affordances* of the environment, and life evolved in a variety of ways to take advantage of what the environment has to offer. One could say an ecological compatibility had evolved between life and the environment. This compatibility can be seen in how inextricably and essentially the environment is involved in the ways of life of the perceiver. Over the next 15 years, the reciprocal relation of affordances and animate ways of life would become an increasingly important theme.

The environment has multiple levels of structure with smaller units embedded in larger units (1966a, p. 8). There is both a spatial and temporal "nesting"; in the latter case, events of lesser duration are embedded in events of longer duration. For example, the day-night cycle is embedded in the seasonal cycle. Ecology deals with the levels of structure relevant to life. In the *Senses*, Gibson again attacks the reductionistic ontology of atomic physics arguing that all levels of nature (and not just the smallest) are real (1966a, pp. 21–22). His basic orientation is

wholistic, treating the "physical world" as possessing inherent organization. The physical world is not elementary atoms in a void. It should be
noted, though, that Gibson does not reject the concepts of analysis and
parts, for finer structures are seen as nested in more global structures.
Gibson is wholistic relative to the one-sided elementarism of reductionistic physics, and is particularly critical of popularized reductionistic physics such as contained in Eddington's *The Nature of the Physical World*
(1929).

There exist both temporal and spatial invariants within the environment. These invariants give the environment stability and provide a
framework for life. Gravity and the earth-sky contrast are two basic
spatial invariants, and the seasonal and diurnal cycles are basic temporal
invariants. Note these invariants are invariant *contrasts* or relationships
of differences. Invariants are relative for nothing is absolutely permanent,
but within the evolutionary history of life there have existed certain
constants. The environment, though, is anything but static and exhibits a
variety of spatial and temporal transformations. Gibson would state that
the environment possesses indeterminate richness in structure (1966a,
p.23).

Aside from the layout of surfaces which provides the spatial structure
of the environment, a second major feature of the environment is the
medium of air (for aquatic life it is the medium of water) (1966a, p. 14).
Animals move across surfaces through the medium of air; the medium
affords locomotion. Gibson would state that the surface layout and
medium "support behavior" (1966a, p. 9). Secondly, the medium, because it is transparent, permits the flow of stimulation. Stimulus information about the environment is "broadcasted" through the medium (1966a,
pp. 14–15).

There is a variety of forms of stimulation transmitted through the
medium. Besides reflected or ambient light, compression waves generated by mechanical vibratory events and distributions of chemical molecules from volatile substances are also propagated through the medium
(1966a, pp. 16–20). The environment due to its physical make-up determines the structure of stimulation and the medium affords its transmission. Information about the environment is specified in the medium.

The guiding principle of investigation in Gibson's ecology of the
environment was to ascertain what the environment affords the animal.
The "facts" of the environment described are selected because of their
relevance to behavior and perception. His description of the environment
"sets the stage" for his examination of perception. Further, the environment is tied to the perceiving animal in two ways: it provides the
conditions for perception and it is what is perceived. The environment is
both ontologically and epistemologically connected to the perceiver.

Traditionally, since the time of Plato, the physical world not only was seen as a set of unrelated particulars, but also it was seen as intrinsically meaningless. There are exceptions to this philosophical perspective, but the most popular view has been to see both order and meaning *imposed* on the world. Gibson, speaking like Aristotle, describes the environment as if perception involved the environment revealing itself to the perceiver. Consequently, the environment is seen as meaningful.

In the historical tradition best exemplified by J. S. Mill and E. B. Titchener, Gibson, circa 1950, appeared to believe that meaning in perception was furnished by the perceiver (Gibson, 1948, p. 184; 1950a, pp. 200, 203, 212–216, 223). Ten years later, Gibson was suggesting that meaning was "given" in stimulation (Gibson, 1958a, pp. 190–191; 1959, p. 485; 1960c, pp. 699–701). By 1966 Gibson had coined the term *affordances* to refer to the meanings of features of the environment (1966a, pp. 273–274, 285). Affordances are what the environment furnishes animals, and, for Gibson, they are directly perceived (see Gibson, Schiff, & Caviness, 1962). Affordances would include graspable and manipulable objects, dangers, edible substances, places to hide or to be sheltered from the weather, the ground to walk on, weapons, and fuel for heat. Gibson would develop his concept of affordances considerably in the 1970s. It is noteworthy that affordances are understood relative to living forms. The affordances of the environment are ontologically tied to the animal.

PERCEPTION, PROPRIOCEPTION, AND THE PERCEPTUAL SYSTEMS

The central theoretical concept of Gibson's *Senses* is the perceptual system. It is proposed as an alternative to the sense organ-sensory channel theory popular in traditional anatomy and physiology. A perceptual system is active rather than passive, obtaining information instead of receiving an input (1966a, p. 5, 31). Perceptual systems are functional rather than anatomical units that overlap both anatomically and functionally, and they are described at a molar and integrative level of analysis (1966a, pp. 52–53). Finally there is an anatomical overlap between the exteroceptive, proprioceptive, and performatory systems (1966a, pp. 32–38, 56–57).

The body of an animal can be described at different levels of analysis. Regarding sense perception, there exist receptor cells that are organized together into receptor units which in turn together form sense organs, such as the eyes or ears. Sense organs can be moved about by means of attached muscles and both these muscles and the sense organs are connected via networks of nerves ("sensory and motor pathways") with the brain. A perceptual system is understood as such a nested organization of structures functionally integrated to detect information (1966a, pp. 40–44). All these levels of analysis are valid. How these units are described and understood is open to question.

Gibson, beginning at the level of receptor cells, objects to traditional physiology on all levels of analysis within his description of a perceptual system. Receptor cells do not respond to stimulus energy per se but to changes in energy. Receptor units, in turn, respond to stimulus structure also, though of more complex kinds. The receptor network does not simply transmit energy to the "sensory channels." Though sense organs are traditionally seen as passive, in normal life the sense organs move about and are active. From the time of Müller, nerves were divided into incoming sensory pathways and outgoing motor pathways; Gibson suggests that recent evidence indicates there are not such distinct pathways (1966a, p. 2). For Müller each sensory pathway, presumably connected with a localized area of the brain, produced a different type of sensation (visual, auditory, touch, etc.). Gibson, though, sees perceptual systems as functionally overlapping. Different perceptual systems can detect the same information and thereby perceive the same facts, e.g., shape is something that can be both seen and felt. The localization theory fitted nicely with Berkeley's heterogeneity of the senses hypothesis and Müller's specific energy of nerves hypothesis; also the brain was thought of as receiving inputs through the sensory channels and in some manner transforming the raw input into perceptions. Gibson does not view the brain as a receiver; rather he views a perceptual system actively obtaining information as a whole. Basically, Gibson rejects the passive, segregated, and reductionistic theory of the senses, instead viewing biological organization in terms of active functional systems with interdependent and overlapping parts.

Gibson distinguishes five basic perceptual systems: The orienting, auditory, haptic, taste-smell, and visual systems (1966a, p. 49). Further, he distinguishes these perceptual systems from the proprioceptive systems that anatomically overlap them (1966a, pp. 35–38). Proprioception, to be discussed more thoroughly later, involves knowledge of the self (body) within the environment. Perception is functionally distinguished from proprioception for perception is knowledge of the environment. Because an animal can both see where it is and also see where features of the environment lie, the same anatomical units can be involved in both processes. The historical concept Gibson turned to in the *Senses* to clarify his distinction between an anatomical and functional description was Lashley's (1929, 1950) idea of vicarious function (Gibson, 1966a, pp.

4–5, 47–58, 264). It seemed reasonable to suppose that the same anatomical unit could be involved in different functions, e.g., the arms and hands can be used to paint pictures or pitch a baseball.

When Gibson defined the perceptual systems as "modes of activity" or "modes of external attention" (1966a, pp. 49–51) he was quick to point out the anatomical overlap of different perceptual systems, e.g., the visual and auditory systems both contain the neck muscles. Each system is a mode of activity rather than some distinct set of anatomical structures (1962b, p. 484; 1962c, p. 230; 1963, p. 10; Gibson & Pick, 1963, p. 386). The modes of activity are all forms of orientation to the environment and include listening, touching, smelling, tasting, and looking (1966a, p. 49).

Besides the anatomical overlap of perceptual systems, there also exists functional overlap (1962b, p. 490, 1966a, pp. 4, 22–23, 54). There exist "natural specificities" for shape, texture, or location that can be registered through either the visual or haptic systems. The modes of attention may differ (i.e., touching versus looking), and the stimulation may differ (i.e., deformation of the skin versus structure in ambient light), but the *information* is identical inasmuch as the natural specificity is to the same feature of the environment. Müller's belief in an absolute segregation of senses is untenable according to Gibson on both anatomical and functional grounds. Further, Gibson sees the senses as working together in coordination, with vision and touch supporting each other to enhance and further clarify perception. The senses exist as a functionally integrated whole. (See also Gibson, 1969c, 1976b, & Gibson & Caviness, 1962 on Gibson's views regarding the relationships between the different senses.)

Taken together, the concepts of perceptual systems and information point to an interesting historical contrast between Gibson and the dualistic theories of perception. If perception is built up from mental experiences based on anatomically distinct phenomenal qualities, it is ontologically separated from the environment. Perceptual systems do not register their own internal states, but rather are different means for registering identical environmental features. Which perceptual system is involved is irrelevant to the perception. For Gibson, perception is relative to the objectivity of information rather than localized internal states. Perceptual systems are given an ecological function.

Gibson points out that empiricism and the specific energies of nerves hypothesis are inconsistent, for if knowledge of the world comes through the senses, how can it be that all the senses convey are states of themselves. A dualistic ontology separates sensory experience from the world, and from Descartes to Müller this approach was developed and defended. Gibson, like Aristotle, is proposing a strict empiricist and nondualistic view of perception. Perception involves knowledge of the world.

The specific energies of nerves hypothesis is also subjected to criticism through Gibson's theory of proprioception (1966a, p. 33). Following the specific energies of nerves hypothesis, there should be specialized receptors and sensory qualities for "self-awareness" (1963, p. 10). Gibson, besides suggesting that there are no specialized receptors, also suggests there are no distinct sensory qualities for proprioception. Gibson, in the 1950s had begun developing an explanation of visual self-perception with a moving observer, but in the 1960s he considerably extended his ideas on proprioception to cover all the senses and treat it as a constant and essential feature of perceptual functioning. He proposed six kinds of proprioception which, though they involve different anatomical structures and different forms of stimulation, may register identical facts about the self. They include muscular, articular, vestibular, cutaneous, auditory, and visual proprioception (1966a, pp. 36–37).

Proprioception and perception are two poles of awareness. Both proprioception and perception have distinct yet related intentional objects, viz., the self and the environment. Both involve a circular and continuous process of biological activity. Gibson, in the *Senses*, clearly advocates the circular-continuous model over the unidirectional-discontinuous model (1963, p. 12; 1966a, pp. 5, 35–39, 267). Both perception and proprioception are continuously ongoing processes, occurring simultaneously, involving activity that circles around through the systems. Awareness is therefore in a fundamental sense ecological for it involves cognizance of the self in an environment. One pole is interospecific; the other pole is exterospecific.

As understood by Gibson, proprioception is distinguished from most "theories of action sensitivity" (von Holst & Mittelstadt, 1950) in that it depends on *re-afference* and not *reefference*. "Motor theories" of visual perception included the hypothesis that the perceiver was aware of body position and movement through muscular sensations produced through sensitivity to muscular action. This form of proprioception would be based on re-efferent data, for example, Lötze's local sign theory or Berkeley's muscular theory of depth cue. Movement exerted (efference) yields muscular sensations (re-efference). For Gibson there is a variety of forms of proprioception aside from sensitivity to muscular exertion; there exists a variety of kinds of stimulation that are afferent and change due to changes in the body. When the observer moves, the skin is deformed, the body rocks back and forth, joints change angles, noises are made, and ambient light is globally transformed.

Traditionally, psychological and physiological processes involved in perception are thought of as intervening between the input and the consequent perception. Organization, inferential, and associative processes operate upon the sensory input originating in the sense organs.

Hence, the functions of perceptual operations are "inner directed." Conversely, the functions of Gibson's perceptual systems are defined with respect to potential information; perception systems obtain, explore, enhance, and pick up information. Gibson described these activities as types of "external attention"; thus the perceptual systems are "outer directed" functionally (Gibson, 1966a, pp. 49–58, 250–265).

Some form of neural transmission has usually been connected with the intervening variable view of perceptual activity. A simple and historically popular view was the projection hypothesis in conjunction with a Hartlian associative representation of the central nervous system. Inputs from the eye are transmitted to the brain with a preservation of retinal patterns, whereupon via cerebral connections, an associative context of ideas (or centrally excited neural activity) is added onto the sensations. The general assumption that the brain (or mind) operates upon a transmitted input is an old idea dating from the ancient Greeks. We have seen how Descartes, Müller, and 19th century physiologists articulated the transmission hypothesis. This whole line of thinking Gibson opposed and disparagingly referred to as the "channels of sensation" view.

For Gibson, the activity of perception involves "outer-directed" or ecological functionings that can only be described in terms of feedback loops. All types of overt attention involve circular activity from the brain to the mucles and peripheral neural units and back again and back *again,* and so forth. There is no end point in this continuous process (Gibson, 1963, p. 12; 1966a, p. 5). For Gibson, the total perceptual system resonates to information. The specificity of these circular activities to the environment perceived is not "contained" in any one part of the system, e.g., the brain, but only within the total "loops" of activity (Gibson, 1966a, pp. 5, 267). Consequently, Gibson has argued against the projection hypothesis (1966a, pp. 262–263). Furthermore, the projection hypothesis serves the function of re-presenting to the inside what is there on the outside; it contains the simulative assumption and the homunculus hypothesis. For Gibson, perception is not a type of inner observation plus inference.

Throughout the 1960s, Gibson continued to employ the term "psychophysics" in characterizing his approach. In addition, the terms *stimulation* and *cause* are still used by him in discussing the optical basis for vision (Gibson, 1962b, p. 477; 1963, pp. 8–12; 1966a, pp. 29, 31, 194–195, 227, 248). These words no longer have the same meanings that they had in *The Perception of the Visual World.* Gibson, in the 1960s, rejected the unidirectional causal theory of perception from which all these terms derived their original meanings.

The formula "perception is a function of stimulation" is no longer considered valid by Gibson since stimulation is just as much a function of the activity of perceiving (Gibson, 1962b, pp. 477–478; 1963, p. 12; 1966a, p. 3, 29–31). There is a circular interdependency. The more appropriate "formula" is that perception is a function of the ability to detect information. The explanation for perception is ecological involving both perceptual activities and information. Consequently, the concept of a psychophysics of perception is no longer applicable to Gibson's approach. What remains of the psychophysical ideal in the ecological approach is the hypothesis that if perception is veridical, there exists registered information specific to those features of the environment perceived. This proposed relationship does not exist because "stimulation causes" perception, but rather because perception involves an active process of resonance to information.

A major theme in Gibson's writings in the 1960s is that perception is not based upon sensations. Specifically concerning vision, he stated that visual perception is not "reducible" to visual sensations (1962b, p. 490); that sensations are "incidental" to visual percepts (1963, pp. 4–8; 1966a, pp. 56, 183); that sensations are not "necessary" (1966a, pp. 47–48); and that visual perception in certain cases (perception of occlusion) is even "sensationless" (1966a, pp. 204–205; 1972b, p. 222).

Gibson offered various "definitions" of "visual sensations."

1. Visual sensations are produced by the "variants of stimulus energy" (Gibson, 1962c, p. 231; 1963, p. 8);

2. Visual sensations result from a "sophisticated pictorial attitude" toward experience (Gibson, 1963, p. 15; 1966a, pp. 235, 306);

3. Visual sensations are determined by the "anatomical pattern of excitation" on the retina (Gibson, 1966a, pp. 237, 256);

4. If the observer "pays attention to the experience" of seeing, then there will be an awareness of visual sensations (Gibson, 1968–1969, pp. 408–409);

5. Visual sensations are experiencing the "states" of nerves (Gibson, 1966a, pp. 38, 47, 55–56, 266).

In 1950, Gibson maintained that the "visual field" was determined by the anatomical retinal image or retinal excitation patterns relative to the anatomy of the retina (Meaning 3). Instead of the word *determine* Gibson often substituted *detect*, hence the visual field depended on a detecting or registration of the anatomically relative retinal mosaic (Gibson, 1966a, pp. 253–256). Because this physical pattern is two-dimensional, the "pictorial attitude" (Meaning 2) amounts to attending to this configuration. Recall that Gibson's visual field was similar to the field of visual sensations implied by the simulative assumption and the picture model of the retinal image.

Because the "picture model of the retinal image" denotes a type of "inner registration" or "observation," detecting internal (anatomically relative) patterns of excitation, visual sensations involve an "awareness of certain aspects of neural states in the eye and optic nerve (Meaning 5). Note that the above connection between the anatomical retinal image and the idea of "inner registration" indicates a relationship between the anatomical retinal image and the homunculus hypothesis. Contrast this type of experience with perception which is resonance to something ecological, viz., information. The activity of visual perception involves neural excitation. These ongoing neural processes are functionally related to information, but if the observer attends to the activity of perceiving (Meaning 4), (which is normally not the case), the perceiver consequently is aware of neurological states included in this "outer directed" activity.

Returning to the anatomical image and the visual field, note that both exhibit numerous types of variations that are not found in the optic array and visual perception. The location, size, and structure of perceived objects remain invariant over changes in the position of the observer because of invariants in the transforming array. If the observer moves, the location and two-dimensional size and form of patterns undergo changes in the anatomical image and visual field. Since optical invariants are not specific to the anatomical image, this latter configuration consists of variants of stimulation (Meaning 1).

Assuming the analysis of Gibson's understanding of the concept of visual sensation is correct, what basic similarity exists across all his various definitions? It would appear visual sensations are distinguishable from visual perceptions in that the former involves sensory awareness considered relative to peculiarities of neurological excitation, while visual perception is specifically related to the information in the optic array. Hence, visual sensations are "incidental" to visual perception because perception is veridical insofar as it is functionally related to the optic array. Visual sensations result from cognizance of subjective aspects of these perceptual activities.

Gibson cited Johannes Müller's "specific energies of nerves" hypothesis as the paramount historical example of "sensation based theories" of visual perception (Gibson, 1966a, p. 38, 47, 55–56, 266). Following in the footsteps of many previous theorists, Müller thought that visual sensations or experience related to the pecularities of the transmitted input (special sensibles) was the first step in visual perception. On the other hand, there is one historical figure with whom Gibson is in agreement regarding the relationship between sensation and perception. For Troland, visual perception is experience functionally related to the "optical ray sheaf" and the "objective" conditions of the response arc, whereas sensation is sensory experience related to neurological states. According to Troland, peception should not be thought of as dependent upon sensations. Basically, this position is very close in meaning to Gibson's 1966 demarcation of sensation and perception.

THE ORIENTING, AUDITORY, AND HAPTIC SYSTEMS

There are certain additional general themes in Gibson's treatment of perceptual systems and perception that become evident in his individual discussions of each of the senses. For Gibson, all the senses are ways to orient to the environment, though there is one sense, the vestibular, that is specialized and basic to this general function. Orientation is an ecological concept. It refers to an actively maintained relationship between an animal and its environment. The vestibular sense involves sensitivity to gravity and the surface of support (equilibrium) and to changes in body position and locomotion relative to gravity and the ground. Though Gibson continued to believe that vision can provide its own spatial framework, the vestibular sense is seen as the basic and most primitive form of orientation. The sense organs include the semicircular canals, the utricle, and the saccule, but equilibrium is active, involving postural adjustments to gravity and bodily acceleration. The vestibular perceptual system involves those muscles of the body that balance or align it to gravity, either when the animal is stationary or moving (1966a, pp. 59–61, 71–72).

Though primitive, the vestibular sense is not sensitive to energy per se but to relations and changes in energy. For example, the semicircular canals react to changes in motion, and to be in constant steady motion is equivalent to being at rest (1966a, pp. 60–63). The vestibular sense together with the haptic sense (pressure on the body from the ground) yield information that is relational and involves two senses integrated together. An animal on an incline has a line of pressure against its body at an angle with the line of gravity—an animal on a level surface has gravity and ground pressure aligned. Variations in alignment between gravity and skin pressure are treated as information by Gibson (1966a, p. 63); it is a relationship between two relationships that is information about alignment and orientation on surfaces of support.

Turning to the auditory system, the sense organs are the ears, but the perceptual system involves the muscles of the neck that orient the head toward sounds. Gibson initially traces the evolution of audition and points out that when the system is active, which it normally is, it is more accurate; audition involves active listening (1966a, pp. 76, 84). Gibson's description of auditory stimulation is ecological and wholistic in orientation; natural sounds and their sources are described at the global level in contrast to the reductionistic and analytic features of sound found in traditional acoustics and psychophysics. (1966a, pp. 86–89). Natural sounds are complex, possessing temporal structure in intensity and frequency variations. Further, given that there are two ears, there exist temporal and intensity differences in sound reaching the ears. Gibson conceives of such variations between the ears as information for the direction of the sound source.

Two points are worth emphasizing about binaural disparity. First, it is clearly an ecological reality, referring to a relatoinship that exists between a sound source and a dual-eared animal. The sound source itself generates a wave train of diminishing intensity as the sound propagates outward through the medium (1966a, pp. 79–81). The two ears receive the sound at slightly different times and correspondingly slightly different intensities. These differences exist in the relationship between a dual-eared perceiver and the propagating sound waves. Second, Gibson states that the variations as such are detected and the brain does not need to perform an internal comparison. Gibson is simply applying his general thesis that differences are directly detected and do not need to be computed by first registering absolute stimulus values. Also note that the first type of variation is a temporal difference, a difference in successive order.

Gibson's approach to auditory stimulation continues his wholistic orientation to stimulation first developed with ecological optics. Consider speech, where although no two speakers produce the same frequency spectrum when articulating the same word, the same word is perceived. Gibson proposed that there exist invariants in structure (frequency relations) that are information for the words being spoken (1966a, pp. 92-94). Never is the same piece of music played identically, yet something in the pattern of sound remains the same. As with light, Gibson looks at higher-order relationships within sound rather than absolute, local values.

The haptic sense is not simply the sense of touch (or skin sensitivity), but the capacity, involving both joints and skin, to "lay hold of" and explore, with the body, features of the environment through direct physical contact. The sense organs are the skin and the joints and the system is active, involving most of the skeletal muscles of the body (1966a, pp. 99–104). There exist both perceptual and proprioceptive poles in the haptic sense, for the perceiver registers both body position and skin deformation as well as the shape, size, and texture of the object being explored (1966a, p. 99). The principle of vicarious function is very evident in the haptic sense. If an object were explored with one finger, against the fingertip there is a flow of variations in skin deformation, but a single, solid, self-enclosed object is perceived. The total informational array specifying the object in its variety of features is registered through one small area of the skin and a few joints (1966a, p. 109). The same information could be registered by using one hand, two hands, or other parts of the body, producing different variations of skin pressure but the same perception.

The information for the haptic sense is not simple energy, but relationships in energy. Neither the skin nor the joints respond to unchanging states. The skin adapts to constant pressure or uniform pressure and the joints adapt to constant angles. It is variations over time on the skin surface that touch reacts to, and it is changes in joint angles that stimulate the articular sense (1966a, pp. 105–106). Temporal discontinuities in stimulation are produced by an active system. There are invariants that specifiy the invariant features of the environment, but these invariants are revealed through changing stimulation. This is the same general theme contained in Gibson's treatment of vision. Stimulus invariants and stimulus transformations are connected together. Information is higher order in another sense, for insofar as two sets of receptors are involved in the haptic sense there exist co-variant patterns between skin deformation and joint articulation (1966a, p. 113). Note that touch is actually involved in two different perceptual systems, orientation and the haptic sense, and for both systems, there exist higher order patterns involving dual forms of energy received through anatomically distinct parts.

Gibson rejects the local sign theory of touch, as he did with the local sign theory of vision. He does not see perceptual learning in the haptic sense involving associations but rather involving increased differentiation (1966a, p. 114). Haptic perception is not built up out of skin and joint sensations; in fact, haptic perception may occur without any concomitant sensations (1966a, pp. 97–98, 109). Gibson carries through with his general thesis that perception is based on objective information rather than subjective sensations.

ECOLOGICAL OPTICS AND THE EVOLUTION OF VISION

Gibson's evolutionary approach to vision is emphatically antianthropomorphic. He discusses both the convex and compound eyes, intending to discredit the idea that the retinal image is necessary for visual perception. He also points out a variety of other major differences between human eyes and other types of visual systems attempting to illustrate how a visual system fits the particular features of a way of life. Gibson's evolutionary approach is also decidedly ecological, for he sees visual evolution within the context of modes of existence within the animal environment (1966a, pp. 154–156).

There exist certain universal constants in which all eyes have evolved.

The sky is above, the earth is below. Night follows day, and day follows night. Ambient light fills the medium (water for fish, air for terrestrial and aerial animals), with diffuse bright light from above and dimmer, reflected light from below. Both the concave and convex eye systems evolved within this ecological context and represent the two main ways in which information is detected in the ambient optic array. What is essential in vision is the array, for the retinal image is peculiar to the concave eye (1966a, pp. 156–159, 163–168).

Gibson applies his functionalism to the evolution and ecology of vision. He introduces the topic of vision by asking what are the eyes good for? He argues that vision's basic functions are: the sky-earth discrimination, involving more detailed discriminations vis-á-vis surface layout; day-night discriminations involving more detailed discriminations of environmental changes; and detection of locomotion (proprioception). In all cases, his analysis proceeds from gross to fine discriminations, reflecting both his wholistic orientation and his differentiation theory of perceptual development (1966a, pp. 156–163).

In Gibson's treatment of the evolution of vision he acknowledges his indebtedness to Walls (1942). Gibson's comparative anatomy and comparative functionalism draw heavily on Walls (1966a, pp. 155, 157, 165, 169, 171–174, 196, 178, 182). Not all eyes are mobile but animals stabilize and orient themselves visually. Animals with mobile eyes turn their eyes to orient to action or the direction of locomotion (1966a, p. 170). Some animals look or fixate, while others without a well-developed fovea do not fixate and look around. Some animals (predators) have frontal eyes, whole others (prey) have lateral eyes (presumably to see a predator coming up from behind) (1966a, p. 174). The dual eye system produces binocular perspective, and the more frontal and overlapping in perspective, the more discriminating is distance perception. In general, anatomy is suited to function and the animal's way of life. Visual anatomy is to be understood within an ecological context.

Ecological optics in the *Senses* (1966a, Chapters 10 and 11), is concerned with the ecological conditions necessary for environmental specificity in the optic array and the actual projective relationships between the environment and the structure of light. Also, ecological optics contains the concept of a medium (Gibson, 1966a, pp. 14, 187–208) because a medium is essential for the rectilinear propagation of light and the steady state of reverberation of "multiply" reflected light. In particular, the medium of air is examined by Gibson in order to explain to his readers why the structure in reflected light is related to the structure in the environment. The special properties of the medium of air (or water) must be presupposed in ecological optics since the fact of optical specificity would not hold if light was reflected through something having a heterogeneous index of refraction.

Ecological optics involves the study of *how* the environment structures light in various ways. In the *Senses* (1966a), Gibson discusses how opaque surfaces structure reflected light through variations in surface inclination, selective reflectance, and differential illumination (1966a, pp. 205–216). He also examines how transparent and mirror-like surfaces structure light (1966a, pp. 216–220), and how "light is structured by artifice or art" (1966a, pp. 224–249). As Gibson stated, the environment is studied "as a source of stimulation" (1966a, pp. 7–30). Gibson's working hypothesis is that there are ecological laws relating an illuminated ecosystem with reflected ambient optical structure.

Consequently, Gibson's ecology of the environment is in two senses part of ecological optics. First the environment is one of the two *relata* in the projective relations studied in ecological optics. Secondly, describing certain underlying features of the environment constitutes an essential ingredient in Gibson's attempt to explain why there are specific relations between the optic array and the environment. An explanation of the natural specificity of structured light involves an understanding of both the medium and the environment and how each effects the propagation and structure of light.

Earlier it was pointed out that Heider proposed that a study of the relationships between proximal stimulation and the environment could be undertaken without having to consider the actual process of visual perception. Similarly, the projective relations between the optic array and the environment investigated in ecological optics are thought of by Gibson as existing independently of the fact of visual perception (1966a, Chapter 10). But is it the case that ecological optics could proceed independently of considerations of the nature of visual perception? And secondly, are all the facts uncovered in ecological optics conceptually disconnected from Gibson's view of animate life?

Regarding the first question, why did Gibson propose to study in his ecological optics projective relations at one special level of analysis? Why isn't radiant light examined for its specifying power and why is structure in light considered so important? Why are invariants of sequential order considered in ecological optics? Gibson was guided in all of the above decisions by considerations of animals and their perceptual capabilities (Gibson,, 1966a, pp. 190–208). What is the real point of doing ecological optics? Simply, it forms part of Gibson's overall attempt to explain why visual perception is veridical.

In Gibson's initial presentation of ecological optics in the *Senses* (1966a, pp. 186–208), one major theme is explaining how the optic array specifies adaptively significant environmental facts of surface layout. Not only is ecological optics geared to the appropriate structural level of analysis, but it is also geared to those functional aspects of the environment relevant to animal evolution and survival. Ecological optics studies and describes facts that do not necessarily involve the presence of a perceiver, but the facts selected presuppose considerations and theoretical ideas about a perceiver. Gibson in the 1950s and 1960s wished to emphasize the objective conditions and support of visual perception, yet the environmental facts studied are related to ways of animate life, making his overall approach ecological. By the 1970s, ecological optics focuses on how ambient structured light specifies environmental affordances for the animal.

The theory of evolution has also had a significant effect upon Gibson's treatment of optic array. It was after he became familiar with Walls' *The Vertebrate Eye* (1942) that Gibson sufficiently emphasized the fact that the retinal image was not necessary for visual perception. In contesting the view that the retinal image is the "stimulus" for visual perception, Gibson emphasized evolutionary considerations. He attempted to demonstrate that the various types of visual sense organs, e.g., chambered eyes and compound eyes, have evolved primarily "to take advantage of the information" in the optic array and not to produce a retinal image (1966a, pp. 163–185). The "retinal image" is only one means by which this evolutionary process has been accomplished.

Throughout the 1970s, Gibson continued to refer to the *fact* of the retinal image, but as can be ascertained from several passages in the *Senses,* he actually no longer believed in its existence as it is traditionally understood (1966a, pp. 172, 226, 262–263). Regarding the focused light on the retina, Gibson believed that it is misleading to refer to it as an image becuase this connotes something to be looked at or seen. The anatomical retinal image is really a "scintillation" due to the continuous tremor and jerking movements of the eye.

In the previous two chapters, the concept of information has been examined as it gradually became explicit in Gibson's thinking. It has been stated that Gibson defined optical information as the projective *specificity* of the optic array to the environment. Throughout the 1970s, Gibson has continued to stress this meaning (Gibson, 1962c, p. 231; 1966a, pp. 187, 242–246).

What is especially noteworthy from the historical viewpoint in Gibson's treatment of information is his contrast of conventional codes or signals with sensory information (1962c, p. 231, 1966a, pp. 242–244). According to Gibson, signs, such as words, are specifically related to facts of the world because of man-made conventions, whereas optical information in Gibson's sense is specific to the environment because of the natural laws of ecological optics. For Gibson, perception, insofar as it is supported by information, will be specific to the environment without any need for associations, mediation, etc. Signs require mediation. Perception is direct without mediation because the relationship between stimulus information and the environment is natural rather than arbitrary.

After 1960, Gibson considered the invariants of optical change as the primary basis of veridical visual perception because they were more environmentally specific than features of a "frozen" or static optic array (Gibson, 1962b, pp. 487–488; 1963, p., 14; 1966a, p. 160; 1967c, p. 20; 1967d, p. 165; 1968d). Again demonstrating the importance of the idea of evolution in his thinking, Gibson argued that the normal ecological situation throughout evolution has been a moving observer. Since the prevalent condition has been a transforming array, animals' visual capabilities must have become primarily adapted to this optical condition. Visual organs evolved to afford survival in ecologically normal conditions (Gibson, 1966a, p. 203; 1966b, p. 145). Especially in his treatment of haptic perception or "active touch," Gibson attempted to show that invariants in transforming stimulation, obtained through exploration, form the basis of perception of the persisting features of the environment.

In *The Perception of the Visual World* (1950a), Gibson maintained that the "stimulus variables" of sequential order did not need to be reconstructed in memory in order for them to be effective in visual perception. Perception is not limited to the instantaneous present. Throughout the 1960s, Gibson continued to argue against memory images or traces in visual perception of sequential order (Gibson, 1966a, pp. 251–252, 262–264, 276; 1966b, p. 142–147). One noteworthy difference in Gibson's thinking on this topic between 1950 and post-1960 is that he no longer maintains that the eye per se responds to sequential order. Instead, he argued that the visual perceptual system (which includes the brain) "resonates" to the transformations and the invariants over transformations in the optic array. There exist different levels of analysis for stimulation that correspond to different levels of analysis in the organizational make-up of the perceptual systems.

In the preceding chapters, there is considerable discussion of many of the substantive problems that interested Gibson, for instance, the visual spatial framework, surface, distance, motion, slant, and shape perception. In the last chapter especially, the concern is with how Gibson approached such issues when the concepts of invariants over transformations and transformations were foremost in his mind. Employing these optical concepts, Gibson throughout the 1960s further developed his explanations of the above perceptual facts (Gibson, 1962a, 1965b, 1966a, pp. 194–208, 253–256; 1966b; 1967c; 1968b; 1968d; 1969a).

Inspired by the work of Michotte (Michotte, 1963; Michotte, Thines, & Crabbe, 1964), one noteworthy new development in Gibson's treatment of the visual spatial framework was the concept of occlusion (1966a, pp. 203–208; 1968d; Gibson, Kaplan, Reynolds & Wheeler; 1969). Gibson hypothesized that a moving observer's ability to see edge depth and surface occlusion in the layout of the environment is based on optical occlusion.

With a moving observer, at the lateral border of the optical projection of an edge, there will be a shearing of texture units, such that the ratio of optical motions is specific to the edge-depth. Texture units for the closer surface will move faster, where the difference in optical motion is specific to differences in distance. Regarding the visual perception of the occlusion of one surfae by another surface, as the observer changes position there is a wiping out of texture at the leading border in the projection of an occluding object, a shearing at its lateral borders, and an unwiping of texture at the trailing optical border. The optical transformation of wiping-out is information for a surface becoming occluded and the unwiping is specific to one surface "emerging from behind" another surface (Gibson, 1966a,, pp. 203–208). Optical accretion (unwiping) and deletion (wiping-out) is information for the "coming into sight" and "the going out of sight" of surfaces (often of objects). These two ecological transformations should be contrasted with a surface coming into existence and going out of existence (Gibson et al., 1969).

Optical accretion and deletion are relevant to the general problems of the persistence and boundlessness of the environment. Assuming accretion and deletion are ecologically specific to surfaces being uncovered and occluded, surfaces need not appear to vanish when they go out of sight and new scenes need not seem as if they are coming into existence when they first come into sight. Neither memory images nor cognitive assumptions are required to explain the permanence and "all-together" character of the perceived environment, since there is information (natural specificity) for the ecological facts that a surface is emerging from behind another surface or that it is going behind an occluding surface. The vistas of the environment encountered as an observer moves along are connected.

PERCEPTION AND KNOWLEDGE

A great deal of recent theoretical history in visual perception revolved around the issue of whether sensory experience was given order through learned or innate mechanisms. Gibson sees either position as presupposing a sensation-based theory of perception, for it is assumed that stimulation does not provide structure (spatial or temporal); hence, it must be added. Gibson's investigation into ecological optics and other forms of stimulation intended to demonstrate structure embodied in stimulation that was naturally specific to the environment, thus discrediting the necessity for organismic organization (1966a, pp. 266–267).

Gibson does not dispute the facts of perceptual learning or inherited mechanisms, but he sees both variables in a different light. In the *Senses* he defends the differentiation theory first proposed in the 1950s with his wife, Eleanor, but he also introduces the hypothesis that attention span increases through perceptual learning. Basically, an animal begins with the inherited ability to detect a limited range of invariants and differentiate a limited range of variants (or transformations). Through a conjoined process of maturation and learning, more complex invariants and more subtle differences are detected. Perception becomes simultaneously more discriminating and abstractive (1966a, pp. 269–271, 1966b).

The concept of association has been central to most empiricist explanations of perceptual order. Since Gibson does not see perception limited to the instantaneous present, he supposes that associated events in the environment can be perceived. A regular sequence which occurs in the environment does not have to be put together in the mind through memory; the regularity exists in the environment and is detected. Gibson's position (though he derives some inspiration from Michotte's work on the perception of causality) stands in opposition to Hume's elementaristic treatment of causality. Sequential order and sequential regularities are ecological realities and perceptual systems become attuned to the corresponding stimulus information (1966a, pp. 271–273). The mind does not need to associate sequential regularities; such regularities only need to be detected. Associations are perceived rather than perceptions associated.

Not only is ecological reality structured spatially and temporally, but it possesses "affordances." Generally, perception has been seen as limited to quality and structure, but Gibson, with the development of the idea of affordances, introduced the hypothesis that "uses" and meanings are perceived. The meaning of an environmental feature is its function vis-á-vis the capabilities of an animal and these *uses* of the environment can be perceived (1966a, pp. 273–274). In the 1970s, the concept of affordances would become an increasingly important topic.

Perception has been seen as a process requiring a variety of other psychological processes, such as memory, expectation, language, and motor responses (1966a, pp. 275–282). All these processes were seen as enriching perception. Basically, Gibson's position in the *Senses* is to treat perception as the primary form of knowledge (empiricism), not requiring these so-called higher level psychological processes. Because Gibson does not see perception limited to the immediate present, memory and expectation are not needed—perception registers the environment's temporal structure as well as its spatial structure. The temporal structure of the environment is detected because the senses are active rather than passive. Perception is not a series of momentary states—it is a continuous process.

Chapter 16 _____

THE DEVELOPMENT
of GIBSON'S ECOLOGICAL
PSYCHOLOGY

CLASSICAL VERSUS GIBSONIAN THEORIES
OF PERCEPTION

Coincident with the publication of the *Senses,* Gibson began the "Purple
Perils" (The "Purple Perils" were short manuscripts printed in purple
ink). For his perception seminar at Cornell, Gibson would write notes,
usually a few pages in length, on a variety of topics and distribute them for
discussion. Most of the material in these notes never reached publication
in the form they were written in, but they served as the foundation for
publications submitted in the late 1960s and the 1970s. They were especially relevant to the germination and development of Gibson's final
book, *The Ecological Approach to Visual Perception* (1979). In this
chapter I overview the "Purple Perils" (hereafter "PP") which number
over 100 and constitute a book in themselves. I do not review the entire
set of "PP"; I have instead selected what seems to be a representative
group, trying to include most of the noteworthy ones.

After completing the *Senses* Gibson spent the next 12 years further
clarifying and developing his ecological psychology, focusing on vision.
His *Ecological Approach* was initially conceived as a rewrite of *The
Perception of the Visual World.* Gibson was extremely concerned with
developing his ideas through historical-theoretical comparison and, in
effect, wrote a history of his ideas concomitant with developing them. In
general, Gibson's "PP" can be seen as working documents on a variety of

topics, revolving around vision, intending to put his ecological approach in the clearest light, both conceptually and historically. They served as a foundation for his *Ecological Approach* (1979), which is examined in a later chapter.

One of the earliest "PP," "Contrasting Assumptions of the Classical Theory of Vision and a New Theory of Vision" (1967f) outlines those major differences, as Gibson saw them, between his ecological theory and traditional views. Those main figures and hypotheses that Gibson most strongly associates with the "accepted" view included Müller, Bell, and Helmholtz (sensory channels, elementary sensations, and sensory areas of the brain), Berkeley, Helmholtz, and Brunswik (depth cues, associationism, and perceptual inference), and Kepler, Fechner, and Newton (retinal and physical optics, atomistic physics and psychophysics). Gibson contrasted the above theorists and their ideas with his theoretical concepts of active perceptual systems and vicarious function, higher order ecological structure, and the ambient optic array.

For Gibson, the environment is described in terms of faces, edges, and borders of surfaces, rather than in terms of points or objects in space. This environmental structure is projected into a "light filled medium" as discontinuities in optical intensity and spectral composition. Traditional views on optics reflected light as individual rays of absolute values (Alhazen). The optic array at a station point consists of invariant discontinuities (ratios of intensity across changes in illumination level), whereas the retinal image is treated as a mosaic of energy points (Kepler).

The visual system is mobile and registers discontinuities, whereas the "passive" eye is traditionally viewed as an image-forming instrument. The visual system responds to the patterns in the light rather than the anatomical patterns of excitation. More generally, where in the traditional view the brain is seen as representing an internal anatomical pattern, for Gibson the function of a perceptual system is not to construct an internal image. The specific anatomical units excited and their own spatial arrangement relative to general anatomy is irrelevant. What is relevant is a preservation of those higher order relationships found in the light.

Gibson's approach to the role of the nervous system in perception reveals some historically noteworthy points. The nervous system does not construct a perception; more accurately, it "extracts" (draws out) perception. The environment, through naturally specific information, reveals its invariant and global features as well as its changes and details. Second, Gibson sees "internal" anatomical patterns much the same way as he approached the problem of the inverted retinal image. If relationships are preserved, which units are excited and how these units are anatomically distributed become secondary. It is the higher order relationships that matter rather than the individual elements or the literal concrete form. Environmental relationships, though realized in a material form, are preserved in energy relationships in stimulation, and these same relationships are preserved in the nervous system. For example, the anatomical facts of two retinal images (two eyes) or two cerebral hemispheres of excitation do not entail that we should see double. Nor must the blind spot be filled in, or a third dimension added, or eye movements cancelled. The retinal image does not have to be reinverted to see the world correctly, nor does any anatomically specific feature of excitation need to be corrected. Perception is specific to information, rather than to anatomy.

ECOLOGICAL OPTICS

One of Gibson's central concerns throughout the "PP" was the clarification and further development of the theory of ecological optics. At a 1970 conference devoted exclusively to ecological optics, Gibson outlined what he saw as those major historical facts that led him to develop ecological optics. It is worthwhile to look at his lecture (transcribed and edited by Anthony Barrand and Mike Riegle) in order to get an inside view of ecological optics' historical development through its creator's eyes (1970f).

First, Gibson lists the Ganzfeld experiments as leading him away from the retinal image toward the ambient optic array. With homogeneous light, the eyes cannot focus or form an image. Heterogeneous light is necessary for the visual system to function. As Gibson stated, it is "differences in different directions" of light energy that are a fundamental condition of vision; consequently, this ambient array is more basic than the retinal image. Several other considerations undermined the retinal image as central to explanations of vision. Gibson points out that the image has connoted something analogous to a picture, yet vision should not be modeled on picture viewing, which is, in fact, ontogenetically and phylogenetically derivative from normal vision. It is questionable if the retinal image is analogous to a picture, for the eyes tremor and dart about producing a continuous scintillation on the retina. Further, whenever either the observer or something in the environment moves, the structure of light transforms; it would be inappropriate to describe such basic optical facts in terms of features of a static "image."

A second set of factors that, according to Gibson, led him toward ecological optics revolved around the general psychophysical formula in psychology. Gibson stated that he came to doubt the applicability of the "variable" concept in describing stimulus information. Information cannot be broken down into a set of qualities that vary quantitatively and can be placed in lawful correspondence with perceptual variables. Gibson, in effect, abandoned any attempt to exhaustively reduce perception or stimulation to some finite set of attributes showing quantitative variation. Boring's "dimensions" were out, as well as Titchener and Wundt's elements. Essentially, information is indeterminately rich and perception is without delimitation, and neither can be analyzed into a set of totally inclusive attributes.

Gibson, as mentioned earlier, objected to the traditional concept of stimulation. He did not like Heider-Koffka's proximal-distal stimulus distinction for the environment is not a stimulus. Physical optics, which treats light as points of energy, had no real application to perception. Gibson believe that in his optical tunnel experiment he was able to separate information from stimulus energy and demonstrate that perception is to be understood through information rather than impinging stimulus energy.

In general, Gibson's historical understanding of ecological optics points to a dissatisfaction with the "picture" and "causal" models of perceptual stimulation. Information is neither a picture viewed by an inner eye nor a physical cause eliciting a perceptual effect. These traditional models would imply that perception is indirect.

In several "PP" Gibson further develops his "dynamic" conception of stimulus information (1966c, 1967k, 1971d, 1971j). The frozen (unchanging) array is a limiting case of the transforming array—a transforming array where there exist sequential as well as adjacent discontinuities is more basic. The transforming array cannot be analyzed into a set of discrete and static arrays, for visual stimulation is continuous, without beginning or end. Further, change is basic and not derivative from a series of static images. Gibson no longer believes point velocities or topology to be appropriate in describing optical transformations. Due to the general fact of occlusion, optical structures (not points) do not merely transform, instead there exist ruptures of structure as new environmental features come into view. Gibson attempts to understand the "stick-in-the-water" illusion in terms of dynamic information. A stick (partially immersed in water) may look bent though in reality it is straight, for in a frozen array there is a double-angled discontinuity. When the stick is rotated or the observer moves around the stick, the double-angle does not change. A stick that was actually bent would project a transforming discontinuity where the angularities would change. Where a stick is actually straight, Gibson argued that the "invariant" within the transforming array is information for straightness.

Invariants within a transforming array are not conceived of as forms or patterns (1972d, 1972e). Invariants are relationships. They have an abstract rather than particular existence. They are formal, though formless.

They exist across time in the transforming array and quite literally cannot be diagramed or "pictured" any more than "triangularity" (what all triangles have in common) could be represented. They have an abstract existence embodied over time and are not static particulars. A "formless invariant" is a temporal, as opposed to a spatial relationship. This idea of "formless invariants" takes us back to the issue between Aristotle and Plato concerning how abstract form could be embodied in transforming particulars. Plato believed that abstract form (e.g., triangularity) existed in a separate realm, whereas Aristotle saw form embodied in particulars. Clearly, Gibson sides with Aristotle.

Gibson attacks Heider's argument that stimulation should be viewed as a set of independent points (1967i). As energy, there are indeed separate "rays" of light, but Gibson assumes perceptual sensitivity to discontinuities and further assumes that such discontinuities have as real an existence as the absolute localized values of stimulus energy. Information involves structure and structure involves relationships. Empiricist psychology and reductionist science give the smallest units of analysis an absolute reality (e.g., sensations, atoms), sharply contrasting such "ultimate" particulars with relationships between particulars. Such an ontology is dualistic.

Gibson describes the structure in the array in terms of "visual solid angles" (1972h), and each angle or unit itself is divisible into smaller nested units indeterminately downward in scale. There are no absolute elements, indivisible and homogeneous, out of which the array is constructed. Instead, there are multiple "levels" (interpenetrating) of structure and the so-called individual rays are no more or less real than any higher level units. Gibson rejects Heider's argument on the same grounds that he rejects Newtonian atomism in general. It is historically noteworthy that although Gibson is an extreme empiricist epistemologically, he rejects elementarism, the ontological cornerstone of modern empiricism, in favor of wholism, an ontology historically associated with rationalism, nativism, and mental subjectivism.

Traditionally, the causal sequence from the environment to stimulation is the first half in the causal chain leading to perception. (Troland's objective phase of the response arc.) Gibson, with his dual concepts of resonance and perceptual loops, rejected the organism (or second) half of the causal chain model. After the *Senses*, Gibson also formulated an alternative interpretation to the causal model as traditionally applied to the relationship between the environment and stimulation.

The environment reflects light energy and in this sense causes the medium to be filled with reverberating light energy. Stimulation *is* transmitted. Information, which is environmentally specific structure, *is not* transmitted. Ambient light exists in a steady state and embodied in this steady state is structure. At any observation point this structure exists—the information is not carried to these points. Whatever may be the natural speed of light energy, it is irrelevant to the omnipresent structure within the sea of energy. Without the energy the structure would not exist, but the structure itself is not transmitted. There are no *eidolae*. Consequently, Gibson would not say that the perceptual systems receive information; perceptual systems resonate to information. There is no causal sequence proceeding from environment to stimulation to organs to brain; rather, there is a unity achieved at the interface of animal and environment by means of resonance to information (1967m; 1968f).

SUBSTANCES, SURFACES, AND SPACE

Gibson, in the "PP," continued to elaborate and systematize his ecological theory of the environment. He was especially interested in supplanting the standard physical ontology of objects or atoms in space and traditional solid and projective geometry. Due to the fact of occlusion, the optic array cannot be seen as a simple projection of the environment. Occlusion occurs because most surfaces in the environment are opaque rather than transparent. Consequently, an opaque solid geometry is needed to describe ecological structure (1968h; 1971n). Gibson, in critiquing the "objects in space" ontology, draws a three-fold ecological distinction between objects, substances, and surfaces. Substances have surfaces, and if a surface closes around itself, there exists an object. It is opaque surfaces (whether they are of objects or not) that occlude. The fundamental ecological concept is surface layout rather than objects in space (1970g; 1971k).

Visible "things" may be divided into tangible and intangible sources. Intangible sources include rainbows and mirror reflections and can be explained through traditional optics; but an intangible source does not *look like what it is*. Tangible sources do look like what they are, and cannot be explained in terms of radiant, divergent optics. Tangible versus intangible is different from opaque versus transparent. Glass is transparent though it is tangible. In general, Gibson's "spatial" ecology concerns itself with tangible opaque surfaces for they are of primary importance in perception and behavior. Visual systems have evolved basically to see the ground rather than rainbows or glass (1970h).

Gibson prefers the word *substance* to *matter,* for the former designates an ecological reality different in meaning from the traditional scientific concept of matter. Matter, though, exists in different states (gas, liquid, solid), and within the environment these different states can be found. Air is a gas and while a state of matter, it is not a substance, rather it is a medium for perception and behavior. Water, relative to fish, is not a substance but a medium. Substance therefore has an ecological relativity whereas matter does not. Gibson's concept of substance is different than the Lockean-Cartesian idea of intrinsic, independent substances. For terrestrial animals, water is a liquid substance and can be distinguished from solid and semisolid (plastic or viscous) substances. Gibson contends that there exists optical information specific to each kind of substance, and this information exists in optical transformations. Time is implicated in the perception of substances. Substances sometimes pass into a gaseous state, i.e., a transformation of matter occurs, yet from the ecological perspective this transformation is perceived as a substance going out of existence. Substances disintegrate or disappear (at the ecological level there is no conservation of substances). There is creation and destruction. Further, going out of sight (occlusion) is not the same as going out of existence; the information is different and the perceptions are different. When one object goes behind another it continues to exist; if it blows up, it does not (1967m).

Another distinction Gibson draws is between the substantial and the insubstantial, though this distinction is more perceptual than environmental. Surfaces are perceived due to structure in light. Heterogeneous stimulation yields a perception of something; homogeneous stimulation yields a perception of nothing. This is not an all-or-nothing phenomenon, for there exists a perceptual transition from the insubstantial to the substantial that is contingent on the degree of optical texture. A fog yields minimal optical texture and, though perceived, is not seen as possessing any substantiality. In general, a gaseous state produces little if any optical texture and is perceived at best as having an indeterminate surface. Anything yielding relatively pure homogeneous stimulation is "seen" as a medium rather than a substance with surfaces. Gibson argues that instead of "form perception" being the more primitive perception relative to "three-dimensional" perception, it is perception of the insubstantial that is more primitive (1968d).

As mentioned, Gibson proposes that an opaque solid geometry be developed to describe environmental surface layout. The opaque quality of surfaces becomes significant when an observation point is involved. The first level of description, though, does not involve any reference to observation and simply considers certain basic features of surfaces. Relative to planarity, a surface may diverge either sharply (an angle) or gradually (a curve). The surface of the ground, though overall an ecological plane, is nested with angles and curves. A surface which achieves relative closure is an object—complete closure would constitute a detached object. In Gibson's ecological geometry, a surface is more basic than an object and ecological space is defined relative to surface layout. Objects are said to have "faces" if they have relatively segregated sides by means of angles across their surfaces. Gibson introduces other geometrical concepts in describing surface layout, and although no initial reference is made to observation points, the ecological size scale of animals is implicit in his description. The ground is not a plane at the cosmological scale; it is a curved, closed surface. The earth is not an object relative to animals, but it is an object relative to astronomy.

Because environmental surfaces are usually opaque, if an observation point is introduced, the fact of occlusion emerges. Angled and curved edges occlude what is behind them relative to observation points. The front of an object will occlude its backside and objects will occlude other objects or surfaces behind them (1968h). Occlusion is ecological.

OCCLUSION AND EDGE PERCEPTION

Beginning in the mid-60s, the ecological fact of occlusion becomes an increasingly important topic for Gibson. Occlusion is an ecological fact, for independent of observation points (a reference point), there is no such thing as occlusion. The importance of occlusion and the perception of occlusion lies in its relevance to the general problems of the unbounded and persistent nature of the environment. Gibson came to believe that understanding occlusion was the key to these problems that had interested him since *Perception of the Visual World*; further, occlusion provided an exemplar case to illustrate several basic hypotheses in his perceptual theory (1965c).

The vistas of the environment are connected and there exists a permanency to the world (1969g; 1971o). As an animal moves about, new features open up from behind edges, and other features become occluded, going out of view. What appears does not seem to come into existence (rather into view) and what disappears does not seem to go out of existence (rather only out of view behind an edge). Objects and surfaces are perceived to continue behind the occluding edge and when they totally go out of view they are perceived as still there. This is perception without sensation. Although it is because of the ecological fact of occlusion (plus a lack of panoramic vision) that all the environment cannot be revealed *simultaneously* to an observer, it is because of the perception of occlusion that the environment can be perceived as spatially coherent and temporally coexistent. Gibson contends that reversible optic transformations constitute information for continuity of existence. Reversible transformations are produced by moving the head and/or body back and forth bringing the environmental features into view and then out of view. This lawful and dynamic feature to perception of occlusion points to a significant element in Gibson's theory of "space" perception.

To quote Gibson,

> The most interesting implication of the experiments to be described is that, even when reformulated in terms of "layout", the ancient problem of space perception is only intelligible in terms of space-time. More concretely, the implication is that we can understand the perception of the environment only when we consider changes in the observer's point-of-view. So, far from visual perception of the world being one problem and the visual experience of movement *through* the world being another problem, the truth seems to be that both are one problem which is simpler when they are considered together (1968d, p. 2).

Through the concept of occlusion, Gibson ties together even more strongly the spatial and temporal dimensions of perception. Continuity of layout entails continuity of existence, and both are perceived with a moving observer (1965c). Throughout the 1950s and 1960s Gibson moved toward explaining "space" perception primarily in terms of a moving observer and a transforming array. The invariants specific to the connectivity of environmental layout are revealed through change. More fundamentally, the spatial and temporal features of the environment are not perceived as two distinct sets of facts; they both derive from optical transformations produced by spatial rearrangements. Simply, ecological movement is the starting point for both "space" and "time" perception.

For a moving observer, occlusion is an ecological event. As an observer moves about, surfaces are revealed and concealed. The event involves a transforming spatial relationship vis-à-vis a moving observer. Though spatial relationships relative to the observer change, the temporal invariance (permanence) of occluded environmental features is perceived. Gibson connects, through occlusion, perception of superposition (a spatial relationship) with object permanence (a temporal fact) (1969e).

In another discussion on occlusion, Gibson distinguishes between the ecological fact of occlusion and the hypothesized "psychophysical" law connecting optical accretion-deletion with the perception of occlusion (1968c). He also gives attention to the rotating object where an object reveals and conceals itself. Perception of the connectivity and integrity of objects is also brought under the concept of occlusion. Gibson also relates occlusion to the problem of depth perception, for seeing one thing behind another involves seeing distance or depth. Increasing distance is seen at the edges of surfaces. Gibson returns to his critique of Berkeley's theory of depth perception arguing that perception of occlusion implies seeing more than one thing in a given direction. A sensation-based theory of perception would imply that only one thing can be seen in any direction—sensations, at best, form a two-dimensional configuration (1969h). Gibson does not deny that occluding edges can be perceived when the observer is stationary, but the information is impoverished ("Psychophysical Hypotheses for Stationary Edge Perception," Undated Manuscript). The natural condition for animals is movement, and under such conditions occluding edges are much more unambiguously specified.

TIME AND EVENT PERCEPTION

As much as Newtonian space is an abstraction not applicable to ecological space, Newtonian time, conceived as a uniform universal flow, is also without ecological significance. Gibson's interest in the temporal aspects of perception burgeons into an ecological theory of time by the late 1960s. The central concept in his theory is the event and he develops his theory of event perception in contrast to Newtonian time and traditional psychological theories of motion perception.

Basically, Gibson ties time to a specific ecological reality the way he tied space to ecological surfaces. Empty time, like empty space, is not perceivable, but events are perceivable. Gibson distinguishes between physical and ecological events; the former are analyzed into uniform rigid motions of determinate velocities; ecological events have beginnings and ends, are fluid and semielastic with abrupt discontinuous changes. A physical motion has reference to empty coordinates (velocity is analyzed into spatial displacement per unit of time) whereas events occur within an ecological context. Gibson downplays the significance of velocity (uniform speed) as such, instead suggesting that acceleration (e.g., starts), deceleration (e.g., stops), and the structure and variations of change are significant (1971e).

Events possess a sequential structure, with shorter events nested in longer events. Events also recur and repeat possessing frequencies or rates. Gibson proposed that there exist laws or regularities of ecological change. For example, things go out of sight through occlusion, darkness, and departure; some changes are reversible while others are not (breaking, cutting); and a thing cannot exist in one place and then another without being moved (1971p). For time and event perception, Gibson follows his general philosophical orientation in looking for variation and higher order structure instead of simple units and absolute dimensions. This approach reflects his wholistic orientation and antielementarism, but it also reflects his empiricism and realism for he attempts to find order embodied in concrete natural particulars instead of transcendent forms. Where Gibson differs from standard empiricism is in emphasizing the primacy of the "difference" over units of absolute values (e.g., sensations). His theory of time contains this relativistic perspective for there are no independent units of ecological time; the ecological temporal structure is "built up" from differential relationships.

Events, for Gibson, became the basic dynamic unit in his description of the environment. Traditionally, motion had been the basic dynamic unit. Gibson's approach to events involved classifications of different types of ecological events and examinations of the stimulus information for these different types. The concept of the dynamic reality of an event is more significant in Gibson's approach, than was motion in traditional approaches. Traditionally, rest or a static condition was treated as perceptually primary and motion was derivative. Gibson sees events as perceptually direct and immediate.

Due to Gibson's increasing interest in occlusion and event perception, his thinking regarding the optic array changed. He came to question the concepts of optical motion and flow velocities. Motion and velocity in the sense used in the physical sciences require a coordinate frame of reference, yet the frame of reference within the optic array is the projection of the horizon and ground. There exist relative displacements but to label them motions with velocities is to apply terms (borrowed from physics) that have a meaning quite different from what happens within an optic array. Gibson attacks the simulative assumption arguing that motion within stimulation is not necessary for the perception of motion (1966c; 1968g). Gibson is interested in developing a new terminology to describe the temporal order of the optic array (1968e).

Gibson also developed reservations about the universal applicability of the concept of transformations. There is always gain-loss or accretion-deletion in the array with a moving observer; structure is not simply transformed (a geometrical concept) but new units appear and old ones disappear. (Such changes are discontinuous). This would be true even without occlusion (though occlusion makes it more salient), for environmental features appear at the frontal horizon and disappear at the rear horizon with a moving observer. Accretion-deletion in a stationary array specifies environmental motion, though accretion-deletion is neither a motion in the array nor a transformation; it is the addition of new units and the subtraction of old units. Consequently, Gibson also sees a limitation in the motion gradient in explaining distance perception. Accretion-deletion is always involved with a moving observer. Even if a surface of support were absolutely flat and empty, the edges of the moving observer's body will produce accretion and deletion.

PERCEPTION AND PROPRIOCEPTION

Perceiving is an activity of the animal and not of the mind or the brain. No specific organ or anatomical location exists in which perception takes place. It is the activity of a system (1972g; 1973c). Neither is perceiving a response to the environment. It involves forms of overt attention such as exploration, adjustment, orientation, and optimization as well as internal neurological activity (1972c). Perceiving does not involve a "processing" of information; at best, active perceptual systems modulate input. Gibson acknowledges that the term *resonate* carries some vagueness, but in examining his ideas on the activity of perception, there are quite a few definite points he does make in describing this activity. It is wholistic, continuous, active, selective, ecological, involving adjustment and equilibration, and circular rather than unidirectional (1971i). Gibson is an empiricist, arguing against innate ideas (1967e), but he distinguishes himself from "associational empiricism" in favor of "discriminational empiricism" (1971l). Perception involves differentiation, the extraction of invariants, and the "separation off of variants." Gibson is opposed to the use of mentalistic jargon as much as behavioristic (S-R) terminology; instead he prefers systems theory, as well as biological and ecological language (1971i). To reinforce a point made earlier, perception is an ecological reality involving both the activity of perceiving and the environment perceived.

Ocular adjustments is one area of anatomy and physiology where Gibson does get more detailed and precise. Adjustments are classified and described relative to the optic array instead of the head, as traditionally done (1969b; 1972f). Gibson prefers the word *adjustment* to *movement* because it is a broader term, and the eyes and head *orient* and *accommodate* to the ecological surround in their normal functionings. Ocular functions operate within an ecological frame of reference. There are different kinds of looking depending on the situation, e.g., looking at the road ahead, looking around a new area, looking out for danger (1967l). Ocular adjustments do not necessarily involve "movement" for Gibson sees their primary function to orient and stabilize; they are functionally nested within the basic orienting system and are "coordinated" vis-à-vis the optic array and not with respect to the anatomy of the body. Though the eyes and head move about, much of the time they are maintained in fixation, foveation, accommodation, and conjugation upon ecological features. Adjustment is a dynamic and functional concept, but movement is only one facet of the overall process.

If the surrounding environment is reciprocal to the surrounded animal there is always a component of proprioception (self-awareness) in perception (awareness of the environment). The environment is never perceived totally without reference to the perceiver for there is no environment totally independent of the perceiver. Aside from the spatial-temporal scale of environmental features perceived, there is a "here-now" relativity that exists in varying degrees in perception. The animal may move about and watch things over a period of time, but the objectivity and invariant quality of the perceived environment is relative. There is no omnipresent and eternal viewpoint, and the environment is at best only extendedly persistent and unchanging (1968i; 1972j; 1974a).

Gibson generally distinguishes proprioception from perception in terms of variants and invariants. Invariants pertain to the environment, whereas variants pertain to the peculiarities of the perceiver. This distinction corresponds closely with his sensation-perception distinction, where sensations are subjective and body-relative and perceptions are objective and environment-relative (1970i). Gibson would say that the invariants of stimulation are exterospecific and the "remainder" propriospecific. It is fairly clear, though, that proprioception is not synonymous with sensation for proprioception is a necessary accompaniment of perception whereas sensation is not. Proprioception is specific to the body-relative aspects of stimulus information, whereas sensation is relative to anatomy and neural excitation (1970d). Gibson ties together perception and proprioception; the perception of a stable environment based on stimulus invariants is reciprocal to the proprioception of a mobile observer based on stimulus variants. If one breaks down, so does the other. Stability is tied to change, where the environment is the relatively stable "pole" and the observer the relatively variant "pole" of ecological reality (1968i).

The objectivity of the perceived environment is relative for the environment is an ecological reality. Its intersubjectivity is based on the fact that observation points are open to multiple observers. Intersubjectivity as a criterion of objectivity implies that the environment is open to public observation and is not private to any one observer (1971e). The objectivity of perception, distinguished from either proprioception or sensation, is based on the relative invariants of stimulation and their intersubjective access due to the open medium and mobile observers. Mobility is tied to objectivity. What is constant (invariant) is revealed through changing perspectives or viewpoints.

Throughout his career, Gibson opposed subjective theories of perception, instead emphasizing the extent and level of objectivity in perception requiring scientific explanation. The statement that objectivity is relative means that the environment is interminately rich both spatially and temporally. Perception is limited to whatever depth the observer attends to and exploes. Gibson stressed the external, intersubjective reality of the environment and stimulus information. For an observer, this natural reality can never be exhausted.

The concept of reciprocity has become increasingly important in Gibson's treatments of perception, proprioception, objectivity, and subjectivity in the late 1960s and early 1970s. Reciprocity has also become central in his understanding of stability and change. Though Gibson is explicitly attacking subjective theories of perception, the deeper issue is between ecological reciprocity and Plato's dualism, for modern subjective theories, as well as materialistic views, are offspring of Plato and mind-matter dualism.

Gibson, objecting to the sensation-based theory of perception, came to argue that information about the environment could not be transmitted across nerves (1971m). Also recall he had objected to the term "transmission" in his ecological optics. Information is something to be explored and adjusted to because it stands extrinsic to the perceiver.

A modern phrasing of constructive theories of perception is that "perception goes beyond what is given to the senses." The concept of transmission is related to the idea of reception and Gibson objects to the applicability of either notion to perception. Information is not given or received. It is available, but it must be obtained. There is no passive (reactive) stage in Gibson's theory. (This makes it extremely ironical that Gibson's theory has been referred to as a "passive theory of perception" by modern critics—more on this later.) Information is an ecological reality that must be actively sought out by the perceiver because it is not given (imposed upon) the observer (1972i). If perception involved any type of "inner observation" it would be subjective based and imply a functional homunculus (1969d). Following the same ecological reasoning, the brain cannot generate a perception. The brain may produce sensations, hallucinations, dreams, illusions, and after-images, but not perceptions. The brain, as part of the integrated animal system, "perceives" the environment, but the objectivity and veridicality of perception is due to information (1970e).

Gibson contends that a subjective experience can in principle be distinguished from an objective (perceptual) experience. Hallucinations cannot be explored, nor can after-images or sensations (1970e). The variant-invariant separation cannot be made (1969d). An experiment can be designed where information is produced, though its natural ecological conditions are absent. The observer "sees" a tunnel though in reality there is none (1967h; 1969f). There is an illusion though the experience is as "real" as if there really were a tunnel. It cannot be stated that the brain produces the experience for there is stimulus information present, but still, it could be argued that the experience is not really objective and the "tunnel" exists only in the mind. Yet it should be emphasized that the perceiver is restricted in examining the experimental conditions, thus the objectivity, or truth, of the situation has been intentionally compromised. There is plenty of information about the actual conditions that normally could be detected.

Presumably, perception evolved toward greater and greater veridicality (1967g). Objectivity itself is not given in perception but must be separated from what is subjective and propriospecific. The exterospecific pole of ecological reality and perception is not an absolute, yet it does not follow that it is intrinsically or ontologically subjective. The abstract notions of absolute truth and absolute reality, which in effect support the complimentary ideas of subjectivity and illusion, are based on Plato's absolute dualism. Coupled with Descartes' theory of the mind and Newton's theory of absolute objective matter, the issue becomes an absolute "either-or": Perception is of the mind or of an independent world. If the observer were allowed to move about and examine an artificial experimental set-up, its "true" nature would be revealed. The perception is still relative to a spatial-temporal scale of objectivity or reality. It is within the context of a Platonic-Newtonian ontology that Gibson seems forces to acknowledge a subjective (mental) core to perception. In fact, all veridical perception brings in the involvement and presence of the perceiver, yet not in the sense of contributing a subjective component to perception. For Plato, it would seem paradoxical to say objectivity is revealed through time, yet if Gibson ties space to time, he also ties ecological objectivity and perceptual veridicality to time (i.e., to movement and exploration).

AFFORDANCES

The ecological ontology of Gibson's approach becomes most explicit in his theory of affordances. Along with occlusion and event perception, the topic of affordances was one of Gibson's main interests after the publication of the *Senses*. His theory of affordances constituted a functional analysis of the environment and was tied to his structural-compositional ecology on one end and his system-theory of animals on the other. Affordances are neither phenomenal (mental) qualities nor physical qualities but ecological facts pertaining to the animal-related functions of the environment. Each basic feature of Gibson's environment (surfaces, edges, objects, medium, events, substances, and animate objects) possesses affordances (1971f). Affordances pertain to environmental features (e.g., a solid surface can be walked upon), but have reference to animals and their capabilities. The geometry and composition of the environment support affordances; for example, the ground is both flat and solid enough to allow for the terrestrial locomotion of animals. The supportability of the ground only extends for creatures up to a certain size. Affordances are not intrinsic, independent, and absolute but relational and reciprocal to the animal.

Gibson notes that historically, a "theoretical gulf" exists between the physics of objects in space and the presumed "meanings" of things. This gulf corresponds with the Cartesian duality of matter and mind. Gibson's structural and compositional ecology (opaque solid geometry, substances, etc.) differs considerably from "objects in space." He can tie a host of animal-related functions to this ecology, e.g., openings afford locomotion, cliffs afford jumping, occluding edges afford concealment, objects afford throwing, holding, plugging, etc. Gibson identifies affordances with meanings. Structure and function are related; what something "is" is related to what it "means"; the gulf between matter and mind is bridged (1971h; 1972a).

Although affordances are reciprocal to the structural and functional features of an animal, they are not "subjective" or contingent upon the moods or needs of the animal. They are relational properties of the environment and exist as *opportunities,* whether or not an animal wants to use them. A banana is edible for a chimpanzee even if the chimp is asleep; a stick is a weapon even if the person is peaceful. Affordances are relative to the species of animal, for a hole that affords concealment for a prairie dog will not hide an elephant. More generally, there are certain fundamental affordances that exist for all members of a basic form of life, for example, water affords locomotion for aquatic creatures, air for aerial creatures, the ground for terrestrial creatures. The environment affords space for life. Gibson's selection of the spatial-temporal scale for a structural description of the environment is determined by the spatial-temporal scale of animal life, and the functions of the environment are tied to the ways of animal life.

Time plays an important part in this ecological ontology, because affordances refer to uses or dynamic relationships involving animals and the environment. An affordance exists as a potential for an interaction between animal and environment. It is the animal which acts, but it acts through utilization of an affordance. Functions in dynamic actualization (to sound Aristotelian) are tied together with affordances in ecological events involving animals and the environment. Affordances exist due to the dynamic dimension of animals. Recall that Gibson tied perceptual functions to the environment; in turn the environment, through affordances, is tied to the animal. One is reminded of the subject-object distinction, but the animal-environment distinction is necessarily reciprocal due to the dynamic features of the relationship. If the concept of affordances moves toward bridging mind-matter dualism it does so by connecting ecological structure (space) and ecological processes (time), or "meaningful matter" with the ways of life of animals.

The environment can be analyzed at different levels. Traditionally, it is broken down into matter, energy, and the interaction of elementary particles. This is the Newtonian concept of the physical world. If we move to the level of ecological relationships, we encounter substances, mediums, surfaces, and surface layout. This level is described in Gibson's opaque solid geometry. Introducing light and ecological optics brings in the structural ecology of energy and matter. When the ecosystem is set in motion, in come affordances (1971g; 1972a). Interestingly, Gibson contends that psychological or epistemic development runs in the reverse order beginning with perception of affordances and culminating in the ethereal abstractions of theoretical physics. Time and function are at the base of perception.

Meaning, and Gibson would include esthetic as well as practical meaning, is not added to raw sensations or given to the world of physical stimuli. Meaning is revealed in the environment. Developmentally, newborns start from the perception of meaning (1975b). Meaning is revealed through change or time, for affordances are specified in the invariants of stimulation over transformations. Perception of affordances is tied to the perception of events. A mother may be perceived as nurturing, comforting, and supportive (affordances) before she is perceived as having long dark hair (1968j). The child perceives affordances and proprioceives capabilities by participation within ecological events.

In conclusion, the topics of occlusion, event perception, proprioception, ecology, ecological optics, and affordances were all of interest to Gibson during his Purple Peril period. Gibson would further extend his investigation into these topics in his *Ecological Approach*. Before discussing his *Ecological Approach*, I will turn away from Gibson's more scientific concerns to epistemological and philosophical issues, areas that especially fascinated him during the last ten years of his career (Gibson, 1965a).

Chapter 17 _____

GIBSON'S ONTOLOGY
and EPISTEMOLOGY

SCIENCE, ONTOLOGY, AND EPISTEMOLOGY

In the first chapter, certain philosophical and scientific themes relevant to the development of Gibson's ecological psychology are described. Included are basic ontologies and epistemologies originating with the Greeks and later developments during the rise of modern science and philosophy. Since Gibson's ecological ideas have now been examined in considerable detail, a more systematic historical and conceptual analysis and comparison can be undertaken of the "philosophical" implications of his views.

To review, the distinction between philosophy and "pure" science is neither historically nor logically clear-cut, but there are certain questions that tend to get identified as "philosophical." As we have seen, such philosophical ideas initially arise in a philosophical context but eventually spill over into the scientific community.

Two fundamental issues within the history of philosophy have been the (ultimate) nature of reality (ontology) and the scope of human knowledge (epistemology). In science, the substantive component of thinking contains an ontology (however explicit it is made), and the methodological component contains an epistemology. Ontology and epistemology, whether we look at philosophical or scientific theories, mutually support each other. Any epistemology assumes both a *what is known* and *how it is known* (its implicit ontology), (e.g., Plato's rationalistic epistemology assumes an ontology of abstract eternal ideas). Any ontology assumes a mode of apprehension and a form in which its knowledge claims are made (e.g., phenomenalism assumes a descriptive observational epistemology). In fact, it is often difficult to distinguish the epistemological and ontological features of a theoretical system. Especially relevant is any scientific ontology that makes claims about the knower and the conditions of knowledge, for such an ontology is relevant to theories of knowledge. The ontological component in Gibson's theory of perception stands in contrast with historically prevalent scientific theories of perception; it leads to an epistemological reformulation of perception and secondarily, other forms of knowledge. In Gibson's approach, the ontological component is his theory of ecological reciprocity and the epistemological component is his direct realism.

The "philosophical" features of science are often so entrenched and fundamental that they do not seem open to revision through scientific experimentation and methodology. Newtonian science contained a central philosophical structure but the science itself was not seriously brought into question until the later 19th century. Newton's science assumed a definitive ontology and metaphysics. Newtonian science also contained an epistemological element that reflected its ontology. Owing its philosophical origins to Parmenides, Plato, Democritus, Kepler, Descartes, and the matter-spirit dualism of the Scientific Revolution, Newton's science will serve as the paradigmatic case of one of the two main philosophies in western history. Its subsequent effects on science and philosophy are seen in Locke, Berkeley, Helmholtz, Müller, scientific atomism, psychophysics, and structuralism-phenomenalism. It was the predominant philosophy within (and of) science until the 20th century (Capra, 1975, 1982).

Newtonian ontology begins from the Cartesian idea of matter (material *substance*). Matter is distributed in space as aggregates of irreducible *elements*. Aggregates are reducible to their parts (the fundamental elements); these elements, all composed of the same substance, form the ultimate substratum of the natural world. These aggregates are collections of objects that are localized in absolute space and absolute time. Substance possesses certain intrinsic qualities, e.g., matter has the qualities of extension (Descartes) and mass (Newton). Units of matter are moved around and rearranged through *cause-effect* relationships. Substance remains unaffected by causal interaction. Elements and/or objects are spatially discrete and distinct from one another. Cause-effect relationships require spatial contact—there is no action-at-a-distance (except for the effect of gravity which Newton found scientifically uncomfortable). Energy (or motion) is passed along through spatial contact. Things happen due to causal sequences across space.

Order is imposed upon matter and motion in the form of "eternal" laws; in fact, the basic features of the natural world are all eternal, viz., the elements of matter, the principle of causality, space, time, and universal laws. There is no fundamental change. From the ontological point of view, the microscopic world of material elements and the set of basic physical laws constitute the ultimate reality of physical world.

Mind and consciousness are localized and causally connected to the physical brain. Knowledge designates a relationship between the knower and the world, but the knower is localized or segregated. Because of the ontological primacy of substance, mind as a substance is self-contained. It may be a second substance (Descartes), the inner reality of matter in the brain (Müller), or the primary substance (Berkeley). To treat mind as a substance (localized and self-contained) separates any individual mind (like any unit of matter) from everything else. Mind possesses the capacity for inference by means of which it can go beyond what occurs within it. What is inferred is not directly known (it is not an inner state of mind), rather it is a thought that "goes beyond" the "here-now" of the substance of mind. Consequently, there is knowledge by acquaintance and knowledge by inference. Knowledge by acquaintance is limited to the mind's own inner states whereas knowledge by inference includes matter and other minds. Relative to mind, matter is an inference.

Knowledge is divided into an abstract and an individualized (particular) component. Sensory consciousness, which is most closely connected with the physical world, is of particulars, whereas thought is abstract. Thought transcends the here and now, whereas sensory consciousness is limited to the here and now. Though empiricism sees knowledge as deriving from sensory consciousness, whether it be nativism, rationalism, or empiricism, fundamental knowledge comes through thought, for thought is abstract or general. The abstract-particular distinction in mind corresponds to the law-element distinction in the physical world. The inference-acquaintance distinction roughly corresponds to the causal relation-inner state distinction in the physical world.

This ontology and epistemology is a simplified description of an intellectual tradition that possessed many variations and exhibited at least two major growth transformations in history. Its origins are found in Parmenides, Plato, and Democritus; it was significantly modified during the Middle Ages, and again during the Scientific Revolution. The other main historical tradition begins with Aristotle and Heraclitus. The shift in emphasis is from eternal (static) units (substances) to dynamic interdependencies. Though Leibnitz typifies this second philosophical perspective, it was not until the 19th century that it had a significant impact on science. Gibson belongs in this second tradition.

The Platonic-Aristotelian traditions tend to interweave; even this basic distinction is relative; further, it would be a mistake to historically reduce Gibson's views to some combination of previous ideas. In the following historical comparison the "Gestalt" quality of an approach and the reality of fundamental change in history must be kept in mind. There is an important sense in which any new theory attempts to go beyond the conflicts or issues of the past, producing a perspective that is distinctively novel.

Though Plato attempts to integrate reality under the umbrella of abstract order and synthetic thought, he begins with an absolute distinction between eternal universals and transient particulars. Following Heraclitus, Aristotle attempts to avoid this absolute division by looking for universals (form) *within* temporal particulars. In his passion for a unified philosophy, Aristotle treats the whole set of basic conceptual distinctions as distinctions of thought rather than actual segregations in reality. Aristotle is well-known for his categories of basic distinctions (e.g., actuality vs. potentiality or form vs. matter), but he relates together these categories in his ontology and epistemology; in reality, form and matter are inseparable. *Relative* to Plato, Aristotle initiates an emphasis on process and internal order. In a sense, he tries to surpass Plato by integrating the dualism embodied in Plato's philosophy. Reality can be seen as dynamic, rather than intrinsically static. At the very least, the persistent dimension can be seen as imbedded within the dynamic dimension. Another expression (Gibson's) would be that invariance and variance are reciprocal. For Aristotle it was potentiality and actuality: Potentiality is the relative invariant manifested in dynamic and transient actualizations. The Heraclitian tradition replaces substance with process as the basic ontological category. Order becomes intrinsic to change (the "Logos"). Permanence is relative to change because it is imbedded within change as regularities. Aristotle's potentials are the regularities of actualizations.

Instead of independent elements (absolute particulars) and distinct laws, order exists as relationships among particulars. The particulars of Aristotelian ontology are not inert and separate, but dynamic and interdependent. Consequently, both the Gestalt tradition and the dynamic view of the natural world tend to be associated with the Aristotelian tradition.

At the height of Newtonian-Cartesian thought, the main spokesman for the Aristotelian tradition was Leibnitz. Absolute space and absolute time also tend to be rejected within a process ontology. Whereas space and time exist extrinsic to the elements of Newtonian science, space and time are relationships *within* Leibnitz's dynamic universe. The relational view of reality is carried further by Hegel, where any particular is intrinsically related to every other particular. Causality in the Cartesian-Newtonian sense also drops out, for causality had been used to relate independent elements and explain the passage of activity across elements. Leibnitz's notion of harmony more closely resembles Gibson's concept of resonance, and where mechanistic causality is a linear series of discrete events, resonance is a circular process of interdependent events.

Aristotle rejects the absolute (substance) dualism of mind and matter and replaces it with a reciprocity of function and structure. Mind is function and integrated; body is the differentiated structure. Parts within themselves are not absolutes (recall Leibnitz's "Always many, never one, therefore never many"); there are no homogeneous elements. Each part of the body is intrinsically a differentiated structure. Function refers to the relational processes and effects of a structure, i.e., how it interacts with other structures.

Similar to Gibson, there are no ultimate units and there is no ultimate level of reality *underneath* nature. There exist multiple levels of reality because there exist multiple levels of relationships. Units (or parts) get their reality in how they are related within the whole. Nature becomes wholistic. Units and relationships can be seen as coexistent and interdependent. If Newton's world was built up from discontinuous (segregated) identities (elements), a wholistic (or ecological) approach views nature as continuous for it is built up out of related differences rather than segregated identities. Plato separated the world of time (all differences) from the eternal realm (the integrated identity); each element in Newton's world is distinct from every other because its identity (inner substance) is self-contained. For Aristotle, order refers to regularities of interaction (process). A wholistic and dynamic universe cannot have a substratum of ultimate parts; it will have multiple levels of entities due to multiple levels of relationships.

Epistemologically, Aristotle was an extreme empiricist for form (the abstract or universal) could be found within the world of perceived particulars. Gibson is a radical empiricist for order, persistence, and invariance can be perceived—they do not have to be inferred from transient particulars. Absolute individual elements (sensations or point stimuli) would lead to an imposition of order, but Gibson *begins* with relationships and differences.

Aristotle does not treat mind as a second substance isolated away from what is "outside" itself; mind is function or subject understood relative to a world of "correlative objects." Strictly speaking, mind is one pole of a larger unit, viz., nature. The "I-other" or "ego-world" distinctions arise in a universe of absolute individuals. If matter is meaningless and intrinsically unknowable in a Cartesian philosophy, for Aristotle it is meaningful vis-à-vis the knower, and therefore matter literally exists to be known. It reveals itself. The whole enterprise of ecological optics is guided by the idea of information; the environment, through information, specifies itself to the perceiver.

Table 1 summarizes the basic contrasting assumptions of the two historical lines of thought being considered.

TABLE 1
Dualism vs. Reciprocity

Parmenides-Plato- Descartes-Newton	Heraclitus-Aristotle- Leibnitz-Gibson
Substance	Process
Elementarism	Organization
External Order	Internal Order
Identities	Differences
Absolutes	Relational Properties
Extrinsic Space and Time	Intrinsic Space and Time
Mind-Matter Dualism	Mind-Matter Reciprocity
Linear Causality	Circular Harmony
Uni-level Reality	Multilevel Reality
Discontinuous	Continuous
Static Invariance	Dynamic Invariance
Epistemological Dualism	Epistemological Realism

Following the preceding conceptual framework, Gibson's ontology divides an intrinsically organized ecosystem into the reciprocal pair of animal and environment. Any unit, inclusive of the ecosystem itself, possesses internal order or structure. Also, any unit exhibits both invariance and variance, where invariants are relatively persistent (rather than absolutely eternal) and refer to constancies imbedded with change. An ecosystem is multilevel in units and relationships: The animal is a multi-level nesting, and the environment is a multi-level nesting. Although an animal exhibits relatively persistent structural features it is a dynamic system interrelated through reciprocal loops with its environment. Space and time are intrinsic to an ecosystem, understood in terms of surface geometry and ecological events. Space and time are multilevel. Both spatial and temporal order are embodied in differences and relationships. Mind, consciousness, and knowledge designate active functions of an animal realized through a dynamic attunement to an organized and meaningful environment that supports the existence of the animal. The environment reveals itself through the flux of ambient energy and the active explorations and adjustments of the perceiver.

At this point the meaning of reciprocity needs to be reemphasized. Though Gibson emphasizes relationships and differences in his descriptions of structured energy and the environment, he does refer to parts, units, objects, and substances, all ideas to be found in Newtonian-Cartesian-Lockean ontology. He does not reject these ideas, but he does reinterpret them within the context of reciprocity, for example, parts are nested within wholes which are themselves parts nested within larger wholes. Gibson wishes to avoid both dualism and derivative monisms. Equally, though Aristotle is a source of the dynamic picture of nature, he also wished to avoid both dualism and materialistic monism, as well as, a totally fluid, chaotic universe or a totally static conception of the cosmos. Relative to the static elementarism of British empiricism, Gibson is wholistic and dynamic. Furthermore, even relative to his intellectual antecedents in the Aristotelian heritage (e.g., Leibnitz or Aristotle himself), he goes beyond them in consistently carrying through the idea of reciprocity. In fundamental theory, Gibson reciprocally ties together at the ecological level permanence and change, units and relationships, temporal and spatial order, and wholes and parts. Most importantly he reciprocally connects the perceiver and the environment, the knower and the known.

One significant ontological factor not yet included in this discussion is the impact of evolution upon Gibson and science in general. Evolution carries the dynamic approach to nature even further than did Aristotle. Plato's forms (basic identities) were considered eternal. Aristotle saw natural forms as dynamic but repetitive. Within Newtonian science, forms or identities (elements of substance) were considered permanent. Prior to Darwin, each species was considered a separate creation, but evolution, adaptation, and natural selection integrated natural forms, bringing them together in a dynamic interchange of cooperation and competition. This interchange is dynamic and ever changing, and although "survival of the fittest" and competition tend to be emphasized in evolutionary thinking, evolution involves progressive attunement, reciprocity, and harmony between animals and the environment. The affordances of an environment are progressively more exploited; interchange is poly-leveled and poly-faceted. To abandon Newtonian ontology at its core, there are no static independent objects—animal existence is an active and progressive harmony *with* the environment.

THE HISTORY OF THE PHILOSOPHY OF PERCEPTION

Perception may seem a self-evident fact. One opens one's eyes and the world is *there*. This perceived world is not private or subjective—other perceivers see the same world. Thoughts may be private to the mind, but the ground below isn't private. Sometimes, we see or hear things that aren't there (illusions and hallucinations), but most of the time *what* is perceived is an objective world that exists independently of perceiving it, and by and large *is* the way it appears to be. What would it mean to say the apple isn't red—one can see it's red. And what could it mean to say the apple is an experience of the mind? The apple isn't in my mind—it's in my hand. Within philosophical and scientific circles, the above position is referred to as naive and/or direct realism (Armstrong, 1961; Austin, 1962). Gibson identifies his perceptual epistemology with direct realism, yet the history of the science and philosophy of perception, to a great extent, has been an attack on direct realism.

The problem of perception begins when an explanation for it is attempted. The ancient Greeks, believing action-at-a-distance was impossible, assumed that the mind and the world somehow made contact during perception. If mind is localized in the perceiver, how could something at a distance from it be perceived? Perception involves awareness and knowledge and these are attributes of the mind, so it is *with* the mind that an observer perceives (even if the body is also involved). Explanation involves causality and causality requires contact, so the mind must make contact with the world. *Eidolae* and emanations were hypothesized to bridge the spatial gap between the perceiver and the world. What is actually perceived must exist *within* the mind (as if the mind had an inside and outside). From the Greeks, with their emphasis on substance and causality, perception turns into an "inner" event within an "inner" observer (homunculus). The Scientific Revolution accepted both these ideas and, by and large, explained and described perception in a similar manner. Perception was the final event in a linear series of spatially connected effects terminating in the perceiver.

Naive realism could be taken to mean that what is perceived is independent (or outside) of the mind, or it could mean simply that perception is qualitatively veridical. (Interpretations of this position vary.) The perceiver may not see the world as such but a perfect copy of it. Naive realism can entail both views taken together: Perception is veridical because it is of the world. The ancient Greeks assumed perception was veridical but involved contact with copies (*eidolae*). With the rise of Newtonian physics, the veridicality of perception was thrown into question for the "world-as-perceived" became increasingly different from the world described by physical science (Ayer, 1956; Feyerabend, 1965; Hayek, 1952; Köffka, 1935; Sellars, 1962). Locke (1690), for one, attempted to salvage some perceptual qualities as actual physical qualities (the primary qualities), but quantum mechanics and the theory of relativity in 20th century physics do not retain any physical qualities comparable to what is perceived. Physics seems to point strongly to the implication that perception is of a different world than the actual physical world. It is assumed that there is only one physical reality, viz., that described by modern physics; therefore the world of perception is subjective and of a different ontological realm. Perception is neither veridical nor of the physical world.

Another argument developed against naive realism derives from perceptual illusions and the supposed facts of cerebral stimulation (Ayer, 1940; Maxwell, 1970a, 1970b). Illusions appear indistinguishable from perceptions; consequently, what reason is there for supposing that perceptions are *of* anything different than illusions, viz., "inner" states? From the time of Descartes, a similar argument has been made regarding cerebral stimulation. If the brain is stimulated directly, a person reports seeing, hearing, or feeling things as if such things were real. Further, Müller's specific energies of nerves hypothesis appeared to clearly demonstrate that perceptual content was a reflection of brain states.

Following Maxwell's distinction, naive realism can be defined as "the world is as it appears to be" (veridicality thesis) and direct realism can be defined as "the world is what is perceived" (ontological thesis). Both these ideas have come under criticism within the history of science and philosophy leading to a variety of "sophisticated" theories of perception, most of which worked their way into psychology. Neither naive realism nor direct realism has had much of a following within the psychology of perception, in great part due to their lack of general plausibility within philosophy and science.

Idealism has never been very popular in psychology. To totally eliminate the physical world and reduce everything to mind (or consciousness) seems unscientific as well as leading to absolute subjectivism and solipsism. If the world is totally a construction of mind, then objectivity seems to vanish, unless one postulates a supra-individual mind that gives the universe a trans-personal reality, (e.g., Berkeley's theistic idealism). However, science in general has tried to explain mind through nature and not nature through mind. One thesis, coming out of idealism, e.g., through Kant and Hegel, that has influenced psychology, is conceptualism. Concepts (or ideas), identified as general mental principles to organize and categorize sensory consciousness, are seen as necessary for intelligible perception. There may be a non-mental element serving as the starting point in perception, but perception requires conceptualization to give it meaningful order.

The two most prevalent ontologies within science and the psychology of perception have been materialism and mind-matter dualism. Materialism, which has been formulated in a variety of ways, seeks to eliminate mind or consciousness from descriptions and explanations of perception. If idealism was ready to assimilate the totality of perception to mind, materialism attempts the opposite, viz., to assimilate perception to "physical" facts. Interestingly, as Feigl (1967) points out, what is meant by "physical" or "material" is neither simple nor uncontroversial. Materialist theories tend to identify perceptions with brain states, though a behavioristic (or action) theory of perception will identify it with responses (Taylor, 1962). The dualistic-based tendencies to equate physical explanations with scientific objectivity, and consciousness with the subjective and ineffable, supported the popularity of materialism.

Beginning from Locke's representational realism (mind copies the physical world) and Descartes' mind-matter dualism, *indirect realism* emerged as the most influential philosophy of perception in modern times. Indirect realism was apparently able to answer the criticisms raised against naive and direct realism without succumbing to the subjectivity of idealism or the extreme reductionism of materialism. Most forms of indirect realism involve mind-matter dualism, though there are some forms of indirect realism that are materialistic. Indirect realism is consequently a many faced doctrine. Though not unanimously held by all versions, its core assumptions are (Armstrong, 1961; Hirst, 1959, 1965):

1. The ontological content of perception is identified with a self-contained and isolated mind or brain clearly distinct from the external physical world existentially and qualitatively.

2. Perception involves an epistemological step from initial data to final perception, or in some sense involves a mental-physiological constructive step.

3. Perception is causally mediated. It is an effect in a series of distinct events beginning outside of the perceiver.

These three ideas describe perception as ontologically indirect, epistemologically indirect, and causally indirect respectively. Given these basic assumptions, a variety of versions of indirect realism developed in modern times. Certain key concepts or hypotheses distinguish each of the most popular versions of indirect realism, though any one position may overlap in spirit or formulation with other positions.

1. Representational Realism: The content of perception, though distinct from the world, copies it in at least some ways (Descartes; Locke; Smythies, 1965).

2. Critical Realism: Though perception may not copy the external world, it is the starting point for knowledge of this world (Feigl, 1967; Henle, 1975; Mandelbaum, 1964).

3. Mental Constructivism: A psychological process of organization is required to produce meaningful and/or veridical perception (Berkeley; Brunswik; Gregory, 1966, 1970, 1972; Helmholtz; Kant; Neisser, 1967, 1976).

4. Physiological Constructivism: A neuro-physiological process of organization is required to produce meaningful and/or veridical perception (Kohler, Koffka).

5. Structural Realism-Identity Thesis: Perceptual consciousness is ontologically identified with the "intrinsic" qualities of brain states (Feigl, 1967; Maxwell, 1968, 1970a, 1970b; Müller; Russell, 1927; Weimer, 1975).

6. Psychological Emergence: The phenomenal qualities of conscious perception "emerge" as global and irreducible characteristics of brain states (Aune, 1967; Meehl & Sellars, 1956; Sellars, 1956, 1962, 1965).

7. Kantian Noumenalism: The phenomenal content and structure of perception is ontologically distinct from things-in-themselves (noumena) and in no intelligible way can be related to this world of noumena.

Though the professional disciplines of psychology and philosophy diverged in the twentieth century, similar themes and issues can be found in each discipline's treatment of perception. The philosophy of perception is presumably concerned with fundamental ontological and epistemological issues, whereas the psychology of perception is concerned with explanations and descriptions of perception. Both disciplines though reflect changes in the general scientific picture and there is cross-fertilization. The previous forms of indirect realism all reflect a Platonic-Newtonian scientific ontology, whether they are more closely associated with the discipline of philosophy or the discipline of psychology. Logically, scientific description and philosophical ontology are tied together on the general question, *"What* is perception?" and scientific explanation and philosophical epistemology are tied together on the general question *"How* can there be perception?" The normative issue of perceptual epistemology is implicit in psychological explanations of the veridicality of perception and the ontological issue is implicit in the classification schemes of psychological facts.

A common idea that clearly ties together the psychology and the philosophy of perception is the belief in a "sensory given" (Firth, 1950; Lewis, 1929; Passmore, 1966). In psychology, this "sensory core" is usually identified with sensations, whereas in philosophy the most common terms are "sense-data" and "sense impressions." Numerous themes have played into the "sensory given" hypothesis. The ideal of analysis led scientists to look for basic building blocks and philosophers to look for conceptually irreducible elements. Atomistic ontology reinforced the results of analysis. Following the causal model of perception, scientists believed there must be "something" in perception caused by the external world, whereas philosophers interested in the veridicality of perception believed some aspect of perception must reflect the external world independent of subjective contamination. Philosophers and psychologists alike followed the active-passive distinction regarding perception. The perceiver must be passive to the world (receptive-reactive) and then active, in some manner or form working on the data of sense. Perception is consequently both ontologically and epistemologically indirect. (Perception is not of the world, it is ontologically indirect, and perception involves an inferential constructive step—it is epistemically indirect. Perception could simply be epistemically indirect if the sense-data is identified as all there actually is, e.g., phenomenalism or idealism.) In a dualistic ontology, interestingly, the component of perception (sense-data) received from the external world is not an accurate indicator of the external world: It is atomized and ego-centric spatially and temporally. The data (the sensory given) is thought impoverished for it is a result of an atomized and analyzed physical world (Plato's impoverished sensory world) and the active intellect must give it order. Order, both spatial and temporal, is imposed—another reflection of Platonic-Newtonian thinking. The active-passive distinction also follows from mind-matter dualism for matter (the body) is passive (reactive), whereas mind is active.

Another distinction inherent in the sensory-given hypothesis is appearance versus reality for the given is appearance, whereas the mind works toward reality and veridicality. The appearance-reality distinction is connected to the extrinsic-intrinsic distinction that is central to a substance ontology. Sense-data (sensations) are *effects* of the world. The true *causes* are comprehended with a mental step. Appearances (sensations) vary, yet there is an intrinsic constancy out in the world. The actual object cannot be brought to the mind, so the mind works backwards from effect and appearance to cause and reality.

GIBSON'S DIRECT REALIST EPISTEMOLOGY

Direct realism has usually been associated with the "common sense" view of perception and common language philosophy, the latter perhaps best exemplified by G. E. Moore's (1905a, 1905b, 1918–1919, 1939) approach to perception. Neither of these perspectives owes much to scientific considerations. More recently, Sellars and Armstrong developed direct realist philosophies that are more sensitive to scientific ideas, but Sellars advocates only epistemological directness (there is no inferential step) while retaining an ontological separation of perception and the world, and Armstrong avoids Sellars' ontological dualism by developing a materialist direct realism. Within scientific theories of perception, the only alternative to indirect realist positions has been behaviorism, but behaviorism reduced perception to associations between stimuli and responses. Gibson's scientific theory of direct perception is consequently unique in modern times.

Given the philosophy of indirect realism and the presumed scientific-philosophical arguments in its favor, what hypotheses and considerations does Gibson offer against indirect realism that support his direct realism? Beginning with the physiology of perception, neurological activity consists of loops "nested" within exploratory activities of a perceptual system (Gibson, 1967c; 1967d, p. 162–163; 1972b, p. 217). At the receptor level, stimuli may *cause* reactions in anatomical units, but a perceptual system does not show one-way transmission; it shows circular resonance (1967b). Causality, in the Newtonian sense, is a micro-level phenomenon. The sequential model of causality is also assumed in Stimulus-Response Psychology and following Koffka's critique of behaviorism (Gibson, 1971c), Gibson opts for the alternative concept of equilibration. Animal and environment are interdependent. The active perceptual system achieves an equilibrium (resonance) with information (1973b). The relationship between stimulation and perception is not a spatial-temporally discrete sequence of cause-effect.

As already noted, Gibson abandoned the idea of a "physiological image" transmitted to the brain. He sees an analogy having developed in history between the retinal image and the cerebral image (1968b, p. 344). However, stimulus invariants of structured energy are not image-like; they are formless (1973a). Invariants are not transmitted from place to place within the nervous system; they are captured across, or better still, "around" a circuit (1967c, 1972b, p. 217). The idea that a percept must be "put together" into a mental or physiological representation misses the dynamic nature of invariants. The order of the percept exists across the process of adjustment and exploration.

Due to Gibson's wholistic orientation, the brain is not seen as adding or contributing to elements. Gibson applies wholistic ideas to both stimulation and the animal-environment relationship-areas the Gestalt psychologists treated in either elementaristic or dualistic terms. Rather, beginning from wholistic relationships, Gibson sees the brain as a discriminator (1970a; Gibson & Gibson, 1972). Variants and invariants in stimulus information are reciprocals and each is detected through discrimination relative to the other. Structure and relationships are therefore primary in perception rather than identification of absolute individual values. Perception is a wholistic process involving relational discriminations rather than being atomistic and additive. The brain does not contribute anything to perception (1967d, 1970a).

Traditionally, sensory awareness is thought to be limited to the present, which, in effect, means that sensory awareness has no sense of time. (Either of change or duration) Memory and expectation (foresight) are clearly separated from sensory awareness. Memory and expectation involve a sense of time, whereas sensory awareness only involves a limited sense of space (1966b). Gibson though believes there is no clear separation between memory and perception, and perception necessarily contains a sense of time *if* it contains a spatial sense. Space and time are reciprocals because the invariants specifying spatial (surface) layout are detected (discriminated) relative to temporal variants.

Perception is conceived of as an activity (1967a) and *what* is perceived cannot be thought of as analogous to a static image or form. Quality and content (in the empiricist-structuralist sense) also seem to be inappropriate terms. Though an observer will view an object from a variety of perspectives (forms) it is the invariants over time that determine the perception and these invariants are not static forms (1967d, p. 165). Gibson points out that images are not necessary for thought and neither are they necessary for perception (1967d, p. 167; 1974a). Perception of occlusion most clearly demonstrates this fact, where there is awareness of something in the environment yet there is no qualitative content of "being occluded" (1972b, p. 222). From the perspective of affordances, perception if *of* ecological *meanings,* a construct clearly not thing-like or image-like.

Viewed from another related perspective, the issue of what is perception *of,* pivots on Gibson's rejection of "sensation-based" theories. Sensations are identified as "image-like" (1968–69; 1972b, p. 215; 1973b). For Gibson, sensations fall into a different category than perceptions; they are not just simpler versions. Sensations are subjective and incidental to perception. Gibson is adamant that perception is not of an inner world constituting a second ontological realm. He thinks that sensation-based theories lead to this absolute dualism (1973b). In effect, he rejects a "mentalistic" interpretation of perception if mind is taken to be a second world populated with mental entities. For Gibson, mind can only mean a functional process of a living form ecologically integrated. The best comparison would have to be with Aristotle's ontology; mind is form and an active form—it is not material, substantial, or absolutely localized. It is clearly an evolutionary emergent form not reducible to neurons, living cells, or molecules, because it is an ecological and active "form" (activity) of the sentient animal.

The topics of illusion and hallucination are also relevant to an ontological understanding of perception. Illusions and hallucinations can be thought to consist of the same "stuff" as perceptions, but the environment can be explored and seen from different perspectives (1970c, 1971a), whereas illusions and hallucinations cannot similarly be explored. There is an exteroceptive reference to perception because in exploring, invariants emerge that cannot be controlled or altered. This revealed independence and objectivity comes through exploration and gives perception its objectivity, which is a quintessential feature of perceiving that is not to be found in illusion and hallucinations. Interestingly, spatial externality or objective independence is revealed over time; the perceiver must be active and involved in order for what is objective and external to be perceived.

Throughout Gibson's ecological period, the concept of reciprocity was extended to cover and integrate an increasing variety of hypotheses and themes. Besides space and time, and invariance and variance, it is central to his description of the animal and the environment. Cartesian dualism led to a clear separation of the mental and the physical and correspondingly the subjective and objective. The concept of reciprocity throws these traditional ideas into question; it is pivotal to the general theoretical shift in Gibson away from Cartesian-Newtonian thought. This type of ontology rejects the isolation of the knower-perceiver and the world.

Perception and proprioception are reciprocal processes, and this reciprocity entails more than just necessary mutual accompaniment. Each is realized relative to the other in the dynamic process of variant-invariant discrimination. The subjective (proprioceptual) and objective (perceptual) poles are not absolute but relative because there are degrees of privacy and degrees of objectivity within a boundary area occupied by the perceiver's body. What is objective is understood as an invariant of perspective and this is only relatively approximated through adopting more and more vantage points. The invariants are realized over perspectives and time, though they are (relatively) timeless and formless. Subjectivity is relative for there seems to be always some information, however difficult to detect, for any supposed subjective or intrinsic state. (In philosophical terms, this rejection of absolute privacy follows from an ontology of interdependence.) What is noteworthy is that the absolute distinctions of intrinsic versus extrinsic, reality versus appearance, phenomena and noumena are, according to Gibson, relative and reciprocal. Gibson's reciprocal theory of perception and proprioception throws all these absolute distinctions into question. Perspectives are relative to observation points (and paths) and it is through such variants that the observer's position is specified, yet this is reciprocal to an objective layout specified by the invariants within an optical flow (1967d, p. 171; 1968b, pp. 341–343; 1971c; 1972b, p. 216; 1973b; 1977b, p. 79).

Gibson's treatment of the ego and affordances attacks the subject–object distinction. Gibson treats the "ego" and the world as an integrated whole, tied together as a dynamic reciprocity (1971c). The ego is proprioceived relative to its ambient environment and the environment is perceived relative to the perceiver. The environment is described in terms of affordances, which objectively depend upon substance and surface properties, yet "fit" and support the ways of life. A rock can be thrown because of its substance and surface properties, but throwing requires certain anatomical, physiological, and perceptual-behavioral attributes specific to only certain species of animals. Affordances are relational features of the environment, where the relationships involve animate ways of life. Gibson would state that the theory of affordances cuts across the traditional subjective-objective distinction as well as the ego and the world. In effect, it calls for an alternative ontology where "physical objects" do not exist as detached "ding-an-sich" (Kantian noumena or Newtonian physical substance) and the mind does not reside in a detached ethereal realm.

The theoretical shift in Gibson's ecological psychology involves an attempt to unite apparently different ontological realms. Gibson rejects any real separation between the artificial and natural worlds, and he views nature as multileveled, such that all natural units and relationships are equally real and coexistent. The apparent conflict between the world of perception and the world of microphysics is resolved by giving up the idea of an ultimate reality (1977b). Reality is wholistic, yet nested.

Through a classification of affordances the functional dimension to the environment is tied reciprocally to the animal and the structural and substantial features of the environment. Affordances give the environment reference to the animal and are grouped together as supporting locomotion, concealment, manipulation, nutrition, and social interaction. Presumably, before more specific features of the environment are perceived, affordances are detected, i.e., the environment is most fundamentally perceived as affordances. Animals exist in ecological niches that are potential ways of life offered by the environment, and a niche, Gibson contends, is a set of affordances. Affordances can also be divided into positive and negative, for if the environment supports life it also embodies features that can harm or destroy life (1977b). Affordances exist in a dynamic ecosystem of life and death.

Affordances tie together the structural-chemical and functional features of the environment; consequently they tie together ecological space and ecological time. Newton had separated space and time as absolute distinct continuum, but Gibson, at an ecological level, treats each as an empirical reality that is manifested concretely through a specific environment feature, viz., layout for space and events for time (Gibson 1975c, 1976a). Affordances are specific ecological functions of structural-chemical environmental features manifested in ecological events. Spatial-compositional features of the environment are relative ecological constants, and affordances persist to the degree to which these constants persist.

The assumption that perception is limited to spatial features is connected to the camera-picture model of perception (1966b, 1968a). If time were brought into the picture, it would be a mistake to view perception as a "moving picture" for a moving picture does not allow for exploration (though it may simulate it). Invariants are extracted over time and details are discriminated—the perceiver "homes in" as much as need be. The idea of an indubitable sensory given is connected with the static concept of perception, as if perception were the viewing of something presented or represented within the observer. The perceiver tunes in to the environment through exploration and sensory adjustments, thus perception can be initially ambiguous and progressively more thorough and discriminating. Perception is a continuous, progressive process, rather than a representation. To put it differently, Gibson rejected the notion of an exhaustive inventory or categorization of perceivables, whether it be in terms of elements, dimensions, or Gestalten. The environment is indeterminately rich.

At the ecological level, what is perceived is the environment and it is important to understand that although this environment is ontologically tied to the animal, it does not follow that it is *in* the perceiver's head or mind. If the question is asked, "is *what* perceived the *real* object, intrinsic and independent to itself?" the question is philosophically loaded; as expressed it assumes a substance ontology and an absolute separation of appearance and reality. Further, it assumes a separation of an object's spatial reality (the matter localized in space) from its temporal reality (the dynamic relationships it has with other objects).

In his discussions of direct realism, Gibson frequently brings up his theory of information as specification. He definitely believed that the impoverished view of stimulation had greatly contributed to the indirect realist theory. The impoverished view of stimulation coupled with the organizational theory of the mind are reflective of mind-matter dualism. Yet, Gibson in his investigations into ecological optics was obliged to redescribe and reconceptualize the environment, to the extent that it would make sense to say the environment is perceived. Within the context of a Newtonian ontology of mechanistic causality and physical objects in space, it is indeed difficult to understand how such a world could be directly perceived. Gibson's direct realism is compatible with an ecological and dynamic ontology—a much different type of universe than the one described by Descartes, Newton, and Locke.

ECOLOGICAL REALISM AND SYSTEMS THEORY

The interest in Gibson's influential theory has often transcended the interest in perception alone. (Ullman, 1980, p. 373)

In reviewing and considering the published discussions and debates about Gibson's ecological psychology, the philosophical significance of Gibson's ideas can be clarified still further. To a degree we will be going beyond Gibson's own writings, yet I believe it will be useful in understanding both his ecological concepts and his direct realist epistemology. Though in the 1950s and 1960s Gibson attracted some attention from psychologists and philosophers (Boring, 1951, 1952a, 1952b, 1967; Epstein, 1964; Gibson, 1957b; Hamlyn, 1977; Postman, 1955; Yolton, 1968–1969), as well as inspiring some of his students to further develop concepts within his theories (e.g., Flock, 1964a, 1964b, 1965; Hay, 1966; Schiff, 1965) in the last decade of his career (the 1970s) interest in his views has heightened considerably. Commentaries on Gibson can be roughly divided into critical and supportive, though there are many that adopt a middle ground, acknowledging the importance and validity of some of his ideas while questioning others (e.g., Boynton, 1974; Halwes, 1974; Hamlyn, 1977; Neisser, 1977; Weimer, 1974). As a measure of Gibson's increasing notoriety and influence some very extensive critiques have appeared (Fodor & Pylyshyn, 1981; Gyr, 1972; Richard, 1976; Ullman, 1980), yet even these generally unsympathetic reviews have acknowledged at least certain aspects of Gibson's ecological approach as important contributions to the psychology of perception.

On the positive side, Gibson attracted numerous supporters. The strongest theoretical contributions to Gibsonian ecological psychology include the works of Bill Mace (1974, 1977; Mace & Pittenger 1975; Mace & Shaw, 1974), Ed Reed and Rebecca Jones (1978, 1979, 1982), Claire Michaels and Claudia Carello (Michaels, 1978; Michaels & Carello, 1981), and Robert Shaw, Michael Turvey, and associates (Shaw & Bransford, 1977; Shaw, McIntyre, & Mace, 1974; Shaw & Pittenger, 1977, 1978; Shaw & Turvey, 1981; Shaw, Turvey, & Mace, 1981; Turvey & Carello, 1981; Turvey & Shaw, 1979; Turvey, Shaw, Reed, & Mace, 1981). All of these psychologists have been associated with either the Universities of Connecticut or Minnesota or both. Gibson, in his *Ecological Approach,* (p. xiv) acknowledges the just cited supportive work, which stretches back to the early 1970s. There are other lines of development through the 1970s and 1980s that are supportive and contributive to Gibson's thinking. With more of an experimental focus, note should be made of Jacob Beck (1972), Eleanor Gibson (Gibson & Walk, 1960, 1961j; Gibson, Owsley, & Johnston, 1978; Gibson, Owsley, Walker, & Megaw-Nyce, 1979), David Lee (Lee, 1974, 1976, 1978, 1980a, 1980b; Lee & Lishman, 1977; Lishman & Lee, 1973), Leonard Mark (1979), John Pittenger (Pittenger & Shaw, 1975a, 1975b; Pittenger, Shaw, & Mark, 1979), Jim Todd (Todd, Mark, & Shaw, 1980), and Rik Warren (Warren, 1976, 1978; Warren & Owen, 1982). Cornell University is well represented in this second group of Gibsonian psychologists, as well as there being additional people from Connecticut and/or Minnesota. In general, Gibson's strongest supporters come from Cornell, Minnesota, and Connecticut.

Gibson also gained general support and acknowledgement outside of the university departments just mentioned. Johansson (1970) and Runeson (1977), Swedish psychologists, have shown considerable interest in Gibson's psychology, though Johansson has debated Gibson on some of the basic points of Gibsonian psychology (Gibson, 1970a). The environmental psychologist Heft (1981) and the developmentalist Costall (1981) have written very positive reviews, applying Gibsonian ecological concepts to their respective areas of interest.

A significant recent development in Gibsonian ecological psychology, that has helped to spread his ideas out toward a much broader audience, has been the formation of an International Society for Ecological Psychology. This group has begun annual conferences and participation and presentations reflect an ever-growing spectrum of psychologists from the United States and around the world.

Given this abbreviated review of contemporary literature pertaining to Gibsonian ecological psychology, it is fair to say that Gibson has attracted a considerable degree of attention. Reed and Jones (1979) characterized Gibson's effect on psychology as at least a potential revolution. As Reed and Jones note the debates, discussions, and developments are still relatively localized. Yet, if viewed in a context broader than just psychology, Gibson's ideas do not exist in isolation. It can be argued that Gibson's ecological approach is one facet of a fundamental and ubiquitous revolution in contemporary science and philosophy. This broader revolutionary context is the evolutionary-dynamic systems approach to nature. (Capra, 1982; Fraser, 1982; Jantsch & Waddington, 1976; Prigogine, 1980, 1984) Within this metatheoretical context, Gibson's ecological approach and his particular ideas concerning perception and psychology are a significant contribution to this more global revolution.

The main areas of similarity between Gibson and dynamic systems theory include a wholistic, relational perspective, a process ontology, where stability and permanence are not seen as independent and separate from change, a strong evolutionary component, an antidualistic position in several respects, and a central theoretical significance (to different degrees) given to the concept of reciprocity. Gibson as early as the 1960s was supportive of systems theory and attempted to describe the senses as perceptual systems. In the 1970s, especially, he has described the subject matter of psychology in terms of an ecosystem. A general anti-Platonic theme seen throughout both Gibson and dynamic systems theory has been to view order, structure, organization, and stability as embedded in change. More generally, time or change is a fundamental concept, rather than being secondary or derivative. Reciprocity comes into systems theory in explaining patterns of change and the organization of natural systems.

Critics of Gibson represent an extremely influential approach in modern psychology, viz., "Information-Processing and Computer Simulation" models of cognition. Such cognitive models adopt a rationalistic-rule governed theory of the mind. Though "internal information processing" could be treated as either learned or innate, the emphasis on organizational and rational-like mechanisms gives this approach a rationalistic form. Further with the emphasis on the need for organization of input and stimulation, there is an elementaristic foundation to this form of psychology. The computer model suggests that the brain performs computations on "input" (harkening back to Kepler's rationalistic model) and synthesizes this "information." Because Gibson has been described in this study as a wholistic empiricist, in contrast, the information-processing computer approach could be described as an analytic (elementaristic) rationalism. Historically, this is an interesting transformation from the wholistic-rationalism and analytic-empiricism controversy of the 18th and 19th centuries.

Gibson's approach embodies much more of a naturalistic-ecological and evolutionary emphasis and this fundamental theme can be tied to the dynamic-open system revolution going on in the biological and natural sciences. Reed underscores the importance of evolution in Gibson's thinking in distinguishing ecological psychology from computer theories (Reed, 1978, 1980a, 1980b). Computer science and information processing speak of "systems," but there are significant differences in how "systems" are defined and understood. A computer system is given information (input) and the system organizes such information, giving it order. Just as significantly, "information" is given a different meaning in computer models than "information" in Gibson's ecological psychology. (See Reed & Jones, 1979).

If one reviews some of the more substantial critiques of Gibson (Fodor & Pylyshyn, 1981; Ullman, 1980), both the language and concepts are reflective of the computer theory, information processing approach. The substantial portion of the criticisms raised miss many of Gibson's basic ecological-evolutionary themes and quite interestingly, from an historical perspective, the criticisms reflect traditional (Pre-Gibsonian) issues and concepts. (Gibson believed that the information processing approach reflected in a new language the traditional explanations of perception he was criticizing through his ecological approach, i.e., he saw nothing fundamentally new in the information processing approach.) Conversely, to a degree, advocates of the computer approach do not see anything new in Gibson. There appears to be almost unanimous agreement among Gibson's critics that Gibson's rejection of an elementaristic description of stimulation was a significant theoretical advance. Yet Gibson's theory of higher order stimulus structure was proposed in his psychophysical period and Gibson felt that in his ecological approach he went far beyond such earlier insights. And these newer ideas are ecological and dynamic, something his critics do not address.

One common argument against Gibson's critics is that they focus on Gibson's psychophysics, perhaps not adequately seeing how his ecological approach goes way beyond his psychophysics. One issue of paramount concern among Gibson's critics is the direct perception hypothesis. They argue that perception is necessarily a causal-sequential chain involving in its last stage psychological contributions and organizational processes. They cannot see, within the context of their understanding of nature and scientific explanation, how perception could be direct. The philosophical context of their arguments, though compatible with Gibson's more traditional psychophysics, is not commensurate with Gibson's ecological approach. The causal chain model conceptually fits with a dualistic ontology that separates mind and matter, e.g., recall Descartes psychophysiology or the Ancient Greek explanations connecting *eidola*, simulation, and the homunculus. If my historical-theoretical analysis of Gibson's ecological approach is correct, then the concept of reciprocity is crucial to understanding modern Gibson, and this concept the critics basically ignore. Further, again if I am correct, Gibson's direct realist epistemology fundamentally involves the notion of animal-environment (ecological) reciprocity. Consequently, Gibson's theory of direct perception and ecological realism cannot be adequately understood except through his basic idea of dynamic ecological reciprocity. Shaw and Turvey have been particularly concerned with developing a new approach to scientific explanations of perception and behavior that incorporates the idea of reciprocity, while rejecting the causal chain explanation of perception (Shaw and Turvey, 1981; Shaw, Turvey, and Mace, 1981).

The nature of mind or mentality and the related issue of the nervous system's role in mentality, are other important issues Gibson's critics address. What is the function of the mind? Does the mind construct percepts? Does it "house" thoughts and perceptions? Are percepts simply subjective states of mind? Are the functions of the nervous system to organize and represent? Such traditional explanations of the mind and nervous system rest upon a dualistic theory of mind and matter. Briefly, if order and organization (integration) are localized in the perceiver, then constructive and representational processes seem to be necessary mental-neural functions, but in abandoning this dualistic split, the functions of mind and neurology could be conceptualized differently.

Let us consider the causal model of perception and the relationship of mind and brain. Fodor and Pylyshyn (1981) argue that even if stimulus structure is lawfully and unequivocally related to the environment, the perceiver, in effect, is directly in contact only with stimulus structure.

The environment is spatially and causally separated from the perceiver, and perceptual awareness of the environment must be a consequence (casual and/or inferential) of stimulation. Perception involves a sequential process of distinct events running from environment to stimulation to neural excitation to perceptual awareness (mental states). One could equate the neural and mental stages (mind-brain identity thesis), but we still are apparently in direct contact only with stimulation (e.g., light, rather than the environment).

First, it should be recalled that Gibson in the 1960s and 1970s argued that relationships within perception involve circular processes rather than linear processes. Also, information is not transmitted through the medium and resonance is not a transmission of impulses from sense organs to brain. To go further than these points already discussed, we should note that awareness is seen within the causal chain model as an event within the chain, localized at its terminal end within the perceiver. Not only is this view dualistic, placing the mind within the animal, aware of nothing but its inner states (homunculus), it is also founded upon a reductionistic error in its conceptualization of perception. There is a confusion of levels of organization.

The perceiver (animal) and the environment exist as a reciprocity. The animal is described as an integration of capacities and ways of life actualized within an environment. The animal perceives, but perception is ecological, for example, humans walk, but walking occurs within an environment. Perception is animal awareness of the environment. Embedded within this ecological reality are perceptual systems and the activities of such systems and stimulus structure and the relationship of specification. Animals perceive with their perceptual systems; it is not the perceptual system that perceives. Animals perceive (veridically) because their systems are sensitive to energy relationships, but they do not perceive these relationships. Animals perceive what the relationships specify, viz., the environment. The reciprocal relation of animal and environment exists at a more global level of organization than those conditions that support their existence. Psychological realities, such as perception, behavior, or motivation, exist at this global and ecological level. We see then that stimulation doesn't cause perception anymore than atoms cause molecules. Perception is a relationship between an animal and an environment—it is not a relationship between neurons and stimulation. Finally, as a relationship achieved by an animal between itself and the environment, it is not a state isolated and localized with the perceiver.

This same line of reasoning applies to understanding the relationship of the brain and the mind. I am reminded of an ingenious title of an article by Bill Mace: "Ask not what's inside your head, but what your head's inside of" (1977). The brain exists within the body and is undoubtedly necessary for perception, but perception (or for that matter any mental function) does not occur in the brain. Perception occurs within an ecosystem. The only way to comprehensively describe what occurs during perception is to describe it at the ecological level of organization. To elaborate on Mace's title, perception does not exist in the head, the head exists within perception (more precisely proprioception). The brain exists at a different level of organization than the mind.

Fundamentally, it is a wholistic interpretation which underlies the theory that perception is ecological. This wholistic organization is a reciprocity, where the perceiving animal and the perceived environment interface with each other, rather than being isolated. They are reciprocal because although each possesses a distinct constituent composition and structure, they possess a set of relational properties necessarily involving the existence of the other. Perception is an epistemic relationship between the knowing animal and the known environment that can exist because of their ontological reciprocity. The term *interface* underscores the fact of contact. At the ecological level, nothing stands between the perceiver and the environment.

At this point, the discussion can be further refined, for strictly speaking, the perceiver is always aware of both itself and the environment. The theory of ecological reciprocity implies that the animal and the environment are interdependent. The reciprocity of perception and proprioception implies that the animal is fundamentally aware of this reciprocity. The epistemic relationship is between the animal as subject and the ecosystem (animal/environment) as object. Knowledge has an ecological support and an ecological epistemic object.

Though the distinction between what is and what is known needs to be maintained or else one's philosophy will collapse into phenomenalism or idealism, Gibson's direct realism implies that what exists are the actual objects of perceptual awareness. If the objects of knowledge are separated from the objects of existence, we end up with a duality of mental objects and physical objects and ontologically indirect perception.

The resolution of this dilemma is to be found in the principle of reciprocity. What exists possesses the potential to be known because of information (though it may not be known) and what knows, viz., the perceiver, possesses the capacity to know because it is sensitive to information. Further, the perceiver is not an entity ontologically distinct from environmental objects of knowledge, in so far as both perceiver and environment are parts of the ecosystem and one perceiver can be part of the environment of another perceiver. The fundamental support for the knowability of what exists in the ecosystem is affordances specified by stimulus information. Affordances and information exist regardless of whether there is perception, but if the perceiver explores and its perceptual systems extract the invariants and variants of stimulus structure, it will be aware of itself and environmental affordances.

Something can exist without being known, but if it is known it must exist. If the animal is aware of something which doesn't exist, we are no longer concerned with perceptual knowledge—we are discussing illusions, hallucinations, and misperceptions. I will go so far as to suggest that existence and knowledge are reciprocals. The perceiver is not aware of itself simply by virtue of its existence. A perceiver must explore, test, and tune into itself, to know itself. Information about the self can be picked-up but there is no necessity for it to occur. Generally, nothing is known simply by virtue of its existence, yet if it exists, then there is information such that it can be known. We continually extend our abilities to detect information, finding new ways to enhance and extend our perceptual awareness. It seems very problematic that there exist noumena in the Kantian sense, such that its existence is forever hidden from our awareness. In summary, though knowledge and existence are distinguishable, they are interdependent for what is known exists and what exists can be known.

The controversy between Gibsonian psychologists and computer information processing theorists is a contemporary event, undoubtedly with many twists and turns to come in the future. Clearly, the question of the nature of psychology is under consideration, as well as the nature of perception. Ullman (1980) notes that Gibson has been so influential, in part, because he is offering a new approach to cognition in general. To return to Reed's contention that Gibson's ecological psychology is a revolution in the making, it is important to see that the revolution goes beyond perception. What is the subject matter of psychology and what constitutes a psychological explanation?

In support of the idea that Gibson's ecological psychology is revolutionary, it is interesting to note the problems of communication and language between Gibsonians and critics of Gibson. There is an element of incommensurability in approaches, a fact about scientific revolutions explored by Kuhn (1962, 1970a, 1970b). It is perfectly understandable that critics would express their ideas in the language and concepts of some assumed philosophy of science, and if Gibson's approach is significantly different, then one would expect problems in understanding. This is not to say that the scientific quest is irrational, simply depending on who yells the loudest. Positions and approaches can be compared and evaluated. Yet it is important to note one's assumptions, language, and philosophy for such fundamental constraints are real, and as this history of Gibson intended to demonstrate, philosophies are varied and changing and they are inextricably bound up with changes in science. Gibson is revolutionary because he offers a rich, new language (e.g., affordances, perceptual systems, surface layout, ecological optics, etc.) and because, through his own efforts, he examined the philosophical foundations of traditional perceptual and psychological science, replacing much of it with a different ontology and epistemology for psychology.

Chapter 18 _____

GIBSON'S "ECOLOGICAL APPROACH to VISUAL PERCEPTION"

THE ECOLOGICAL ENVIRONMENT

During the last decade of his scientific career, Gibson's major theoretical project was a book that would systematically, yet with considerable empirical detail, treat vision from an ecological perspective. The "Purple Perils" plus those philosophical-theoretical articles cited in the last chapter were all steps along the way toward this final theoretical integration. Though Gibson's *Ecological Approach to Visual Perception* (1979a) is both integrative in format and historically self-conscious, it has a definite naturalistic and descriptive flavor. It attempts to outline and fill in as much as possible the facts of ecological psychology. Especially in the early sections of the book, one has the feeling of listening to a naturalist describe the world around him. The *Ecological Approach* does not carry the explicit evolutionary emphasis contained in the *Senses*. Gibson is more concerned with reconceptualizing natural science in order to distinguish and define his ecological approach. The *Ecological Approach* is a clear advance over the *Senses,* and though its focus is vision, it embodies a scientific and psychological perspective as general in scope as the *Senses*. It is Gibson's final and most uniquely personal statement, and while it is grounded in history and a lifetime of research, it points toward the future, opening the doors to a new investigative approach for psychology.

The term *environment* means a surrounding, thus the concept implies something surrounded. Though Gibson's treatment of the environment in the 1960s to some degree involved considerations of the animal, in 1979 the concept of the environment is explicitly ecological. Animate life is understood in terms of distinctive "ways of life" (perception and behavior), and the idea of *surround* or *ambience* is explicitly tied to animate ways of life. How does the surround afford perception and behavior? What conditions, structural and dynamic, must it satisfy? The environment is that special type of surround in which animate life exists.

Consequently, Gibson's starting point in his *Ecological Approach* is not simply the environment but the reciprocity of the animal and the environment (1979a, pp. 7–8). Though the reciprocity of animal and environment is implicit in the beginning of the *Senses* (1966a, p. 7), the environment is primarily treated in this earlier work as "what is perceived" and as the "source of stimulation." Gibson no longer relates the environment just to those conditions relevant to understanding perception, but rather to the totality of psychological facts. Further, it is very clear that the environment is subsumed under the more basic concept of an ecosystem. Gibson's concept of the environment is more general in the 1979 book: It is what affords animate life.

The key concept in Gibson's 1979 treatment of the environment is ambience, designating the ecological fact that the environment surrounds animals. The environment is tied to the animal via this concept before any discussion of *what* is perceived or *how* the environment is the source of stimulation. Animate life is to be understood as existing within an ecological context. The subject matter of psychology is not of a separate realm independent of the world. Animals, unlike plants and non-living things, are both animate and sentient, hence they are not surrounded by an environment the way "space" surrounds a celestial body or even the way a forest surrounds a tree. The environment supports animate life, providing not only those necessary vegetative and non-cognitive conditions, but also supporting both perception and behavior. In the most general sense, its ambient structure affords these animate functions. It is not an empty ambience, but a differentiated surround that allows for animal life. Surfaces surround animals and provide rigid support and differentiated structure, making orientation possible. The medium affords room for locomotion, yet it is significant that the medium is adjacent to surfaces (it is not unsupported space) such that animals move *through* the medium and *across* the surfaces. The surface differentiation is reflected in the ambient optic array, thus providing information specific to position and path. Energy reverberates through the differentiated ecosystem, thus surrounding animals with a differentiated energy ambience. Significantly, the structure within this energy ambience is a consequence of both the surrounding environment and the surrounded perceiver.

According to Gibson, traditional physics leads one to treat animals as objects, subject to the laws and descriptive concepts of mechanics. Not only are the spatial and temporal scales in physics inappropriate, but "animals within an environment" constitutes a different kind of *relationship* than objects in space (1979a, pp. 8, 15, 43). Animals move about in a differentiated ambience; objects move through a relatively undifferentiated emptiness. The environment has an absolute frame of reference and a surface of support. Space has a relative and variable frame of reference without a demarcated surface layout. Conversely, animal behavior is not analogous or reducible to mechanical motions. Animals orient to the environmental frame of reference and control their behavior relative to what they perceive. Behavior is elastic, intentional, and multinested in complexity; it cannot be reduced to rigid translations through space; in fact, there are no behavioral atoms, and control is not through physical forces but by means of ecological information. Nesting is not purely hierarchial because there are transitions and overlaps between size levels. Further animals control, manipulate, and modify the environment in various ways. Animate behavior is not reactive motion to independent external causes. Behavior should be described as coordinative in organization and function. Both traditional S-R psychology and mechanistic physiology view psychological processes as purely dependent reactions within a causal chain; animals are objects that are moved. Gibson opposed this Cartesian-Newtonian model in his theory of perception. His *Ecological Approach* opts for an intentional and modulatory theory of behavior, where behavior is seen as controlling and adjusting (see also Gibson, 1975d). Behavior both varies as a function of the ecological situation and changes the situation to achieve the animal's ends. Behavior is reciprocally related to the ecosystem.

The crux of Gibson's theory of animal-environment reciprocity is to avoid mechanistic reductionism, as well as dualistic psychology, by functionally interrelating each member of the ecosystem. What environmental conditions afford perception and behavior? What must perception and behavior be like given the environment within which life exists? For perception and behavior, differentiated rigid surfaces and a relative homogeneous transparent medium are necessary. The medium provides paths of locomotion and paths of observation. Surfaces support behavior and are the source of stimulation. In general, the environment is described in terms of meaningful affordances that are functionally related to the capacities of animals. It is within this global level of ecological organization that all the basic features of perception are nested. (See also Gibson, 1978c, 1979d.)

Gibson's introduction to his ecological approach is an elaboration on the idea of reciprocity founded on a description of ecological ambience.

He rejects traditional physics, especially Newtonian mechanics, substituting spatial and temporal scales of description appropriate to animal life (1979a, pp. 9–11). He substitutes a description of nested natural units for the building block units of physics, geology and chemistry. Ecological motions, whether pertaining to animal behavior or other events, are not reducible to Newtonian motions (p. 15). Surfaces, substances, and mediums are described in terms of higher order properties relevant to perception and behavior (pp. 23–31). In effect, Gibson sketches out an ecological geometry of surfaces and an ecological physics and chemistry for substances and events that exhibit the meaningfulness of the world in which animate life exists. The word *ecology* comes from the Greek *oikos,* a house, and Gibson's ecological description focuses appropriately on the floor plan, composition, and furnishing of the house of life.

It would be a mistake to attribute a teleological interpretation to Gibson's description of the environment, as if the environment was created to furnish animate life with what it needed to exist. Animate life is evolving and changing and the necessary conditions for its existence in numerous respects could not, in principle, be anticipated. The environment, according to Gibson, had a *potential* existence prior to life filling its niches, viz., its opportunities for existence. The harmony between environment and animate life is due to the latter developing abilities which use those opportunities potential in the former (1979a, p. 8). Yet the level of analysis selected and those features of the environment emphasized clearly assumes the animal and animate ways of life. The theoretical study of the environment cannot logically precede the study of animals and in *functional actuality* the environment exists because of animals. I would add that animals create new opportunities by their very presence. Many significant features of our environment have been constructed by us, and it is noteworthy that much of our environment involves the presence and effects of other living forms.

The concept of evolution is relevant to our understanding of the compatibility and reciprocity of the animal and the environment. If nature shows harmony and order, how do we explain this fact? One explanation is that organization ultimately derives from an organizer, be it God or the human mind. The theory of evolution postulates that order arises within nature, rather than being imposed. Evolution rejects the dualistic split of order and particulars. Gibson accepts the theory of evolution, but with one significant qualification. The order found in the environment is tied to life. An environment only potentially exists prior to life, and though to a degree life *creates* new environmental order, it is always implicated in the order existing in the environment. Since his psychophysical period, Gibson was concerned with the veridicality and objectivity of perception, viz., perception for him was of something real and objective. Yet for

Gibson the term "objective" took on a new meaning in his ecological approach. The environment is not a "ding-an-sich" or intrinsic substance; it is understood relative to animate ways of life. Its reality, objectivity, or "invariant" characteristics exist embodied within an ecosystem involving life. The environment and the animal are *reciprocal* and evolution in reality has been an ecological fact, rather than simply a fact of "life." It is ecosystems that have evolved.

Gibson's shift to an ecological perspective is clarified by the concept of ambience because traditionally, psychological explanations begin *within* the animal (or mind). Gibson begins *outside,* yet always with reference to the animal, describing the ambience in which life exists. The environment is a frame of reference both theoretically and psychologically but he avoids reductionistic environmentalism and physicalism by finding the appropriate level of analysis for the environment and functionally tying the "physical" ecology to animate life.

"What is perceived" follows from his ecology. Instead of the standard list of qualities, such as depth, color, shape, size, motion, and so forth, Gibson substitutes places, attached and detached objects, substances, and events (1979a, pp. 240–242). This is a list of environmental features relevant to animate life. Comparing this approach with Gibson in 1950 and 1966, the starting point is neither a phenomenology (1950a) nor an ecology of stimulation (1966a), but a description and explanation of the ecological support for animate life. Its functionalism is tied to the idea of a surround or ambience which is necessary for behavior (locomotion, manipulation and communication) and ambient ambulatory perception (1979a, p. 2). Its wholistic orientation is tied to the same concept—the animal is not separated from the environment, but supported (surrounded) within the whole.

As noted earlier, Gibson in the 1960s substituted a description of the environment for a phenomenology of perception. Phenomenology, as practiced by Gibson and Gestalt psychologists has a subjective dualistic foundation. By identifying the "objects" of perception with the environment, Gibson avoided both the subjectivism and dualism inherent in his phenomenology. Yet in his ecological approach, Gibson did not abandon the quest to describe accurately and correctly *what* is perceived. It is, in fact, an ecological reality, involving both "subject" and "object." Recall that "subjective" and "objective" take on relative, relational meanings in Gibson. Further, a description of "what" is perceived cannot be done independent of an explanation of perception. The ideal of a presuppositionless description is a mistake, founded upon an absolute separation of theory and fact (Feyerabend, 1962, 1965, 1970a, 1976). What is of value in the Gestalt critique of introspection is not that structuralists were assuming a theory in their description of perception, but that the theory assumed was wrong. One can not first describe the facts of awareness and then try to explain them. Gibson's description of what is perceived is intended to capture both its animal significance (its meaningfulness and relation to the living form) and its objectivity. Such a description requires an ecological theory of reality.

The environment is objective or intersubjective because of its ambience. An animal can move about and occupy different positions within the surround. Also, different animals can occupy identical positions over time. An animal, unlike a plant, is not cemented to one position and perspective; animals can exchange positions or perspectives. There exists one ambience for all animals due to their mobility. Ambience then has a different quality for animals than for immobile objects because over time, animals share the same surround. The objectivity of the surround is due to the mobility of animals realized over time. Ecological objectivity is this shared engulfing permanence, yet it should be emphasized that it can only be defined by assuming animate life. Ambience, though the ground of objectivity, pertains to a relational or ecological property vis-à-vis mobile creatures.

With the development of a theory of events and event perception in the 1960s and 1970s, Gibson completed his critique and abandonment of the Newtonian concepts of space and time. Gibson in the 1950s had replaced space (depth) perception with surface perception. By the 1970s, he replaced time with events (Gibson, 1975c). Neither empty space nor empty duration is perceived. Rather, there is perception of adjacent and sequential order embodied within differentiated particulars (1979a, p. 101). Further, as illustrated in the concept of ecological ambience, space and time cannot be absolutely separated. Gibson notes how space has been separated from time in abstract geometry, but ecologically there are no frozen forms. All spatial structures and relationships are realized within a dynamic ecology (1979a, p. 74). Consequently, Gibson drops the concept of absolute "empty" frames of reference and their presumed mutual independence. The presumed atomistic independence of "elements" in physical and psychological domains depends on the mutually independent absolute frames of reference of space and time. For Gibson, spatial and temporal frames of reference are built into the "particulars" of the ecosystem. In contrast to elements defined and described intrinsically, Gibson's ecological units cannot be described independently of how they are related together. Reciprocity of natural kinds in Gibson's ecology assumes the idea of interdependency.

The environment is a blend of permanence and change, where neither is an absolute. Reconsider the Parmenidian-Heraclitian split taken up with various refinements by Plato and Aristotle respectively. Gibson rejects the idea that all change is reducible to continuous transformations.

Ecologically there are disruptions of structure and objects come and go out of existence (1979a, pp. 13–14). Gibson in the 1960s spoke of "transformations" in describing change, but ecologically there are also disruptions of structure, i.e., examples of discontinuous change. Gibson rejects the applicability of "motion" in describing ecological change for it is more than (or different than) simple reshuffling of parts (1979a, p. 15). In defining invariance and variance as reciprocals, Gibson sticks to the idea of relative invariants, yet certain invariants, for example, the vertical axis of the horizon, are so basic to the environment that for them to change, the environment itself would have to be redefined. The ecological horizon, embedded in the optic array, is changeless and fixed (1979a, pp. 75, 163–164). Consequently, nested within the dynamic structure of the ecology rather than standing above as eternal Platonic laws, there are invariants of the environment that do not change over time. The environment can neither be characterized in terms of Parmenides' absolute dualism of permanency and change nor Heraclitus' absolute flow. Simply, change and stability are reciprocal (see also Gibson, 1975e).

At times, Gibson appears to substitute the terms *invariance* and *variance* for space and time, giving the former pair an ecological-empirical meaning not found in the latter (1979a, p. 12). Though historically time is often identified with change, spatial structures do change and in some respects temporal structure shows regularity and invariance. From Heraclitus and Aristotle through Galileo and Newton the concept of a natural law implied a temporal invariance, and Gibson, in his theory of events, clearly emphasizes the idea of temporal regularities. In general, there exist both spatial and temporal constancies that ecologically do not change.

The temporal structure of the environment is composed of events. Gibson developed a classification scheme of events, thus providing a set of categories for natural temporal units to go along with his classification of ecological spatial structures. Events are divided into changes in surface layout, change in color and texture, and changes in surface existence (1979a, pp. 94–99). Some events are reversible, whereas others are not, thus giving ecological time a direction. Movements of animate bodies and rearrangements of detachable objects are generally reversible, whereas chemical changes, biological growth, and the destruction of surfaces are irreversible. Events have temporal structures, thus similar events or repeating events will possess transformational invariants. For both atomic and celestial mechanics, there are a variety of temporal regularities known as the laws of mechanics, but Gibson contends that ecological events cannot be simply reduced to atomic events. There is a level of existence of ecological temporal units irreducible to smaller units. Where there is atomic complexity, there may be ecological simplicity (1979a, pp. 99–101). This argument for the temporal reality of ecology corresponds with Gibson's argument for the spatial reality of ecology above the level of atoms. Basically, it assumes a wholistic orientation consistently applied to all aspects of ecology.

In his *Ecological Approach,* a distinctive Aristotelian flavor emerges concerning ecological events. Gibson divides events into "episodes" that begin and end. Episodes are integrated units where beginning and end are naturally tied together. The development and end of an ecological episode is implicit in its beginning (this is also similar to Leibnitz's concept of a monad) (1979a, p. 102). There is a rhythm to the flow of time captured in those natural episodes found in the environment. The idea is not that an event in the future determines an event in the present but that there are natural relationships between how events begin and how they end.

In the late 60s and throughout the 70s, Gibson paid more attention to the concept of substance because surfaces had been defined as the interface of substances and the medium, and surfaces presumably contained information about substances. Though surfaces are clearly a relational concept, the term *substance* hearkens back to Cartesian-Lockean ontology seemingly connoting something intrinsic and independent of possible relationships with other substances. Such a concept of substance would fall within Newtonian ontology, but Gibson ties ecological substances to both surfaces and affordances and avoids giving it a purely intrinsic characterization.

Due to their texture and pigmentation, surfaces reveal the composition of substances. Substances have other properties such as hardness, viscosity, and density, and such properties related to the capacities of animals constitute the affordances of substances. According to Gibson, when an animal perceives substances it perceives the various affordances of the substance. Second, a surface is not a veil of appearance covering the inner reality of a substance, but rather the interface of a substance with a transparent medium. A surface reveals a substance (1979a, pp. 19–21) (see also Gibson, 1979c, 1980).

Overall, there exist certain parallels between Newtonian physical ontology and Gibson's ecological ontology. For Newton there is matter, space, planes, and lines of motion; for Gibson there is substance, medium, surfaces, and events. Yet Gibson's ontology is intended to be referential to animate life and each concept is significantly different in meaning than its Newtonian counterpart. Also, there is a definite integration of time into ecological space; this is an especially noteworthy change in Gibson's approach to the environment between 1950 and 1979, and a fundamental difference between Newton and Gibson.

ECOLOGICAL INFORMATION

Ecological optics begins precisely where Gibson's psychophysics leaves off—circa 1960. Gibson in the 1960s became dissatisfied with traditional optics, especially its reductionistic and ecologically irrelevant nature. Radiant light is an inadequate starting point for vision, for it does not possess the higher order structure necessary for vision and it is not ambient to a perceiver. In effect, the optical starting point for ecological vision is a dynamic structured ambience, viz., the ambient optic array. Animate life literally exists in an engulfing sea of energy. Gibson's definition of the environment as a spatial-temporal ambience is carried over into his theory of stimulus information. The spatial-temporal ambience is now embodied within an energy flux rather than the substances of the environment (1979a, pp. 48–49). Ecological optics involves a level of analysis (differentiation) and order commensurate with the meaningful ecology of animate life.

Ambient light is a consequence of an ambient ecology, and the dynamic structure in light is a consequence of the dynamic structure of the ecology. The term *information* has been used by Gibson to refer to the unique relationship stimulus structure has to the environment, but Gibson has also emphasized how stimulus structure is related to the perceiver. In effect, information is ecological for stimulus structure possesses "concurrent specification" of both the perceiver and the environment (1979a, p. 76). The concept of ambience implies something surrounded and something surrounding and information pertains to this ecological reciprocity.

In his *Ecological Approach,* Gibson continues many of the familiar themes developed over the previous 20 years in ecological optics (see also Gibson 1974b, 1977a). He continues to put special emphasis on the distinction between stimulus energy and information (1979a, pp. 50–57). Gibson contends that light energy as such is never seen although a radiant source may be seen (1979a, pp. 54–55). Information, unlike light energy, is specific to the ecology, and is *not* propagated through the medium. Gibson criticizes the idea that information is sent or transmitted by the environment and received by the perceiver (1979a, pp. 63–64). The ancient Greeks had three basic meta-theories of perception emphasizing motion from the perceiver, motion from the world or a meeting of motions in between perceiver and world. All three approaches assume a linear causal process, and Gibson's theory of perception based on ecological information attacks this assumption. When Gibson moved from the psychophysical to the ecological framework he moved away from the causal process approach. It was during this same transitional period that the concept of information became increasingly important. Energy may be "transmitted," but information is not transmitted. Complementarily, the perceiver does not receive an input of information though energy may flow within the animate life form. Neither specification nor detection are linear causal processes.

Another theme that Gibson continues to elaborate on within his *Ecological Approach* is ambient structure (1979a, pp. 65–76). He stressed that the ambient optic array is the central concept in ecological optics, but he no longer speaks of observation "points" (an unnaturalistic geometrical fiction). Rather, there are "positions" and "paths" localized within the ambient environment. Solid angles, rather than rays, make up the structure of the optic array because angles have "form" whereas rays do not. Gibson in the 1960s spoke of "rays projected to a point." He sees "solid angles" as a continuation of ancient and Medieval perspective optics before the reductionistic optics of Kepler came to dominate thinking. Natural perspective, though, has limitations for it geometrizes the world, omitting motion and time. Further, optical structure cannot be considered simply a projection for optical structure contains information for occluded surfaces. The dynamic flow of the array cannot be construed as *motions*; more descriptive terms would be *disturbances* or *disruptions*. The array is completely filled with nested solid angles and this multi-nested structure undergoes both continuous and discontinuous changes. Gibson distinguishes between perspective and invariant structure in the optic ambience. The former will change as an observer moves about, but the latter will change only as there is some change in the environment. Invariant optical structure underlies perspective structure, and it is within changing perspective structure that invariant structure is embedded.

The concept of specification of ecological structure by optical structure can now be more adequately explicated and summarized. From the Greeks comes the idea of projection of geometrical forms, producing some degree of geometrical simulation of the world reaching the perceiver. Physical science provided a linear causal model of energy transmitted from the world to the perceiver, but the energy flux was considered a poor geometrical representation of the world. From the empiricists comes the idea of correlation between stimuli and the world, but correlations were between individual properties of stimulation and individual properties of the world. Twentieth century psychology saw these individual correlations as limited and equivocal, e.g., Brunswik. Gibson initially saw stimulus-environment relations as projective and correlational, though correlations were to be found between global properties of stimulation and the environment. He vehemently attacks the necessity of geometrical simulation in his 1950 book as if light were something to be seen. Instead, in 1950, he speaks of lawful and projective relations. In his *Ecological Approach*, Gibson returns to his attack on the simulative assumption, this time with special consideration being given to motion and event perception. Disturbances in optical structure are not "copies" of physical motion, though they are information for events. Further, event information does not involve "point to point correspondence" between optical and environmental structure (1979a, pp. 102–105). The dynamic features of the optic array are not always geometrical transformations, e.g., loss by substitution is information for going out of existence and loss by deletion is information for going out of sight. Gibson by 1979 clearly wishes to avoid both the simulative and projective models of information. Given our discussion of levels of organization in the previous chapter, we can see that simulation and the homunculus hypothesis involved a confusion of levels. Stimulation is not perceived, though it is embedded within the ecological reality of perception.

In discussing Gibson's psychophysical approach and how it differed from Berkeleian approaches, it was pointed out the Gibson meant something stronger than "correlation" in describing the relationship of stimulation and the environment. Though Gibson in 1979 rejects the linear chain model of causation, he does believe in lawful relationships between optical structure and ecological structure. Natural laws, though, are not simply correlations. Further, though Gibson in writing and research analytically isolates single features of optical and ecological structure to give examples of specification, what he theoretically has in mind is a wholistic relationship between the integrative spatial-temporal order of the optic array and the integrative spatial-temporal order of the ecology. Integrative designates the fact that adjacent and successive order in both the optic array and the ecology involve a nesting and organization of finer details embedded in more global structures. Optical structures are organized and related together rather than being a set of separate facts. The same is true of ecological organization.

AFFORDANCES AND ECOLOGICAL PSYCHOLOGY

There have been numerous and often divergent systematic approaches within 20th century psychology. These different approaches produced different definitions of the subject matter of psychology. The nature of basic facts and basic relationships is different for structuralism, functionalism, Gestalt psychology, and behaviorism. Perception as part of the domain of psychology has been described and explained differently, depending on the overall systematic orientation of the psychologists. In reaction to the restrictions of S-R behaviorism, over the last twenty years modern cognitive psychology (Neisser, 1967, 1976) has been dominated by mentalistic and information-processing concepts and has altered the ontological territory of psychology. Representational and inference-based theories of perception have become popular again. As noted in the previous chapter, some of Gibson's strongest critics advocate an information processing approach. Gibson, as explained in earlier chapters, began from a systematic orientation combining features of functionalism, psychophysics, and Gestalt phenomenology. In developing an integrative approach to the problem of perception (1950a, 1966a), Gibson laid the seeds for a new systematic approach to the entire domain of psychology (1979a). As Gibson had been critical of traditional empiricist and nativist approaches to perception, his ecological approach critiques both behavioristic and information-processing approaches to psychology.

Gibson's systematic approach to psychology begins with the concept of a dynamic animal-environment reciprocity. As noted earlier, this view places Gibson at odds with mental monism, physical monism, and mind-matter (body) dualism. Gibson states that he sees the mind-body problem to be a false dichotomy (1979a, p. xiii). The environment, if not reduced to animal-neutral physical variables, is tied to the animal ontologically. The animal, equally so, is more than its molecular or cellular parts. Gibson also rejects treating the mind as a thing, distinct from the body, in which thoughts, precepts, and affective states occur. Mentalistic psychology, rejecting the physical reductionism of behaviorism, has introduced a dualistic ontology extremely reminiscent of Descartes and Locke. Further, with the restrictions of associationism removed from psychological relationships, information-processing has acquired a rationalistic flavor. Gibson, due to his Gestalt background, rejects reductionism, and proceeding from his functionalism background, he sees the importance of relating together knower and known, subject and object. "Mind" involves global functions of the body with respect to the environment. Mind-matter dualism ontologically split the universe in two and epistemologically faced the tremendous problem of connecting them together again. Gibson, in fact, avoids using the term *mind* and related terminology because he wishes to avoid being interpreted as a dualist. Gibson's insight into the multi-nested and multi-ordered nature of reality offers a way of understanding the relationship of the functioning mind to the body.

The reciprocity between the animal and the environment undercuts both dualism and reductionism, for the "matter" of the environment and the "mind" of the body are ontologically and epistemologically connected through the functional and informational unity of the ecosystem. One could also state that the perceiver is not simply mental for it perceives with its perceptual systems, and the perceiver exists within the ecosystem. Complimentarily, the environment is not simply physical in the traditional dualistic sense, for it possesses affordances and is meaningful to the animal-perceiver. Animal and environment are not treated as disjointed entities; consequently the linear chain model of causation, e.g., in S-R behaviorism or standard psychophysics, is inappropriate (1979a, p. 2). Lawful relations between the animal and the environment are not understood as cause-effect relations. The perceiving (and acting) animal and the environment stand in a dynamic reciprocal relation where neither instigates the life processes. It is a circular, mutually supporting reciprocity. The sentient animal does not organize an unordered physical input because order and organization exist in the ecosystem.

According to Gibson, psychology is concerned with animate ways of life, a distinctly ecological definition for a way of life occurs in an ecosystem within some niche (1979a, p. 7). The "world" the animal perceives and behaves within is commensurate to that animal in spatial and temporal scale but most importantly in terms of its affordances. The set of affordances available for the living process of an animal constitutes the environmental niche (1979a, pp. 127–129). The dynamic-functional complementation of the environment to the animal is the set of the environment's affordances. Complimentarily, the psychological facts of the animal are functions ecologically tied to the affordances of the environment.

Affordances are what the environment "furnishes" or "provides" the animal, and they are "measured" and understood relative to the animal (1979a, p. 127). Surfaces, objects, substances, and events can have affordances, in fact, multiple affordances (1979a, p. 36), for example, fire can be used to cook or provide light, a stick can be used to move something or make marks. Gibson devotes considerably more attention to affordances in his *Ecological Approach* than in his *Senses*. Aside from a descriptive taxonomy, based on previous writings (Gibson, 1971f, 1971g, 1971h, 1972a, 1977b), he puts considerable theoretical stress on how affordances undercut the subjective-objective dichotomy (1979a, pp. 128–138). Affordances constitute part of the domain of psychology proper, for a way of life is not just what goes on inside an animal nor simply the animal's movements. Behaviors are descriptively tied to affordances; for example, the animal walks across a supporting surface, eats an edible apple, and mates with a cooperative female. A way of life necessarily includes reference to affordances and the environment.

Perception of affordances is a "primitive" process, for the perception of edibility, for example, can occur without discriminating and identifying the particular qualities of a piece of fruit. Affordance perception involves neither classification nor conceptualization. From an ecological and evolutionary viewpoint, perception of affordances is crucial and basic to animate ways of life (1979a, pp. 134–135). Survival depends on affordance perception. Regarding affordance perception, Gibson is again resisting the popular rendency to intellectualize perception. Affordances depend on compound features within the environment, for instance, as a surface of support depends upon both the rigidity of a surface and its inclination. Gibson believes that the affordance of supportability is specified in structured light and the perceiver does not have to perceive rigidity and inclination separately and then decide after some type of intellectual process if it would support locomotion. A perceiver may discriminate or differentiate rigidity or inclination, but it is the affordance relevant to action that is primary (1979a, p. 141).

Affordances exist at a level of organization commensurate with animate ways of life. Though the structural and compositional support for an affordance may be complex, it exists at a finer level of organization. The affordance, existing at a more global level, may be relatively simple in comparison to its constituent support. Consider how simple the affordance of "writability" is for a pencil or pen in comparison to the complexity of factors that make up a pencil or pen. First, there is no one set of complex, constituent factors that is necessary; they can be made of wood, plastic, or metal, or be short, fat, thin, long, green, blue, heavy, light, and so forth. Second, one can analyze pens or pencils into a series of finer and finer levels of organization down to atoms, protons, and quarks. Must we perceive the parts before the whole? At what point do we stop?

Another general point about affordances is that it is a novel concept and consequently it is difficult to subsume under any traditional conceptual category within psychology. I have used the terms *function* and *use* to introduce the idea of affordances, but the concept of affordances actually is more basic and encompassing. Affordances are relational properties of the environment defined relative to the ways of animate life. At times we would be stretching the meaning of *use* in describing affordances, for instance, if we were to say environmental ambience affords locomotion, surface layout affords orientation, and people afford companionship. Generally, I would say that while uses or functions of the environment are affordances, not all affordances are uses.

Considering a typical case where available stimulus information co-specifies environmental affordances and the perceiver, it is clear now that reciprocal features of the optic array (invariants and variants) specify reciprocal features of the ecosystem, viz., affordances and the animate life form (1979a, p. 141). Affordances are potential ways in which an environmental feature relates to an animal, and animate ways of life are capabilities requiring affordances for their "actualization." Though both the animal and the environment are composed of a variety of substances, it is their dynamic interdependencies that tie them together into an ecosystem. Historically, mind and matter have been associated with subject and object. Aristotle believed such pairs could be separated in thought, though not in reality; dualists in modern times separate them both in thought and reality. Gibson contends that affordances and the animal are interdependently defined, and inconceivable separately. The environment had a potential existence (at least in some respects) prior to life; there was a ground and the compositional and structural features of substances and surfaces necessary for affordances existed also, for example, the ground possessed degrees of density, rigidity, and reflectance (1979a, pp. 128–129). On the other hand those relationships which support the affordance reality of the environment did not and could not exist until the animals also existed. Basically, it would be a "chicken or the egg question" to ask which came first, the affordance or the animate way of life.

Two noteworthy facts of the environment especially relevant to the topic of affordances are tools and other animals of the same species. *Homo sapiens* are not the only animals who make or use tools, but we appear to be far more advanced than any other species in this regard. Tools have affordances, but, interestingly, these affordances are constructed into the tools. Tools are made with affordances (uses) in mind (1979a, p. 41). Through the development of tools and complex instruments, the affordances of the environment are increased and refined to better suit human life. Other humans, possessing a wealth of social affordances, are also understood in terms of the concept of reciprocity. Human interaction is seen in terms of dynamic complementation involving behavioral loops (1979a, p. 42). The basic circular model of interdependency is applied in the social ecosystem as it was in understanding perceptual processes. Gibson, therefore, hopes to integrate the social-technological spheres into his general theoretical framework of dynamic reciprocity. Social psychology and the psychology of technology and instrumentation can both be assimilated within the theory of ecological reciprocity.

PERCEPTION AND PROPRIOCEPTION

Gibson's theory of perception can be divided into a theory of the environment, a theory of information, and a theory of the perceiver. The concept of ecological reciprocity is central to all three main theoretical topics. Gibson in the *Senses* began theoretically integrating perception and proprioception and he counted his treatment of their relationship as one of the most novel aspects of his overall theory. As has been explained in the earlier sections of this chapter, the idea of reciprocity is crucial to his treatment of the environment, ecological information, and ecological psychology. In his *Ecological Approach*, perception and proprioception are tied together via the principle of reciprocity. Many of the significant ways in which Gibson's treatment of perception differ from traditional views have been discussed extensively in previous chapters (e.g., direct vs. indirect, resonance vs. causal chain model of the nervous system, and passive senses vs. active perceptual systems). These topics are reviewed in his *Ecological Approach* (see also Gibson, 1976c), but what is most noteworthy is how ubiquitous and developed is the theme of perceptual-proprioceptual reciprocity. It is also noteworthy that when Gibson discusses perception and proprioception he emphasizes the concepts of space-time reciprocity and permanence-change reciprocity.

The classic subjective-objective dichotomy is transformed by Gibson into the ecological relationship of here-there. The two poles are connected in information via the gradients of texture density and optical flow with the nose and horizon fixing the two ends of the relation (1979a, p. 116). Gibson abandons the idea that the gradients, static, or dynamic, simply specify distance. There is no such thing as depth or distance per se; distance is perceived as a relationship between where the animal is and features across the terrain (1979a, p. 148). Because the subjective-objective pole is reciprocal, Gibson does not believe either type of experience ever exists in a pure form. Contrary to popular belief, children do not begin life with an egocentric awareness for proprioception and perception are reciprocal. The former cannot exist without the latter (1979a, p. 201). Also, Gibson believes all animals must possess self-awareness, for if they perceive the environment they also sense themselves (1979a, p. 205).

The transition from here-to-there or subjective-to-objective is not abrupt. Proprioceptually, the ego tends to be localized in the head (1979a, pp. 111–114), specifically in the "blind area" of occlusion due to the head (1979a, p. 208). Other parts of the body appear in the field of view, and though they are seen as objects, they cannot shrink in optical projection past a certain point. You cannot walk away from your hands, unless they were severed from you because they are part of you and seen as part of you. Gibson refers to the body as a subjective object (1979a, p. 121). Awareness is ecological, and the perceiver, as well as the surrounding environment, is within the perceiver's field of view. Gibson considers the "field of view" a fact of ecological optics. The field of view is distinguished from the visual field as described in *Perception of the Visual World*. The visual world was an experience; the field of view is that angular section of the environment within sight (1979a, p. 114). Gibson states that the "sweeping" and "wheeling" of the field of view over the optic array specifies head turns and tilts (1979a, p. 118). In this case body movement is not being specified by optical flow but rather by accretion-deletion within optical structure. Body movements break down into three types distinguished by the general type of information specifying each one: head movements relative to the body, limb movements relative to the body, and body movements relative to the environment (1979a, p. 126).

Gibson connects space and time in his treatment of perceptual-proprioceptual reciprocity. He state that what is "seen-now" and "seen-from-here" specify the self rather than the environment (1979a, p. 195). "Here-now" is the limiting case of restricted perspective. But, reciprocally there is an awareness of environmental persistence as well as environmental ambience "behind the head" (1979a, pp. 208–209), concurrent with the "here-now." Moving extends the "here-now," introducing optical flow and the uncovering of surfaces. Both the coexistence and concurrence of environmental features become more determinate, but the objective and invariant features revealed remain reciprocal to perspective structure and flow (1979a, pp. 122–123). Objectivity is extended the more the "here-now" is extended. Because there are only certain very basic features of the ecosystem that are absolutely invariant (within the defined limits of the ecosystem), e.g., the horizon-ground framework of orientation, all other environmental invariants have some relative limit. The "here-now" and the reality of the observer are implicated to some degree in any discussion of ecological invariants (1979a, p. 195).

In his review of research in the perception of surface layout, Gibson still sees optical texture and gradients as significant facts, but he states that observers never merely see a surface or the ground. The self is always seen in relation to the surface (1979a, pp. 151–157). Units of texture yield a scale for distance and size, but the ratios of units apply to both perception and proprioception. Here-to-there and there-to-there are both registered via the same scale of texture units and relative sizes; of special significance for behavior, the sizes of objects and surfaces involve the same scale as the body (1979a, p. 162). Gibson also wishes to emphasize perception of the layout's affordances, which, of course, further ties environment and perceiver together. In effect, Gibson further redefines the classic problem of depth perception: the question is now how the animal perceives the ecological (animal relative) layout. An "edge" is no longer simply a geometrical concept; rather, it is steep, deep, or rough relative to the size and behavioral capabilities of the animal. Recall that environmental ambience is tied to *what* is surrounded. "Space" is perceived relative to what the animal can do in it. Animals move, orient, and manipulate within ecological space. The empty space (and depth) of Newton and Berkeley completely disappears in Gibson's *Ecological Approach*. Though Gibson's ground theory of space in 1950 was a significant theoretical advance over the "air theory" and was a step toward an ecologically more valid conceptualization of space, Gibson further developed his views on the spatial environment over the next 30 years (see also Gibson, 1975a).

The topic of occlusion continues to occupy a position of importance in Gibson's treatment of layout perception (1979a, pp. 76–86, 189–202). Occlusion is an ecological fact of a cluttered environment with localized observers; reversible occlusion, due to reversible locomotive and looking behavior, provides an explanation for the spatial connectivity of the environment (see also Gibson, 1978b). Gibson criticizes both S-R and mental map theories of orientation and oriented locomotion; vistas (the environmental reciprocal to field of view) are spatially connected via reversible occlusions. Animals perceive environmental connectivity rather than associating responses to stimuli or constructing internal maps of the terrain (1979a, pp. 198–200). Though there exist relative invariants for a layout that underlie all possible perspectives and reversible occlusions, it is important to note that these invariants are defined reciprocal to the variants of stationary and moving observation. The possibility of public or objective knowledge depends on discriminating the invariants from variants, but these are ecological invariants, existing within the ecosystem of an ambient layout and moving animals. Gibson states that when an observer moves, it is the whole rather than perspectives that are noticed (1979a, p. 197), yet this whole is not a Platonic whole. It is the whole reciprocal to the observer related perspectives. In essence, Gibson's visual framework became an ecological framework with an exploratory subject.

The principle of ecological reciprocity as it applies to layout perception is also implicit in the concept of the horizon. The horizon divides the sphere of observation—it is the vanishing limit and the ecological interface between the ground below and the sky above. All terrestrial features are nested within the membrane of the horizon. Objects in the terrestrial environment will transverse the horizon, projecting above it, but the structures are connected (or continuous) with features under the horizon; the horizon serves as the framework for relative size, direction, distance, and slant (1979a, pp. 163–166). The horizon demarcates the extent of terrestrial locations and movements. The horizon of the earth exists only for observation relatively close to the earth's surface. As an observer moves outward into space, the earth's surface continues to have a surrounding edge, yet the earth becomes an object in space and its edge no longer orients the observer to up and down. The horizon exists for observers whose heads are not too far above the ground relative to the extent of the ground. Past that point the horizon becomes the occluding edge of an object. The horizon is an ecological reality.

Gibson sees considerable promise in understanding various perceptual phenomena by means of the framework of the horizon. Besides texture unit ratios, the horizon provides an ecological scale for relative size (height). In the 1950s Gibson attempted to explain slant perception in terms of optical slant, but in his *Ecological Approach,* geographical slant is seen as a nesting of surface slants relative to the horizon. In addition he suggests that the animal's body orientation is seen within this framework (1979a, pp. 164–166). The horizon also provides a good example of the global reality of optical information; ecological information exists as a nesting of finer structures within more global structures.

True to form, temporal considerations are integrated into Gibson's treatment of the perception of occlusion, the spatial framework, and environmental objects. Optical accretion and deletion and the general phenomena of reversible occlusion are events in the broadest sense, being regularities of certain types of change. Reversible occlusion ties together the spatial principal of ecological coexistence with the temporal principal of ecological concurrence. Reversible occlusion takes time, and Gibson remarks that the perception of persistence of surfaces being hidden and uncovered indicates perception extends into the future and into the past (1979a, p. 190).

In reviewing the research and theory on the kinetic depth effect (Johansson, 1950; Wallach & O'Connel, 1953), Gibson remarks that such studies inspired his research on transformation of projected shadows and the perception of shape (Gibson, 1957a). Such research by Gibson eventually led him to the idea of "formless invariants" as information for the perception of objects (1979a, pp. 173–178). In retrospect, Gibson sees his 1950s research as still assuming that object perception could be explained through a psychophysics of form perception. Yet even in his *Perception of the Visual World* (1950a), the concept of lawful transformations of form (derived from D'Arcy Thompson plus Boring's dimensions of consciousness) was leading Gibson away from the traditional "fixation" on static form. In his *Ecological Approach,* it is invariants (formless) of optical change that specify an object's integrity, its shape, and its rigidity.

Even in reconsidering the problems of the perception of surface texture, brightness, and color, time enters in vis-à-vis the daily cyclic pattern of illumination (1979a, pp. 86–91). Optical texture varies throughout the day as the direction of illumination changes. Gibson proposes that it is invariant ratios of light intensity and spectral composition that serve as information for surface texture and pigmentation. Once again, it is the spatial-temporal structure of the optic array that is lawfully related to the environment. Gibson, in his earlier treatments of surface texture and pigmentation (1950a, 1966a), had emphasized only the spatial structure. In his *Ecological Approach* the diurnal illumination cycle and its systematic effects are integrated with the spatial structure of the array. This development in theory is another example of how time played an increasingly important role in Gibson's ecological thinking.

Any theoretical position possesses a conceptual integrity whatever the ontology, implicit or explicit; the concepts fit together and support each other through related definitions and common themes or principles. Even if we take as examples the dualistic and atomistic approaches inherited from Plato, Newton, and British empiricism, though the ontologies portray a world of distinct, absolute entities, the primary concepts (e.g., mind, matter, objects, and space) used to describe this segregated universe are themselves interrelated. Mind-matter dualism, and the related dichotomies of subject–object and perceiver-world are not, strictly speaking, conceptual dualisms. Consequently, traditional treatments of matter, objects of knowledge, and the world naturally, if not logically, fit with traditional approaches to the mind and knowing subject. Questions of being and questions of knowledge within a general philosophical or scientific system are related together through the conceptual geography of the system. It is quite understandable that Gibson, in reformulating the theory of the environment, should have also reformulated the theory of the perceiver; for example, if the environment already possesses a spatial-temporal order, the function of perceiving cannot be to construct order. Also, there are certain common themes to be found between Gibson's theory of the environment and his treatment of the perceiver. The concepts of nesting, dynamic order, and reciprocity are found in Gibson's treatment of the perceiver as well as in his treatment of environment. The inevitable relationship between ontologies and epistemologies is supported by the conceptual integrity of a general theoretical position, and one reason that scientific-philosophical positions, such as outlined in the previous chapter, fall into certain common groups of concepts and (usually) not others is the compatibility of certain ideas with each other.

Gibson's treatment of the perceiver differed significantly from traditional psychological approaches in many respects. Processes are not linear chains; elements are not contextually independent; time is not a disjointed series of immediately vanishing present instants; there are no ultimate natural units; mind and body, and observer and world are not absolutely distinct; space does not have precedence over time; and knowledge and life are not processes intrinsic to the animal-observer. Gibson views psychological and ecological processes as nested loops; the spatial structure is a multigrained nesting of mutually supportive units; time has both extent and order and is perceived just as directly as space; and the animal-observer and the physical environment are reciprocals within an integrated ecosystem.

Perception does not involve a linear transmission of images or input from body to brain (1979a, p. 61). Separating body from mind leads to the idea that the body must transmit something to the mind. Treating the body as a concatenated set of physical elements entails that the mind must build an organized perception, but according to Gibson, the "mind" is not spatially localized and segregated in the brain. It is the animal who perceives, and its body is not a set of elements, but a dynamic functional system. The perceptual systems are nested together in the body, and perception as a psychosomatic activity is a hierarchy of adjustments to the environment (1979a, pp. 218, 239). Such adjustments are circular rather than linear reactions. The modern metaphor of "input processing" implies that physical input is somehow in need of being related to the psychological reality of the animal. Gibson rejects this approach as just another example of the traditional belief that the mind must operate upon the meaningless deliverances of the physical senses (1979a, p. 251). More generally, the input processing model is an example of mind-matter dualism, where matter must somehow be related to mind. But, as Gibson stressed, information cospecifies and relates the perceiver and the environment.

Traditionally, the body is treated as a passive reactive object and the senses as channels that receive and transmit. Newtonian matter simply reacts. Perceptual systems are active exploratory mechanisms—mind-matter dualism reserved activity for the mind (1979a, pp. 245–246). Classical psychophysics grew out of a similar idea, viz., treating experience and behavior as reactive to stimulation. The world is treated as an independent variable that determines reactions in the body. According to Gibson, vision is ambient and ambulatory (1979a, p. 2); thus the animal is active in perception.

In the previous chapter, a basic distinction was drawn between the Platonic, Newtonian heritage and the dynamic wholism of Aristotle, Leibnitz, and Gibson. Further, toward the end of the chapter, a brief contrast was developed between Gibsonian perceptual theory and the information processing approach. The dynamic systems revolution in contemporary science and philosophy, in which Gibson's ecological psychology has emerged, reflects the philosophical heritage of dynamic wholism. As Gibson argued, the information processing approach appears to reflect the heritage of traditional perceptual theory, a heritage combining the dualism of Plato and the reductionism of Newton.

Perception is an accomplishment, but it should not be seen as a series of discrete acts with beginnings and endings. Perception is continuous (1979a, pp. 239, 253). Limiting perception to an immediate present, separate from the past and the future, assumes that perception is exclusively spatial, but there is a temporal dimension to perception as well. The invariants and variants of structured energy can only be detected over time, and though there are episodes and events in the environment as well as shifts in attention, both environmental and perceptual activities are nested temporally. Exploration may continue revealing finer details and novel perspectives; the temporal order of perception cannot be naturally divided into non-overlapping separate experiences. If perception is not limited to the immediate present, what are the functions of thought, expectation, and memory, the cornerstones of traditional rationalistic and empiricist explanations of perception?

KNOWLEDGE, PERCEPTION, AND BEHAVIOR

In his *Ecological Approach*, Gibson develops a general theoretical framework that integrates many areas of psychology. Perception is connected to behavior; his ecological concept provides an environmental context in which all psychological facts are to be understood; his theory of affordances relates animate ways of life to the environment; and toward the end of his book, Gibson explores the relationship between perception, reformulated ecologically, and higher forms of cognition and knowledge (1979a, pp. 253–291). The overarching theme is animal-environment reciprocity coupled with a rejection of dualistic psychology.

Perception and behavior are reciprocal. Perception serves behavior, for what is perceived are facts of the environment relevant to ways of life. Behavior, in turn, is controlled by perception for orientation, posture, and action stay attuned to the perceived facts of the environment (1979a, p. 223). Affordances provide the "connection" between perception and behavior, for it is affordances which are perceived and it is affordances that are used and adjusted to vis-à-vis behavior. Gibson's concept of affordances was developed to provide a description of the environment relevant to ways of life. Though behavior may be "divided" into acts, behavior, in the most general sense including postural orientation, is continuous and nested with temporally overlapping "units" (1979a, p. 12). Locomotion and manipulation are neither reflexes (S-R behaviorism) nor commands initiated in the brain (mentalism); the relationship between perception and behavior is not cause-to-effect. Both processes are continuous and each is continuously being adjusted to the other; again the best model is circular rather than linear. Gibson states that behavior is controlled by information in the animal-environment system. It is not ignited specifically in the brain anymore than is perception; both are ecological events (1979a, pp. 225, 232–233).

When Gibson says behavior is controlled by ecological information he means that invariants and variants of the stimulus array, which specify stable and changing relationships of the self and the world, are used by the animal to guide its behavior (1979a, pp. 232–236). It would be useless to simply perceive either the environment or the self separately; the perceptual-proprioceptual reciprocity is integral to behavior control. Behavior, therefore, is the reciprocal to perception-proprioception, and the totality of animate ways of life are reciprocal to the affordances of the environment. Turvey, Shaw, and Kugler have been working on an ecological theory of behavior ("effectivities") that would complement the theory of affordances (Kugler, Kelso, & Turvey, 1980; Shaw & Turvey, 1981; Shaw, Turvey, & Mace, 1981; Turvey, 1977; Turvey, Shaw, & Mace, 1978). A second relevant line of development is the work of David Lee (1974, 1976) and Rik Warren (1976) on visual proprioception.

Gibson's general theory of knowledge follows from his ecological realism and wholistic empiricism. Gibson does not wish to introduce either an epistemological or ontological separation between perception and "higher" forms of knowledge. All forms of knowledge must pertain to the world specified through information; instruments may extend sensitivity to a wider range of features of the world not presently within view, but knowledge is obtained from the empirical world and pertains to this same empirical world. This empirical world is multileveled or multinested, such that it cannot be reduced to a single level of description, as attempted in analytic empiricism or phenomenology. Perception, however, is viewed as continuous with higher forms of cognition. Cognition is the process of finding both order and detail in this multi-nested reality. Gibson wishes to avoid a mind-body split, therefore he avoids relegating any type of cognition to a "detached" mind. Perception is functionally and ontologically continuous with mnemonic, linguistic, imaginative, and abstractive processes (1979a, pp. 253–263).

Since the time of Plato, abstraction has traditionally been limited to thought, whereas perception provided bare individuals or unrelated particulars. Thought pertained to timeless universals; perception was of fleeting particulars. This psychological dualism reflects Parmenides distinction between the eternal one and the temporal many. Further, whereas memory and expectation extend into the past and the future, perception was limited to the immediate present. In general, it was higher cognitive functions that apprehended relationships, whether they be temporal relations, spatial order, or relationships of identity and similarity.

First I would note that the dualistic distinction is itself an abstraction of the highest order, and the concept of particulars is a creation of philosophical thought. The concept of particulars, as well as the concept of the present, derive their significance by distinguishing them from abstraction and the past-future. Could one conceivably experience unrelated particulars in a timeless present?

Gibson rejects the psychological dualism of thought and perception. Perception is not limited to a perpetually vanishing series of instants. Perception has temporal extension, necessarily both into the past and into the future, for perception involves temporal order—constancy and change nested over time. In fact, nested constancy and change is ecological time. Perception involves the detection of temporal regularities, for example, rhythms of nature and patterns of growth and decay. As Aristotle believed, through perception we discover laws. In discussing temporal order, Gibson will talk in terms of event structure, rather than empty abstractions. We should also note that the temporal order or event structure of the ecosystem exists at a higher level of organization than time spans as conceptualized in sub-atomic physics or neuronal-receptor physiology.

Ironically, though perception was limited by Plato to the realm of time, time disappears in this type of theory, being replaced by the timeless edge of the present. The present disappears without the past-future, and without an awareness of persistence, awareness of change disappears.

As the Gestalt psychologists realized, without relationships there are no units or individuals. Gibson believes we can perceive relationships as well as individuals. A perceiver can see that two things are identical or similar, as well as seeing that they are different. The principle of reciprocity ties together the dualism of Plato and Parmenides, and Gibson, through ecological optics (and acoustics, etc.) demonstrates how the various ecological realities are reciprocally related in stimulus structure and information.

If we ask what is thought or memory or conceptualization, I suggest that we keep in mind that such psychological abilities are reciprocally tied to perception and behavior. The higher cognitive functions will guide perception and behavior, but equally perception and behavior will guide thought. Further, the objects of thought and memory should not be separated from the objects of perception, as in Plato's eternal realm of ideas. Theory and fact are reciprocals and every advance in thought is coupled with an advance in observational capabilities and instruments.

Cognition is not two separate types of awareness, for the same reciprocal principles that apply to perception, apply to the mnemonic, linguistic, graphic, and technological activities of the scientist, artist, and philosopher. For Gibson, language provides a means for making explicit and communicable tacit perceptual knowledge, as well as providing a relatively standardized and systematic repertoire of symbols, rules, and meanings. Language enhances public perception and organized social action. One should not, though, model perception on language, as Berkeley and information processing psychologists have, for this is putting the cart before the horse. Pictures and other graphic forms are depictions used to record and convey observations (Gibson, 1954d, 1960e, 1971b, 1977c, 1978a, 1980). Again, it would be a mistake to model perception on pictures and images, as retinal image-picture perspective theorists have, for art and representation is an extension and elaboration of perception and not the other way around. Imagination and fantasy are also extensions of perception, though they are more subjective and consequently, in principle, distinguishable from perception through perceptual tests. Again we can find a tradition which attempted to model perception on a psychological process that actually requires perception. For many constructivist theorists, perception was built up out of sensation and imagination. In all cases of cognition Gibson follows an Aristotelian realist epistemology. Knowledge begins with perception-proprioception and all knowledge pertains to the same world as first apprehended through our senses (1979a, pp. 256–258, 267–291).

EPILOGUE

What we call the beginning is
Often the end
And to make an end is to make a
Beginning.

—T. S. Eliot

My first contact with perceptual theory was Bishop Berkeley's idealistic philosophy. I found Berkeley extremely convincing, though I wouldn't say he destroyed my belief in realism. I had never thought about perception or the reality of perceptual objects. I was not a realist before I read Berkeley—I wasn't anything. Berkeley had a powerful impact on me. He raised a question never considered. The world of perception suddenly appeared to me, yet it appeared in a strange and disquieting way. I soon found that much of modern perceptual psychology pointed in the same direction as Berkeley's philosophy. When I first read Plato and Descartes I had similar experiences: A strange sense of new found clarity and revelation, yet a suspicion that something wasn't right.

When I first began to read Gibson, I did not experience a sudden and penetrating "Gestalt switch," but at some point (now lost to my memory) I started to believe that Gibson was on to something important and challenging to traditional psychology. The road to understanding Gibson has been long, though I must say perpetually fascinating. I began thinking about perception in idealistic and indirect realist terms, but over the years I have come to appreciate and understand Gibson's direct realism. Though direct realism is the presumed philosophy of perception of the common person, at best it is a totally intuitive and tacit philosophy. My first thoughts and history's first thoughts on perception are the opposite.

My investigation into Gibson eventually led me back to the ancient Greeks and the concepts of *eidola*, emanation, simulation, and the homunculus. I researched my way through the Cornell University History of Science Library studying Medieval and Renaissance thought and encountering Alhazen, Pecham, da Vinci, and others. It was at Cornell that I first saw the strong connections between Alhazen's elementaristic optics and psychology and Helmholtz and nineteenth century empiricism. Perhaps most significantly, I was able to study translations and commentaries on Kepler and see how his ideas fit with the mind-matter dualism of the Scientific Revolution and Descartes' mind-body dualistic psychology.

These early scientific and philosophical approaches to perception provided the context and support in which Berkeley's ideas germinated. Empiricist psychology with its emphasis on elements, association, and mediation fitted well within the epistemology and ontology of the Scientific Revolution. As I have tried to show, 19th century perceptual physiology (specific energies, projection, and the local sign hypothesis) supported elementaristic structuralist psychology and the sensation perception distinction. Kepler, Locke, Berkeley, Müller, Helmholtz, Lötze, and others were the architects of this complex theoretical, experimental paradigm. This approach was the traditional psychology of perception I learned at Minnesota reading Boring's *History of Experimental Psychology* (1950).

History shows many interesting twists and turns, and it is often happenstance that provides an essential ingredient to its development. Though Gibson was breaking new ground in perception through his adaptation studies, it was his Air Force experiences away from academia and the logical progression of ideas that instigated his psychophysical theory of perception. Seeds had been planted in Gibson's mind, notably from Troland, Carr, Boring, and Koffka, but one can never totally explain originality and creative insight or else it would not truly possess novelty. Something out of the ordinary must occur, something unexpected, and then the unusual must be seized upon and perceived as an opportunity for growth rather than being a nuisance. Gibson showed this openness to change in his adaptation studies and their unexpected results.

It is an interesting fact that Kepler, Newton, and Descartes, while bound to the ground, peered upward into space and modeled terrestrial depth perception on astronomy. Gibson, leaving the ground and flying through the air above, discovered the significance of the ground for perception.

Though Gibson's theory of higher-order stimulation was very original, as well as his perceptual psychophysics running counter to empiricist, nativist, and Gestalt explanations of perception, Gibson retained in the 1950s many traditional concepts. He supported phenomenology, the causal chain model, and the retinal image. Gibson would eventually discard these traditional ideas. On the other hand, there were certain noteworthy traditional ideas that Gibson rejected in his psychophysics. In particular, he was especially critical of the simulative assumption and the reductionistic theory of physical reality.

One of the main forces behind Gibson's eventual abandonment of a psychophysics of perception was his functionalism, though it was his functionalism, in part, that initially motivated his psychophysics. How can perception be veridical? Gibson's psychophysical answer involved the highly significant idea that wholistic relationships in stimulation, both temporal (successive) and spatial (adjacent) were as real and psychologically significant as point stimuli. Gradients and the ordinal retinal image could explain distance, arrangement, motion, persistence, and boundlessness in the visual world.

As I mentioned, Gibson's functionalism was one of the primary factors that transformed his psychophysics into an ecological psychology. In the *Senses,* Gibson develops the concept of active, functionally integrated perceptual systems, proposing a psychology extremely reminiscent of Dewey and Aristotle. Perception involves exploratory activity, that scans, orients, and selects, thus making effective stimulation contingent upon psychological processes. It is also in the *Senses* that the concept of ecological reciprocity begins to emerge. Perceiver and environment are functionally tied together. A description of the environment replaces phenomenology and affordances appear in Gibson's psychology.

My first contact with Gibson was the *Senses,* which I read as an undergraduate. I read the *Visual World* later as a graduate student. If I recall correctly, some fellow graduate students bought me the *Visual World* as a birthday gift. In retrospect, reading the *Visual World* turned me into an historian of Gibson, for I read it looking for antecedents of ideas in the *Senses.* Though the *Senses* introduced many new ideas not found in the *Visual World,* one line of thought continued and further elaborated in the *Senses* was Gibson's concept of higher-order stimulation. In the 1960s Gibson spoke of stimulus information, and the retinal image was dropped in favor of the optic array. The retinal image caused perceptions; the optic array specified the environment and the perceiver. Stimulus information was both exterospecific and propriospecific. Gibson reemphasized his rejection of the simulative assumption with the concept of information. Information is specification, not simulation. The reciprocal concepts of invariants and transformations come to the forefront in Gibson's description of ambient structured energy, whether it be in the optic array or the acoustic array.

My interest in Gibson could be divided into two periods. The first period culminated in my years of teaching Gibsonian perceptual psychology at Indiana University N.W. Every academic year, besides teaching Gibson, I also taught a history of psychology course. It was in the history course that I began to explicate and develop a comparative analysis of Platonic and Aristotelian psychologies and philosophies. Then, there was a break of approximately three years. When I came back to academia and psychology, Gibson, Plato, and Aristotle had become strongly connected together in my mind. Thus began my second period of interest in Gibson.

Philosophy had had as one of its most fundamental problems how knowledge is possible. There have been skeptics who have rejected the possibility of true knowledge and there have been dogmatists who believed they had access to an indubitable source of certainty and truth. Yet knowledge could be taken as a puzzle, as something to be understood. Einstein stated that knowledge was a puzzle of the highest order, the most baffling feature of the universe. Science, of course, set out to understand and know nature, assuming that a method had been discovered to gain knowledge about the world. What this method is, how it works, and why it works has been the subject of continuous controversy since Copernicus and Galileo laid the foundations of the scientific enterprise. Plato believed that knowledge about nature was impossible. Aristotle believed it was possible and set out to explain and understand the conditions of knowledge. I like the statement by Einstein (quoted at the beginning of this book) because he brings nature itself—the object of knowledge—into the epistemological puzzle. Knowledge can not simply be understood by asking what our minds are like, such that we can know. What is nature like, such that it can be known? Humanity has apparently made great progress in understanding nature, both prior to science and since its rise. The more we study and observe the world, the more we know. How is this possible?

Perception enters into the epistemological puzzle when we try to develop a scientific explanation of it. Perception is integral to scientific knowledge, as well as other forms of knowledge. Paradoxically, explanations invariably take the form of separating perceptual awareness from the world of nature, as well as the sphere of truth, thus throwing the whole concept of knowledge about nature into question. Traditional scientific explanations of perception lead to the conclusion that scientific knowledge is impossible and the world is incomprehensible. We are supposedly caught in an inner world of mental states. Berkeley noted the inherent problems in the ontological dualism of Descartes, Locke, and Newton and opted for idealism.

Gibson comes into the picture at this point: Indirect and dualistic theories of perception lead to paradox and inherent contradiction, whereas idealism leads to solipsism. Materialism, the antithesis of idealism, fares no better, for if we recall Democritus' views, we end up trapped not in our minds, but in our brains viewing copies of the world. The beginnings of a resolution to the problem of knowledge, I believe, can be found in Aristotle. What Aristotle contributed was a way of relating body and mind without conflating the two or separating them ontologically. Secondly, he rejected Plato's separation of eternal universals and transforming particulars, instead proposing an ontological inseparability of form and matter and order and temporal flow. Finally, he saw a functional connection between the mind and the world and a complimentary connection of the world to the mind, where the world of nature is seen as intelligible, with the potential to be known. I came to the conclusion that Aristotle and Gibson bore a striking resemblance, and further, I concluded that the common adversary was Platonic dualism. Although Gibson's explicit focus of criticism was modern indirect, dualistic theories of perception, the foundations of such theories is Plato. Gibson went further than Aristotle, but in fundamental approach there is considerable agreement. Gibson offers a scientific solution to how perceptual knowledge (and consequently all natural knowledge) is possible by demonstrating that there is a comprehensibility and meaningfulness to nature that can be related to the capacities and ways of life of the knower.

How is the Scientific Revolution reflective of Plato? I have attempted to answer this question in considerable depth throughout earlier chapters. To summarize, the Scientific Revolution inherited both the ontological dualism of mind and matter and the epistemological-psychological dualism of particulars and universals-abstractions. Not unexpectedly, the conclusion of this approach was similar to Plato: Perceptual knowledge is impossible. I wish to reemphasize that Plato's dualism has often been attacked and rejected in monistic ontologies, but both materialism and idealism, as well as extreme elementarism and wholism, actually accepted whichever half of Plato's dualism the monist thought was sufficient to explain everything. But how can we have matter without form, or vice versa? The answer is that we are not dealing with an incomprehensible dualism, but a reciprocity.

Where Gibson especially takes tradition to task is in trying to understand what the world of nature is like, such that it can be known. This constitutes a direct attack upon the natural reality of comprehensibility. We can state that ecological optics, the theory of ecological information, his ecological description of the environment, and the concept of affordances are all pieces to Gibson's answer. Specifically regarding the environment, in his *Ecological Approach,* we find extended treatments of events, occlusion, ecological substances, the medium, the opaque geometry of surface layout, the horizon, ecological ambience, and affordances. If Gibson does not seem to be doing psychology when he discusses the environment, it is because we think dualistically. The key to understanding how we can know is not just a description of the knower, but equally a description of the known, for knowledge involves a reciprocity of knower and known.

Though in the early 1970s I believed that what fundamentally separated Gibson's approach from tradition could be captured in the contrast between ecological reciprocity and mind-matter dualism, I did not fully appreciate the significance and ramifications of this contrast. In the last ten years, I have explored the ramifications, and thought a great deal about the concept of reciprocity. I believe Gibson makes even more sense to me now. Many of the basic themes in Gibson's approach can be expressed in terms of the principle of reciprocity. In Table 1 is a tentative list of reciprocal concepts in Gibson's ecological psychology.

TABLE 2
Gibsonian Reciprocities

Animal	Environment
Perceiver/Behaver	Environment
Ways of life	Affordances
Perception/Proprioception	Behavior
Proprioception	Perception
Propriospecific information	Exterospecific information
Perceptual activity	Effective stimulation
Change	Persistence
Time	Space
Stimulus Transforma'ion	Stimulus invariant
Parts/Elements	Wholes/Systems
Perceptual differentiation	Perceptual constancy
Ambulatory perception/Behavior	Environmental Ambience
Subjective	Objective

I am sure this list can be extended. There are other important ideas in Gibson that, given some additional thinking and exploration, could probably be expressed as reciprocities. Some that come to mind are coexistent and concurrent, substances and events, deletion (going out of view) and accretion (coming into view), going out of existence and coming into existence, reversible and irreversible events, and surfaces and the horizon vis-à-vis substance-medium and ground-sky.

Since I became fascinated with the concept of reciprocity, I have considered other topics and issues that may be more understandable if interpreted and explored in terms of this idea. I have mentioned within the book that ontology (existence) and epistemology (knowledge) are reciprocals, as well as theory and fact. Shaw and Turvey's (1981) concept of coalitions, an extension of Gibson's thinking, can be conceptualized as a reciprocity. Fraser, the philospher of time, presents a theory of temporal evolution founded upon the idea that order and chaos are reciprocals (1978). Prigogine talks about being and becoming, reversible and irreversible processes, and order and chaos as reciprocities (1980, 1984). The territory ahead seems to be exploding with possibilities. Evolution, conceptualized as an ecological reciprocal process between life and the environment, could replace the Darwinian theory of adaptation—more precisely it may encompass it. All things considered, we have a very fruitful concept emerging in 20th century science and philosophy.

For me, this journey began with Gibson, for he was the person who initially explored and developed the idea of reciprocity before my eyes. He made direct realism comprehensible in terms of this idea. He brought me back to my intuitive starting point, though as a naïve realist, I did not consider or try to explain perception. What Gibson gave to me and to psychology, was a rich new language and a whole new territory to be explored. Gibson's ecological psychology is full of light and color and real and lasting clarity. I studied Plato, Descartes, and Berkeley before Gibson and understood traditional perceptual psychology before I understood ecological optics, affordances, and animal-environment reciprocity. Gibson illuminated the layout and extended the horizon. Gibson helped me to see.

REFERENCES

Abbott, T. K. *Sight and touch: An attempt to disprove the received (or Berkeleian) theory of vision.* London: Longman, Roberts, & Green, 1864.

Abbott, T. K. Bishop Berkeley and Professor Fraser. *Hermathena,* 1879, *3,* 1–39.

Agassi, J. Towards an historiography of science. *History and theory: Studies in the philosophy of history.* Beiheft: Gravenhage, Mouton, 1963, 1–117.

Agassi, J. The nature of scientific problems and their roots in metaphysics. In M. Bunge, (Ed.), *The critical approach to science and philosophy.* London: Collier-MacMillan, Ltd., 1964.

Agassi, J. Sensationalism. *Mind.* 1966, *LXXV.*

Agassi, J. *Science in flux. Boston studies in the philosophy of science,* Vol. XXXVIII. Dordrecht-Holland: D. Reidel, 1975.

Alberti, L. B. *De pictura.* 1435. In M. Pollionis *De architectura libri decem.* Vitruvii: Amsterdam, 1649.

Alhazen (Ibn al-Haitham). *Opticae thesaures.* ca. 1000, In F. Risnero (Ed.), 1572.

Alkindi *De aspectibus.* ca. 850 AD. Leipzig, 1912.

Allport, F. *Theories of perception and the concept of structure.* New York: Wiley, 1955.

Angell, J. *Psychology, an introductory study of the structure and function of human consciousness.* New York: Holt, 1904.

Angell, J. The province of functional psychology. *Psychological Review,* 1907, *14,* 61–91.

St. Thomas Aquinas *Summa theologica.* ca. 1270. In A. Pegis (Ed.), *Introduction to Saint Thomas Aquinas.* New York: Modern Library, 1948.

Armstrong, D. Discussion: Berkeley's new theory of vision. *Journal of the History of Ideas,* 1956, *17,* No. 1, 127–129.

Armstrong, D. *Berkeley's theory of vision.* London: Cambridge University Press, 1960.

Armstrong, D. *Perception and the physical world.* London: Routledge & Kegan Paul, 1961.

Asch, S. E. & Witkin, H. A. Studies in space orientation. I. Perception of the upright with displaced visual fields. *Journal of Experimental Psychology,* 1948, *38,* 325–337. (a)

Asch, S. E. & Witkin, H. A. Studies in space orientation. II. Perception and the upright with displaced visual fields and with body tilted. *Journal of Experimental Psychology,* 1948, *38,* 455–477. (b)

Asch, S. E. & Witkin, H. A. Studies in space orientation: Further experiments on the perception of the upright with displaced visual fields. *Journal of Experimental Psychology,* 1948, *38,* 603–614. (c)

Aune, B. *Knowledge, mind and nature.* New York: Random House, 1967.

Austin, J. L. *Sense and sensibilia.* London: Oxford University Press, 1962.

Avicenna. *Avicenna's psychology: An English translation of the Kitab al-Najat.* London, 1952.

Ayer, A. J. *Foundations of empirical knowledge.* London: MacMillan, 1940.

Ayer, A. J. *The problem of knowledge.* London: Penguin Books, 1956.

Bacon, R. The "Opus Majus" of Roger Bacon. 1263. J. H. Bridges (Ed.). London, 1900.

Bailey, S. *Review of Berkeley's theory of vision: Designed to show the unsoundness of that celebrated speculation.* London: Ridgeway, 1842.

Bailey, S. *Letter to a philosopher in reply to some recent attempts to vindicate Berkeley's theory of vision.* London: Ridgeway, 1843.

Bain, A. *The Senses and the intellect.* London: Longmans, Green, 1868.

Bain, A. *Mental and moral science.* London: Longmans, Green, 1872.

Bain, A. *Mind and Body.* New York: Appleton, 1873.

Bartley, W. W., III. Rationality versus the theory of rationality. In M. Bunge (Ed.), *The critical approach to science and philosophy.* London: Collier-MacMillan, 1964.

Beare, J. I. *Greek theories of elementary cognition from Almaceon to Aristotle.* Oxford, 1906.

Beck, J. *Surface color perception.* Ithaca, NY: Cornell University Press, 1972.

Berkeley, G. *Philosophical commentaries.* 1707–1708. In A. A. Luce & T. E. Jessop (Eds.), *The works of George Berkeley* (Vol. I). London: Thomas Nelson, 1964.

Berkeley, G. *An essay towards a new theory of vision.* 1709. In A. A. Luce & T. E. Jessop (Eds.), *The works of George Berkeley* (Vol. I). London: Thomas Nelson, 1964.

Berkeley, G. *Principles of human knowledge.* 1710. In A. A. Luce & T. E. Jessop (Eds.), *The works of George Berkeley* (Vol. II). London: Thomas Nelson, 1964.

Berkeley, G. *Three dialogues of Hylas and Philonous.* 1713. In A. A. Luce & T. E. Jessop (Eds.), *The works of George Berkeley* (Vol. II). London: Thomas Nelson, 1964.

Berkeley, G. *Alciphron, or the minute philosopher.* 1732. In A. A. Luce & T. E. Jessop (Eds.), *The works of George Berkeley* (Vol. III). London: Thomas Nelson, 1964.

Berkeley, G. *The theory of vision or visual language, vindicated and explained.* 1733. In A. A. Luce & T. E. Jessop (Eds.), *The works of George Berkeley* (Vol. I). London: Thomas Nelson, 1964.

Boring, E. G. *The physical dimensions of consciousness.* 1933. New York: Dover, 1963.

Boring, E. G. *Sensation and perception in the history of experimental psychology.* New York: Appleton-Century-Crofts, 1942.

Boring, E. G. *A history of experimental psychology* (2nd ed.). New York: Appleton-Century-Crofts, 1950.

Boring, E. G. Review of J. J. Gibson's The perception of the visual world. *Psychological Bulletin,* 1951, *48,* 360–363.

Boring, E. G. Visual perception as invariance. *Psychological Review,* 1952, *59,* 141–148. (a)

Boring, E. G. The Gibsonian visual field. *Psychological Review,* 1952, *59,* 246–247. (b)

Boring, E. G. Review of J. J. Gibson's The senses considered as perceptual systems. *American Journal of Psychology,* 1967, *80,* 150–154.

Boring, E. G., & Harper, R. S. Cues. *American Journal of Psychology,* 1948, *101,* 112–123.

Boyle, R. The origin of forms and qualities. 1666. In P. Shaw (Ed.), *The philosophical works of the honourable Robert Boyle . . .,* 1, 2nd ed. London, 1738.

Boynton, R. The visual system: Environmental information. In E. C. Carterrette & M. P. Friedman (Eds.), *Handbook of perception* (Vol. 1). New York: Academic Press, 1974.

Brentano, F. *Psychologie vom empirischen standpunkte.* Leipzig: Meiner, 1874.

Brett, G. S. *Brett's history of psychology.* R. S. Peters (Ed.). Cambridge: MIT Press, 1962.

Brown, T. *Lectures on the philosophy of human mind.* 1820. Hallowell: Glazier, Masters, & Co., 1834.

Brunswik, E. Organismic achievement and environmental probability. *Psychological Review,* 1943, *50,* 255–272.

Brunswik, E. Distal focusing of perception: size constancy in a representative sample of situations. *Psychological Monographs,* No. 254, 1944.

Brunswik, E. *The conceptual framework of psychology.* Chicago: University of Chicago Press, 1952.

Brunswik, E. Representative design and probabilistic theory in a functional psychology. *Psychological Review,* 1955, *62,* 193–217. (a)

Brunswik, E. In defense of probabilistic functionalism. *Psychological Review,* 1955, *62,* 236–242. (b)

Brunswik, E. *Perception and the representative design of psychological experiments.* Berkeley, CA: University of California Press, 1956.

Brunswik, E., & Tolman, E. The organism and the causal texture of the environment. *Psychological Review,* 1935, *42,* 43–77.

Capra, F. *The Tao of physics.* Berkeley: Shambhala, 1975.

Capra, F. *The turning point*. New York: Simon & Schuster, 1982.

Carnap, R. Testability and meaning. *Philosophy of Science, 1936, 3*.

Carr, H. A. *An introduction to space perception*. New York: Hafner, 1935.

Cassirer, E. The concept of group and the history of perception. *Philosophy and phenomenological research, 1944, 5, 1–35*.

Condillac, E. *Essai sur l'origine des connoissances humanies*. 1746. In *Oeuvres Philosophiques de Condillac*. Paris: Presses Universitaires, 1947.

Condillac, E. *Traite des sensations*. 1754. In G. LeRoy (Ed.), *Oeuvres Philosophiques de Condillac*. Paris: Presses Universitaires, 1947.

Costall, A. On how so much information controls so much behavior: James Gibson's theory of direct perception. In G. Butterworth (Ed.), *Infancy and epistemology*. Brighton, England: Harvester Press, 1981.

Courant, R., & Robbins H. *What is mathematics?* New York: Oxford University Press, 1941.

Crombie, A. C. The mechanistic hypothesis and the scientific study of vision: Some optical ideas as a background to the invention of the microscope. In S. Bradbury & G. Turner (Eds.), *Historical aspects of microscopy*. Cambridge: Heffner & Sons, 1968, 30–86.

Dallenbach, K. M. The history and derivation of the word "function" as a systematic term in psychology. *The American Journal of Psychology, 1915, 26, 473–484*.

Darwin, C. *The origin of species*. London, 1859.

Darwin, C. *The descent of man, and selection in relation to sex* (2nd ed.). 1871. New York, 1886.

Darwin, C. *The expression of the emotions in man and animals*. London: Murray, 1872.

della Porta, G. G. *Magia naturalis*. Naples, 1589.

della Porta, G. G. *De refractione*. Naples, 1593.

Descartes, R. *Rules for the direction of the understanding*. 1628. In T. V. Smith & M. Greene (Eds.), *From Descartes to Locke*. Chicago: University of Chicago Press, 1940.

Descartes, R. *Le traite de l'homme*. 1637. In F. Alguie (Ed.), *Euvres philosophique de Descartes, 1*. Paris: Garnier, 1963.

Descartes, R. *Dioptric*. 1638 (a). In N. K. Smith (Ed.), *Philosophical writings*. New York: Random House, 1958.

Descartes, R. *Discourse on the method of rightly conducting the reason*. 1638 (b). In *The philosophical works of Descartes*. New York: Dover, 1955.

Descartes, R. *Dioptric*. 1638 (c). In W. S. Sahakian (Ed.), *History of psychology*. Itasca, IL: Peacock Publishers, 1968.

Descartes, R. *Meditations on first philosophy*. 1641. E. S. Haldane & G. R. Ross, (Trans.). In *The philosophical works of Descartes*. New York: Dover, 1955.

Descartes, R. *The principles of philosophy*. 1644. E. S. Haldane & G. R. Ross, (Trans.). In *The philosophical works of Descartes*. New York: Dover, 1955.

Descartes, R. *The passions of the soul*. 1649. E. S. Haldane & G. R. Ross, (Trans.). In *The philosophical works of Descartes*. New York: Dover, 1955.

Desmond, A. J. *The Hot-blooded dinosaurs*. New York: Dial Press, 1975.

Dewey, J. The reflex arc concept in psychology. *Psychological Review, 1896, 31, 357–370*.

Duncker, K. Uber induzierte bewegung. *Psychol. Forsch., 1929, 12*. (Trans. in Ellis, 1938.)

Eddington, A. S. *The nature of the physical world*. New York: MacMillan, 1929.

Ellis, W. D. *A source book of Gestalt psychology*. New York: Harcourt-Brace, 1938.

Epicurus Letter to Herodotus. ca. 300 B.C. Trans. by C. Bailey. In W. J. Oats (Ed.), *The Stoic and Epicurean philosophers*. New York: Random House, 1940.

Epstein, W., & Park, J. An examination of Gibson's psychophysical hypothesis. *Psychological Bulletin, 1964, 62, 180–196*.

Euclid. The optics of Euclid. *Optica*. ca. 300 B.C. H. E. Burton, (Trans.). In *Journal of Optical Society of America, 1945, 35*.

Farber, M. *The aims of phenomenology*. New York: Harper & Row, 1966.

Feigl, H. *The mental and the physical*. Minneapolis: University of Minnesota Press, 1967.

Ferrero, N. Leonardo da Vinci: Of the eye. *American Journal of Opthamology*, 1952, *35*, 507–521.

Ferrier, D. Experimental researches in cerebral physiology and pathology. *Journal of Anatomy and Physiology*, 1874, *8*.

Feyerabend, P. K. Explanation, reduction and empiricism. In H. Feigl & G. Maxwell, (Eds.), *Minnesota studies in the philosophy of science, 3*, Minneapolis: University of Minnesota Press, 1962, 28–97.

Feyerabend, P. K. Realism and instrumentalism: Comments on the logic of factual support. In M. Bunge (Ed.), *The critical approach to science and philosophy*. London: Collier-MacMillan, 1964.

Feyerabend, P. K. Problems of empiricism. In R. Colodny (Ed.), *Beyond the edge of certainty*. Englewood Cliffs, NJ: Prentice-Hall, 1965, 145–260.

Feyerabend, P. K. Problems of empiricism II. In R. Colodny, (Ed.), *The nature and function of scientific theories*. Pittsburgh: University of Pittsburgh Press, 1970. (a)

Feyerabend, P. K. Consolations for the specialist. In I. Lakatos & A. Musgrave (Eds.), *Criticism and the growth of knowledge*. London: Cambridge University Press, 1970. (b)

Feyerabend, P. K. Against method: Outline of an anarchistic theory of knowledge. In M. Radner & S. Winokur (Eds.), *Minnesota studies in the philosophy of science* (Vol. IV). Minneapolis: University of Minnesota Press, 1970. (c)

Feyerabend, P. K. On the critique of scientific reason. In R. S. Cohen, P. K. Feyerabend, & M. W. Wartofsky (Eds.), *Essays in memory of Imre Lakatos. Boston Studies in the Philosophy of Science, Vol. XXXIX*. Dordrecht-Holland: D. Reidel, 1976.

Firth, R. Sense-data and the percept theory. *Mind*, Vol. LVIII, 1949, Vol. LIX, 1950.

Flock, H. R. Some conditions sufficient for accurate monocular perceptions of moving slant. *Journal of Experimental Psychology*, 1964, *67*, 560–572. (a)

Flock, H. R. A possible optical basis for monocular slant perception. *Psychological Review*, 1964, *71*, 380–391. (b)

Flock, H. R. Optical texture and linear perspective as stimuli for slant perception. *Psychological Review*, 1965, *72*, 505–514.

Fodor, J. A., & Pylyshyn, Z. W. How direct is visual perception? Some reflections on Gibson's "Ecological Approach". *Cognition, 9*, 1981, 139–196.

Fraser, A. C. Berkeley's theory of vision. *North British Review, 41*, 1864, 199–230.

Fraser, A. C. *The works of George Berkeley*. Oxford: Clarendon Press, 1871.

Fraser, J. T. *Time as conflict*. Boston: Birkause Verlag, 1978.

Fraser, J. T. *The genesis and evolution of time*. Amherst: The University of Massachusetts Press, 1982.

Fuchs, W. Untersuchungen uber das sehen der hemianopiker und hemiamblyopiker. II. Die totalisierende Gestaltauffassung. *Zts. f. Psych.*, 1921, *86*. (cited in Koffka, 1935.)

Galen. *On the utility of the parts of the human body*, ca. 200 A.D. From *Oeuvres anatomiques, physiologiques, et mediacales de galien, . . .*

Gibson, E. J. A systematic application of the concepts of generalization and differentiation to verbal learning. *Psychological Review*, 1940, *47*, 196–229.

Gibson, E. J. Improvement in perceptual judgments as a function of controlled practice or training. *Psychological Bulletin*, 1953, *50*, 401–431.

Gibson, E. J. *Principles of perceptual learining and development*. New York: Appleton-Century-Crofts, 1969.

Gibson, E. J., Owsley, C. J., & Johnston, J. Perception of invariants by 5-month-old-infants: Differentiation of two types of motion. *Developmental Psychology*, 1978, *14*, 407–415.

Gibson, E. J., Owsley, C. J., Walker, A., & Megaw-Nyce, J. Development of the perception of invariants: Substance and shape. *Perception*, 1979, *8*, 609–619.

Gibson, E. J., & Walk, R. D. The visual cliff. *Scientific American*, 1960, 202, 64–71.

Gibson, E. J., & Walk, R. D. A comparative and analytical study of visual depth perception. *Psychological Monographs*, No. 15, 1961, *75*.

Gibson, J. J. The reproduction of visually perceived forms. *Journal of Experimental Psychology*, 1929, *12*, 1–39.

Gibson, J. J. Adaptation, after-effect, and contrast in the perception of curved lines. *Journal of Experimental Psychology*, 1933, *16*, 1–31.

Gibson, J. J. Retroaction and the method of recognition. *Journal of Genetic Psychology*, 1934, *10*, 234–236. (a)

Gibson, J. J. Vertical and horizontal orientation in visual perception (abstract). *Psychological Bulletin*, 1934, *31*, 739–740. (b)

Gibson, J. J., (Ed.). Studies in psychology from Smith College. *Psychological Monographs*, 1935, *46*(210).

Gibson, J. J. A note on the conditioning of voluntary reactions. *Journal of Experimental Psychology*, 1936, *19*, 397–399. (a)

Gibson, J. J. Review of Ellis Freeman's social psychology. *Psychological Bulletin*, 1936, *33*, No. 8. (b)

Gibson, J. J. Adaptation with negative after-effect. *Psychological Review*, 1937, *44*, 222–244. (a)

Gibson, J. J. Adaptation, after-effect, and contrast in the perception of tilted lines. II. Simultaneous contrast and the areal restriction of the after-effect. *Journal of Experimental Psychology*, 1937, *20*, 553–569. (b)

Gibson, J. J. The Aryan myth. *Journal of Educational Sociology*, 1939, *13*, 164–171. (a)

Gibson, J. J. Why a union for teachers? *Focus*, 1939, *2*, No. 1. (b)

Gibson, J. J. A critical review of the concept of set in contemporary experimental psychology. *Psychological Bulletin*, 1941, *38*, 781–817.

Gibson, J. J. History, organization, and research activities of the psychological test film unit. Army Air Forces. *Psychological Bulletin*, 1944, *41*, 457–468.

Gibson, J. J., (Ed.). *Motion picture testing and research*. (Report No. 7, AAF Aviation Psychology Research Reports). Washington, DC: U.S. Government Printing Office. 1947.

Gibson, J. J. Studying perceptual phenomena. In T. Andrews (Ed.), *Methods of psychology*. New York: Wiley, 1948, 158–187.

Gibson, J. J. *The perception of the visual world*. Boston: Houghton-Mifflin, 1950. (a)

Gibson, J. J. The perception of visual surfaces. *American Journal of Psychology*, 1950, *63*, 367–384. (b)

Gibson, J. J. The implications of learning theory for social psychology. In J. G. Miller, (Ed.), *Experiments in social process*. New York: McGraw-Hill, 1950. (c)

Gibson, J. J. What is form? *Psychological Review*, 1951, *58*, 403–412. (a)

Gibson, J. J. Theories of perception. In *Current trends in psychological theory*. Pittsburgh: University of Pittsburgh Press, 1951, 85–110. (b)

Gibson, J. J. The relation between visual and postural determinants of the phenomenal vertical. *Psychological Review*, 1952, *59*, 370–375. (a)

Gibson, J. J. The visual field and the visual world: A reply to Professor Boring. *Psychological Review*, 1952, *59*, 149–151. (b)

Gibson, J. J. Social perception and the psychology of perceptual learning. In M. Sherif & M. O. Wilson, (Eds.), *Group relations at the crossroads*. New York: Harper, 1953, 120–139.

Gibson, J. J. Review of M. D. Vernon's "A Further Study of Visual Perception." *Psychological Bulletin*, 1954, *51*, 96–97. (a)

Gibson, J. J. Ordinal stimulation and the possibility of a global psychophysics. *Proceedings of the Fourteenth International Congress of Psychology*. Amsterdam: North Holland, 1954, 178–179. (b)

Gibson, J. J. The visual perception of objective motion and subjective movement. *Psychological Review*, 1954, *61*, 304–314. (c)

Gibson, J. J. A theory of pictorial perception. *Audio-visual Communication Review*, 1954, *1*, 3–23. (d)

Gibson, J. J. The optical expansion-pattern in aerial locomotion. *The American Journal of Psychology*, 1955, *68*, 480–484.

Gibson, J. J. The non-projective aspects of the Rohrschach experiment—IV. *Journal of Social Psychology*, 1956, *44*, 203–206.

Gibson, J. J. Optical motions and transformations as stimuli for visual perception. *Psychological Review*, 1957, *64*, 288–295. (a)

Gibson, J. J. Technical and scientific communication: A reply to Calvert. *American Journal of Psychology*, 1957, *70*, 129–131. (b)

Gibson, J. J. Review of E. Brunswik's Perception and the representative design of psychological experiments. *Contemporary Psychology*, 1957, *2*, 33–35. (c)

Gibson, J. J. Visually controlled locomotion and visual orientation in animals. *British Journal of Psychology*, 1958, *49*, 182–194. (a)

Gibson, J. J. Research on the visual perception of motion and change. In *Second symposium on physiological psychology*. Washington: Office of Naval Research (ONR Symposium Report No. ACR-30), 1958. (b)

Gibson, J. J. The registering of objective facts: An interpretation of Woodworth's theory of perceiving. In G. S. Seward and J. P. Seward (Eds.), *Current psychological issues*. New York: Holt, 1958, 39–52. (c)

Gibson, J. J. Review of P. McEwen's after-effects: Figural and negative. *British Journal of Psychology Monographs Supplements*, 1958, *31*, 294–295. (d)

Gibson, J. J. Perception as a function of stimulation. In S. Koch (Ed.), *Psychology: a study of a science*. New York: McGraw-Hill, 1959, *1*, 457–501.

Gibson, J. J. Pictures, perspective, and perception. *Daedalus*, 1960, *89*, 216–227. (a)

Gibson, J. J. The information contained in light. *Acta Psychologica*, 1960, *17*, 23–30. (b)

Gibson, J. J. The concept of the stimulus in psychology. *American Journal of Psychology*, 1960, *16*, 694–703. (c)

Gibson, J. J. Perception. In *Encyclopedia of science and technology*. New York: McGraw-Hill, 1960, 1–20. (d)

Gibson, J. J. Review of E. H. Gombrich: Art and Illusion. *American Journal of Psychology*, 1960, *73*, 653–654. (e)

Gibson, J. J. Ecological optics. *Vision Research*, 1961, *1*, 253–262. (a)

Gibson, J. J. The contribution of experimental psychology to the formulation of the problem of safety—a brief for basic research. In *Behavioral approaches to accident research*. New York: Association for the Aid of Crippled Children, 1961, 77–89. (b)

Gibson, J. J. The apparent distance of mountains. *The American Journal of Psychology*, 1962, *75*, 501–503. (a)

Gibson, J. J. Observations on active touch. *Psychological Review*, 1962, *69*, 477–491. (b)

Gibson, J. J. The survival value of sensory perception. *Biological prototypes and synthetic systems*. New York: Plenum Press, Inc. 1962, *1*, 230–232. (c)

Gibson, J. J. Introduction to *The formation and transformation of the perceptual world*. Kohler, I. New York: International Universities Press, Inc., 1962, 5–13. (d)

Gibson, J. J. The useful dimensions of sensitivity. *American Psychologist*, 1963, *18*, 1–15.

Gibson, J. J. Review of R. J. Hirst's Perception and the external world. *American Journal of Psychology*, 1965, *78*, 700. (a)

Gibson, J. J. Constancy and invariance in perception. In G. Kepes (Ed.), *The nature and art of motion*. New York: Brazilier, 1965. (b)

Gibson, J. J. *Four related problems in the visual perception of environmental layout*. Unpublished manuscript, 1965. (c)

Gibson, J. J. *The senses considered as perceptual systems.* Boston: Houghton-Mifflin, 1966. (a)

Gibson, J. J. The problem of temporal order in stimulation and perception. *The Journal of Psychology,* 1966, *62,* 141–149. (b)

Gibson, J. J. *A further note on the perception of the motion of objects as related to the perception of events.* Unpublished manuscript, 1966. (c)

Gibson, J. J. *The stick-in-water illusion.* Unpublished manuscript, 1966. (d)

Gibson, J. J. James J. Gibson. In E. G. Boring and G. Lindzey (Eds.), *A history of psychology in autobiography.* New York: Appleton-Century-Crofts, 1967, 127–142. (a)

Gibson, J. J. On the meaning of the term 'stimulus'. *Psychological Review,* 1967, *74,* 533–534. (b)

Gibson, J. J. Invariant properties of changing stimulation as information for perception. *The Organization of Human Information Processing: Symposiumbericht vom XVIII Intenatinalen Kongress fur psychologie.* Berlin: Academie-Verlag, 1967, 5–22. (c).

Gibson, J. J. New reasons for realism. *Synthese,* 1967, *17,* 162–172. (d)

Gibson, J. J. *A note on innate perception.* Unpublished manuscript, 1967. (e)

Gibson, J. J. *Contrasting assumptions of the classical theory of vision and a new theory of vision.* Unpublished manuscript, 1967. (f)

Gibson, J. J. *Do animals have illusions?* Unpublished manuscript, 1967. (g)

Gibson, J. J. *Apparatus for the experimental study of visual perception.* Unpublished manuscript, 1967. (h)

Gibson, J. J. *Note on an elaboration of the distinction between the proximal and the distal stimulus.* Unpublished manuscript, 1967. (i)

Gibson, J. J. What is perceived? Notes for a reclassification of the visible properties of the environment, 1967 (j). In Reed, E., and Jones, R. (Eds.), *Reasons for realism.* Hillsdale, NJ: Lawrence Erlbaum Associates, 1982.

Gibson, J. J. *Note on illumination and space.* Unpublished manuscript, 1967. (k)

Gibson, J. J. *Situations requiring different types of exploratory ocular behavior.* Unpublished manuscript, 1967. (l)

Gibson, J. J. *The direct observation of matter in relation to its physical state.* Unpublished manuscript, 1967. (m)

Gibson, J. J. *Is there a mathematical model appropriate for a general analysis of optical motion?* Unpublished manuscript, 1967. (n)

Gibson, J. J. Depth perception. *International encyclopedia of the social sciences.* New York: MacMillan Co., 1968, 540–544. (a)

Gibson, J. J. What gives rise to the perception of motion? *Psychological Review,* 1968, *75,* 335–346. (b)

Gibson, J. J. *A tentative psychophysical law for progressive occlusion.* Unpublished manuscript, 1968. (c)

Gibson, J. J. *An outline of experiments on the direct perception of surface layout.* Unpublished manuscript, 1968. (d)

Gibson, J. J. *Temporal organization.* Unpublished manuscript, 1968. (e)

Gibson, J. J. *Wave-train information and wave-front information in sound and light with a note on ecological optics.* Unpublished manuscript, 1968. (f)

Gibson, J. J. *Memo on motion.* Unpublished manuscript, 1968. (g)

Gibson, J. J. *The perception of surface layouts. A classification of types.* Unpublished manuscript, 1968. (h)

Gibson, J. J. *On the difference between perception and proprioception.* Unpublished manuscript, 1968. (i)

Gibson, J. J. *The construction of meaning vs. the detection of meaning.* Unpublished manuscript, 1968. (j)

Gibson, J. J. Are there sensory qualities of objects? *Synthese,* 1968–1969, *19,* 408–409.

Gibson, J. J. Further thoughts on the perception of rigid motion. In J. Jarvinen (Ed.),

Contemporary research in psychology of perception. Porvoo, Finland: Werner Soder-
strom Osakeyhtio, 1969, 1–5. (a)

Gibson, J. J. *A reconsideration of eye-movements and eye postures based on ecological optics.* Unpublished manuscript, 1969. (b)

Gibson, J. J. *On the conflict between vision and touch.* Unpublished manuscript, 1969. (c)

Gibson, J. J. *The theory of images transmitted to the brain.* Unpublished manuscript, 1969. (d)

Gibson, J. J. *A further note on occlusion.* Unpublished manuscript, 1969. (e)

Gibson, J. J. *Experiments on perception considered as illusions.* Unpublished manuscript, 1969. (f)

Gibson, J. J. *The perception of a permanent world.* Unpublished manuscript, 1969. (g)

Gibson, J. J. *Transparency and occlusion, or how Bishop Berkeley went wrong in the first place.* Unpublished manuscript, 1969. (h)

Gibson, J. J. On theories for visual space perception. *Scandanavian Journal of Psychology,* 1970, *11,* 67–79. (a)

Gibson, J. J. Size and distance. *Science,* 1970, *170,* 723–724. (b)

Gibson, J. J. On the relation between hallucination and perception. *Leonardo,* 1970, *3,* 425–427. (c)

Gibson, J. J. *The visual ego.* Unpublished manuscript, 1970. (d)

Gibson, J. J. *Memo on the relation between hallucination and perception.* Unpublished manuscript, 1970. (e)

Gibson, J. J. A history of ideas behind ecological optics. Ed. by Anthony Barrand and Mike Riegle, 1970. (f) In Reed, E., and Jones, R. (Eds.), *Reasons for realism.* Hillsdale, NJ: Lawrence Erlbaum Associates, 1982.

Gibson, J. J. *A terminology for describing the layout of opaque surfaces and the occluding of one surface by another.* Unpublished manuscript, 1970. (g)

Gibson, J. J. *On the visual perception of tangible and intangible things.* Unpublished manuscript, 1970. (h)

Gibson, J. J. *Inquiry into sensations.* Unpublished manuscript, 1970. (i)

Gibson, J. J. On hallucination and perception. *Leonardo,* 1971, *4,* 405–412. (a)

Gibson, J. J. The information available in pictures. *Leonardo,* 1971, *4,* 27–35. (b)

Gibson, J. J. The legacies of Koffka's principles. *Journal of the History of the Behavioral Sciences,* 1971, *7,* 3–9. (c)

Gibson, J. J. *Concerning onset and cessation of stimulation and disturbances in an array of stimulation.* Unpublished manuscript, 1971. (d)

Gibson, J. J. The problem of event perception, 1971. In Reed, E., and Jones, R. (Eds.), *Reasons for realism.* Hillsdale, NJ: Lawrence Erlbaum Associates, 1982.

Gibson, J. J. A preliminary description and classification of affordances, 1971. (f) In Reed, E., and Jones, R. (Eds.), *Reasons for realism.* Hillsdale, NJ: Lawrence Erlbaum Associates, 1982.

Gibson, J. J. More on affordances, 1971. (g) In Reed, E., and Jones, R. (Eds.), *Reasons for realism.* Hillsdale, NJ: Lawrence Erlbaum Associates, 1982.

Gibson, J. J. Still more on affordances, 1971. (h) In Reed, E., and Jones, R. (Eds.), *Reasons for realism.* Hillsdale, NJ: Lawrence Erlbaum Associates, 1982.

Gibson, J. J. *The problems of information pickup.* Unpublished manuscript, 1971. (i)

Gibson, J. J. *Invariants in the changing ambient optic array and what they specify for an observer in an environment.* Unpublished manuscript, 1971. (j)

Gibson, J. J. *On the distinction between objects and substances.* Unpublished manuscript, 1971. (k)

Gibson, J. J. *A note on the muddle of extrasensory perception.* Unpublished manuscript, 1971. (l)

Gibson, J. J. *The crisis in sensory physiology.* Unpublished manuscript, 1971. (m)

Gibson, J. J. *On the concept of optical texture.* Unpublished manuscript, 1971. (n)

Gibson, J. J. *Note on terrestrial orientation.* Unpublished manuscript, 1971. (o)

Gibson, J. J. *A note on conjuring tricks and the psychology of event perception.* Unpublished manuscript, 1971. (p)

Gibson, J. J. The affordances of the environment, 1972. (a) In Reed, E., and Jones, R. (Eds.), *Reasons for realism.* Hillsdale, NJ: Lawrence Erlbaum Associates, 1982.

Gibson, J. J. Outline of a theory of direct visual perception. In J. R. Royce and W. W. Rozeboom (Eds.), *The psychology of knowing.* New York: Gordon and Breach, 1972. (b)

Gibson, J. J. *Note on the differences between a sensory modality and a perceptual system.* Unpublished manuscript, 1972. (c)

Gibson, J. J. *Note on the concept of "formless invariants" in visual perception.* Unpublished manuscript, 1972. (d)

Gibson, J. J. *Note on the distinction between stimulation and stimulus information.* Unpublished manuscript, 1972. (e)

Gibson, J. J. *The exploring, selection, and enhancing of optical stimulus information.* Unpublished manuscript, 1972. (f)

Gibson, J. J. *With what do we see?* Unpublished manuscript, 1972. (g)

Gibson, J. J. *On the concept of the "visual solid angle" in an optic array and its history.* Unpublished manuscript, 1972. (h)

Gibson, J. J. *Note on the concept of "what is given".* Unpublished manuscript, 1972. (i)

Gibson, J. J. *A note on visualizing conceived as visual apprehending without any particular point of observation.* Unpublished manuscript, 1972. (j)

Gibson, J. J. On the concept of "formless invariants" in visual perception. *Leonardo,* 1973, *6,* 43–45. (a)

Gibson, J. J. Direct visual perception: A reply to Gyr. *Psychological Bulletin,* 1973, *79,* 396–397. (b)

Gibson, J. J. *What is meant by the processing of information?* Unpublished manuscript, 1973. (c)

Gibson, J. J. Visualizing conceived as visual apprehending without any particular point of observation. *Leonardo,* 1974, *7,* 41–42. (a)

Gibson, J. J. A note on ecological optics. In E. Carterette and M. Friedman (Eds.), *Handbook of perception* (Vol. 1). New York: Academic Press, 1974. (b)

Gibson, J. J. The Implications of experiments on the perception of space and motion. Office of Naval Research Final Report (Contract No. N000 14-67A-077-0005). Arlington, VA: Office of Naval Research (Environmental Physiology), 1975. (a)

Gibson, J. J. Pickford and the failure of experimental esthetics. *Leonardo,* 1975, *8,* 319–321. (b)

Gibson, J. J. Events are perceivable but time is not. In J. T. Fraser and N. Lawrence (Eds.), *The study of time, II.* New York: Springer-Verlag, 1975. (c)

Gibson, J. J. Note for a tentative redefinition of behavior, 1975. (d) In Reed, E., and Jones, R. (Eds.), *Reasons for realism.* Hillsdale, NJ: Lawrence Erlbaum Associates, 1982.

Gibson, J. J. On the new idea of persistence and change and the old ideas that it drives out, 1975. (e) In Reed, E., and Jones, R. (Eds.), *Reasons for realism.* Hillsdale, NJ: Lawrence Erlbaum Associates, 1982.

Gibson, J. J. Three kinds of distance that can be seen or how Bishop Berkeley went wrong. In G. B. Flores D'Arcais (Ed.), *Studies in perception: Festschrift for Fabio Metelli.* Milano-Firenze: Giunte Editore, 1976. (a)

Gibson, J. J. Commentary and a further note on "The relation between audition and vision in the human newborn": by M. J. Mendelson and M. M. Haith. *Monographs of the Society for Research in Child Development,* 1976, *41,* (4, Whole No. 167). (b)

Gibson, J. J. The Myth of Passive Perception: A reply to Richards. *Philosophy and Phenomenological Research,* 1976, *37,* 234–238. (c)

Gibson, J. J. On the analysis of change in the optic array. *Scandinavian Journal of Psychology,* 1977, *18,* 161–163. (a)

Gibson, J. J. The theory of affordances. In R. Shaw and J. Bransford (Eds.), *Perceiving, acting, and knowing*, Hillsdale, NJ: Lawrence Erlbaum Associates, 1977. (b)

Gibson, J. J. Notes on direct perception and indirect apprehension. 1977 (c). In Reed, E., and Jones, R., (Eds.), *Reasons for realism*. Hillsdale, NJ: Lawrence Erlbaum Associates, 1982.

Gibson, J. J. The ecological approach to visual perception of pictures. *Leonardo*, 1978, *11*, 227–235. (a)

Gibson, J. J. The perceiving of hidden surfaces. In P. Machamer and R. Turnbull (Eds.), *Studies in perception*. Columbus: Ohio State University, 1978. (b)

Gibson, J. J. A note on what exists at the ecological level of reality. 1978 (c). In Reed, E., and Jones, R., (Eds.), *Reasons for realism*. Hillsdale, NJ: Lawrence Erlbaum Associates, 1982.

Gibson, J. J. *The Ecological Approach to Visual Perception*. Boston: Houghton-Mifflin, 1979. (a)

Gibson, J. J. A note on E. J. G. by J. J. G. In A. D. Pick (Ed.), *Perception and its development: A tribute to Eleanor J. Gibson*. Hillsdale, NJ: Lawrence Erlbaum Associates, 1979. (b)

Gibson, J. J. What is involved in surface perception? 1979 (c). In Reed, E., and Jones, R., (Eds.), *Reasons for realism*. Hillsdale, NJ: Lawrence Erlbaum Associates, 1982.

Gibson, J. J. Ecological physics, magic and reality. 1979 (d). In Reed, E., and Jones, R., (Eds.), *Reasons for realism*. Hillsdale, NJ: Lawrence Erlbaum Associates, 1982.

Gibson, J. J. Forward, A prefatory essay on the perception of surfaces versus the perception of markings on a surface. In M. A. Hagen (Ed.), *The perception of pictures* (Vol. 1). New York: Academic Press, 1980.

Gibson, J. J., & Backlund, F. An after-effect in haptic space perception. *The Quarterly Journal of Experimental Psychology*, 1963, *15*, 145–154.

Gibson, J. J., & Beck, J. The relation of apparent shape to apparent slant in the perception of objects. *Journal of Experimental Psychology*, 1955, *50*, 125–133.

Gibson, J. J., & Bergman, R. The negative after-effect of the perception of a surface slanted in the third dimension. *The American Journal of Psychology*, 1959, *72*, 364–374.

Gibson, J. J., & Carel, W. Does motion perspective independently produce the impression of a receding surface? *Journal of Experimental Psychology*, 1952, *44*, 16–18.

Gibson, J. J., & Cavinnes, J. The equivalence of visual and tactual stimulation for the perception of solid forms. Paper read at Eastern Psychological Association. Atlantic City, April, 1962.

Gibson, J. J., & Cornsweet, J. The perceived slant of visual surfaces—optical and geographical. *Journal of Experimental Psychology*, 1952, *44*, 11–15.

Gibson, J. J., & Crooks, L. E. A theoretical field-analysis of automobile driving. *American Journal of Psychology*, 1938, *51*, 453–471.

Gibson, J. J., & Dibble, F. Exploratory experiments on the stimulus conditions for the perception of a visual surface. *Journal of Experimental Psychology*, 1952, *43*, 414–419.

Gibson, J. J., & Fernberger, S. W. Perception. *Psychological Bulletin*, 1941, *38*, 432–468.

Gibson, J. J., & Gibson, E. J. Retention and the interpolated task. *American Journal of Psychology*, 1934, *46*, 603–610.

Gibson, J. J., & Gibson, E. J. The identifying response: A study of a neglected form of learning. *American Psychologist*, 1950, *7*, 276.

Gibson, J. J., & Gibson, E. J. Perceptual learning in relation to training. In *Symposium on psychology of learning basic to military training problems*. Department of Defense, HR-HTD-201-1, 1953.

Gibson, J. J., & Gibson, E. J. Perceptual learning: Differentiation or enrichment? *Psychological Review*, 1955, *62*, 32–41. (a)

Gibson, J. J., & Gibson, E. J. What is learned in perceptual learning? A reply to Professor Postman. *Psychological Review*, 1955, *62*, 447–450. (b)

Gibson, J. J., & Gibson, E. J. Continuous perspective transformations and the perception of rigid motion. *Journal of Experimental Psychology,* 1957, *54*,129–138.

Gibson, J. J., & Gibson, E. J. The senses as information-seeking systems. *The London Times Literary Supplement,* June 23, 1972, 711–712.

Gibson, J. J., Gibson, E. J., Smith, O. W., & Flock, H. Motion parallax as a determinant of perceived depth. *Journal of Experimental Psychology,* 1959, *58,* 40–51.

Gibson, J. J., & Hudson, L. Bilateral transfer of the conditioned knee-jerk. *Journal of Experimental Psychology,* 1935, *18,* 774–783.

Gibson, J. J., Jack, E. G., & Raffel, G. Bilateral transfer of the conditioned response in the human subject. *Journal of Experimental Psychology,* 1932, *15,* 416–421.

Gibson, J. J., Kaplan, G., Reynolds, H., & Wheeler, K. The change from visible to invisible: A study of optical transitions. *Perception and Psychophysics,* 1969, *5,* 113–116.

Gibson, J. J., & Mowrer, O. H. Determinants of the perceived vertical and horizontal. *Psychological Review,* 1938, *45,* 300–323.

Gibson, J. J., Olum, P., & Rosenblatt, F. Parallax and perspective during aircraft landings. *American Journal of Psychology,* 1955, *68,* 372–385.

Gibson, J. J., & Pick, A. Perceptions of another person's looking behavior. *American Journal of Psychology,* 1963, *76,* 386–394.

Gibson, J. J., Purdy, J., & Lawrence, L. A method of controlling stimulation for the study of space perception: The optical tunnel. *Journal of Experimental Psychology,* 1955, *50,*1–14.

Gibson, J. J., & Radner, M. Orientation in visual perception: The perception of tip character. *Psychological Monographs,* 1935, *46*(210), 48–65.

Gibson, J. J., & Radner, M. Adaptation, after-effect, and contrast in the perception of tilted lines. I. Quantitative studies. *Journal of Experimental Psychology,* 1937, *20,* 453–467.

Gibson, J. J., & Raffel, G. A technique for investigating retroactive and other inhibitory effects of immediate memory. *Journal of Genetic Psychology,* 1936, *15,* 107–116.

Gibson, J. J., & Robinson, D. Orientation in visual perception: The recognition of familiar plane forms in differing orientations. *Psychological Monographs,* 1935, *46*(210), 39–47.

Gibson, J. J., Schiff, W., & Caviness, J. Persistent fear responses in rhesus monkeys to the optical stimulus of 'looming'. *Science,* 1962, *136,* 982–983.

Gibson, J. J., & Smith, O. W. The perception of motion in space. In Symposium on *Physiological Psychology* (ONR Symposium Report ACR-1). Washington, DC: Office of Naval Research, 1955.

Gibson, J. J., & Smith, O. W. Apparatus for the study of visual translatory motion. *American Journal of Psychology,* 1957, *70,* 291–294.

Gibson, J. J., Smith, O. W., Steinschneider, A., & Johnson, C. W. The relative accuracy of visual perception of motion during fixation and pursuit. *The American Journal of Psychology,* 1957, *70,* 64–68.

Gibson, J. J., & von Fieandt, K. The sensitivity of the eye to two kinds of continuous transformation of a shadow-pattern. *Journal of Experimental Psychology,* 1959, *57,* 344–347.

Gibson, J. J., & Waddell, D. Homogeneous retinal stimulation and visual perception. *The American Journal of Psychology,* 1952, *65,* 263–270.

Greene, J. *The death of Adam: Evolution and its impact on western thought.* Ames, IA: The Iowa State University Press, 1959.

Greene, J. *Science, ideology and world view.* Berkeley: University of California Press, 1981.

Gregory, R. L. *Eye and brain.* New York: McGraw-Hill, 1966.

Gregory, R. L. *The intelligent eye.* New York: McGraw-Hill, 1970.

Gregory, R. L. Seeing as thinking: an active theory of perception. *The London Times Literary Supplement,* June 23, 1972, 707–708.

Grosseteste, R. De iride. ca. 1250. In L. Baur (Ed.), *Die philosophischen werke des Robert Grosseteste.* (Beitrage zur Geschichte der philosophie des Mittelalters, 9) Munster, 1912.

Gruber, H. E. *Darwin on man*. Chicago: The University of Chicago Press, 1981.

Guilford, J. P., and Dallenbach, K. M. A study of the autokinetic sensation. *American Journal of Psychology*, 1928, *40*, 83–91.

Gyr, J. Is a theory of direct visual perception adequate? *Psychological Bulletin*, 1972, *77*, 246–261.

Halwes, T. Structural realism, coalitions, and the relationship of Gibsonian, constructivist, and Buddhist theories of perception. In W. Weimer and D. Palermo (Eds.), *Cognition and symbolic processes*. Hillsdale, NJ: Lawrence Erlbaum Associates, 1974.

Hamlyn, D. W. *Sensation and perception*. London: Routledge and Kegan Paul, 1961.

Hamlyn, D. W. The concept of information in Gibson's theory of perception. *Journal for the Theory of Social Behavior*, 1977, *7*, 5–14.

Hartley, D. *Observations on man, his frame, his duty, and his expectations*. London: Richardson, 1749.

Hay, J. C. Optical motions and space perception: An extension of Gibson's analysis. *Psychological Review*, 1966, *73*, 550–565.

Hayek, F. A. *The sensory order*. Chicago: University of Chicago, 1952.

Heft, H. An examination of constructivist and Gibsonian approaches to environmental psychology. *Population and Environment: Behavioral and Social Issues*, 1981, *4*, 227–245.

Heidbreder, E. *Seven psychologies*. New York: Appleton-Century-Crofts, 1933.

Heider, F. Thing and medium. 1927. In On perception, event structure and psychological environment. *Psychological Issues, 1*, No. 3, International Universities Press, 1959, 1–34.

Heider, F. The function of the perceptual system. 1930. In On perception, event structure, and psychological environment. *Psychological Issues, 1*, No. 3. International Universities Press, 1959, 35–52.

Helmholtz, H. *Treatise on physiological optics*. 1866. J. P. S. Southall (Ed.), Optical Society of America, 1924. New York: Dover, 1962.

Helmholtz, H. The recent progress of the theory of vision. 1873. In R. Warren & R. Warren (Eds.), *Helmholtz on perception*. New York: Wiley, 1968, 61–136.

Helmholtz, H. The facts of perception. 1878. In R. Warren & R. Warren (Eds.), *Helmholtz on perception*. New York: Wiley, 1968, 207–231.

Helmholtz, H. The origin of the concept interpretation of our sensory impressions. 1894. In R. Warren and R. Warren (Eds.), *Helmholtz on perception*. New York: Wiley, 1968, 249–260.

Henle, M. On naive realism. In R. B. MacLeod and H. Pick (Eds.), *Studies in perception: Essays in honor of J. J. Gibson*. Ithaca, NY: Cornell University Press, 1975.

Herrnstein, R., and Boring, E. G. *A source book in the history of psychology*. Cambridge: Harvard University Press, 1965.

Hicks, G. D. *Berkeley*. London: Benn, 1932.

Hirst, R. J. *The problems of perception*. New York: Humanities Press, 1959.

Hirst, R. J. *Perception and the external world*. New York: MacMillan and Co., 1965.

Hobbes, T. *Leviathan*. 1651. In T. V. Smith & M. Green (Eds.), *From Descartes to Locke*. Chicago: University of Chicago Press, 1940.

Hochberg, J. Nativism and empiricism in perception. In L. Postman (Ed.), *Psychology in the making*. New York: Knopf, 1962, 255–330.

Hochberg, J. Perception-space and movement. In J. W. Kling & L. A. Riggs (Eds.), *Experimental Psychology*, 3rd ed. New York: Holt, 1971, 475–550.

Holst, E. von, and Mittelstadt, H. Das reafferenzprinzip. *Naturwiss*, 1950, *37*, 464–476.

Holt, E. B. Response and cognition. In *The Freudian wish*. New York: Holt, 1915, 153–207.

Holway, A. H., and Boring, E. G. Determinants of apparent visual size with distance variant. *American Journal of Psychology*, 1951, *54*, 21–37.

Hull, C. L. *Principles of behavior*. New York: Appleton-Century-Crofts, 1943.

Hull, C. L. *A behavior system*. New Haven: Yale University Press, 1952.

Hume, D. *A treatise of human nature*. 1739. In V. C. Chappell (Ed.), *The philosophy of David Hume*. New York: Random House, 1963.

Husserl, E. *Ideas*. New York: Collier Books, 1931.

Husserl, E. *Phenomenology and the crisis of philosophy*. Trans. by Q. Lauer. New York: Harper and Row, 1965.

Huygens, C. *Dioptrica*. 1667–1691. In *Opera Posthuma*. Louvain, 1703.

James, W. *The principles of psychology*. 1890. New York: Dover, 1950.

Jantsch, E., & Waddington, C. H. (Eds.), *Evolution and Consciousness: Human systems in transition*. Reading, MA: Addison-Wesley, 1976.

Johansson, G. *Configurations in event perception*. Uppsala: Almkvist and Wiksell, 1950.

Johansson, G. On theories of visual space perception. *Scandinavian Journal of Psychology*, 1970, *11*, 67–74.

Kant, I. *Critique of pure reason*, 1781. New York: St. Martins Press, 1965.

Katz, D. *The world of colour*. Trans. by R. B. MacLeod & C. W. Fox. London: Kegal Paul, Trench, Trubner and Co., 1935.

Kepler, J. *Ad vitellionem paralipomena, quibus astronomiae pars optica traditur*. 1604. Trans by A. C. Crombie. In I. Cohen & R. Taton (Eds.), *Melanges Alexandre Koyre: L'aventure de la science*. Paris: Herman, 1964.

Kepler, J. *Dioptrice seu demonstratio eorum quae visui & visibilibus propter conspicilla non its pridem inventa accidunt*. Ausburg, 1611.

Kirk, G. S., & Raven, J. E. (Eds.), *The Presocratic Philosophers*. Cambridge: Cambridge University Press, 1966.

Kockelmans, J. (Ed.), *Phenomenology*. Garden City, NJ: Doubleday, 1967.

Koestler, A. *The act of creation*. New York: MacMillan, 1964.

Koffka, K. Some problems of space perception. In *Psychologies of 1930*. Worcester: Clark University Press, 1930, 161–187.

Koffka, K. *Principles of Gestalt psychology*. New York: Harcourt-Brace, 1935.

Kohlhans, M. J. *Tractatus opticus*, etc. Lipsiae. 1663.

Kohler, W. Ueber unbemerkte empfindungen und urteilstauschungen. *Zsch. f. psychol.*, 1913, *66*.

Kohler, W. Physical Gestalten. 1920. Trans. and abridged by W. Ellis (Ed.), *A sourcebook of Gestalt psychology*. New York: Harcourt-Brace, 1938.

Kohler, W. On the nature of associations. *Proceedings of the American Philosophical Society*, 1941, *84*, 489–502.

Kohler, W. *Gestalt psychology*. New York: Liveright, 1947.

Kugler, P. N., Kelso, J. A. S., & Turvey, M. T. On the concept of coordinative structures as dissipative structures: I. Theoretical lines of convergence. In G. E. Stelmach & J. Requin (Eds.), *Tutorials in motor behavior*. Amsterdam: North Holland Publishing Co., 1980.

Kuhn, T. *The structure of scientific revolutions*. Chicago: University of Chicago Press, 1962.

Kuhn, T. Logic of discovery or psychology of research. In I. Lakatos & A. Musgrave (Eds.), *Criticism and the growth of knowledge*. London: Cambridge University Press, 1970. (a)

Kuhn, T. Reflections on my critics. In I. Lakatos & A. Musgrave (Eds.), *Criticism and the growth of knowledge*. London: Cambridge University Press, 1970. (b)

Lakatos, I. Criticism and the methodology of scientific research programmes. *Proceedings of the Aristotelian Society*. Vol. LXIX, 1968.

Lakatos, I. Falsification and the methodology of scientific research programmes. In I. Lakatos & A. Musgrave (Eds.), *Criticism and the growth of knowledge*. Cambridge: Cambridge University Press, 1970, 91–195.

Lakatos, I. History of science and its rational reconstructions. In R. C. Buck and R. S. Cohen, *Boston studies in the philosophy of science, 8,* Reidel, 1971.

Lamarck, J. *Philosophie Zoologique . . .*, 1809.

Lashley, K. S. *Brain mechanisms and intelligence*. Chicago: University of Chicago Press, 1929.

Lashley, K. S. In search of the engram. *Physiological mechanisms in animal behavior*. (Symposium No. 4). New York: Academic Press, 1950.

Lee, D. N. Visual information during locomotion. In R. MacLeod & H. Pick (Eds.), *Perception: Essays in honor of James J. Gibson*. Ithaca, NY: Cornell University Press, 1974.

Lee, D. N. A theory of visual control of braking based on information about time-to-collision. *Perception*, 1976, *5*, 437–459.

Lee, D. N. On the functions of vision. In H. Pick & E. Saltzman (Eds.), *Modes of perceiving and processing of information*. Hillsdale, NJ: Lawrence Erlbaum Associates, 1978.

Lee, D. N. The optic flow field: The foundation of vision. *Philosophical transactions of the Royal Society, London*, (B), 1980. 290, 169–178. (a)

Lee, D. N. Visuo-motor coordination in space-time. In G. Stelmach & J. Requin (Eds.), *Tutorials in motor control*. Amsterdam: North Holland Press, 1980. (b)

Lee, D. N., & Lishman, J. R. Visual control of locomotion. *Scandanavian Journal of Psychology*, 1977, *18*, 224–230.

Leibniz, G. W. *New essays concerning the understanding*. 1765. Trans. by A. G. Langley. New York: MacMillan, 1896.

Liebniz, G. W. *The Leibniz-Clarke correspondence*. 1717. Edited by H. G. Alexander. Manchester, England: Manchester University Press, 1956.

Leonardo da Vinci. *The notebooks of Leonardo da Vinci*. ca. 1500, E. MacCurdy (Ed.), London: Duckworth, 1910.

Leonardo da Vinci. *The literary works of Leonardo da Vinci*. J. P. Richter & I. Richter (Eds.). London: Oxford University Press, 1939.

Lewin, K. *Principles of topological psychology*. New York: McGraw, 1936.

Lewis, C. I. *Mind and the world order*. New York: Dover, 1929.

Lindberg, D. C. *John Pecham and the science of optics*. Madison, WI: University of Wisconsin Press, 1970.

Lindberg, D. *Theories of vision from Al-Kindi to Kepler*. Chicago: University of Chicago Press, 1976.

Lishman, J. R., & Lee, D. N. The autonomy of visual kinesthesis. *Perception*, 1973, *2*, 287–294.

Locke, J. *An essay concerning human understanding*. 1690. New York: MacMillan, 1965.

Locke, J. *An examination of P. Malebranche's opinion of seeing all things in God*. 1706. In *The works of John Locke, 9*, Germany: Scientia Verlag Aalen, 1963.

Lombardo, T. J. *J. J. Gibson's Ecological Approach to Visual Perception: Its historical context and development. Doctoral dissertation*. University of Minnesota, 1973. Dissertation Abstracts International, 1973–1974, *34*, 3534–3535B (University Microfilms No. 74-721).

Lombardo, T. J. Gibson, Berkeley, and psychophysical simulation. Paper presented at University of Connecticut psychology symposium, Storrs, CT, 1975.

Lötze, R. *Outlines of psychology*. Trans. by G. T. Ladd. Boston: Ginn, 1886.

Luce, A. A. (Ed.), *Berkeley's philosophical commentaries*. Edinburgh, 1944.

Luce, A. A. *Berkeley's immaterialism*. Edinburgh, 1946.

Luce, A. A. *Berkeley and Malebranche*. Oxford: Clarendon Press, 1934, 2nd Ed., 1967.

Mace, W. M. Ecologically stimulating cognitive psychology. In W. Weimer and D. Palermo (Eds.), *Cognition and symbolic processes*. Hillsdale, NJ: Lawrence Erlbaum Associates, 1974.

Mace, W. M. James J. Gibson's strategy for perceiving: Ask not what's inside your head, but what your head's inside of. In R. E. Shaw & J. Bransford (Eds.), *Perceiving, acting, and knowing*. Hillsdale, NJ: Lawrence Erlbaum Associates, 1977.

Mace, W. M., & Pittenger, J. Directly perceiving Gibson. *Psychological Bulletin*, 1975, *82*, 137–139.

Mace, W. M., & Shaw, R. E. Simple kinetic information for transparent depth. *Perception and Psychophysics*, 1974, *15*, 201–209.

Mach, E. *The analysis of sensations*. 1906. (5th ed.) New York: Dover, 1959.

Mach, E. *The science of mechanics*. Trans. by Thomas J. McCormack. LaSalle, IL: Open Court, 1960.

Mandelbaum, M. *Philosophy, science, and sense-perception*. Baltimore: Johns Hopkins Press, 1964.

Mann, C. W., Berry, N. H. B., & Dauterive, H. J. The perception of the vertical. I. Visual and non-labyrinthine cues. *Journal of Experimental Psychology*, 1949, *39*, 538–547.

Mark, L. S. A transformational approach toward understanding the perception of growing faces. Unpublished doctoral dissertation. University of Connecticut, 1979.

Marx, M., & Hillix, W. *Systems and theories in psychology*. (2nd ed.) New York: McGraw-Hill, 1973.

Mason, S. F. *A history of the sciences*. New York: Collier, 1962.

Maxwell, G. The ontological status of theoretical entities. In H. Feigl & G. Maxwell (Eds.), *Minnesota studies in the philosophy of science*. III. Minneapolis: University of Minnesota Press, 1962.

Maxwell, G. Scientific methodology and the causal theory of perception. In I. Lakatos & A. Musgrave (Eds.), *Problems in the philosophy of science* III. Amsterdam: North Holland Publishing, 1968.

Maxwell, G. Theories, perception, and structural realism. In R. Colodny (Ed.), *Pittsburgh studies in the philosophy of science, 4*. Pittsburgh: University of Pittsburgh Press, 1970, 3–34. (a)

Maxwell, G. *Russell on perception: A study in philosophical method*. Unpublished manuscript, 1970. (b)

Mead, G. H. *Movements of thought in the nineteenth century*. Chicago: The University of Chicago Press, 1936.

Meehl, P., & Sellars, W. The concept of emergence. *Minnesota Studies in the philosophy of science*, Vol. I, H. Feigl & M. Scriven (Eds.). Minneapolis: University of Minnesota Press, 1956.

Michaels, C. F. *The information for direct binocular steropsis*. Unpublished manuscript, 1978.

Michaels, C. F., & Carello, C. *Direct perception*. Englewood Cliffs, NJ: Prentice-Hall, 1981.

Michotte, A. *The perception of causality*. New York: Basic Books, 1963.

Michotte, A., Thines, G., & Crabbe, G. Les complements amodaux des structures perceptives. *Studia Psychologica*. Louvain: Publ. Univ. de Louvain, 1964.

Mill, J. *Analysis of the phenomena of the human mind*. 1829. 2nd ed. J. S. Mill (Ed.). London: Longmans, Green, Reader, and Dyer, 1878.

Mill, J. S. *An examination of Sir William Hamilton's philosophy*. 6th ed. London: Longmans, Green, 1865.

Mill, J. S. Bailey on Berkeley's theory of vision, 1842. In *Dissertations and discussions, 2*, Boston: Spencer, 1865–1868. (a)

Mill, J. S. Rejoiner to Mr. Bailey's reply, 1843. In *Dissertations and discussions, 2*, Boston: Spencer, 1865–1868. (b)

Mill, J. S. Berkeley's life and writings. *Fortnightly Review, 10*, 1871.

Mill, J. S. *A system of logic, ratiocinative and inductive*. (6th ed.) New York: Harper, 1874.

Molyneux, W. *Dioptrika nova*. London, 1692.

Moore, G. E. The objects of perception. *Proceedings of the Aristotelian Society*, VI, 1905. (a)

Moore, G. E. Refutation of idealism. *Mind*, 1905. (b)

Moore, G. E. Some judgments on perception. *Proceedings of the Aristotelian Society*, XIX, 1918–1919.

Moore, G. E. Proof of an external world. *Proceedings of the British Academy*, XXV, 1939.

Müller, J. *Zur vergleichhenden physiologie des gesichtssinnes*. Leipzig, 1826.

Müller, J. *Elements of physiology*. Trans. by W. Baly. Philadelphia: Lea & Blanchard, 1843.

Müller, J. *The physiology of the senses, voice, and muscular motion, and with the mental faculties*. Trans. by W. Baly. London: Taylor, Walter & Maberly, 1848.

Neisser, U. *Cognitive psychology*. New Jersey: Prentice-Hall, 1967.

Neisser, U. *Cognition and reality*. San Francisco: W. H. Freeman & Co., 1976.

Neisser, U. Gibson's ecological optics: Consequences of a different stimulus description. *Journal for the Theory of Social Behavior*, 1977, 7, 17–28.

Newton, I. Mathematical principles of natural philosophy, 1687. In *Sir Isaac Newton's mathematical principles of natural philosophy and his system of the world*. Florian Cajori edition. Berkeley, CA: University of California Press, 1934.

Noble, C. E. The perception of the vertical. III. The visual vertical as a function of centrifugal and gravitational forces. *Journal of Experimental Psychology*, 1949, 39, 839–850.

Ockham, William. *In Quattor Libros sententiarum*. Lyons, 1495.

Passey, G. E. Perception of the vertical. IV. Adjustment to the vertical and with normal and tilted visual frames of reference. *Journal of Experimental Psychology*, 1950, 40, 738–745.

Passmore, J. *A hundred years of philosophy*. Baltimore: Penguin Books, 1966.

Pastore, N. Samuel Bailey's critique of Berkeley's theory of vision. *Journal of the History of the Behavioral Sciences*, 2, 1965, 321–337.

Pastore, N. *Selective history of theories of visual perception*. New York: Oxford University Press, 1971.

Pavlov, I. P. *Conditioned reflexes*. Trans. by G. V. Anrep. London: Oxford University Press, 1927.

Pavlov, I. P. *Selected works*. Trans. by S. Belsky (Ed.), J. Gibbons. Moscow, 1955.

Pecham, J. *Perspectiva communis*. ca. 1275. In D. C. Lindberg, *John Pecham and the science of optics*. Madison, WI: University of Wisconsin Press, 1970.

Pittenger, J. B., & Shaw, R. E. Aging faces as visual-elastic events: Implications for a theory of nonrigid shape perception. *Journal of Experimental Psychology: Human Perception and Performance*, 1975, 1, 374–382. (a)

Pittenger, J. B., & Shaw, R. E. Perception of relative and absolute age in facial photographs. *Perception and Psychophysics*, 1975, 18, 137–143. (b)

Pittenger, J. B., Shaw, R. E., & Mark, L. S. Perception information for the age level of faces as a higher-order invariant of growth. *Journal of Experimental Psychology: Human Perception and Performance*, 1979, 5, 478–493.

Pitts, W., & McCullock, W. S. How we know universals: The perception of auditory and visual forms. *Bulletin of Mathematical Biophysics*, 1947, 9, 127–147.

Plato. *Timaeus*. ca. 350 B.C. In F. M. Cornford (Ed.) *Plato's cosmology*. London: Routledge and Kegan Paul, 1937.

Platter, F. *De corporis humani structure et usu*. 1583. Basel, 1603.

Plotinus. *Enneads*, ca. 200 A.D.

Poincare, H. *Science and hypothesis*. 1905. New York: Dover, 1952.

Polyak, S. *The vertebrate visual system*. Chicago: University of Chicago Press, 1957.

Popper, K. *The logic of scientific discovery*. New York: Harper & Row, 1959.

Popper, K. *Conjecture and refutations: The growth of scientific knowledge*. New York: Harper & Row, 1963.

Postman, L. Association theory and perceptual learning. *Psychological Review*, 1955, 62, 438–446.

Prichard, J. *Researches into the physical theory of man*. London, 1813.

Prigogine, I. Order through fluctuation: Self-organization and social systems. In E. Jantsch and C. H. Waddington (Eds.), *Evolution and consciousness: Human systems in transition*. Reading, MA: Addison-Wesley, 1976.

Prigogine, I. *From being to becoming*. San Francisco: W. H. Freeman & Co., 1980.

Prigogine, I., & Stengers, I. *Order out of chaos*. New York: Bantam Books, 1984.

Randall, J. H. *Aristotle*. New York: Columbia University Press, 1960.

Ray, J. *The wisdom of God manifested in the works of the creation* . . . 3rd ed. London, 1701.

Reed, E. Darwin's evolutionary philosophy: The laws of change. *Acta Biotheoretica*, 1978, *27*, 201–235.

Reed, E. Why do things look as they do? A review of J. J. Gibson's *The ecological approach to visual perception*. Unpublished manuscript, 1980. (a)

Reed, E. Information pickup is the activity of perceiving. *The Behavioral and Brain Sciences*, 1980, *3*, 397–398. (b)

Reed, E., & Jones, R. Gibson's theory of perception: A case of hasty epistemologizing? *Philosophy of Science*, 1978, *45*, 519–530.

Reed, E., & Jones, R. J. J. Gibson's ecological revolution. *Psychology of the Social Sciences*, 1979, *8*, 189–204.

Reed, E., & Jones, R. *Reasons for realism*. Hillsdale, NJ: Lawrence Erlbaum Associates, Inc., 1982.

Reichenbach, H. *Experience and prediction*. Chicago: University of Chicago Press, 1938.

Reisch. *Epitome omnis philosophiae, alais margarita philosophica, tranctans de omni genere scibili*. Freiberg, 1486.

Ribot, T. *German psychology of today*. New York: Scribner's, 1886.

Richards, R. J. Gibson's passive theory of perception: A criticism of Müller's specific energies hypothesis. *Philosophy and Phenomenological Research*, 1976, *37*, 221–234.

Ritchie, A. D. *George Berkeley: A reappraisal*. New York: Barnes and Noble, 1967.

Romanes, J. *Animal intelligence*. London, 1882.

Ronchi, V. *Optics: The science of vision*. Trans. by E. Rosen. New York: New York University Press, 1957.

Ronchi, V. Complexities, advances, and misconceptions in the development of the science of vision: What is being discovered? In A. C. Crombie (Ed.), *Scientific change*. New York: Basic Books, 1961.

Ronchi, V. *The nature of light*. Trans. by V. Barocas. Cambridge: Harvard University Press, 1967.

Runeson, S. On the possibility of "smart" perceptual mechanisms. *Scandinavian Journal of Psychology*, 1977, *18*, 172–179.

Russell, B. *The analysis of matter*. London: Allen and Unwin, 1927.

Sambursky, S. *Physics of the Stoics*. London, 1959.

Scheiner, C. *Oculus hos est: fundamentum opticum, etc.* Innsbruck, 1619.

Schiff, W. Perception of impending collision: A study of visually directed avoidant behavior. *Psychological Monographs*. No. 604, 1965, *79*.

Sellars, W. Empiricism and the philosophy of mind. In H. Feigl & M. Scriven (Eds.), *Minnesota Studies in the philosophy of science*, Vol. I. Minneapolis: University of Minnesota Press, 1956.

Sellars, W. Philosophy and the scientific image of man. In R. Colodny (Ed.), *Frontiers of science and philosophy*. Englewood Cliffs, NJ: Prentice-Hall, 1962.

Sellars, W. The identity approach to the mind-body problem. *Review of Metaphysics*, April 1965. (a)

Sellars, W. Scientific realism or irenic instrumentalism. In R. Cohen & M. Wartofsky (Ed.), *Boston Studies in the philosophy of science*, Vol. II. New York: Humanities Press, 1965. (b)

Shaw, R. E., & Bransford, J. Introduction: Psychological approaches to the problem of knowledge. In R. E. Shaw and J. Bransford (Eds.), *Perceiving, acting and knowing*. Hillsdale, NJ: Lawrence Erlbaum Associates, 1977.

Shaw, R. E., McIntyre, M., and Mace, W. The role of symmetry in event perception. In R. B. MacLeod and H. L. Pick (Eds.), *Perception: Essays in honor of James J. Gibson*. Ithaca, NY: Cornell University Press, 1974.

Shaw, R. E., & Pittenger, J. B. Perceiving the face of change in changing faces: Implications for a theory of object perception. In R. E. Shaw and J. Bransford (Eds.), *Perceiving, acting and knowing*. Hillsdale, NJ: Lawrence Erlbaum Associates, Inc., 1977.

Shaw, R. E., & Pittenger, J. On perceiving change. In H. Pick & R. Saltzman (Eds.), *Modes of perceiving and processing information*. Hillsdale, NJ: Lawrence Erlbaum Associates, Inc., 1978.

Shaw, R. E., & Turvey, M. T. Coalitions as models for ecosystems: A realist perspective on perceptual organization. In M. Kubovy & J. Pomerantz (Eds.), *Perceptual organization*. Hillsdale, NJ: Lawrence Erlbaum Associates, Inc., 1981.

Shaw, R. E., Turvey, M. T., & Mace, W. Ecological psychology: The consequence of a concommitent to realism. In W. Weimer & D. Palermo (Eds.), *Cognition and the symbolic processes*, II. Hillsdale, NJ: Lawrence Erlbaum Associates, Inc., 1981.

Sherover, C. M. *The human experience of time*. New York: New York University Press, 1975.

Singer, A. *A short history of scientific ideas to 1900*. Oxford: Oxford University Press, 1959.

Smart, J. J. C. *Between science and philosophy: An introduction to the philosophy of science*. New York: Random House, 1968.

Smythies, J. R. The representative theory of perception. In J. R. Smythies (Ed.), *Brain and mind*. London: Routledge & Kegan Paul, 1965, 241–264.

Spencer, H. *The principles of psychology*. London, 1855.

Spiegelberg, H. *The phenomenological movement*. The Hague: Martinus Nijhoff, 1965.

Spinoza, B. *Ethics*, 1677. Trans. by W. H. White. London: Truber and Co., 1883.

Stavrianos, B. K. The relation of shape-perception to explicit judgments of inclination. *Arch. Psychol.*, New York, 1945, 296.

Stratton, G. M. Some preliminary experiments on vision without inversion of the retinal image. *Psychological Review*, 1896, *3*, 611–617.

Stratton, G. M. Vision without inversion of the retinal image. *Psychological Review*, 1897, *4*, 341–360, 463–481.

Stratton, G. M. *Theophrastus and the Greek physiological psychology before Aristotle*. London, 1917.

Suppe, F. *The structure of scientific theories* (2nd ed.). Champaign-Urbana, IL: University of Illinois Press, 1977.

Taylor, J. G. *The behavior basis of perception*. New Haven: Yale University Press, 1962.

Ternus, J. Experimentelle untersuchungen urber phanomenale identitat. 1926. Trans. and edited in Ellis, 1938.

Thompson, D. W. *Growth and form*. New York: MacMillan, 1942.

Titchener, E. B. *An outline of psychology*. New York: MacMillan, 1896.

Titchener, E. B. Postulates of a structural psychology. *Philosophical Review*, 1898, 6, 449–465.

Titchener, E. B. Structural and functional psychology. *Philosophical Review*, 1899, 7, 290–299.

Titchener, E. B. *Lectures on the experimental psychology of the thought processes*. New York: MacMillan, 1909.

Titchener, E. B. *Textbook of psychology*. New York: MacMillan, 1910.

Titchener, E. B. Sensation and system. *American Journal of Psychology*, 1915, 26, 258–267.

Titchener, E. B. *Systematic psychology: prolegomena*. 1929. Ithaca, NY: Cornell University Press, 1972.

Todd, J. T., Mark, L. S., Shaw, R. E., & Pittenger, J. B. The perception of human growth. *Scientific American*, 1980, *242*(2), 132–144.

Troland, L. *The principles of psychophysiology, 1, The problems of psychology and perception*. New York: Van Nostrand, 1929.

Troland, L. *The principles of psychophysiology, 2, Sensation*. New York: Van Nostrand, 1930.

Troland, L. *The principles of psychophysiology, 3, Cerebration and action*. New York: Van Nostrand, 1932.

Turbayne, C. M. Berkeley and Molyneux on retinal images. *Journal of the History of Ideas, 16*, 1956, 339–355. (a)

Turbayne, C. M. The influence of Berkeley's science on his metaphysics. *Philosophy and Phenomenological Research, 16*, June 1956, 476–487. (b)

Turbayne, C. M. Berkeley and Ronchi on optics. *Proceedings XII International Congress of Philosophy*, 1961, 453–460.

Turbayne, C. M. *The myth of metaphor*. New Haven: Yale University Press, 1962.

Turbayne, C. M. (Ed.). *Works on vision: George Berkeley*. Indianapolis: Bobbs-Merrill Co., 1963.

Turbayne, C. M. The origin of Berkeley's paradoxes. In W. Steinkraus (Ed.), *New studies in Berkeley's philosophy*. New York: Holt, Rinehart, & Winston, 1966.

Turvey, M. T. Preliminaries to a theory of action with reference to vision. In R. E. Shaw & J. Bransford (Eds.), *Perceiving, acting and knowing*. Hillsdale, NJ: Lawrence Erlbaum Associates, Inc., 1977.

Turvey, M. T., & Carello, C. Cognition: The view from ecological realism. *Cognition, 10*, 1981, 313–321.

Turvey, M. T., & Shaw, R. E. The primacy of perceiving: An ecological reformulation of perception for understanding memory. In L. -G. Nilsson (Ed.) *Perspectives on Memory Research: Essays in honor of Uppsala University's 500th Anniversary*. Hillsdale, NJ: Lawrence Erlbaum Associates, Inc., 1979.

Turvey, M. T., Shaw, R. E., & Mace, W. Issues in the theory of action: Degrees of freedom, coordinative structures and coalitions. In J. Requin (Ed.), *Attention and performance VII*. Hillsdale, NJ: Lawrence Erlbaum Associates, Inc., 1978.

Turvey, M. T., Shaw, R., Reed, E., & Mace, W. Ecological laws of perceiving and acting: In Reply to Fodor and Pylyshyn. *Cognition, 9*, 1981, 237–304.

Ullman, S. Against direct perception. *The Behavior and Brain Sciences*, 1980, *3*, 373–415.

Vesalius, A. *De humani corporis fabrica*. Basel, 1543.

Wallach, H. Brightness constancy and the nature of acromatic colors. *Journal of Experimental Psychology*, 1948, *38*, 310–324.

Wallach, H., & O'Connell, D. N. The kinetic depth effect. *Journal of Experimental Psychology*, 1953, *45*, 205–217.

Walls, G. L. *The vertebrate eye*. Bloomfield Hills, MI: Cranbrook Institute of Science, 1942.

Ward, J. *Psychological principles*. London, 1918.

Warren, H. C. *A history of association psychology*. New York: Scribner's, 1921.

Warren, R. The perception of ego motion. *Journal of Experimental Psychology: Human Perception and Performance*, 1976, *2*, 448–456.

Warren, R. The ecological nature of perceptual systems. In E. C. Carterette & M. P. Friedman (Eds.), *Handbook of perception*, Vol. X. *Perceptual ecology*, New York: Academic Press, 1978.

Warren, R., & Owen, D. Functional optical invariants: A new methodology for aviation research. *Aviation, Space and Environmental Medicine, 53*, 1982, 977–983.

Wartofsky, M. W. The relation between philosophy of science and history of science. In R. S. Cohen, P. K. Feyerabend, & M. W. Wartofsky (Eds.), *Essays in memory of Imre Lakatos. Boston Studies in the Philosophy of Science* Vol. XXXIX. Dordrecht-Holland: D. Reidel Publishing, 1976.

Watson, J. B. Psychology as the behaviorist views it. *Psychological Review*, 1913, *20*, 158–177.

Watson, J. B. *Psychology from the standpoint of a behaviorist*. Philadelphia: Lippincott, 1919.

Watson, J. B. *Behaviorism*. Chicago: University of Chicago Press, 1930.

Watson, R. *The great psychologists*. (2nd ed.) Philadelphia: Lippincott, 1968.

Webster's new world dictionary of the American language. Cleveland: World Publishing, 1968.

Weimer, W. Overview of a cognitive conspiracy. In W. Weimer & D. Palermo (Eds.), *Cognition and symbolic processes*. Hillsdale, NJ: Lawrence Erlbaum Associates, Inc., 1974.

Wertheimer, M. Experimentelle studien uber das sehen von bewegungen. *Zsch. Psychol.* 1912, *61*, 161–265.

Wertheimer, M. Untersuchungen zur lehre von der Gestalt. *Psychol. Forsch.*, 1921, *1*, 47–58; 1923, *4*, 301–350.

Whitrow, G. T. *The nature of time*. Baltimore: Pelican Books, 1975.

Witasek, S. *Psychologie der raumwahrnehmung des auges*. Heidelberg, 1910.

Witelo. *Vitellonis thuringopoloni opticae lebri decem . . .* ca. 1275. F. Risnero (Ed.), Basel, 1572.

Woodworth, R. S. Reinforcement of perception. *American Journal of Psychology*, 1947, *60*, 119–124.

Woorworth, R. S. Functional and structural psychology. In *Contemporary schools of psychology*. New York: Ronald, 1948, 13–58.

Wundt, W. *Outlines of psychology*. (4th ed.) Trans. by C. H. Judd. Leipzig: Englemann, 1902.

Yolton, J. On Gibson's realism. *Synthese*, 1968–1969, *19*, 400–406.

AUTHOR INDEX

SUBJECT INDEX